We Rest Here Content

We rest here content

The monuments and headstones of the

Imperial Light Horse Regiment

Compiled by Robin Smith

We rest here content

The monuments and headstones of the Imperial Light Horse Regiment

first published in South Africa by Robin W. Smith

Copyright 2013, 2023 © Robin W. Smith

ISBN: 978-1-915660-49-7

The right of Robin Smith to be identified as the author of this work has been asserted by the author in accordance with the UK Copyright, Designs and Patents Act 1988.

ll rights reserved. No part of this publication may be reproduced, stored in a retrieval system or transmitted, in any form or by any means without the prior written permission of the publisher, nor be otherwise circulated in any form of binding or cover other than that in which it is published and without a similar condition being imposed on the subsequent buyer.

Robin W. Smith

Military history researcher of Anglo Boer War sites.

We Rest Here Content

FOREWORD

We Rest Here Content is not the history of the Imperial Light Horse Regiment — that was written by the regiment's Intelligence Officer, Lieutenant George fleming Gibson and published in 1937 as *The Story of the Imperial Light Horse in the South African War 1899-1902*. Gibson was one of the original members of the 1st I.L.H. and was present at many of their engagements. There seems to have been some kind of exclusivity to membership of the 1st I.L.H. for he makes no mention at all of the 2nd Regiment! *The Story of the Imperial Light Horse* is written largely with first-person accounts and covers all the engagements of the 1st I.L.H. and more.

We Rest Here Content approaches the subject of the I.L.H. from a different viewpoint. Gibson reproduced the report of C. Ellis, Secretary of the Imperial Light Horse Memorial Committee, which lists the memorials and headstones that were erected in all four of the old provinces of the Union of South Africa from 1903-05. We, that is, myself and Robin Smith who has compiled and edited all the material, set out some years ago to establish the whereabouts of all of these. Each and every one that still exists has been located and photographed.

Some narrative is necessary and the Light Horse Regiment is in possession of an unpublished manuscript which has been edited and presented here exactly as it was originally written. The author is unknown but was clearly an Australian for there were many Australians in the two regiments. When once our book is published we hope that the identity of the author will come to light. His principal source was the Karri-Davies Papers in the archive of Museum Africa in Johannesburg. We freely acknowledge that this account is deserving of publication.

We Rest Here Content has been some years in preparation. I have few reservations in endorsing it as a worthwhile addition to our store of knowledge about the Imperial Light Horse Regiment.

Under the Crossed flags,

Heinrich E. Janzen (Lt Col)
Officer Commanding — Light Horse Regiment

Officers of the Imperial Light Horse.
From Photo by Nicholls, Johannesburg.

I.L.H. in camp, Pietermaritzburg, Natal.

I.L.H. in camp, Pietermaritzburg, Natal.

Introduction

John Stirling in his book *The Colonials in South Africa, 1899-1902* stated that "no other corps can point to a prouder history" than the Imperial Light Horse "as far as the South African War is concerned." Sir Archibald Hunter called the regiment "the finest corps I have ever seen anywhere in my life." Supported by the substantial finances of the Rand mining companies, the nucleus of the regiment was organised in secret in Johannesburg before the war even began. The significant political influence of the sponsors of the I.L.H. must surely have been a considerable factor in the naming of the regiment – apparently Queen Victoria herself was approached for her approval that the regiment should be called the "Imperial Light Horse."

In the course of the Anglo Boer War, four members of the regiment were awarded Britain's highest award for valour, the Victoria Cross, seven were decorated with the Distinguished Service Order and thirteen the Distinguished Conduct Medal. There were numerous mentions in despatches and the regiment gained battle honours for Elandslaagte, the Defence of Ladysmith, the Relief of Mafeking and South Africa 1899-1902. No other colonial regiment could match this record although it has to be said that the I.L.H. certainly had opportunities that others did not.

At the time of the centenary of the Anglo Boer War, the present O.C. of the Light Horse Regiment, Lieutenant Colonel Heinrich Janzen (he was an N.C.O. then), and the writer began to do what might be described as an inventory of the regimental monuments. These are spread around South Africa in each of the four historical provinces, Natal, the Cape, Transvaal and the Orange Free State. The regiment too has changed its name, "Imperial" being dropped in 1961 on the orders of then National Party government intent on severing all ties with the British Commonwealth that they had just left.

It turned out to be a considerable task and more than twelve years later we believe we have visited and photographed all the places where the Imperial Light Horse's distinctive gravestones, obelisks and monuments still exist. Understanding where members of the regiment fought and died tells a great deal about the Anglo Boer War history of the regiment. Steve Watt, the ultimate expert on South African war graves has provided the raw data that we required and re-directed us when we failed to find what we were looking for.

Between 1903 and 1905 ninety-two single tombstones were erected together with fourteen obelisks. The plaques for the headstones and the obelisks were made in Pietermaritzburg from white Carrera marble by J. Smith & Co., that company now long gone. These were then transported to the grave and battle sites and erected by contractors. In those days this was no light undertaking. Some of the sites were close to the railway, Ladysmith for example, but several of the obelisks would need to have been carried by wagon for a considerable distance from the nearest station or siding.

The headstones are quite distinctive. The base is cast in concrete and most were probably made on site. Onto the base is fixed a marble plaque with the regimental coat of arms, the soldier's name, where he fell and the date. The letters are all inlaid in lead and looters have been busy on many graves removing the lead letters. Many of the headstones have disappeared but all of the obelisks still exist and are in good condition. There are now only fifty-five headstones still in place. Where graves have been relocated from other places, on farms away from urban areas, only occasionally were the headstones replaced on the new grave. In Ladysmith Borough Cemetery and at Intombi Hospital outside the town the headstones have been built into a wall along the side of the Garden of Remembrance. In Bethlehem there are eight headstones out of the ten Imperial Light Horse men buried in the British Boer War Cemetery. They are all intact and several of them were re-interred there after burial elsewhere.

Apparently the regimental chaplain's casualty list was used for the placement of the headstones. Later research has turned up many more casualties marked only with the metal crosses supplied by the army or some with no known resting place. Pietermaritzburg war graves expert, Steve Watt, includes no less than 203 names in his list in his book *In Memoriam* but only 92 headstones were placed. Named on obelisks were 88 – many on more than one and some with headstones as well. The regiment therefore commemorated 160 of the dead. We have discovered two more names on National Monument Commission columns that do not appear on Steve Watt's list. Three members of the I.L.H. were drowned in the course of their service – one in the Albert Docks in Cape Town, one in the Tugela River and one in Compies River outside Piet Retief near the border with Swaziland. Their graves are not known.

The chapters that follow are made up of accounts written by eye-witnesses of the various events, wherever possible. These were either actual members of the regiment as participants or observers such as war correspondents. To make the narrative readable and understandable a minimum of text has been added to make a coherent story. Among many others, these are the principal sources from which have quoted:

- George fleming Gibson's *The Story of the Imperial Light Horse in the South African War 1899-1902* is a mine of information and anecdotes about the members of the regiment but he does not cover the Second Imperial Light Horse, raised towards the end of 1900. Gibson, as a Lieutenant was the Intelligence Officer of the regiment. He wrote numerous articles and historical pieces about the regiment for magazines and newspapers before he wrote the book.

- An unsigned and unpublished manuscript, evidently written by R.L. Wallace whose other work is *The Australians at the Boer War*. The manuscript that has been used here was acquired by the Ladysmith Siege Museum a number of years ago.

- John Stirling *The Colonials in South Africa, 1899-1902* has a concise summary of the regiment's movements, activities and actions during the war as well as a valuable listing of medals and decorations awarded.

- Brigadier General Duncan Mackenzie commanded the 2nd Imperial Light Horse, raised towards the end of 1900 when Lord Roberts considered that the war was "practically" over. His son wrote *Delayed Action*, part of which covers his father's time with the I.L.H. He was mostly in the southern Orange Free State, or Orange River Colony as it then was, and the western Transvaal in the latter stages of the war.

The Epitaph

"Tell England, ye who pass this monument,
We, who died serving her, rest here content."

This inscription has evolved from the original Greek text in Herodotus. Simonides, a Greek lyric poet, composed a well-known epigram, which was engraved as an epitaph on a commemorative stone placed on top of the burial mound of the Spartans at Thermopylae. According to Herodotus, the historian of the Greek-Persian wars, 300 Spartans died defending the pass at Thermopylae against overwhelming odds. The epigram was a message to the Spartans from their king, Leonidas, who was killed in the battle. The translation according to William Lyle Bowles reads:

Go tell the Spartans, thou who passest by,
That here, obedient to their laws, we lie.

The Imperial Light Horse was by no means the first to use this couplet as an epitaph. The version used on the obelisks of the Imperial Light Horse seems to have been suggested by the writings of Fydell Edmund Garrett. Garrett had been editor of the *Cape Times* and a Member of the Cape Parliament until his health broke down in 1899. He eventually returned to England and spent some time in the East Anglian Sanatorium in Nayland, Suffolk undergoing treatment for tuberculosis. He wrote a number of books at this time including a book of lyrics and poems from Ibsen, translated from the originals in Norwegian.

One of his poems dating from this period is 'Three Epitaphs':

> TELL England, you that pass our monument,
> Men who died serving Her rest here, content.
> Together, sundered once by blood and speech,
> Joined here in equal muster of the brave,
> Lie Boer and Briton, foes each worthy each:
> May peace strike root into their common grave,
> And blossoming where the fathers fought and died,
> Bear fruit for sons that labour side by side.
>
> Where'er I fall, like yonder ripped
> Old elm, there lay me ; so but one
> Small brass hang where the solemn crypt
> Gives respite from the Cape Town sun,
> Hard by the hurrying street, alive
> With strength and youth : 'tis all I claim,
> That where the heart is, there survive
> The dust and shadow of a name.

The first two lines, only slightly altered appear on the Imperial Light Horse marble obelisks erected at 9 different locations around South Africa. They are all still intact; however, a number have been moved from their original sites. They can be found at:

> Elandslaagte – Battle Ridge.
> Wagon Hill – Ladysmith.
> Wagon Hill Cemetery – Ladysmith.
> Intombi Cemetery – Ladysmith.
> Ladysmith Town Cemetery.
> Braamfontein Cemetery – originally erected at Witklip, Delmas.
> Krugersdorp Cemetery – originally erected at Naaupoort Nek, Cyferfontein.
> Maritzani – south of Mafikeng.
> Hartbeesfontein Cemetery, west of Klerksdorp, North West Province.

GENERAL SIR ARCHIBALD HUNTER

General Sir Archibald Hunter, giving evidence before the War Commission said, inter alia: "Sir Walter Hely Hutchinson drove up on to the grounds as he wanted to see them (the Imperial Light Horse), and he asked me to go round and look at them. I had not long come from a tour abroad, where I had seen nothing but the picked Guards of Sweden, Denmark, Russia, Prussia and Saxony, and there was nothing I saw on the Continent then, and nothing I have ever seen here except the Irish Constabulary, that could put a patch on them. You can tell men when you look at them. Every man was a picture of manhood; he was beaming with intelligence. They were a great success, a most undoubted success. They were the finest corps I have ever seen in my life."

<u>Lieutenant-General Sir Archibald Hunter's testimony to the British Government enquiry into the conduct of the war, 1903.</u>

14570. And what do you say of the auxiliary forces? – The greater bulk, I should say, of the inhabitants of Natal are Scotch, or of Scotch extraction. I was associated with the Natal Mounted Volunteers; they went by different names – the Border Mounted Rifles, the Natal Carbineers, the Umvoti Rifles, and some rather unpronounceable names – but the one general descriptive name that included them all was the Natal Mounted Rifles. They were all excellent material; they were almost all young farmers and farmers' sons; there were a few men like young doctors, young lawyers, and lawyers' clerks, and there were a few men out of the towns like Durban and Pietermaritzburg but the vast majority of them were men accustomed to riding and a hard outdoor life – men who had been brought up in raising stock, and all of them accustomed to handle arms, and game shooting and riding.

14571. You – are speaking now of the irregular corps raised in Ladysmith? – Yes. Then the other force was the Imperial Light Horse; they were the picked 1,200 men out of about 12,000 refugees from Johannesburg; all the British refugees from Johannesburg were well-to-do men; they were all men getting big wages; they were either mine owners or mine managers, or electrical engineers, experts of one sort or another; many of them were men on the Stock Exchange, lawyers, doctors, solicitors, and very few of them were engaged in trade – shopkeepers and suchlike; and they were all men who had either in prospecting, or as contractors, or as wood merchants, or in one form or another, done a lot of transport riding to and fro; they were the pick and the cream of the intelligent men who were going out to South Africa, and naturally, physically, they were very fine. The first time I ever saw them was on the first day I arrived at Pietermaritzburg. It was the first day they had ever been on parade as a regiment; up to that time they had only paraded as squadrons under their squadron leaders; it was the first day that Colonel Chisholme had ever had them under his command. Sir Walter Hely Hutchison drove up on to the ground, as he wanted to see them, and he asked me to go round and look at them. I had not long come from a tour abroad, where I had seen nothing but the picked Guards of Sweden, Denmark, Russia, Prussia, and Saxony, and there was nothing I saw on the Continent then, and nothing I have ever seen here, except the Irish Constabulary, that could put a patch on them. You can tell "men" when you look at them. Every man was a picture of manhood; he was beaming with intelligence. They were a lot of very highly-educated men; there were 10, I should think, or 20 of them with incomes of £10,000 a year; I should think over 100 that had over £1,000 a year of their own; they had been in the enjoyment of that, I mean, in Johannesburg. For a long time I do not suppose there were over 200 or 300 men who ever touched their pay; they all put it back into the regimental funds. Out of those regimental funds Government allowed, I think it was, £35 for a horse; they gave £45 for their horses. If there was anything to be procured for love or money, they got it. They all had Zeiss glasses; not a single British officer had a Zeiss glass unless he got it out of his own pocket. But they had them as a corps, and their physique, their intelligence, their morale, and their knowledge of the country were all excellent. Amongst them were men who talked Dutch, Kaffir, and Basuto, and they had every element of success in them, and they were a great success, a most undoubted success. They were the finest corps I have ever seen anywhere in my life.

Regimental Origins

The Imperial Light Horse Regiment was ready to take the field in October 1899. It had been raised in anticipation that war between Great Britain and the Boer Republics was inevitable. With the discovery of gold on the Witwatersrand in 1886 and the realization that this was the richest gold field ever discovered, thousands of prospectors and fortune-seekers of all kinds descended on the Transvaal. The Boer government of the South African Republic had to make some hasty improvisations as there was not even a system to peg out claims but soon a large and unruly town came into being named Johannesburg. As the President's names were Stephanus Johannes Paulus Kruger and the surveyor-general was Johan Rissik so Johannesburg would seem to have been named after them. Kruger rather disliked the place so he would not have considered it an honour.

Foreigners, Uitlanders[1] to the Boers, grew increasingly dissatisfied with the Kruger government's refusal to grant them the franchise. Within seven years of the discovery of gold, Johannesburg had grown from nothing to a city as large as the capital, Pretoria. The Transvaal rapidly changed from a poor Boer farming community to the most prosperous state in South Africa, then a region and not a single sovereign state as it has become from 1910 onwards.

The Johannesburg population was predominantly uitlander and English-speaking. The Boers feared losing control of their country if they allowed all these newcomers to vote and the cry of the American colonists of a century or more before, "no taxation without representation", was the uitlanders' same grievance. The uitlanders attempted to persuade President Paul Kruger to see reason from their point of view but attitudes became entrenched on both sides with the refusal of the Boers to budge from their position. The fact that the Boers were now able to arm themselves with the money gathered from taxation of the mineral wealth garnered from the Witwatersrand by the gold mining companies rankled even more. Petitions were presented but ignored and the British High Commissioner at the Cape, Sir Henry Loch, went up to the Transvaal in 1893 to be accorded a rousing reception in Johannesburg. His interview with Kruger gained no concessions for the Uitlanders.[2]

Loch came again in 1894 when there was an uproar over the commandeering of uitlanders to fight in the campaign against Malaboch in the northern Transvaal. Uitlanders who refused to serve were jailed but in June 1894 Loch managed to persuade the Transvaal government to abandon the commandeering claim. Such was the feeling of enthusiasm by the British population that he was requested by the Boers not to visit Johannesburg lest his presence lead to an armed demonstration against the Pretoria authorities. Later that year a petition with more than 38 000 signatures was presented to the government who once again refused to countenance any but minor changes to the electoral law. No wonder that the Boers were concerned about losing their country – in the Presidential election of 1892 the total of votes cast was a little more than fifteen thousand. Johannesburg then had a white population considerably more than that. Kruger, it was said, "wanted the gold without the diggers".[3]

Johannesburg people who styled themselves Reformers under the chairmanship of lawyer Charles Leonard became convinced that "coercive measures" were necessary for them to gain their rights as citizens of the Zuid Afrikaansche Republiek. Cecil Rhodes was consulted by Leonard and Lionel Phillips, a wealthy financier, and it was agreed that an armed force consisting largely of police from the British South Africa Company, the administrators of Rhodesia, be kept on the frontier as "moral support". The force commander was Doctor Leander Starr Jameson, a close confidant of Rhodes. Meanwhile the Reformers would secretly put together an armed force so as to stage an uprising in Johannesburg.[4]

Although advised by the Reformers and by Rhodes himself not to cross the frontier into the Transvaal, Jameson made a speech to his troopers and quoted from a letter written by the Reformers. This was supposed to be an "invitation" from the Uitlander population of the Transvaal and averred that "thousands of unarmed men, women and children of our race will be at the mercy of well-armed Boers. We cannot but believe that you and the men under you will not fail to come to the rescue of people who will be so situated." It was Sunday 29th December 1895 and the speech "was received with the greatest enthusiasm by the men who cheered most heartily".[5] The letter, written a month before and left undated, was only to be used after the Johannesburg rising had begun and Jameson's copy was only a kind of alibi in case of need. That evening the raiders set out from Pitsani in Bechuanaland and met up at Malmani with another contingent from Mafeking.

It turned out to be a disaster. finally cornered at Doornkop, south of Krugersdorp, Jameson fought hard but surrendered after losing 17 killed, 35 missing and 55 wounded. The surrender terms were obtained in writing from Commandant P.A. Cronjé by Sir John ("Johnny") Willoughby and guaranteed their lives. This was a political decision that Cronjé was not empowered to make but Kruger later endorsed his commandant's terms. The raiders were jailed for three weeks and then handed over to the British Government on the Natal border to be taken back to England for trial in the Bow Street police court in London.

The Reform Committee had been set up to negotiate with Kruger when the news came of the armed incursion into the Transvaal. Bobby White, one of Jameson's officers had carried a dispatch case with copies of all the telegrams that had passed between the Reformers, Rhodes and Jameson as well as the details of the cipher. The "women and children" letter was among the documents but this had already been published (with the fictitious date 28th December) in *The Times* of London. Signed by Charles Leonard, Lionel Phillips, Frank Rhodes (brother of Cecil), John Hays Hammond and George Farrar, all wealthy Johannesburg men, the letter was close to treasonous. All 64 members of the Reform Committee were rounded up and incarcerated in Pretoria Jail. This in spite of the British Agent in Pretoria, Sir Jacobus de Wet giving advice that were they to give up their arms they would go free.[6]

Brought to trial, the four ringleaders (Leonard had left Johannesb6urg and gone to the Cape to see Rhodes and then to England) were sentenced to death and the rest to two years in jail after which they were to be banished from the Transvaal for three years. Kruger was prevailed upon, perhaps by his wife and some of the other Boer wives to reduce the sentences. Within 24 hours the death sentences were commuted to 15 years imprisonment and after some months of negotiation to a fine of £25 000, a huge sum in those days. The remaining prisoners were released on payment of £2 000 except for Aubrey Wools-Sampson and Walter Karri-Davies. In protest against the breach of faith by the Transvaal government they declined to pay the fine and went to prison for 15 months.

Wools-Sampson and Davies stuck it out in spite of entreaties from their friends and letters from Wools-Sampson's mother in Cape Town who begged him to pay the fine. The two became something of an embarrassment for the Transvaal government and on the occasion of Queen Victoria's Diamond Jubilee they were released unconditionally on 22nd June 1897.[7]

Jan Smuts said that the Jameson Raid was the real declaration of war. In spite of the four years of truce, both sides prepared for the inevitable.[8] The South African Republic had spent considerable sums on armaments and the Boer commandos were equipped with modern Mauser rifles. Some still preferred Martini-Henry and Westley-Richards single-shot rifles and many of the wealthier Boers equipped themselves with expensive sporting weaponry. The Mauser with its 5-cartridge clip was quicker to load than the 10-round Lee Metford used by the British which had to be loaded with single cartridges. The Martini-Henry and the Westley-Richards had a Martini mechanism and was favoured by many of the Boers. French Creusot and German Krupp artillery was supplied to the South African Republic's and Orange Free State's artillery and, trained by German instructors, the British were to find themselves outranged when hostilities began.[9]

Aubrey Wools-Sampson and his friends determined to raise a regiment from the citizens of Johannesburg. On release from prison Aubrey Wools-Sampson went to live with his mother in Cape Town while Walter Karri-Davies, Charles Mullins, Percy Fitzpatrick and others in

Johannesburg met initially in the Rand Club but later in secret on Parktown Ridge so as to be safe from eavesdroppers. There they provisionally formed the regiment and chose its Officers. From among their friends it was obvious that a one thousand man regiment could be raised for service in the war which was clearly coming soon. Sir Percy Fitzpatrick and Lionel Phillips and their business associates provided the financial assistance sufficient to arm and mount such a force.[10]

In Cape Town, Wools-Sampson approached the Imperial authorities to offer them the services of the uitlander regiment. The High Commissioner, Sir Alfred Milner referred him to Lieutenant General Sir William Butler, the General Commanding at the Cape. Rather naturally there seems to be no record of exactly when these meetings took place but it was probably in the first half of 1899. Sir William was in no position to sanction such a force under Imperial auspices and Wools-Sampson was disappointed to hear from Butler that "England is not preparing for war even if the Transvaal is preparing." In view of the political situation prevailing at the time, some weeks or months before the Bloemfontein Conference of May 1899, Butler could hardly have responded differently. Wools-Sampson therefore approached Sir Walter Hely-Hutchinson, the Governor of Natal, armed with a letter from Sir Alfred Milner. Again, there is no record of this letter, but after the failure of the Bloemfontein Conference and President Kruger's closing remarks that he was "not ready to hand over my country to strangers", the political situation was markedly different. This time the military authorities agreed to the formation of a 500-man mounted regiment, stipulating that the Commanding Officer be a British regular officer and that the Adjutant and the Regimental Sergeant Major be likewise British regulars. The name of the regiment was to be the Imperial Light Horse, a name approved of by Her Majesty Queen Victoria who always took a keen interest in the affairs of the British army.[11]

Lieutenant Colonel John James Chisholme was commanding officer of the 5th (Royal Irish) Lancers and had been in South Africa since 1898 as part of the garrison in Natal. An irregular corps of horse was being raised in secret in the safely guarded enclosure of the Pietermaritzburg Agricultural Show grounds. Chisholme was supposedly retired on half pay from the 5th Lancers but in fact was in command of this new force, responsible for its equipment and training and promoted to Colonel.[12] The Adjutant was Lieutenant Reginald Barnes of the 4th Hussars, then in India. The position was offered to him by the War Office "Provided that you will personally discharge the cost of your passage to Natal, and that of your servants and horses." Reggie Barnes jumped at the opportunity – had he remained with his regiment he would not have made it to the war. The 4th Hussars was one of only three British regiments that did not serve in South Africa.[13]

The majority of the regiment was English-speaking men from Johannesburg who had made their way to Pietermaritzburg especially to offer their services as well as others from Natal and the Cape and even some Australians, New Zealanders, Canadians and Americans. The first call for volunteers saw five thousand keen to serve but there was room only for five hundred in the 1st Imperial Light Horse. Those five hundred were an elite and Lieutenant General Sir Archibald Hunter, no mean judge of fighting men, described them as "a great success, a most undoubted success. They were the finest corps I have ever seen in my life."[14] The methods of selection were drastic and only those whose horsemanship, shooting, physique and character met the highest standards were accepted. During the period of training, if any Squadron Leader was not satisfied with any man's keenness or efficiency, he was discharged. As many of the officers and men were personal friends and business associates or members of the same sporting bodies, the relations between all ranks was excellent.

Ten members of the Reform Committee became officers, all of them prominent citizens of Johannesburg. Aubrey Wools-Sampson and Walter Karri-Davies, being the prime movers in its formation were gazetted majors in the I.L.H. before the war began. Charles Mullins and Douglas Gilfillan were lawyers and Gilfillan a partner in Bowman, Gilfillan and Blacklock, a firm that still to this day is prominent in the legal profession in Johannesburg. W.T.F. Davies was a prominent surgeon who served as the first medical officer but became a combatant later in the war. Another Major was D.E. Doveton, a mining man and Manager of the Village Deep Gold Mine until his fellow directors asked him to stand down because of his heavy involvement in the controversial Uitlander politics. His house in Doveton Road, Parktown still stands. His successor at Village Deep was Frederick Creswell, a Lieutenant in the I.L.H. who later became Minister of Defence in the Union government. John Orr, a Captain owned a shop in Johannesburg that later became the department store named after him. John Donaldson, Captain and Quartermaster to start with rose to become Lieutenant Colonel and C.O. of the regiment after the war.[15]

Aubrey Wools-Sampson probably had more military experience than any of the other Colonials. He had been involved in actions against the native inhabitants of the Northern Transvaal and was present at Ulundi in the Zulu War of 1879 as a Captain in Ferreira's Horse. When Pretoria was besieged by the Boers in 1881, Wools-Sampson joined a volunteer horse troop raised by Captain Henry Nourse of the Transvaal Mounted Police and commanded by Wools-Sampson when Nourse became too ill to lead. He was wounded in a foray to attack the Boers at Zwartkopje, outside Pretoria as was the Boer Commandant Hans Botha. Together in hospital recovering from their injuries, Wools-Sampson and Botha became friends and Botha was one of those who were instrumental in bringing pressure to bear on the authorities for Wools-Sampson's release from Pretoria prison in 1897. Connected with a number of gold mines in Barberton and Johannesburg, Wools-Sampson was reasonably well off by the middle of the 1890s. At the outbreak of war Aubrey Wools-Sampson was 43 years of age.[16]

Walter Karri-Davies was an Australian born in 1867 and involved in the mining industry in Australia until ill-health forced him to undertake a long sea voyage. Rather fortuitously he came to be in South Africa when the mining industry was flourishing on the Rand. He became an importer of jarrah and karri timber from Australia (South Africa was practically treeless in those days) used in the mining industry and for railway sleepers. Both he and Wools-Sampson offered their services without reward of pay, promotion or award although Wools-Sampson did accept a number of promotions as we will see.[17]

The equipment of the regiment was purchased wherever it could be found as the Ordinance Department could supply very little. The rifle issued to the regiment was an outdated

Martini Metford or Martini Enfield – a Martini mechanism fitted to a Metford or Enfield barrel firing the standard .303 ammunition. This was standard issue to Colonial units and had the virtue of simplicity and ease of maintenance. Being a carbine it lacked stopping power and accuracy but for the first few engagements in which the I.L.H. were involved this may not have been much of a disadvantage. Many of the Boers were armed with Westley Richards rifles with the Martini mechanism but with a larger calibre .45 bullet in the early stages of the war. Later on when ammunition became scarce or unobtainable they perforce used captured Lee Metfords. It was only on 8th January after the battle of Wagon Hill that the I.L.H. were issued with Lee Metford rifles, one of the troopers writing home expressing his delight at being given a brand new magazine rifle. There were then so many British soldiers in hospital with enteric and dysentery, to say nothing of casualties from the various actions and sorties, that the supply of rifles exceeded the demand of the I.L.H.[18]

In little more than a month Colonel Chisholme declared the "men trained and the horses broken" and after inspection by Brigadier James Wolfe-Murray permission was given for the regiment to proceed to the front. During September and October a number of generals visited the Royal Showgrounds in Pietermaritzburg and presumably were impressed with what they saw. General Sir Archibald Hunter's remark has already been noted but other visitors were General Sir George White, Major General Sir William Penn Symons and Major General John French whose comments seem not to have been recorded.[19]

On 14th October 1899 'A' Squadron arrived in Estcourt under Captain D.E. Doveton with Lieutenants H. Bottomley, Douglas Gilfillan (the Riding Master and a superb shot) and Campbell Ross. Under Major General John Hildyard their responsibilities were scouting from the Oliviershoek and Van Reenen's passes over the Drakensberg to Weenen in the east. The remaining five squadrons went by train to Ladysmith on 16th October and were similarly engaged in patrolling and scouting. On the 18th October they marched to Colenso, camped for the night and returned on the 19th after thoroughly searching the area for signs of the enemy.[20]

The first major action of the war took place on 20th October when the British garrison of Dundee attacked the Boers who had occupied Talana hill, north east of the town. It was a victory of sorts but Major General Sir William Penn Symons was mortally wounded among ten officers and thirty-one N.C.O.s and men killed and nearly four hundred wounded, captured or missing. This was more than ten percent of the Dundee Field Force and although they had driven away the Boers from Talana Hill, the British found themselves in an untenable position and in danger of being outnumbered and trapped in Dundee by the Boer force of General Lukas Meyer. Major General Yule, who had succeeded to the command on the wounding of Symons, decided on retreat to Ladysmith and the weary column managed to reach safety four days later.

In the meantime, another Boer advance guard had captured a supply train at a station on the line between Ladysmith and Dundee and General Sir George White, in command of the Natal field Force, decided to take action to keep open his lines of communication with Dundee. The station was Elandslaagte and this was the first major action of the Imperial Light Horse.

Notes:

1. The word "uitlander" in Afrikaans or Dutch merely means foreigner just as the word "boer" merely means farmer. Capitalising the words gives them a different connotation – "Uitlanders" being those of British nationality who were foreigners to the Transvaal government just as "Boers" refers to the Dutch or Afrikaans-speaking inhabitants of South Africa. The Imperial Light Horse Regiment was formed largely of men who came from the Uitlander community in Johannesburg although a number of men with Afrikaans surnames were among them.

2. See Diana Cammack *The Rand at War 1899-1902* pp 1-11 for a description of Johannesburg and its population in the 1890s. Sir Percy Fitzpatrick's *The Transvaal from Within* is largely propaganda but is hugely informative for all that. For the aims and objects of the Reformers, but interesting nonetheless – see pp 108-119. A modern account is in Martin Meredith's *Diamonds, Gold and War* which may be more acceptable to modern readers, pp 365-415. Elizabeth Longford *Jameson's Raid*, pp 38-49 describes the few years before the Jameson raid and the two visits of Sir Henry Loch.

3. From J.L. Garvin, Chamberlain's biographer, quoted in Elizabeth Longford *Jameson's Raid*, p 39. See Diana Cammack *The Rand at War 1899 – 1902* pp 3.

4. Martin Meredith's *Diamonds, Gold and War* pp 323-361 describes the intrigue behind this ill-starred adventure.

5. Sir John Willoughby's report to the War Office. See H.M. Hole *The Jameson Raid*. The report is reproduced in full in Sir Percy Fitzpatrick's *The Transvaal from Within*.

6. Elizabeth Longford *Jameson's Raid*, pp 88-89.

7. Victor Sampson and Ian Hamilton *Anti-Commando* pp 98-100. L.S. Amery *The Times History of the War in South Africa* vi p 179.

8. "The Jameson Raid was the real declaration of war in the Great Anglo-Boer conflict. ... And that is so in spite of the four years truce that followed ... [the] aggressors consolidated their alliance ... the defenders on the other hand silently and grimly prepared for the inevitable." *Jan Smuts, 1906.*

9. Darrell Hall *The Darrell Hall Handbook of the Boer War* p 2 and pp 7-8.

10. Gibson *The Story of the Imperial Light Horse* pp 16-17.

11. Gibson *The Story of the Imperial Light Horse* pp 17-18. Victor Sampson and Ian Hamilton *Anti-Commando* pp 103. L.S. Amery *The Times History of the War in South Africa* i p 281 for detail of the Bloemfontein conference.

12. Walter Temple Willcox *The fifth (Royal Irish) Lancers in South Africa 1899-1902*. Introduction.

13. Gibson *The Story of the Imperial Light Horse* p 23. This in time of war!

14. Gibson *The Story of the Imperial Light Horse* p 25. Diana Cammack *The Rand at War 1899-1902* p 54 tells of David Robertson, a 28-year old Scot working for the Clydesdale (Transvaal) Colliery who was arrested in late September for recruiting uitlanders for the I.L.H. This was reported in the *Standard and Diggers News*. He had been sending men down to Natal for some time and spent several months in jail. He must have been released only once Lord Roberts entered Johannesburg because he then joined the 2nd I.L.H. as Trooper #430.

15. See Gibson *The Story of the Imperial Light Horse* p 19.

16. Victor Sampson and Ian Hamilton *Anti-Commando* pp 80-81.

17. R.L. Wallace *The Australians at the Boer War* p 40.

18. Ron Bester and Associates *Small Arms of the Anglo-Boer War 1899-1902*, p 50 has a picture of Corporal Taylor with a Martini Enfield carbine.

19. Gibson *The Story of the Imperial Light Horse* p 24.

20. Gibson *The Story of the Imperial Light Horse* p 26-7.

The originators of the Imperial Light Horse Regiment

Sir Aubrey Wools-Sampson

Major Walter David "Karri" Davies

Captain Charles Mullins

Captain John Donaldson

Sir Percy Fitzpatrick

Colonel John James Scott Chisholme

The marble obelisk on Elandslaagte.

Sketch by Melton Prior.

Top: An equestrian photo of Colonel Scott Chisholme in Pietermaritzburg probably in early September 1899.
Below: An informal picture taken at Government House, Pietermaritzburg on 9th October, 1899.

Uplands School

Uplands School is now St Christopher's Boarding Establishment in Uplands Road, Pietermaritzburg. In those days it must have seemed quite a distance from the city and there were three stations before Blackridge on the line up the hill to the ridge at Hilton Road, as it then was. The station name was Blackridge, an Anglicization of the nearby hill, Zwartkop.

From Miss Rowe, later Mrs Colepepper, headmistress of Uplands School, Pietermaritzburg:

One of the first troop trains brought to our station that splendid body of men, the Imperial Light Horse. On a late sunny afternoon their train was delayed for over an hour, and the men were glad to stretch their limbs and have a spell of friendly intercourse on their journey to unknown perils. Among our party several sisters and cousins and aunts were found, to such an extent indeed that the regiment then and there dubbed itself Uplands Own and gave many promises of future meetings. The fiancé of one member of my party re-passed us wounded a few days later, and was I think the first victim of that war to fill a grave in the military cemetery.* On the opening day of school in February a message, heliographed from L. to W.** reached us in the form of a telegram, "I.L.H. Ladysmith to Uplands School love and best wishes write by return care of magistrate Estcourt." How did they know in Ladysmith the date of our re-opening?

*Trooper C.D.B. White died at Fort Napier military hospital on 25th October 1899 after being severely wounded at Elandslaagte.
** Ladysmith to Weenen.

Source:
From an account of happenings at Upland School during the Anglo Boer War in the archive of the Killy Campbell Library, Durban.

'A' Squadron, Imperial Light Horse marching to the station, Pietermaritzburg, on 13th October, 1899. It could have been these men whose train was delayed for an hour at Uplands Station. And the same scene many years later.

The engagements of the Imperial Light Horse Regiment, 1899 – 1902

Colony of Natal:
('B','C', 'D', 'E', 'F' Squadrons)

Elandslaagte	21st October 1899
Rietfontein	24th October 1899
Ladysmith	30th October – 27th February 1900
Ladysmith – the Long Valley	3rd November 1899
Mounted Infantry Hill	3rd November 1899
Gun Hill	8th December 1899
Ladysmith – Wagon Hill	6th January 1900

('A' Squadron)

Willow Grange	23rd November 1899
Colenso, Hlangwane	15th December 1899
Acton Homes	18th January 1900

Cape Colony:
(All six squadrons)

The Relief of Mafeking	5th – 17th May 1900
Maritzani	13th May 1900

Transvaal:

Witklip	7th July 1900
Nelshoogte (Barberton)	12th September 1900
Frederickstad	16th October 1900
Doornpan	1st January 1901
Ventersdorp	1st January 1901
Cyferfontein (Naauwpoort Nek)	5th January 1901
Vlakfontein	27th January 1901
Bothwell (Lake Chrissie)	6th February 1901
Hamelfontein	10th February 1901

Amsterdam	22nd February 1901
Rietvlei	2nd March 1901
Geduld Farm	22nd March 1901
Hartebeestfontein	22nd March 1901
Rietkuil	17th April 1901
Palmietfontein	9th May 1901
Oog van Marico	6th July 1901
Rietvlei	31st July 1901
Sterkfontein (Bloemhof)	14th August 1901
Compies River	25th February 1902
Diamantuur	8th May 1902

Orange Free State:

Fauresmith	8th March 1901
Concordia	7th September 1901
Roodepoort	24th September 1901
Tygerkloof	28th September 1901
The raid on Reitz	21st October 1901
Paardeplaatz	25th October 1901
Brandkop	7th November 1901
Vischgat	11th November 1901
Tygerskloof Spruit	18th December 1901
Tygerskloof	16th January 1902
Klipkraal	25th January 1902
Pramkop (Kalkfontein)	27th January 1902
Newmarket Farm	5th February 1902
Katkop (Heilbron)	7th February 1902
Craven's Rust, Lindley	8th March 1902

Other places with I.L.H. monuments or headstones:

Colony of Natal:

Ntombi Camp	1899 – 1900
Ladysmith Borough Cemetery	1899 – 1900
Mooi River	1900
Charlestown (now Newcastle)	1901
Durban	1900
Fort Napier (Pietermaritzburg)	1899 – 1900
Howick	2nd April 1902

Cape Colony:

Mafeking	2nd June 1900
Norval's Pont	17th June 1901
Kimberley	26th August 1901

Transvaal:

Elandsfontein (now in Braamfontein)	1900 – 1902
Standerton	25th February 1901
Piet Retief (now Wakkerstroom)	16th April 1901
Pretoria	1901
Krugersdorp	1901

Orange Free State:

Bethlehem	1901
Harrismith	1902

The Imperial Light Horse Regiment

From an unsigned manuscript apparently by an
Australian author

Anglo Boer War 1899 – 1902

Contents

Chapter 1 Before 11th October 1899.
Chapter 2 The raising of the Imperial Light Horse.
Chapter 3 The strength of the opposing forces.
The early battles in Natal.
Chapter 4 In Ladysmith — 2nd November – 31st December 1899
Chapter 5 The Defence of Wagon Hill and Caesar's Camp, 6 January 1900.
Chapter 6 The activities of 'A' Squadron, Imperial Light Horse October 1899 – April 1900.
Chapter 7 A summary of the marches undertaken by the British army to the fall of Pretoria, 5th June 1900.
Chapter 8 The Relief of Mafeking, 17th May 1900, the Light Horse enters Johannesburg, 23rd June and camps outside Pretoria, 27th June.
Chapter 9 The campaign in June-July 1900 — Witklip 7th July — the drive through the Eastern Transvaal — the Light Horse marches with General French to Barberton.
Chapter 10 Western Transvaal — October 1900 – August 1901 — actions at Frederikstad — Cyferfontein — Geduld near Hartebeestfontein — Wildfontein — marching with Major-General Babington.
Chapter 11 The establishment of the 2nd Imperial Light Horse — with Smith-Dorrien in the eastern Transvaal — chasing de Wet along the Orange River in the Cape Colony.
Chapter 12 September 1901 – February 1902
The Imperial Light horse Brigade — action in the Harrismith-Bethlehem-Reitz region in the Orange Free State.
Chapter 13 March 1902, the 1st Light Horse returns to the western Transvaal — Peace proposals and the last great drives of the War.
Chapter 14 The Peace Treaty of 31st May 1902.
Appendices Names of the fallen, the imperial Light Horse. Honours, the posthumous award of the Victoria Cross to Trooper Hermann Albrecht, no. 459 1st Imperial Light Horse.

CHAPTER 1
BEFORE 11th October, 1899.

On 11th October 1899, Squadron-Sergeant-Major T. Sulivan, Imperial Light Horse, recorded in his Diary: "What Ho! At last the Boer bravado has come to a head. War is declared. The enemy is fast invading our territory and Old England is going to have a rough time, but her sons are willing." On l6th June 1902, the following appraisal of the Imperial Light Horse appeared in the columns of the Johannesburg *Star*: "The Regiment was the first Johannesburg regiment to be formed and has been peculiarly associated with the place of its origin from the beginning. It was raised with the deliberate intention of vindicating the honour and the courage of the English of the Rand,[1] upon which an unhappy combination of incidents had cast a doubt".

The formation in 1899 of the Imperial Light Horse Regiment, sprang from the bitterness engendered by the momentous racial and political struggle within the South African Republic. The struggle was between the foreign population in Johannesburg and the Witwatersrand and the Boer population of the Republic, a voting minority with almost exclusive electoral rights.

The founders of the imperial Light Horse were the South African born Aubrey Woolls-Sampson[2] and the Australian born Walter Karri-Davies.[3] Both men served 15 months imprisonment in 1896-97 for revolutionary activities against the Republic. In 1899 when war between Great Britain and the South African Republic seemed certain, a number of prominent industrialists provided finance for the raising of the Regiment, recruited almost solely from the ranks of the foreigners living on the Rand.

The South African Republic had its origin in 1836, when the first dissentient pastoral farmers trekked away from British rule in the Cape Colony to the interior previously unsettled by Europeans. Some of the Boers, as the migrating farmers were called, by settling on the plains between the Orange and the Vaal Rivers, pioneered the Orange Free State. With the sanction of Britain the Orange Free State became an independent republic on 23rd February 1854.

The Trekkers also formed settlements in the territory beyond the Vaal. On 16th January 1852, with the signing of the Sand River Convention the Transvaalers gained the right to govern themselves under their own laws, without interference from Britain. For some time there was no unity among the Transvaal Boers. It was not until 1858 that a constitution for a united republic called the South African Republic was drawn up. The establishment of the Boer republics meant that South Africa was now politically divided.

From the beginning the newly formed South African Republic turned out to be unstable. The country was not at all developed and the loosely knit Boer community continued to display all the old traits of failure to readily respond to the bonds of government. The burghers, as the citizens were called, were unable to submit their characteristic individuality to the authority of their own Government and prospects of stability vanished to the point where the country was on the verge of bankruptcy and chaos.

At this time European powers were displaying an interest in southern Africa, particularly imperial Germany. During a visit to Europe President T. Burgers had sought alliances for the Republic with several countries including Germany. Anxious lest Germany should gain a sphere of inluence in the Transvaal, the British Government sent Sir Theophilus Shepstone with an escort of 25 mounted police to Pretoria for discussions with President Burgers. On 12th April 1877, after talks with the President spread over eleven weeks, the South African Republic was annexed for Great Britain by Proclamation without a shot being fired and in the absence of any form of intervention from the Volksraad.[4]

Before long the Transvaalers, previously so divided, were united in their discontent under British rule. Paul Kruger, emerging as the leader of a national movement striving for independence, led two ineffectual deputations to London. On 16th December 1880, the Boers rose in revolt, besieging a number of weak British garrisons. A column on the march on the road to headquarters in Pretoria was attacked and heavily defeated at Bronkhorstspruit. A relieving British force advancing from Natal suffered several defeats on the Natal–Transvaal border, culminating in the humiliating defeat at Majuba Hill. Troops were still being mobilised when the British Government arranged an armistice. Terms of peace were negotiated and the Pretoria Convention was drawn up and signed on 3rd August 1881.

The Pretoria Convention gave the Transvaalers limited self-government. Certain restrictions were placed upon internal affairs and the boundaries of the country, called the Transvaal State, were set. The Convention also provided that in external affairs a negotiated treaty made with any country, other than the Orange Free State, might not be concluded without the agreement of the British Government empowered with the right of veto. In 1883, the year of his election to the office of President of the Transvaal State, Kruger journeyed to London seeking a revision of the terms of the Pretoria Convention. The London Convention, which was signed on 24th February 1884, omitted the clauses covering the internal affairs of the Transvaal, although foreign policy with nations other than the Orange Free State, still required the consent of Queen Victoria. The Transvaal State was once again called the South African Republic.

Article 4 of the Convention stated: "The South African Republic will conclude no treaty or engagement with any State or Nation other than the Orange Free State, nor with any native tribe to the eastward or westward of the Republic, until the same has been approved by Her Majesty the Queen."

In March 1886, a young Australian named George Harrison found a main gold bearing reef in a rocky outcrop on the Witwatersrand, 35 miles from Pretoria. In a report made to President Kruger in Pretoria, Harrison wrote: "I have had a long experience as an Australian gold digger and I think it is a payable goldfield." It proved to be the richest goldfield in the world. George Harrison was granted the discoverer's claim. In November 1886, he sold his right for £10 and disappeared.

The great discovery drew a new wave of white immigrants to the Republic. Capitalists, miners and associated industrial workers flocked in from all over the world. They came mainly from Britain, but also from Europe, the United States and Australia. The newcomers established the town of Johannesburg and raised the South African Republic from the poorest to the wealthiest State in South Africa.

The Government believed in 1886 that the foreigners would produce wealth from which the State would benefit and that when the gold had been mined out the foreigners would go and things would be just as they were before. But the reef was followed deeper and deeper, until it became clear that the Rand mines and the miners were going to remain. The inrush of immigrants completely upset the balance of the population. Within six years of the discovery, the immigrant population equalled the adult Boer citizens. By 1899 the immigrants outnumbered the adult Boer citizens by more than two to one. The immigrants were also better educated and culturally different from the pastoral farmers.

President Kruger decided that if the old citizens were to retain control of the Republic, the mining community must be treated as a foreign colony. The foreigners, or Uitlanders as they were called, paid nine-tenths of the taxes, yet were without electoral rights, either in the election of the Government, or in the municipal administration of Johannesburg, the town they had established. The President realised that if the Government granted the Uitlanders the franchise, the burghers would be outvoted and overruled in the country they had made their own. The Government made the franchise almost beyond the reach of the Uitlanders by progressively raising the qualifications for citizenship.

The Uitlanders formed a Transvaal National Union which over some years petitioned the Government in Pretoria for the redress of grievances held by the mining and business community. Within the mining community there were many settlers of South African birth, men from Natal and the Cape, whose status in the South African Republic was no different to the settlers from overseas. They shared the grievances of the Uitlanders with no less bitterness.

President Kruger usually received the petitioners grudgingly and with scant respect. In reply to one deputation he claimed; "Protest! Protest! What is the good of protesting? You have not got the guns, I have." The people of Johannesburg were regarded as nothing better than troublemakers and rebels.

When a petition for the extension of the franchise was debated in the Volksraad, one Member, a Mr Otto, in the course of a speech delivered a challenge: "Come on and have it out and the sooner the better. I cannot help it, Mr Chairman. I must speak out. I say I am prepared to fight them and I think every burgher of the South African Republic is with me."

When it seemed quite clear that no further amount of constitutional agitation was likely to have any effect on the Government, the National Union turned to revolutionary means to solve the Uitlander's grievances. Rifles and ammunition were smuggled into Johannesburg, concealed, in railed freight trucks and stored in and near the mines in oil drums and in machinery cases.

Prominent Rand industrialists took a leading part in the activities of the National Union. The Union also co-operated closely with Cecil Rhodes, the managing director of the British South Africa Company holding a Royal Charter for the development of Rhodesia. Rhodes was Prime Minister of the Cape Colony and manager of Consolidated Goldfields, a company with mining interests on the Rand.

By the end of 1895 plans were well ahead for an armed uprising. The plot depended heavily for success on the seizure of the barracks at Pretoria with its arsenal of 10,000 rifles and millions of rounds of ammunition. Only a few men guarded the establishment at night and at the time a section of the wall was down while repairs and additions were being carried out. The plan called for the trucking of arms and ammunition from the arsenal to Johannesburg by rail and for the demolition of the building. As a preliminary move, 300 rifles together with mules and wagons were sent to a place of concealment 10 miles from Pretoria.

The National Union accepted an offer from Rhodes to provide a mounted column, backed by artillery on the Bechuanaland–Transvaal border, ready to ride in ride in with support when the uprising took place. Under instructions from Rhodes, a column led by Dr Leander Starr Jameson, the Administrator of the South Africa Company, was stationed at Pitsani about 25 miles north of Mafeking. Dr Jameson had orders to wait on a signal from Johannesburg before crossing the border. Ostensibly, the purpose of the mixed column of South Africa Company Police and Bechuanaland Border Police was to guard the railway then being extended from Mafeking into. Rhodesia.

Although the uprising was expected to take place in Johannesburg during the Christmas–New Year period, a difference of opinion within the body of the National Union caused a postponement. For some, the intention of replacing the Kruger regime with a government more progressive and more fully representative of the white population was enough. They wanted to retain a fully independent Republic under the old Republican flag. Others favoured the concept held by Rhodes of a new State with a British link under the Union Jack.

In the meantime, while Jameson waited impatiently at the border, he received news of the postponement from Rhodes in Cape Town and from the Union in Johannesburg. Two independent couriers sent by the Union arrived at Pitsani, one after travelling overland on horseback and the other by train. Both couriers carried clear instructions forbidding any move over the border without an authorative direction from Johannesburg.

On 29th December 1895, Dr Jameson took matters into his own hands by setting out for Johannesburg with a column of about 500 mounted men. Although it was a somewhat smaller force than Jameson had hoped to lead, the column possessed armaments made up of one 12½ pounder gun, two 7 pounder guns and eight machine guns.

In an attempt to maintain telegraphic silence, the wires to the Cape south of Mafeking were cut and also those to the north of Mafeking. Wire spans were also dropped and removed along the route running in the Republic between Ottoshoop and Zeerust and between Zeerust and Lichtenburg. The cutting of the lines within the borders of the Republic mattered very little after a well-mounted burgher rode 18 miles to Zeerust to alert the Landdrost,[5] with the result that the Government in Pretoria was informed of the invasion by 2 p.m. on 30th December. From that time, fairly constant communications from the western Transvaal kept President Kruger well informed of the movements of the Raiders.

By the end of the first day the commandant at Marico had made contact with the column and unsuccessfully ordered Jameson to turn about. The column had covered two-thirds of the distance to the Witwatersrand when it was overtaken by a fast messenger from Mafeking, bringing a telegram from the British High Commissioner, Sir Hercules Robinson, ordering the immediate withdrawal of the column to beyond the boundaries of the Republic. As the advance continued the Boers started to appear in force, flanking the column in a running fight for 10 miles. Approaching the Witwatersrand, riflemen engaged the Raiders near the Queen's Mine outside Krugersdorp. Forced to bivouac for the night on a low rise in the open veldt[6] near Luipaardsvlei, the column came under sniping fire: several times before morning.

On the morning of 2nd January the Raiders swung south towards Johannesburg, skirting the Witwatersrand ridges and marching through the village of Randfontein. For the next 10 miles the column was continually harassed by burghers and all the time was being gradually pressed in towards a line of ridges where overnight Commandant[7] Piet Cronje had positioned riflemen and artillery.

Outnumbered and outmanoeuvred, Jameson and his men surrendered to Cronje soon after 9 a.m. near the Kopje[8] known as Doornkop. The Commandant promised to spare their lives. Over the march of 169 miles to Doornkop in 86 hours, the Raiders lost 18 men killed and 55 wounded. Within a few hours of the surrender the Raiders found themselves shepherded temporarily into the Market Square Krugersdorp. The wounded were taken to the Krugersdorp hospital. Nightfall saw the Raiders securely locked up in the Pretoria gaol.

Meanwhile, in Johannesburg the tidings that Jameson and his men were across the border were received with dismay. A Reform Committee was hastily organized to deal with an emergency situation, for it was thought that President Kruger, who had for long suspected that some kind of plot was being hatched on the Rand, would order reprisals. Rifles were hurriedly unpacked and issued from the Consolidated Goldfields Office to more than 2,000 men. Trenches were speedily dug on the ridges around the town.

Well aware of what was taking place, the Government withdrew the police force. The Committee met the emergency by enrolling a special force to maintain order. The President sent two representatives to meet the committee and a 24-hour truce was arranged. On New Year's morning a deputation from the Committee left for Pretoria by train to negotiate. The deputation told a Government Commission of the agreement with Dr Jameson and that the Raiders had entered the Republic without waiting for instructions from Johannesburg. In the course of interrogation the deputation told the Commission that the Uitlanders would lay down their arms if the Government agreed generally to meet their grievances. The Commission indicated that no armed action would be taken against Johannesburg provided the town remained peaceful. The Commission meanwhile, reported back to the Government.

With the Raiders under lock and key in Pretoria, the town of Johannesburg was still under arms. On 6th January 1896 the people of Johannesburg received a 24-hour ultimatum to lay down arms unconditionally. The British Agent in Pretoria, Sir Jacobus De Wet visited Johannesburg. In an address delivered from outside the Rand Club to a large gathering in the street, the Agent advised the crowd to lay down their arms, otherwise the lives of the imprisoned Raiders would be in jeopardy.

Johannesburg surrendered without firing a shot. The Government Police returned and the commandos encircling the town were withdrawn. Some weeks later Dr Jameson and his men were handed over to Sir Walter Hely-Hutchinson, the Governor of Natal and sent to Britain to stand trial in London. The British Government entirely disassociated itself from the Raid and the plotting of the Revolutionaries on the Rand.

As the result of his association with the Jameson Raid, Cecil Rhodes lost his position as Prime Minister of the Cape Colony for activities regarded as: "Not consistent with his duty as Prime Minister of the Colony."

Upon the surrender of arms President Kruger granted a general amnesty to the people of Johannesburg. Even so, on the evening of 9th January and on the morning of l0th January the members of the Reform Committee, comprising most of the leading men on the Rand were placed under arrest. In custody in Pretoria they faced a charge of high treason for endangering the independence of the State. The various nationalities of the arrested men reflected the cosmopolitan population of the Rand; 35 from Britain, 16 South Africans, 6 Americans, one Canadian, one Australian and several Europeans.

The trial in Pretoria ended on 28th April 1896. Four Committee leaders, George Farrar, Lionel Phillips, John Hammond and Frank Rhodes were sentenced to death, but provision was made for the sentences to be commuted to a fine of £25,000 each, together with an undertaking to never again interfere in the politics of the Transvaal. Only Frank Rhodes refused to be bound. Upon the payment of the fine he was transferred over the border and banished from the Republic for 15 years.

The other Reformers received lesser sentences of two years' imprisonment, or a fine of £2,000 in default. An assurance was also required from them that they would take no further part in the internal affairs of the Republic or would suffer three years' banishment. Only Walter Karri-Davies and Aubrey Woolls-Sampson refused either to pay the fine or to give the necessary assurances.

On the Rand the news of the release of the Reformers was received with relief. On arriving at the station in Johannesburg in a special train the party was greeted by an enthusiastic crowd. In the music halls and theatres performances were interrupted while the released men were welcomed and applauded. At the Stock Exchange, Lionel Phillips and George Farrar were carried shoulder high.

Walter Karri-Davies and Aubrey Woolls-Sampson served 15 months' imprisonment in the Pretoria gaol. On 22nd June 1897, as an act of grace to mark the occasion of Queen Victoria's Diamond Jubilee, President Kruger released both prisoners unconditionally. The pair returned in triumph to Johannesburg.

The Raid widened the division between the two white groups in the Republic. It made more difficult the chances of finding a solution to the problem of how the original white settlers in the country could live side by side with the new arrivals without too much friction. The Government began the construction of a fort on a hill overlooking Johannesburg, to impress and overawe the townspeople. Work also commenced on forts outside Pretoria.

In the aftermath of the Raid the German Emperor was quick to despatch a telegram to President Kruger couched in the most congratulatory terms. "I express to you sincere congratulations that you and your people; without appealing to the help of friendly Powers, have succeeded by your energetic action against armed bands which invaded your country as disturbers of the peace and in maintaining the independence of the country against attack from without."[9]

A hasty reaction on the part of the German Government resulted in a proposal to despatch to Pretoria several hundred soldiers from German East Africa and Marines from a warship in Delagoa Bay. On reflection, no such German troop movements occurred. These outward expressions of interest in the Transvaal together with the known and avowed aims of German colonial expansion in southern Africa, did nothing to lessen British insistence on the preservation in southern Africa of the Convention of London.

In March 1897, the Orange Free State after having kept aloof from the war in 1880–81, entered into an offensive and defensive alliance with the South African Republic. In April of the same year, President Kruger declined an invitation to visit London to discuss the grievances of the Uitlanders, on the ground that Britain had no right to interfere with the internal affairs of the Republic. When it became clear that petitions to the Volksraad were meeting with no more success than in the days before the Raid, the Uitlanders directed their appeals and petitions to Queen Victoria.

Great Britain, the paramount power in South Africa, was concerned at the constant friction between the two white groups. The atmosphere of instability issuing from the South African Republic affected the whole of South Africa. Mr John X. Merriman, South African born and a member of the Cape Colony House of Assembly, wrote to President M. Steyn of the Orange Free State on 11th March 1898: "Yet one cannot conceal the fact that the greatest danger to the future lies in the narrow attitude of President Kruger and his vain hope of building up a State on a foundation of a narrow bigoted minority." In the long run the solution seemed to the British to be one that granted a fair measure of enfranchisement to the great bulk of the white population willing to accept it.

President Steyn attempted to settle the differences between Britain and the South African Republic by inviting the parties to meet in Bloemfontein in the Free State. At the conference held on 31st May, 1899, to a background of longstanding distrust and suspicion, there was disquiet on the part of Sir Alfred Milner[10] the British High Commissioner, at the hurried and heavy building up of arms by the Republic. This seemed to the British to bear out the alleged long terms aim of the South African Republic to undermine the position of British supremacy in South Africa.

When President Kruger left the Bloemfontein Conference deadlocked on the franchise question he declared: "It is my country you want." At the time of the war in 1880–81, when he had appealed without success to the Free State for support, Kruger had also said: "Then shall it be, from the Zambesi to Simon's Bay, Africa for the Africander." Subsequent negotiations on the vexed question of the franchise failed. Kruger was willing to concede amendments to the law on the franchise on certain conditions, mainly that Britain should agree to submit any further matters of contention to arbitration.

Great Britain rejected the proposal of arbitration, or any form of interference on matters affecting the suzerain relationship held under the terms of the Conventions and which over the years had been so plainly irksome to the Kruger Government.

On 26th July, the Governor of Natal, Sir W. Hely-Hutchison in a cable to the Secretary of State for the Colonies, Mr J. Chamberlain, said: "Men from all categories in Natal have rendered their hearty support and their belief that permanent peace and prosperity can only be secured by securing equal rights and privileges for Dutch and English throughout South Africa and of their earnest desire that there should be obtained, even if necessary at the cost of war, a real and effectual settlement."[11]

Of the 10,000 white male adults in Natal, 7,497 signed a petition to the Queen, supporting the action of the British Government by intervening on behalf of the Uitlanders. The report also stated: "The support which is thus given to Her Majesty's Government is given in the firm alliance that they will accept nothing but a real and permanent settlement. The acceptance of any terms short of this would be at lowest resented seriously and almost universally".[12]

On 5th July 1899, the *Transvaal Leader* published a report of a meeting of merchants and traders convened by the Johannesburg Chamber of Commerce. The meeting resolved that members: "Wanted to live in a country where all white men should have equal rights".

War seemed certain after the failure of the Bloemfontein Conference. Britain took steps to strengthen the small garrisons stationed in South Africa with reinforcements from overseas. From the colonial Empire offers of troops reached London.

On 9th October 1899, the British Agent in Pretoria was handed an ultimatum demanding the withdrawal of all troops from the frontiers, the removal from the country of troops arrived since June and the turning about of troopships on the high seas in transit for South Africa. The ultimatum expired at 5 p.m. on 11th October 1899. It forestalled a British ultimatum that otherwise must have been forthcoming. The demands were such that Great Britain was not willing to discuss them. On 12th October the first shots in the war were fired. The Orange Free State, having no quarrel of its own with Great Britain, entered the war on a point of honour under the terms of the Treaty with its sister Republic.

---

[1] Witwatersrand
[2] Born Aubrey Sampson
[3] Born Walter Davies
[4] Parliament of the South African Republic
[5] Magistrate
[6] plain
[7] Senior officer of a commando
[8] A small rocky hill or rising ground
[9] *The Jameson Raid*, van der Poel
[10] Afterwards Lord Milner
[11] From Official British Correspondence Relating to South Africa, September 1899, Her Majesty's Stationery Office, London, 1899
[12] From British Official Correspondence Relating to South Africa, September 1899

CHAPTER 2
THE RAISING OF THE IMPERIAL LIGHT HORSE

At about the time of the Bloemfontein Conference a movement was started by certain Uitlanders in Johannesburg to raise a mounted corps to take the field in the war which most were convinced was bound to come. After the first discussions in the Rand Club and in the privacy provided by the rather solitary environment of the Parktown ridges on the outskirts of the town, the idea was set in motion by Aubrey Woolls-Sampson, who approached the officer commanding in Cape Town, Lieutenant-General Sir William Butler, with an offer to raise a corps to be placed at the service of the Imperial Government. General Butler declined to accept the offer on the grounds that Britain was not about to go to war.

Undeterred by the refusal, Woolls-Sampson found the military command in Natal more receptive. The result was that representations were made to the Secretary of State to sanction the formation in Natal of a mounted infantry corps of 500 strong, to be recruited mainly from Johannesburg volunteers. On 9th September 1899, Sir Alfred Milner sent a message to the Governor of Natal, advising him of approval received from the Secretary of State, with the provision that "the matter should be kept quiet until the men have been got out of Johannesburg".[1] Unofficial recruiting had been going on for some time in Pietermaritzburg, although it was not considered wise to recruit openly.

Meanwhile, at the Victoria Club in Pietermaritzburg, Woolls-Sampson and Karri-Davies were busy planning, raising funds and buying up horses, saddlery, equipment and transport wagons. At the end of August a subscription of £20,000 was remitted from England by Lionel Phillips and others and lodged in a bank in Pietermaritzburg.

The Imperial authorities stipulated that the corps be commanded by a regular British Army officer. The name – Imperial Light Horse – was approved by Queen Victoria. In the first week in September 250 men began to arrive from Johannesburg and camped in the Agricultural Showground in Pietermaritzburg. Other than exercising the horses, little more was done at the time. Permission to recruit publicly was withheld until 20th September.

On 22nd September news of the raising of the Uitlander Corps was published in the Rand newspapers. A few days later, Karri-Davies received a letter from an English woman residing in Johannesburg: "Seeing yours and Mr Woolls-Sampson's names in our local papers in connection with a corps to be formed in 'Maritzburg, I thought I should like to write and wish you both every possible success in your venture and hope sincerely that you may both have an opportunity of again showing the world what manly courage really is. We shall indeed give you the heartiest welcome and most cordial congratulations when you enter Johannesburg with flying colours. I am writing this under cover to a friend in 'Maritzburg, as I know your name is as a red flag to a bull and in all probability this would never reach you. My sisters and friends have all left the town, but I am staying on to see the game right through."[2]

Open recruiting proceeded rapidly in Pietermaritzburg, where thousands of young men from all parts of southern Africa rushed to join the Imperial Light Horse Corps, and to sign up to serve for such a period as their services may be required. Only those who could ride and shoot well were accepted. Conditions of pay were the same as for the established Cape Colony and Natal colonial forces. The Natal Government supplied Martini-Metford .303 single shot rifles without bayonets or ammunition. In addition to providing horses and equipment for themselves, Woolls-Sampson and Karri-Davies also contributed to the cost of raising the corps from their personal funds. Both men elected to serve for the duration of the war without military pay.

Lieutenant-Colonel J. Scott-Chisholme of the 5th Royal Lancers was appointed to command the corps, with Woolls-Sampson second in command. Both Woolls-Sampson and Karri-Davies were appointed majors. Lieutenant R. Barnes[3] 4th Hussars came from India to take up the duties of adjutant. The corps divided into six squadrons. Most of the officers were members of the Reform Committee.

The Imperial Light Horse wore a tunic buttoned up to the neck, with twill riding breeches, khaki puttees, tan ankle boots and a slouch felt hat. Over the shoulder a bandolier was draped diagonally down to the right waist. A Light Horse Diarist[4] from 'F' Squadron described the uniform and equipment issued from the store in Pietermaritzburg: "Our uniform was khaki tunic and riding breeches, putties, ankle boots and spurs and smasher hat.

"Our saddles were what are termed semi-military, like a civilian saddle only they had the D's on rings for attaching wallets, blanket straps and rifle buckets. We carried a macintosh rolled up in front of the saddle. Two blankets, a water-proof sheet, a kit bag containing a spare tunic, shirt, socks, towels etc. completed our kit. Each man carried an identification card with name, regimental number etc. and a packet of first field dressing. We were armed with a rifle with Lee-Metford bore and Martini-Henry action. Each man carried 200 rounds of ammunition."

Two informative letters describing the raising of the corps written from Pietermaritzburg and dated 26th September, appeared in the London *Times* on 30th October 1899: "The corps is divided into six squadrons and each squadron into three troops. As the corps is 500 strong, there are quite a few men in each troop under a lieutenant. The corps is not quite formed yet, but enlisting is going on daily. Everyone is trying to get in. Applications come from all parts of South Africa; Salisbury, Beira, Kimberley, Cape Town – everywhere.

"Men of every class and kind are applying. Even boys still at school. You never saw such keenness. The greatest care is being exercised in the selection of men. There is no doubt that when the corps is formed it will be equal to anything previously raised in South African wars. As one man said, it will be the flower of South Africa. At present they are rejecting 25 percent of the applicants. There has been some terribly hard cases of fellows who have come hundreds of miles to join up. They have been rejected, perhaps for some minor defect they were quite unaware of.

"It is awful to see some of them going away and trying to hide tears of disappointment. I think that if some of the so-called 'peace' people in England could see and understand the spirit of the thing; the keenness of the men, the material and other sacrifices they are making, it would open their eyes a bit to the true position in South Africa.

"The tests are pretty severe. first riding under the eyes of Woolls-Sampson, Douglas and Gilfillan. Next, a most careful medical examination at the hands of doctors Billy Davies and Bobby Mitchell. Lastly, rifle shooting. Unfortunately, most of the mines are still working and that prevents many a good man from coming down yet. Many of the men who are rejected for riding are old soldiers who have service records. If the Imperial authorities would only allow more recruiting, several splendid corps could be formed."

The second letter from Natal published in the *Times* said: "There is terrible disappointment here among those who cannot get into the Imperial Light Horse. Old hands are turning up from everywhere. Sambo (Woolls-Sampson), Karri-Davies, Charles Mullins, Doveton, Jack Orr, corps surgeons Billy Davies and Mitchell are dead set on having only the best. I believe we could easily get together 3,000 men out of the Johannesburg men now in Natal. There must be plenty more in Cape Town and the other coast towns, but the Imperial Government has not agreed to take them.

"Perhaps they think it is quicker and better to bring soldiers from overseas than train them here. Still, there is much virtue in the volunteer and our chaps are so keen.

"I was reckoning out and find that for every 1,000 men volunteering from the Johannesburg population, there would be half a million from the British Isles in the same proportion. And that makes no allowance for the non-British Uitlanders. It's funny to see how well the Britisher, the poor working beggar of a clerk, workman nondescript and Jack of all trades, has taken his gruel for months and rolled up to fight now. And to think that these are the chaps who were called the traitors of Judasburg in Jameson's time.

"But I never believed in the theory that a community of Britishers could cut up dead against the race traditions simply because they happened to be not in England."

On 9th September 1899, the date when official permission to raise the corps was received, Woolls-Sampson placed on record in a report[5] to Lieutenant-General Sir William Penn-Symons, the Commanding Officer in Natal, the steps taken for the formation of the corps: "I have at your request the honour to place on record the circumstances under which Mr Karri-Davies, certain friends and myself have asked to be allowed to form a corps of irregulars 500 strong for the purpose of co-operating with the Imperial forces in the event of hostilities with the Transvaal.

"In the month of May last, certain of my friends in Johannesburg and others placed themselves in communication with me to ascertain from Sir Alfred Milner in what manner they could be most useful should a contingency arise. Many asked that their personal services as combatants be accepted. Others, who through age and other circumstances could not proceed on active service expressed the wish to assist in the formation of a corps by furnishing it with the necessary funds and helping by any means in their power.

"Milner provisionally accepted in Cape Town when I visited him. I passed through Johannesburg and found much support. In visiting Natal I found my friend Karri-Davies just arrived from England. From the very inception Karri-Davies had been associated with me in every sense and did everything possible to secure financial assistance from friends in London. He will be linked with me in carrying out the proposal. We asked permission to purchase the necessary horses etc., with funds provided by our friends and ourselves.

"Finding that there might be some difficulty in getting the equipment for the proposed corps set aside, we again on behalf of our friends, expressed our willingness to equip the whole force and now we thank his Excellency and yourself for accepting the offer.

"Now that the question is no longer the redress of the grievances of the Uitlanders in the Transvaal, but the much wider one of the British supremacy in South Africa, we feel if possible more keenly the honour and privilege of being allowed to assist Her Majesty's Government by any means in our power and are willing to make every sacrifice in supporting the policy of Sir Alfred Milner.

"As I have already informed the High Commissioner and yourself, it is Mr Karri-Davies' wish as well as my own, that we should be allowed to serve in any capacity at our own expense. I feel sure that it will be the wish of all officers and men who are in a position to do so to offer their services upon the same terms."

Aubrey Woolls-Sampson was born at the Cape where he spent his boyhood days. As a young man he went to the Barberton goldfields in the eastern Transvaal. He also served in the Zulu War in 1878–79 and was at the battle of Ulundi. Woolls-Sampson returned to the Transvaal to take up a position as Clerk and Interpreter to a Native Commissioner. The post served as an introduction to the duties of Native Commissioner which he later held in the Waterberg district about 60 miles from Pretoria.

When the Boer uprising broke out in 1880, Commissioner Woolls-Sampson trekked to Pretoria through country thick with hostile commandos,[6] guarding a bag containing Government Revenue. He enlisted in a mounted squadron about 60 strong raised by Captain Henry Nourse to reinforce the garrison. After Nourse fell ill the command went to Captain Woolls-Sampson. The Squadron suffered casualties in active daily patrolling and foraging expeditions on the outskirts of the town. On the morning of 28th December, Captain Woolls-Sampson took a 50-man strong patrol south of Pretoria, skirmishing with Boers at Six Mile Spruit.[7] In a foraging expedition to outlying farms on New Year's Eve, Captain Woolls-Sampson gathered in 500 sheep, cattle and poultry.

On the 6th January 1881 after a night march, a British force of 120 mounted men and 280 infantry under Lieutenant-Colonel G. Gildea, Royal Scots Fusiliers the garrison commander – attacked a Boer laager at Swart Kopje, about 12 miles east of Pretoria. The infantry travelled on wagons drawn by mules to Struben's Farm, about three miles in advance of Swart Kopje. The attack on the Kopje lasted an hour. The laager and contents were destroyed. Most of the commando, numbering about 1,000 burghers, got away. Only 16 prisoners were taken.

From Struben's Farm, Captain Woolls-Sampson had advanced ahead of the main body to the right of the kopje with 25 men. Woolls-Sampson and the Boer leader, Commandant Hans Botha, a crack shot, who had fought at Bronkhorstspruit, engaged at short range from behind ant-hills. In the duel Botha received seven bullet wounds. Woolls-Sampson was wounded in the arm, in the shoulder and had his jugular vein almost severed. Commandant Botha was picked up on the field by the British. Captain Woolls-Sampson was carried under heavy fire across the Pienaar's River by Lance-Corporal H. Hampton of the Fusiliers. Corporal Hampton was later awarded the Distinguished Conduct Medal for his action. Woolls-Sampson and Botha occupied adjacent beds in the British Army Hospital, where they became friends.

At one time Woolls-Sampson was very near to death. Word actually reached the Cape that he had died. The family went into mourning and obituary notices appeared in the Cape newspapers at the very time when Woolls-Sampson was making a recovery.

When the British Government decided not to continue the war and commenced the peace negotiations that ended with the Convention of Pretoria. .Woolls-Sampson joined the group of dismayed Britishers who burnt an effigy of Mr Gladstone, the British Prime Minister, and buried the Union Jack that had flown over the British garrison camp. The flag was placed in a coffin and buried in a grave dug in vacant land opposite the British Residency where the Treaty was being signed.

For the next five years Woolls-Sampson lived at the Cape. He served in Rhodesia at the time of the Matabele War. When hostilities ended in 1894 he stayed on for some time, hunting and prospecting. Eventually, he returned to Johannesburg and became a member of the National Union. As stated earlier after the Jameson Raid, Woolls-Sampson and Karri-Davies served 15 months of a two year sentence, until President Kruger released them on the occasion of Queen Victoria's Diamond Jubilee.

Aubrey Woolls-Sampson was severely wounded at the battle of Elandslaagte on 21st October 1899. He recovered and served for a time as Commanding Officer of the Imperial Light Horse. Early in 1901, he transferred to the Intelligence Corps where he was an outstanding success. Before the end of the war Lieutenant-General Ian Hamilton described him as "an unrivalled Intelligence Officer."[8]

On 26th June 1902, he was appointed an Honorary Colonel in the British Army. At a later date he was knighted. For a brief period after the war he became the Member for Braamfontein in the parliament of the Union of South Africa. Colonel Sir Aubrey Woolls-Sampson died in Johannesburg on 19th May 1924 at the age of 68 years. He was buried in the Brixton Cemetery.

Walter Davies was born in 1867 and educated at Scotch College, Melbourne. He qualified as a consulting engineer and was associated with mining at the Broken Hill field in New South Wales, until ill-health forced him to make a sea voyage. Davies arrived in South Africa where he was destined to spend the most important years of his life at the period when the Rand mines were being developed. He established a successful business with the importing from Western Australia of the Karri and Jarrah timbers, used on the rapidly developing South African railways. Besides being used for railway sleepers the timber was also in demand in the mines. In Western Australia the Davies family was also engaged in the timber industry.

In South Africa the name of Walter Davies became almost synonymous with the Australian timbers which he imported and traded. So he decided to change his name to Walter Karri-Davies. During the crisis in Johannesburg at the time of the Jameson Raid, Australian volunteers

reported to the office of the Australian Association. An Australian Corps 800 strong was enlisted to assist in the defence of the town. The chief duties of the Corps turned out to be the protection of life and property and keeping the streets free and open. As an active member of the Reform Committee, Karri-Davies was posted to the Robinson Deep mine close to the town with 150 armed men, nearly all of whom were from the Australian Corps. A lookout was kept from the mine headgear.

After his release from Pretoria with Woolls-Sampson in 1897, Karri-Davies visited England. When war seemed certain in 1899, the two men renewed their close association and joint confrontation of the Kruger Government by directing all their efforts towards the raising of the Imperial Light Horse. Karri-Davies wrote from the field with the Light Horse: "So long as a single Boer remains in the field with a rifle, so long will I remain to fight it out."[9]

Walter Karri-Davies took neither pay nor accepted promotion for his military service. He turned down offers of awards and the honour of a knighthood. In a letter to General Kitchener he asked to be permitted to decline, as the privilege of serving was of itself sufficient reward. In correspondence in 1905 he disclosed: "That by order of the King, I was graciously granted the privilege of serving throughout the 1899–1902 war without decoration or distinction or any kind."

Major Karri-Davies served for the duration of the war with the corps that he helped to raise. He was prominent in the defence of Ladysmith and was slightly wounded on Wagon Hill. He led the first relieving patrol through to the besieged town of Mafeking. Towards the end of the war he was responsible for imperial Light Horse supplies and organized recruiting for the Corps.

After the war Karri-Davies resumed business in Johannesburg as a consulting engineer. He was commissioned by Lord Milner to make recommendations for the establishment of irrigation works and dams and for the improvement of the methods of production in the wool-growing industry. After some years he returned to Western Australia where the Davies family had a property at Karridale about 200 miles south of Perth.

In 1915 Karri-Davies arrived in England to offer his services in World War I. With the rank of Honorary Colonel in the British Army, he represented the British Government Mission on the west coast of the United States. As Liaison Officer he had staff and offices in Los Angeles and San Francisco. Colonel Walter Karri-Davies deserves to be remembered as co-founder of the Imperial Light Horse and a patriot who defended fervently the interests of the British Empire. He died in London on 28th November 1926.

The volunteers in the Imperial Light Horse engaged in the war with a real sense of grievance. The Corps fought for nothing less than the unconditional surrender of the Boer forces. Mr G.W. Steevens, the correspondent in Ladysmith of the London *Daily Mail*, reporting on the attitude taken by the Light Horsemen wrote: "The men enlisted mainly with a view of vengeance on the Boers". Mr Steevens died in Ladysmith during the siege from enteric fever.

An English doctor serving in military hospitals in South Africa, wrote after a talk with a wounded Light Horseman: "What I don't like and can't understand is the intense and implacable bitterness against the Boers which all South Africans such as him show. Nothing is too bad for the Boers." Early in the war Major Woolls-Sampson summed up the general feeling in the Corps: "My natural inclination is to keep the field as long as a single Boer remains in arms".[10]

The Imperial Light Horse was made up mainly of South Africans, Britons and Australians. Louis Creswicke, a British historian wrote: "The Imperial Light Horse formed by Majors Karri-Davies and Woolls-Sampson was largely composed of Australians".[11] Another illustration of how the Australians were identified with the Corps is indicated by a statement of Guiseppe Garibaldi, the son of an Italian nobleman: "I went to the headquarters of the Imperial Light Horse, an Australian Mounted Corps, presented my credentials and signed on for service."[12]

The Light Horse was the first of the many volunteer colonial corps raised in South Africa. Nearly 30,000 volunteers enlisted in the other colonies of the Empire. Although the numbers are not accurately known, double that number enlisted in the Cape and in Natal. In addition to long standing regiments like the Natal Carbineers and the Cape Mounted Rifles, there were a good number of irregular corps raised in the early days of the war, such as the South African Light Horse and Thorneycroft's Mounted Infantry. Within the ranks of all the corps raised in South Africa were large numbers of volunteers from the far flung Empire – Australia, New Zealand and Canada who either worked a passage or paid their way to the front.

Lieutenant-Colonel John Adye, Assistant Adjutant-General for Colonial Forces – South Africa, giving evidence before the Royal Commission on the War in London in 1902-1903 stated:[13] "I cannot give you accurate numbers and I doubt whether anybody an, because there was considerable irregularity in raising the corps at the start. The fact that there was no staff officer right through the war dealing with all colonial forces, meant that scarcely any record was kept of many of them. Once I got to Pretoria I tried to get the matter more into shape for the whole of the Colonial Forces. Some men undoubtedly enlisted in various corps and very often under different names after obtaining a discharge. So that you may have counted a man more than several times over and in that way it is impossible to give an absolute correct statement. I should say from my experience that from 50,000 to 60,000 men enlisted in South Africa under all the various categories, right down to the lowest."

Field-Marshal Lord Roberts said in the House of Commons: "No less than 46,858 South African Colonials took part in the war. Of these 3,080 were killed or died of wounds or disease and 3,333 were wounded."[14]

In a common appraisal of colonial troops, Lieutenant-General P. Methuen stated at the Royal Commission: "The shrewdest men I have ever dealt with are the Colonials. Anything they do not know is not worth knowing. They were quite the Boers equal in everything but courage, in which quality they excelled him greatly."

The Imperial Light Horse was the only South African irregular corps not disbanded at the end of the war. The Corps fought in both World Wars and became the most famous of all the South African regiments. Today, the great regiment is simply called – The Light Horse Regiment.

In a speech at Pietermaritzburg on 5th December 1900 in praise of colonial troops Lord Roberts said: "I can tell you that these corps have rendered magnificent service and I do not know what we should have done without the colonial contingents."

To this day, the Imperial Light Horse Memorials of the 1899–1902 campaign on the battlefields all over South Africa, bear these enduring words: "Tell England, ye who pass this Monument, we who died serving her, rest here content."

---

[1] From a document in the Karri-Davies Papers
[2] A letter in the Karri-Davies Papers
[3] Later Major-General Sir Reginald Barnes. K.C.B., D.S.O.
[4] Typed Diary of 'F' Squadron. 1st Light Horse in the Karri-Davies Papers
[5] In the Karri-Davies Collection of Papers
[6] A Boer military unit of any size
[7] A small watercourse or creek
[8] In *Anti Commando* by Victor Sampson & Ian Hamilton
[9] From a paper in the Karri-Davies Collection
[10] From a paper in the Karri-Davies collection
[11] *South Africa and the Transvaal War* L. Creswicke
[12] *A Toast to Rebellion* G. Garibaldi
[13] Minutes of Evidence taken before the Royal Commission on the War in South Africa – 1902–03
[14] *The Colonials in South Africa* J. Stirling

CHAPTER 3

THE STRENGTH OF THE OPPOSING FORCES – THE EARLY BATTLES IN NATAL.

In the four months following the expiration of the Ultimatum on the 11th October 1899, all the fighting took place within the British colonies. By the end of August the number of British troops in South Africa was not more than 10,000. Another 5,000 men landed in Durban from India only a few days before the war began. In Britain, the Army received orders to mobilize on 7th October. On 14th October, General Sir Redvers Buller, appointed Commander-in-Chief in South Africa, sailed from Southampton. By 20th October the mobilized troops were embarking.

On 11th October the Republics had about 38,000 burghers ready to take the field. The numerically superior and more highly mobile commandos of the Republican forces invaded the colonies on three fronts in an effort to strike a knockout blow before the landing of British reinforcements. Seasonal spring rains provided fresh veldt grass for the ponies crossing the frontiers. From the western frontier the commandos attacked and placed under siege the towns of Kimberley and Mafeking lying along the railway from Cape Town to Rhodesia. The railway ran almost parallel with the western borders of the Republics.

Another Republican thrust occurred over the Orange River in the weakly held northern Cape Colony midlands. By crossing at Norval's Pont[1] the commandos occupied the railway town of Colesberg. A second crossing took place not many miles upstream at Bethulie. The commandos advanced to the railway junction at Stormberg. The British fell back, leaving small garrisons to hold the railway south of Stormberg and the junctions at Naaupoort and De Aar, maintaining the rail links with the southern ports.

The strongest thrust was directed east of the Drakensberg. Range, through mountain passes into Natal and extending some distance south of the Tugela River towards Pietermaritzburg. A few miles north of the Tugela the small garrison town of Ladysmith came under siege on 2nd November, after General Buller had disembarked at Cape Town on 31st October.

The British decision to defend northern Natal, lying wedged in a narrow apex between Orange Free State and Transvaal boundaries, was a political rather than a military decision. It was thought that an immediate withdrawal to Ladysmith would have an undesirable effect on the morale of the population. Nevertheless, within a few weeks commandos invading on two fronts, forced the British to retire from Dundee to Ladysmith.

The total number of burghers taking part in the war is not known exactly, for the loose system under which the commandos entered the field, did not allow for accurate returns. The actual number of burghers engaged in military service from the two Republics during the course of the war must have been about 50,000. There were as well, some 10,000 men from the Cape – called rebels by the British – who joined the commandos, and something like 2,500 foreign sympathisers; making a total of between 60,000 to 65,000. The greatest number in the field at a given time was about 45,000 in December 1900.

In September 1899, a young burgher wrote to his brother in Ottoshoop, a village just north of Mafeking. In October 1900, the letter was found in a deserted house in Ottoshoop by a London *Times* correspondent who sent it to his newspaper from Zeerust:[2] "We are going to have a bloody war and can expect the same every day, nay, every hour, just as sure as I am writing this. We must be brave and faithful to our country. The English Government will not declare war because they say we are a subordinate State.

"The troops will cross our borders at a certain hour to occupy our country. Of course, as soon as they cross they will be fired on. Our country will be bathed in blood and tears, our bravest men will fall in battle, but we will gain the victories. Our cause is just and righteous. Besides, according to statistics, an army of 17,000 on the defensive is equal to an advancing army of 50,000. Well, Orange Free State and Transvaal can have 34,000 men in the field in eight days. Then we will be twice as strong as the 50,000.

"Their artillery will not do so much harm, we fight guerrilla fashion. Our artillery will play havoc with the 25,000 or 30,000 *voetgangers*.[3] We are all mounted. We have the advantage of selecting our own battlefields. They say England can send more than 50,000. They must prove this first. But our Republican armies will also be reinforced from the discontented population from Natal and Cape Colony. I think we have a good chance of wounding England for life."

The British Army in South Africa in 1899–1902 reached a total of 448,000. It was the largest overseas army to leave Britain up until that time. It was also the first khaki-clad arm to a major campaign. In a healthy climate, carelessness and neglect of sanitary precautions caused dysentery and enteric fever. These scourges were responsible for more casualties than the effect of shot and shell. Losses from death by disease were 13,250. Officers and men killed in action or died from wounds amounted to 7,792 in a total of 21,844 deaths in South Africa. The losses of the Boer forces in battle are difficult to determine, although the number was relatively small. Estimates vary from several thousand to 6,000.

With the exception of the Artillery Corps and the Corps of the South African Republic Police,[4] the commandos wore no uniform. Every burgher was mounted and well adapted to the countryside. Armed with both Mauser and Martini-Henry rifles, they carried no bayonet. Disembarking British troops were predominantly infantry and commonly marched straight from the ship, along the pier, into the railway carriages and away to the front. The Boer gunners were equipped with the most modern German and French artillery. These, although fewer in number, had the capacity to outrange the British guns. To overcome the disparity, the British hurriedly improvised by mounting, a limited number of long range naval guns on specially built mobile carriages, some of which were used most effectively in the siege of Ladysmith.

The war was fought over an area about the size of Germany and France, in country where roads were primitive and bridges were few. Railways were narrow gauge with over 5,000 miles of single track. Thousands of troops were tied down, guarding the tracks from raids by the elusive commandos. Sunken rivers winding across the veldt impeded convoys and were often crossed between breaches in high banks leading down to a drift.[5]

Speaking in London on 6th November 1899, Lord Wolseley, Commander-in-Chief of the British Army referred to the need to: "Bring this curious army of ours up to the level of the modern armies of the world."

Conditioned for years to being more or less engaged regularly in fighting small colonial wars the Army also suffered from being steeped in tradition. It was largely an Army on foot about to meet, in open country, a force with the advantage of selecting its own battlefields against an advancing foe. At first the soldiers made easy targets, being slow to take cover against the long range magazine rifle. The burghers usually waited behind a protective sangar[6] built on a kopje, for the soldiers to attack across the open veldt. Things began to change when officers left swords behind and any necessary part of a soldier's equipment that glittered in the sun was painted dull khaki.

On 11th October 1899, the six squadrons of the Imperial Light Horse were camped on the showground at Pietermaritzburg. On Thursday, 12th October, 'A' Squadron under Captain DE Doveton marched out from the showground and scouting widely, headed towards Estcourt in the direction of Colenso and the Tugela River. On 16th October, 'B-C-D-E'-Squadrons entrained for Ladysmith, in carriages and open trucks. The horses also went by truck. Travelling overnight the Light Horse arrived in Ladysmith in the early hours of 17th October, going into camp on a river flat on the east side of the town in the direction of the railway station. 'F' Squadron, the last to leave Pietermaritzburg, arrived without tents or baggage as they had gone astray. At midnight on the same day, the Light Horse was ordered back 17 miles to Colenso, followed by infantry and artillery to reinforce a small garrison of Natal Volunteers. It was feared that Free State commandos were about to attack the small garrison guarding the village and the rail bridge linking the town with Ladysmith. Within a few days the Light Horse returned to Ladysmith without meeting the enemy and camped alongside British regulars in the valley to the west of the convent.

Lieutenant-General Sir George White landed at Durban from Southampton on 7th October, to take command of the reinforced Army in Natal. Within a few days he moved to Ladysmith where all available troops were concentrated. The first battles in Natal occurred north of Ladysmith in the narrow apex between the boundaries of the Republics. Through the apex ran the Durban–Pretoria railway. The Republican forces, numbering about 20,000, advanced across the frontiers through the Drakensberg passes from the Free State and over Laing's Nek[7] on the Natal–Transvaal border.

After some hesitation, General White allowed Lieutenant-General Sir W. Penn-Symons to defend Dundee, situated in the middle of the narrow apex. General Penn-Symons had a force of about 4,000 men. On 20th October the Boers were defeated in a hard fought battle with British infantry and artillery at Talana Hill, on the outskirts of the town. General Penn-Symons was mortally wounded. Under pressure from the rapidly converging commandos the British were soon compelled to undertake a forced march back to the base at Ladysmith.

While the battle was being decided at Talana Hill, General Johannes Hermanus Kock, by advancing from the Transvaal, established a commando made up mainly of Johannesburg and Krugersdorp burghers, astride the railway at Elandslaagte station, 15 miles north-east of Ladysmith on the line to Dundee. This commando seized a mixed goods train with trucks full of military stores and livestock assigned for the Dundee garrison. Mr Mitchell, the correspondent for the London *Standard* was apprehended on the train, together with a number of other civilians.

"On 21st October five squadrons of the Imperial Light Horse under Colonel Scott Chisholme ('A' Squadron was at Estcourt) moved out from Ladysmith towards Elandslaagte before daylight, along slippery and muddy roads in a mist so thick that not much could be seen ahead. The Light Horse was in support of half a battalion of infantry – 330 men from the 1st Manchester Regiment, the Natal Volunteer Field Battery and a Railway Construction company of Royal Engineers, under the general command of Major-General Sir John French".[8]

After reconnaissance with Major Woolls-Sampson, 'B' and 'C' Squadrons located the enemy at Elandslaagte station and on a ridge of kopjes a mile and a half south-east of the station.to the right front of the column. The Natal Field Battery shelled the railway sheds at a range of 1,900 yards from a flat rise west of the station between the railway and the Newcastle road killing eight burghers and forcing the enemy to withdraw from the railway completely. Mr Mitchell and the other passengers taken the previous day, escaped when the first shell fell. In the meantime, Boer gunners on the kopjes started to drop shells within 50 yards of the Light Horse drawn up near the Natal battery, which, with its outmoded 7-pounder muzzle loaders, was unable to reach the Boer position at the range of more than 2,000 yards.

Fortunately a considerable number of shells from the Boer guns failed to explode. One shell landed close to Colonel Scott Chisholme and another landed almost under Major Karri-Davies' horse. After about half an hour, when it seemed that 'E' Squadron in occupation of the station under Captain John Knapp might be cut off, Karri-Davies galloped across and gave the order to retire. Although the Boers kept up a rapid fire, no one was hit on the gallop back. finding the enemy in such strength and his obsolete guns outranged by about 500 yards, French retired back almost four miles to Modder Spruit and waited for the arrival of reinforcements from Ladysmith.

Colonel Ian Hamilton, in command of the infantry, accompanied troops assigned to one armoured train and two trains made up of carriages and open trucks. Colonel Hamilton had seven companies – 1st Battalion Devonshire Regiment, five companies 2nd Battalion Gordon Highlanders – sent to reinforce the 1st Manchester Regiment. One squadron of the 5th Lancers and a squadron of the 5th Dragoon Guards travelled by road. The 21st and 42nd Royal field Artillery galloped up from Ladysmith with double teams. The first reinforcements arrived by 11 a.m. By 3.30 p.m. the force under General French had grown to 3,500 officers and men.

French quickly established artillery superiority over the two Boer guns on the ridge to the south east and enemy position. By taking what scant cover they could from behind ant-hills in broken ground, the Devons formed a line 850 yards from the Boer position. Under strong rifle fire they waited for the right flank attack to develop over rocky spurs. By about 2 p.m. the Light Horse and the 5th Lancers, having cleared Boer outposts on the south-west extremity of the ridges, secured a low spur over two miles from the main enemy position, selected by French to be the launching point for the flank attack.

By 4.30 p.m. the turning movement was in motion. The Manchesters, Gordon Highlanders and dismounted Imperial Light Horse advancing in that order on the veldt on the extreme right, the 5th Lancers patrolled the left. The main ridge, not more than 300 feet above the veldt was broken by rising rocky spurs. Taking cover wherever they could behind rocks and small boulders, the troops gradually pushed the Boers back, towards the main position, although the combined effect of heavy rifle fire and slight cover incurred casualties. Pushing forward and veering towards the north of the objective, the troops were held up and suffered casualties at an intersecting barbed wire farm fence near the bottom of a long slope. Rifle fire caught the Gordon Highlanders and the Light Horse bunched up at the fence. The men covered the final 350 yards in a broken and confused advance.

By 5.55 p.m. the infantry had fought its way to the summit, a plateau of 400 yards by 200 yards across. The Boer guns fell to the Devons, who after waiting for their comrades to advance on the flank, pressed home the frontal attack to join in the final assault. From the crest of the plateau with almost all resistance broken, Light Horsemen firing into the laager[9] below were in some danger from sharp shooters on a sugar-loaf kopje to the left and from burghers firing from the protection of laagered wagons. Meanwhile, on the plateau some of the troops were looking for their respective companies and others were resting.

After leading the advance to the summit at the head of his men waving a red and yellow silk scarf attached to the end of a cane, Colonel Scott Chisholme rested on a rock, and was chatting to a major in the Gordons, when his attention was drawn to the plight of Corporal Robert Tinsley suffering from a wound in the leg. With the assistance of Trooper Charles Lamb, the Colonel bound the wound and together they started to carry Tinsley to a place of safety.

A group of about 50 Boers, previously concealed and lying low, suddenly staged a counter-attack by opening up a severe cross fire at fairly close range. About six Boers led by a man with a big black beard and wearing a blue mackintosh fired directly at the pair carrying the wounded man. Colonel Scott Chisholme was hit in the leg. Trooper George Ferrand went to his assistance as he fell and got him to his feet. Almost at once the Colonel was shot through the lungs. Troopers Ferrand and Lamb got him to his feet again, but almost instantly he was killed by a bullet in the head. Captain Charles Mullins shouted an order for the men to leave the Colonel and take cover. With Lieutenant Robert Johnstone and Lieutenant Arthur Brabant and officers of the Gordons, he rallied the men to hold the position they had won. Between them, the Gordons and the Light Horse stopped the desperate counter-attack. The 5th Lancers pursued and cut down about 50 burghers as they fled away to the north. This was the only occasion in the war when the lance was used with any effect.

Major Karri-Davies surrounded a farm house used as a concentration post by the enemy. The house was enclosed with a wire fence. There was also a stable and several mud walled thatched kraals.[11] Leaving a party to cover the house from the kraal, Karri-Davies took some men around to the verandah in front of the house and called upon the burghers inside to surrender. Altogether, 23 prisoners were taken at the farm house.

British casualties in the battle of Elandslaagte were 36 killed and 228 wounded. The Imperial Light Horse and the Gordon Highlanders suffered the highest percentage of casualties, the Light Horse losing 14 killed and 32 wounded.

Major Woolls-Sampson, fell, wounded, at the head of his men, about 150 yards from the main, plateau. With his right thigh badly smashed he was carried from the field on a litter made from rifles by a party of Gordons and Light Horse. Major Karri-Davies wrote: "I had the good fortune when taking the Regiment home in the darkness to discover Woolls-Sampson near the place where he received his wound. He was placed upon a rough litter made of three rifles and carried over rocky ground to Elandslaagte station."[12] Trooper Nixon, who was a doctor, attended Woolls-Sampson until he arrived in Ladysmith.

An Imperial Light Horse Diarist wrote: "The Devons set up a picket on the kopje where they lit a fire and sent out fatigue parties in conjunction with the Light Horse. The less severely wounded were taken to the farm house used as a makeshift hospital. The more severely wounded were taken across to the fireside and wrapped in blankets."[13] Many of the regular troops were attended by doctors at a camp set up in the Boer laager. A great many soldiers took shelter near the railway station, clustering in front of fires built up from stacks of coal in the railway yard.

All through the night search parties continued to bring in the wounded but owing to the rough nature of the ground it meant, that the wounded could not be moved easily. In any case the column was without ambulance wagons. Trooper J. O'Hara, although shot three times in the leg, kept firing at any burgher within sight after he had dressed his wounds himself. Eventually, he was picked up and laid on a garden seat on the verandah at the farm house until the morning. The Light Horse Medical Officers, Surgeon-Major W.T. Davies and Surgeon Lieutenant C.E. Ligertwood, worked unceasingly throughout the night, assisted by Troopers T. Crean and Nixon, both doctors fighting in the ranks.

Some of the wounded lay out in the drizzle and the cold all night. The next morning Trooper Hubert Wolseley was found dead. Unable to walk because of a wound in the leg, Wolseley fainted from loss of blood and died overnight from exposure. From the position in which he was found some unaccounted for rifle shots fired off at 9 a.m. were thought to have come from his efforts to attract attention. Trooper Wolseley was the nephew of Lord Wolseley, the Commander-in-Chief of the British Army.

That night, on his way back to Ladysmith from the battle at which he had been a distant observer, General White received information that the town was in some danger from the west, where commandos were reported coming through the Drakensberg Mountains at Van Reenen's Pass. Acting on the intelligence report, White decided to abandon Elandslaagte and withdraw completely to Ladysmith.

From the five Light Horse squadrons at Elandslaagte, not more than 200 dismounted troopers took part in the assault with the infantry. 'F' Squadron escorted the guns of the 42nd Royal field Artillery, but expended no ammunition while coming under shell fire. Some men in camp in Ladysmith and horseholders accounted for the rest.

Strangely enough, the Corps went into its first action against a commando drawn to a large extent from Johannesburg. The result was when the battle was over, there were many opportunities for some rather unexpected mutual recognitions: "There we met and destroyed a picked contingent of mischief makers and old time British opponents hailing from Krugersdorp and Johannesburg."[39] Furthermore, at Elandslaagte, the Uitlanders effectively silenced the taunts of indecision under which they had smarted since the days of the Jameson Raid.

For gallantry at Elandslaagte two Imperial Light Horse officers, Captain Charles H. Mullins and Lieutenant Robert Johnstone were awarded the Victoria Cross. Captain Mullins, a Johannesburg solicitor and a member of the Reform Committee was wounded, The citation read: "On 21st October 1899 at Elandslaagte, when at a most critical moment the advance became momentarily checked, these two officers very gallantly rushed forward under heavy fire and rallied the men, thus enabling the flanking movement which decided the day, to be carried out."

In General Kock's commando there were a number of Government officials from Johannesburg, Hollanders and German sympathisers, serving in the artillery and the Zuid-Afrikaans Republiek Police. A Diarist[14] in 'F' Squadron commented on the general appearance of the burghers: "They were a rough looking lot and resembled cattle drovers." General Kock died in Ladysmith from wounds received at Elandslaagte. The British arranged for his body to be sent to the Transvaal. Dr H. Koster, a prosecutor in the trial of the Reformers in Pretoria, died bravely while serving as a field-cornet.[15]

Colonel Adolf Schiel, a German gunnery instructor was shot in the legs. He was once commandant at the Johannesburg Fort and was Governor of Pretoria Gaol when Karri-Davies and Woolls-Sampson were prisoners. Some months after Elandslaagte, Schiel wrote from the prisoner of war camp at Simonstown: "It was strange feeling at Elandslaagte, when lying wounded on the battlefield and recovering from unconsciousness. The first faces I saw were Johannesburg friends in the Imperial Light Horse. The officer who took me prisoner was one of my best friends, an Australian named Karri-Davies. That really is the fortune of war."[16]

Starting early on the morning of 22nd October, the Light Horse under Major Karri-Davies, marching back to Ladysmith were subjected to sniper fire for most of the way. A working party under Lieutenant Arthur Brabant stayed until 8 a.m., moving the wounded and escorting the captured guns and ambulance wagons to Elandslaagte station.

At 7.30 a.m. on 23rd October, a burial party of 12 men under Lieutenant Brooking left Ladysmith by train for Elandslaagte. The train, made up of an engine and several carriages with a white flag on a staff tied to the funnel, had only gone seven miles before it was fired at and forced to shunt slowly back to Ladysmith. Headquarters in the town obtained a letter from the wounded General Kock and by the early afternoon the train was again travelling towards Elandslaagte. Near Modder Spruit about four miles out, the track was blocked with large rocks. With the services of Trooper Clem Gardner as interpreter, a party of Boers was persuaded to allow the train to proceed. Only a short distance further along the track, the wooden Modder Spruit bridge came into view burning fiercely. The burial party left the train and set out on foot. For more than ten miles they walked all the way to Elandslaagte, accompanied by a party of Boers on horseback. That night the Light Horsemen slept at Elandslaagte station.

The next morning it was found that all the dead had been buried by a working party of 150 Africans. Accompanied by a chaplain, Lieutenant Brooking and his men went to the spot where Colonel Scott Chisholme was buried. A service was read before the body was exhumed and carried on a stretcher to a cart. No mules were provided by the Boers, so the men were forced to haul the cart themselves. Some distance was covered before the Boers came up with mules and the party again set out along the road back to the train waiting near Modder Spruit. Lieutenant Brooking and party reached Ladysmith that night, together with two Boer doctors to attend to General Kock and the other wounded prisoners.

On 23rd October mounted patrols from Ladysmith reported a concentration of Free State commandos on heights overlooking the road and railway to Newcastle from the west, seven miles north of Ladysmith. General A Cronje with a force of 6,000 riflemen supported by artillery was extended over six miles along the crests of the heights. Cronje's position gave General White reason for anxiety for the safety of the column withdrawing from Dundee. With the objective of containing the enemy long enough to ensure a clear passage for the Dundee column, White marched out of Ladysmith at 5 a.m. on the 24th October with 5,300 officers and men.

Led by Major-Karri-Davies, in temporary command following the death of Colonel Scott Chisholme and in the enforced absence from the field of Major Woolls-Sampson, four squadrons of the Imperial Light Horse marched at 4 a.m. with the Natal Volunteers, the Hussars and the 5th Lancers under General French. Leaving 'C' Squadron Light Horse with the baggage train and followed at 6 a.m. by infantry, the 10th Mountain Battery and the 42nd and 53rd Royal field Artillery, the mounted column soon came under fire from the hills on the left.

By ousting burghers from advanced positions on low ridges sloping towards the road, the 5th Lancers cleared the way for the infantry to take up ground at about 8 a.m. on a ridge near Rietfontein Farm. For some hours the opposing forces directed heavy rifle fire across the bushy valley from protected positions on the crests. Mounted troops supporting the infantry screened both flanks of the British position. Field artillery drawn up near Rietfontein Farm silenced several Boer batteries on the hills, setting the positions aflame with burning grass arid stampeding the battery teams.

In a lull before midday about 150 Gloucestershire infantrymen with a machine gun detachment suddenly and unaccountably dashed up and away down the open slope into the valley in the face of intense rifle fire losing six killed and 40 wounded within a very short time. The Gloucester's commanding officer, Colonel E. Wilfred was killed. After 30 year's service with the regiment it was the first time he had been under fire. The losses of the Gloucesters accounted for almost half of the British casualties on the day. 'D' Squadron, Light Horse, joining the Gloucester infantry on the right in the advance down the hill, fortunately suffered no casualties under fire.

Patrolling with British Mounted Infantry to the left of the road and railway between Rietfontein Farm and Modder Spruit, 'E' and 'F' Squadrons Light Horse engaged riflemen at 1,400 yards and forced them to retire. Attached to the rear screen, most of the Light Horse reached Ladysmith by about 7 p.m. with the last of the returning troops. Trooper Phillip Tucker wrote:[17] "We 'B' Squadron led by Captain Knapp, patrolled the battlefield all night after the fight. It rained all night and we were miserable, having been something like 28 hours without sleep and little food and almost all the time in the saddle." The only Light Horse casualties in the battle of Rietfontein were three troopers in 'E' Squadron who were wounded.

Early on the morning of 25th October, General White sent the 19th Hussars and squadrons of Light Horse patrolling towards Rietfontein. The squadrons returned late in the day when the security of the Dundee column was assured from any threat from the right flank. On 26th October the retiring column with Brigadier J. Yule in command reached Ladysmith without loss at the end of five weary days on the march under difficult wet weather conditions. They came in, guided all the way back clear of the enemy, by Colonel J. Dartnell,[18] Chief Commissioner of the Natal Police. With the linking up of the Free State and Transvaal commandos only a few days after Rietfontein, the Republican forces were spread over a 20 mile front, east and west of the road leading to Newcastle. With a strength of about 12,000 men, the commandos were only five miles from Ladysmith. General White decided to loosen the tightening cordon by launching dawn attacks preceded by night marches. In these actions fought on 30th October and known as the Battle of Ladysmith, British losses were about 1,200 killed, wounded or taken prisoner. The losses of the Boers were about 200.

On the night of 29th – 30th October, Colonel E. Grimwood marched with the main infantry brigade four miles north-east of the town to a ridge near Farquhar's Farm. From that point soon after dawn, the main attack was planned against the left of the Transvaalers line between Long Hill and Pepworth Hill. Before any attack could be launched, the brigade was surprised at dawn and caught on the right flank in the fire from 4,000 Mausers. A degree of support provided by the arrival of detachments of French's dismounted cavalry was not enough to prevent the retreat from Farquhar's Farm. Only the most resolute rearguard covering fire by the 53rd and 13th batteries enabled the infantry to complete a three to four mile rather disorderly retreat to Ladysmith, across

A bush plain, under the range of the 94-pounder shells from a 6-inch gun on the long flat-topped Pepworth Hill.

Lieutenant-Colonel F. Carleton led a column on the night of 29th October to Nicholson's Nek, four miles to the left of Pepworth Hill, to provide cover on the left flank of the main Pepworth-Long Hill position. Colonel Carleton's progress was slower than anticipated. Rather than risk being caught at dawn crossing the valley leading up to the pass in the Nek, he decided to camp for the night on Tchrengula Hill, about two miles in front of the Nek. The column suffered a severe reverse when untrained mule teams carrying ammunition and mountain guns became restive after several large boulders rolled noisily down the hillside. The team stampeded in the darkness and shots were fired from a Boer outpost. Without the guns and without ammunition other than the rounds carried in bandoliers, the troops climbed to the top of the hill, one of the two high points of a long ridge. The night was spent on the southern end of the ridge where some sangars were built. Lord Roberts described the sangars as:[19] "Almost pitiful, they were so insignificant and badly placed."

From early daylight General Christian De Wet advanced his commando from rock to rock along the ridge, stalking and pinning the soldiers down l behind the hastily constructed sangars. The morning passed with Boer reinforcements increasing from the north. By 10.30 a.m. the engagement was general on all sides, with the Boers on hills only 1,000 to 1,400 yards away and shooting strongly. The soldiers were surrounded. At noon a heliographed order was received to retire to Ladysmith, but this was impossible. With ammunition running low, short of food and without water in the heat of the day, the column surrendered, the ceasefire coming not long after noon. In the column of 1,100 men (297 were killed or wounded), about 100 unwounded men escaped back to Ladysmith, more than 700 prisoners were taken to a prison camp set up on the racecourse in Pretoria.

In the battle of Ladysmith the Light Horse was attached to the column under Colonel Ian Hamilton, made up of 5th Dragoon Guards and two squadrons of mounted infantry located near Limit Hill, midway between Farquhar's Farm and Ladysmith. Because of the defeat of Grimwood's infantry brigade, a projected frontal attack by Hamilton's column against Pepworth Hill did not eventuate. The column retired in good order. General French, with a force near Lombard's Kop north-east of Ladysmith, could make no headway. When French got the signal to retire he signalled back his ability to hold on, but White insisted on a withdrawal.

Meanwhile, Colonel Hamilton ordered 'E' and 'F' Squadrons Light Horse to occupy two kopjes west of the Newcastle road, to stop the possibility of a Boer advance from the direction of Nicholson's Nek on the left flank. The Light Horse held the kopjes unopposed for two hours. On the way back they passed some wounded and a few mules with several gun carriages; the remnant of Carleton's 10th Mountain Battery coming from the direction of Nicholson's Nek.

With Major Karri-Davies in command, 'B-C-D' Squadrons were engaged in covering Grimwood's infantry in the withdrawal from Farquhar's farm, the withdrawal that owed so much to the gallant gunners of the field batteries. The Light Horse was called upon to protect the rear of the marching Leicester Regiment and the 60th King's Royal Rifles.

The failure of the rather unwieldy operation planned by General White was due to unexpected pressure – not anticipated by British Intelligence – from the extreme right and the extreme left.

Colonel Hamilton testified before the Royal Commission in London in 1902–03: "We returned to Ladysmith in a state in which a large number of the troops were discouraged and which for a day or two we had lost the power of any vigorous initiative. If the Boers had really pressed, if they had some disciplined body to which they could have given the order to vigorously attack and pursue, I think it might have been a bad business."

Mr John Stuart, correspondent for the Morning Post wrote:[20] "The men straggled into town and lay under stoeps[21] along the main street and under trees by the roadway. dead beat." On 31st October shells fell on Gordon Hill in the north-west sector, just beyond the town. The fire was drawn by the presence of the long range guns of the Naval Brigade. A number of shells landed in the Light Horse camp below Gordon Hill. The Corps moved across the Klip River to the eastern side of the town, close to where the camp was on 16th October. This was a pleasant spot called Mulberry Grove, shaded by trees, where the soil was dry and sandy. The Light Horse camped on this spot until the lifting of the siege.

When the Regiment was moving camp a shell dropped close to the rear of the column and another landed in front of the leaders. A shell also fell near Major Karri-Davies, covering his horse with dirt.

---

[1] A ferry-boat moved by ropes or chains
[2] Published in the London *Times*, 6th December, 1900
[3] Footsloggers
[4] Called "Zarp" i.e. Zuid Afrikansche Republiek Politie
[5] A ford
[6] Anglo-Indian word for a low breastwork
[7] A low strip or pass between two hills
[8] Later field-Marshall Earl French. Commander of British Forces in France in 1915
[9] Army camp
[10] Huts forming a native village, an enclosure for cattle
[11] From a paper in the Karri-Davies Papers
[12] From an unknown Diarist in the Karri-Davies Papers
[13] In a paper in the Karri-Davies Papers
[14] An unknown Diarist in the Karri-Davies Collection
[15] Lieutenant
[16] From a letter in the Sydney *Morning Herald*, 1900
[17] In his Diary in the Karri-Davies Collection
[18] Presently Major-General Sir John Dartnell
[19] In evidence to the Royal Commission 1902–03
[20] *Pictures of War*, 1900. John Stuart
[21] A verandah

CHAPTER 4
IN LADYSMITH – 2nd NOVEMBER – 31st DECEMBER 1899

Ladysmith had been an important centre for the marketing of sheep and cattle since before the establishment of Johannesburg. In 1897, not long after the Jameson Raid, Ladysmith became a frontier military base. Although the site was not a particularly easy one to defend, the position was chosen chiefly because it happened to be the most important railway junction in Natal. Situated some miles north of the Tugela River, it was close to the junction of the railway leading from Natal to the Orange Free State and to the Transvaal.

It was a most convenient place for military stores and had the type of small engineering equipment and locomotive sheds that went with a railway centre. The Klip River provided the town with its water supply and the drifts over the river near the town were not difficult. There was also the open space around required for rifle and artillery ranges.

The military establishment consisted of nothing more than an open camp, with corrugated iron barracks housing a garrison of about 1,800, made up of infantry, cavalry and usually two batteries of field artillery. Nothing was ever done to fortify the post. Both the camp and the town were completely open. None of the big hills almost overlooking the town had ever been surveyed and scarcely a British officer had ever set foot on any one of them.

By 2nd November Ladysmith was completely invested by about 22,000 Boers. On the same day telegraphic communication with the south was cut. The British perimeter, extending for some 14 miles, was defended by about 13,000 men holding positions on a ring of heights rising from the Ladysmith plain and varying in distance from a mile to about three miles from the town. The veldt around was covered with grass and low scrub. Along the eastern side the Klip River skirted the town, forming a natural trench on the plain as it wound away crookedly at a sunken level to the south-east. The Republican forces encompassed Ladysmith in a wider circle of ridges and kopjes, all well within artillery range of the town. Generally the defence had a clear field of fire for three-quarters of a mile, although to the north-east in the direction of Gun Hill and Lombard's Kop there was some cover up to half a mile from the British lines. On Mounted Infantry Hill south of the town, the Boers set a gun only 900 yards from the British position on Wagon Hill.

With 22 guns, the Boer artillery was only half as strong numerically as the British but had long range superiority. With an effective range of 3,500 yards, the British 15-pounder field guns were outranged and were only effective in repelling a close assault. General White telegraphed for naval guns. Four naval 32-pounders and two 4.7 guns on improvised mobile carriages arrived from Simonstown by the last train to get through before the railway was cut. Captain P. Normand,[1] Light Horseman and one of the Jameson Raiders wrote from Ladysmith: "The guns out here at present are absolutely inferior to Boer guns, which is a disgrace to the British Army. Blame the War Office, not the Generals."

General White told the Royal Commission: "The naval guns arrived and were in action on 30th October." He also said of the naval guns: "They could reply to the enemy's guns and I have no doubt kept the enemy's guns at a greater distance from us than they otherwise would have been." General White testified that the 6-inch Creusot guns: "fired 10,000 yards into my position." He also described the standard Army field gun: "Our field gun which was a 15-pounder, the effective range of which was 3,500 yards and when directed at any objective 4,000 yards off, began to fall off rapidly." White concluded: "These 4.7 and 12-pounder naval guns outranged my soldier's guns by 100%."

The decision of General White to hold Ladysmith not only prevented large quantities of military stores from falling into enemy hands, but also had the effect of stopping a rapid advance south by the Boers beyond Pietermaritzburg to Durban. White wrote in despatches:[2] "I was confident of holding out at Ladysmith and I saw clearly that so long as maintained myself there I could occupy the great mass of the Boer armies."

When the bombardment commenced on 2nd November, General Piet Joubert was confident that the effect of the long range gun would be enough to bring about a quick surrender. J.D. Kestell, a Dominie[3] with the commandos wrote:[4] "We were living in constant expectation that Ladysmith would speedily fall into our hands."

On the morning of 2nd November, General French directed a successful probing reconnaissance south of the town into Long Valley. On the afternoon of the same day, French was recalled to Cape Town. The train carrying French and his Chief Staff Officer, Major Douglas Haig[5] came under heavy rifle fire near Pieter's station. It was the last train to pass rough to the south. On the same afternoon, a goods train was forced to turn back.

After the recall of General French, the cavalry command in Ladysmith passed to Major-General J. Brocklehurst. At 4.30 a.m. on 3rd November, 'B-C-E-F' Squadrons Imperial Light Horse under Major Karri-Davies, proceeded to the Ladysmith railway station. The Light Horse was part of a strong mixed detachment, under General; Brocklehurst, with orders to reconnoitre in force and if possible to dislodge the laager that General French had located and attacked on the previous-day on the lands of Dewdrop Farm. The laager was situated in Long Valley, a wide plain stretching south from Ladysmith. The valley ended at a line of rugged hills through which a road twisted in descending to a bridge over the Tugela River alongside Colenso village.

General Brocklehurst's column was made up of the 18th and 19th Hussars, the 5th Lancers, the 21st field Artillery and the four Light Horse Squadrons. The other Light Horse Squadron left the same morning to scout along the Helpmekaar road in the direction of Lombard's Kop. The column advanced down Long Valley with patrols on both flanks and 'E' Squadron patrolling ahead. Both to the east and to the west lay a broken line of hills about a mile away. After four miles 'E' Squadron came under fire. Captain Knapp reported the position of the enemy with a big gun on a forward kopje.

Advancing with half of 'B' and half of 'F' Squadron to protect the left flank, Captain T. Fowler occupied a ridge to the south of Wagon Hill, near the nek of Bester's Valley, about six miles from Ladysmith, called Middle Hill. A troop under Lieutenant John Pakeman found cover on the top of the kopje, forming a semi-circle facing the east in the direction of the Boer shelling. A troop under Lieutenant G.M. Mathais took cover short of the summit on the eastern shoulder of the kopje. Maintaining a good rate of fire they steadied the riflemen on the plain below.

Before midday the Light Horse on Middle Hill was reinforced by the Natal Carbineers and the Border Mounted Rifles. Soon after, 'B' squadron on the western end of the kopje, moved to better cover. In doing so, Trooper McLeod was wounded. Lieutenant Arthur Brabant, stopping to help McLeod, was shot through the lungs. Sergeant Kirk received three slight wounds in taking Brabant to a place where he could be reached by the ambulance. Lieutenant Brabant died about a week later.

He was the son of Major-General E. Brabant, the member for East London in the Cape House of Assembly.

Between 9.30 a.m. and 4.30 p.m. the position was continually under shell and rifle fire. The bombardment came from two guns Mount Bulwana from a range of 3,000 yards. Captain Fowler reported:[6] "The ridge was valuable as it saved the main column from a flank fire."

A Diarist[7] wrote: "Immediately on occupying the top of the kopje, the Boers began to shell us from away over on our left. We kept down as soon as we saw the guns fired. Away down below, the ground was covered with bush giving good cover for the enemy and interspersed with dongas. Explosive bullets were pattering and bursting on the rocks behind us and our men returned the fire." The squadrons retired in the late afternoon, each troop covering the other until every man was out of range. Captain Fowler reported: "I found it impossible to retire when I first received instructions. The enemy were at the time close enough to have gained the kopje and fired down from the crest upon us, before the men could have reached the horses."

From a knoll in front of the main Boer position on the ridge, the six guns of the 21st Battery quickly silenced the single Boer gun. Believing that the Boers were about to leave the hill, 'C' and 'F' Squadrons galloped along the valley towards the enemy position, then about 3,000 yards ahead. After covering 2,000 yards the men dismounted, leaving the horses in the shelter of a donga near flagstone Spruit. Running forward at the double in skirmishing order, the Light Horse came under severe fire in open country.

Some of the men, becoming short winded were compelled to lie flat down without cover on the open veldt. In this situation Captain Knapp was killed instantly. While Lieutenant Jardine and Lieutenant Campbell were carrying Captain Knapp's body back to the donga it was hit twice more. From there the body was sent to the rear strapped to a horse. Trooper C.S. Mann wrote:[8] "Just as the Captain got flat down a bullet hit him right in the head. I found he was quite dead, so then I ran for a donga which I reached in safety, quite exhausted."

In the cover of the donga the Light Horse commenced firing at a range of 800 to 1,000 yards from the Boers on the ridge. In this position the men were not only subject to fire from the front but to sharp cross fire from the left. Trooper Phillip Tucker wrote:[9] "In the donga one bullet just about nicked my ear without drawing blood."

In the race to reach the donga, Sergeant Harbord stumbled and fell, lying exhausted on the open. He at once became a target for a hail of bullets without being hit once. He lay so still that the enemy apparently believed him dead. As soon as the stream of bullets died down, Harbord got up and ran wildly to the safety of the donga.

From the donga Major David Doveton started a sortie with the intention of getting around the enemy position on the ridge to try to capture the gun. Major Doveton advanced diagonally to the right with Lieutenants Johnstone and Cresswell and 16 troopers from 'C' Squadron. Aided by good luck under intense rifle fire, the party reached the protection of a rocky outcrop without a man being hit. At this point Doveton's party came under fire from a slight ridge at almost point blank range and under fire as well as from 1,000 yards away on the left.

Because of the uncertainty of the advanced position of the Light Horse the artillery was ordered to cease fire. The Boers reacted by returning to the gun and the small arms fire was intensified by the enemy, by this time reinforced up to about 800 in number. Major Doveton had advanced the small party into a salient from where it was impossible to go forward. To retire was hazardous.

Major Karri-Davies took Captain J. Orr and a few men across to the right in support of Doveton, then realising that Doveton's party was in extreme danger of being cut off, he signalled Doveton to retire. At the same time a message was sent back for the artillery to cover the retreat. Because of the heavy rifle fire, Major Doveton was at first unable to carry out the order. Eventually the men ran back at the double in groups of four, until they all reached the donga.

The Light Horse in the donga in front of the Boers on the ridge retired from the zone of fire. They were covered by the volleys of the 5th Dragoon Guards, by the 21st Battery and supported by the 42nd and 53rd Field Batteries hurriedly provided by General White to extract the Light Horse from a position in which they were in danger of being cut up. With the road to Ladysmith under fire from guns on Mount Bulwana, 'E,F' and 'B' Squadrons rode back for most of the way in a dry spruit running to the east of the road. 'C' Squadron made a wide detour south-west in the cover of scrub. Within a short time the Boers held all the ground occupied during the day by General Brocklehurst's column.

Following closely on the withdrawal the ambulance brought in the bodies of Captain Knapp and Trooper Fred Dearlove. Captain Brabant and Trooper A. Short died from wounds, the last named at Intombi Hospital on 24th January 1900. The Light Horse lost 11 other troopers wounded. *The Times History* stated:[10] "The chief conclusion to be drawn from the reconnaissance was that the rare qualities essential to a cavalry leader were lacking in the officer to whom General French's departure had left the command of the mounted troops in Ladysmith."

Before dawn on 4th November, 'F' Squadron Light Horse, crossed the Klip River Drift near the camp. The Squadron rode along Murchison Street, past the Town Hall being used as a hospital for the wounded, and turning right at the deserted railway station, crossed the open ground beyond the cemetery and moved out along the Helpmekaar road: "After we passed the end of Helpmekaar Ridge and crossed the dry donga we came to the open country and there was not a sign of anything moving, although we knew that there were plenty of Boers on Bulwana and Lombard's Kop, which loomed up two miles away.

"We extended at about 10 horses lengths interval. Some shots were fired at us, landing a few yards in front near a dead horse. We retired to some bushes and had a look through field glasses. I could see the enemy making a sangar on Gun Hill, where they were fixing up a gun and could see the horses grazing on the slopes of the hill. The Boers had a good look at us from the hills. After two hours we reported back to camp."[11]

Before long a post was established for patrolling parties close to the cemetery, north-east of the centre of the town and facing Gun Hill: "Patrolling every morning just before sunrise up towards the Boer lines. The mounted infantry from the Liverpool Regiment along Boer lines. The mounted infantry from the Liverpool Regiment doing the same. Our Farrier-Sergeant brought his portable forge down here in order to shoe the horses. A continual stream of artillery horses pass up and down to the river for water. The Boer shells pass over continually on their way to the town. The flies down here are terrific and it is impossible to get a mouthful of anything to eat without swallowing one or two. Dust, flies and heat. On a wet day the place is ankle deep in mud."

On a drizzling day, when mist on the hills prevented the enemy from seeing very much movement, the Light Horse destroyed a farm house known as the Red House, situated between the river and Mount Bulwana and often used as cover by the Boers.

On 4th November, General White negotiated by letter with General Joubert. The Boer General agreed to the establishment of a hospital for the sick and wounded and certain non-combatants in flat country along the railway near Intombi Spruit, four miles south-east of the town. From 5th November, one train left Ladysmith daily with food and medicines for the hospital. The Boers entrained to Ladysmith from Dundee, 98 British wounded, accompanied by Indian orderlies, with 16 Royal Army Medical Corps personnel.

On 5th November, Major Karri-Davies asked to be relieved from the position of temporary command of the Corps, because of his lack of military experience. Major A.H.M. Edwards – 5th Dragoon Guards – with the local rank of Lieutenant-Colonel was appointed to the command until Major Woolls-Sampson had recovered. Fatigue parties dug emergency shelters for civilians into the banks of the Klip River and gouged out caves in the banks for the storage of ammunition.

Situated only about 3,000 yards to the south, the ridge known as Caesar's Camp rose over 300 feet above the plain, dominating the town. flat-topped, it ran for 2,500 yards from east to west, varying in width from 500 to 800 yards. The south-east corner was covered with small trees. Elsewhere it was bare and rocky. The southern side fell steeply away into Bester's Valley. In the north an underfeature known as Maiden's Castle sloped away to the point where the Klip River wound its way in a loop around the southern approach to the town. A nek linked Caesar's Camp with Wagon Hill, a plateau 1,200 yards long and 400 yards across. Wagon Hill tapered away to a smaller plateau covered with stunted trees, about 200 yards by 50 yards, called Wagon Point. The entire Caesar's Camp-Wagon Hill sector was under the command of Colonel Ian Hamilton.

From dawn on 7th November, a general bombardment with all guns, mixed with heavy rifle fire opened against the entire British perimeter. Companies of the 1st Manchester Battalion posted on the Caesar's Camp-Wagon Hill ridge returned fire from burghers in the valley south of Wagon Hill, in the direction of Middle Hill and Mounted Infantry Hill. From mid-morning the rifle fire slackened although the sniping continued throughout the day. The Manchesters lost one killed and seven wounded. 'D' and 'E' Squadrons Light Horse, were sent to reinforce the Manchesters. They took up a position on Wagon Hill which had been held by less than 20 Manchesters.

Wagon Hill was again strengthened by the arrival from Ladysmith in the late afternoon of 'B' and 'C' Squadrons under Major Doveton. The Light Horse endured a cold night in mackintoshes in the wind and the rain. On the same night the 42nd Field Battery was entrenched in pits along the northern crest of Caesar's Camp. On 8th November three companies of 1st King's Royal Rifles occupied Wagon Hill. On the same day General White reported:[12] "A 6-inch gun opened fire from the top of Bulwana Mountain. Throughout the siege this gun proved most troublesome." On 9th November the posts around the perimeter again came under heavy bombardment. In the north, attacks with rifle and gun fire were concentrated on Devonshire Post and Observation Hill without being pressed at short range at any point.

In the south, shells from Mount Bulwana began to fall on the Caesar's Camp Plateau from 5 a.m. The pickets in the sangars came under shell and rifle fire from across Bester's Valley. Salvoes from the 42nd Battery, replying to the guns on Mount Bulwana, also had the effect of checking burghers advancing in the valley. The burghers waited, concealed in thorn bush and broken ground seamed with dongas along Fourie's Spruit, in expectation of the Manchesters retiring from the crestline.

On Wagon Hill, 130 Light Horse troopers and the King's Royal Rifles exchanged long range shots until nightfall with riflemen on Mounted Infantry Hill and in Bester's Valley. On the next day under a flag of truce the Boers were allowed to remove the dead and wounded. In repulsing the half-hearted attacks on the perimeter the British lost only four killed and 23 wounded. After 9th November, Wagon Hill was drawn more into the defence scheme and strengthened. From this date, two squadrons of Light Horse were permanently in occupation with the King's Royal Rifles.

In a bungalow in the centre of Ladysmith, Jim Crow a horse trainer, formerly of Johannesburg, set up a coffee shop. The shop became popular with the Light Horse, for the men liked to meet there and relax: "With an eye to business, Jim set up a stand in his bungalow, selling coffee and biscuits at six pence. When the biscuits ran out, Jim sold just coffee, when the tinned milk ran out – coffee without milk. Then coffee with milk or sugar and in the end something hot in a cup – probably made from Indian corn burnt up and ground. It was rumoured that Jim made a profit of £500 in four months. There was also Jim's dry humour and witty anecdotes."[13]

On 14th November, General Brocklehurst took a mounted column with artillery to test the enemy strength on Rifleman's Ridge on the western side of Long Valley from Wagon Hill and if possible dislodge them and capture the single gun positioned on the ridge. The column was well supported by the 21st and 67th field Batteries. At 11.30 a.m. General Brocklehurst detached 'C' and 'D' Squadrons Light Horse, and ordered them to occupy Star Hill, a low ridge 2,000 yards north-east of Rifleman's Ridge. One battery also took up a position near Star Hill. The other battery with the 5th Lancers and the 18th Hussars moved on to field's Farm. For the next two hours the batteries shelled Rifleman's Ridge where about 450 burghers were posted with the gun. Just before 2 p.m. Brocklehurst ordered a cease fire.

As the column withdrew to Ladysmith the enemy became very active, the burghers on Rifleman's Ridge allowing themselves to be seen as they opened fire. The column also came under fire from nearby hills. Only four men were wounded. The Light Horse returned to camp without firing a shot. In some quarters[14] the reconnaissance was described as a waste of shells already in short supply.

On 18th November, Trooper James, a Light Horseman, was passing along Murchison Street near the Royal Hotel on the opposite side of the street, when he received a scalp wound from a howitzer shell fired from Gun Hill. James was lifted off his feet and took a week to recover. On the same day Dr Stark, from Torquay in England, was killed by a shell from the gun on Rifleman's Ridge. The shell passed through the roof of the Royal Hotel in Murchison Street, where correspondents and officers were at dinner. It went through the building before exploding on the footpath taking off the legs of Dr Stark and wounding three others. H. Watkins-Pitchford, an officer of the Natal Volunteer Medical Staff, wrote:[15] "I turned aside to see the effect of a 60-pound shell upon the Royal Hotel. It had struck a corner of the roof and almost demolished the house, breaking down walls and floors and going to earth before exploding."

On 21st November shells from a 6-inch gun on Gun Hill landed in the Light Horse camp: "One shell passed over Karri-Davies' tent, knocking down the furniture and nauseating him with the fumes and narrowly missing Lieutenant Mathias who was lying under a tree. A few minutes later a shell dropped on the aloe field where the sports were held early in the day. Orders were issued for the men to sleep under cover of the river bank on the west side of the camp. Tents were toned down to something like khaki in colour, as white was known to be drawing the enemy fire".[16] "A shell hit a cottage where certain officers went for meals, only a few minutes ahead of the time when Colonel Ian Hamilton, Lord Ava and Colonel Frank Rhodes normally breakfasted."

The Boers set up a 6-inch Creusot gun firing a 94-pound shell on Middle Hill. The gun went into action against Wagon Hill for the first time on 27th November. The British reacted by dragging up two howitzers onto the nek between Wagon Hill and Wagon Point and a 12-pounder naval gun onto Caesar's Camp. The howitzers shelled Middle Hill on the 28th. Some days later the enemy withdrew the Creusot after it was hit and damaged. The howitzers were removed to Ration Post on 11st December.

On 30th November a shell from the 6-inch Creusot gun on Gun Hill east of the town struck the Town Hall, in use at the time as a hospital killing one and wounding 10 of the patients and orderlies. The hospital was transferred to a sheltered gorge under tents where the protection from shell fire was better.

Major-General Sir Archibald Hunter,[17] Chief of Staff to General White, led a night raid on 7th December with the objective of destroying the guns on Gun Hill, a spur of Lombard's Kop over 300 feet above the veldt. The main armament on Gun Hill was a 6-inch Creusot gun known as "Long Tom" and a 4.7 howitzer. Gun Hill lay to the north of the Helpmekaar road, four miles from the centre of Ladysmith. The raiding party of more than 600 was made up of 500 Natal Volunteers under Colonel J. Royston, 105 selected from Squadrons 'B-E-F' Light Horse under Colonel Edwards and smaller units from the No. 10 Mountain Battery, Royal Garrison Artillery and Royal Engineers with explosives and sledge hammers. Major Karri-Davies who had been in bed for a week, made one of the party. Every Light Horse officer who could manage to be included went: Captains Mullins, Fowler, Cordington and Lieutenant P. Fitzgerald, who had replaced Lieutenant Barnes as adjutant after he had been wounded at Elandslaagte. General Hunter only received permission to undertake the sortie at 9 p.m. on the 7th. The march began with the officers riding and the men on foot as far as the cemetery, about half a mile east of Ladysmith station. From the cemetery everyone went on foot.

"Colonel Edwards and Major Karri-Davies proceeded to Colonel Royston's house at 9 p.m. where instructions were received from General Hunter as to the part to be taken in conjunction with the Natal Volunteers from an attack on Gun Hill. The rendezvous was on the Helpmekaar road. No firing until the hill had been taken – absolute silence. When the gun had been taken, the squadrons were to form up 30 yards around the embrasure, in order to check any possible counter-attack while the gun was being disabled by the engineers. General Hunter personally commanded the attack."[18]

On an unusually dark night the party advanced through cactus and low thorn bushes at a slow pace along a rough route interspersed with stony dongas.[19] The base of the hill was reached without a challenge soon after 2 a.m. Leading the way up the long slope facing Ladysmith, made difficult by small loose stones shifting underfoot, the Light Horse took the left of centre position to the Carbineers in open order on the right. A Boer picket far to the right on the side of the hill turned and fired back in running down the hill, on being disturbed by the Carbineers, who after doing all they could to avoid the picket, returned some shots into the darkness.

At the sound of the shots the Light Horse fell flat to the ground momentarily, before running forward, cheering, when Colonel Edwards and then Karri-Davies shouted – "fix bayonets" an item which the Light Horse did not have. Within 15 yards of the summit the burghers on the top of the hill ceased firing: "Some of the Boers ran across the sloping plateau to the Lombard's Kop position. 'F' Squadron fired volleys in the direction of Lombard's Kop to prevent a counter-attack, provoking nothing more than a few stray shots."[20]

The men took up defensive positions while the engineers prepared to demolish the guns. After 15 minutes on the hill Captain Foulkes of the engineers was ready to blow up the guns. Karri-Davies knocked out the pin hinging the breech-block of the Creusot, using a small hammer on the sighting rod of the gun after efforts with a sledgehammer alone proved unsuccessful. The harness for hauling the guns was also found and destroyed. 'E' Squadron found a third gun pit with a gun carriage but no gun. Karri-Davies in his explorations in the dark discovered a maxim gun. The troops were half way down the steep slope before the explosion took place. Tired and sore, the men reached the Devonshire on the eastern side of the town, where General White was waiting to meet them just as daylight was breaking.

Carrying the maxim gun and the breech block from the "Long Tom" as trophies, the Light Horse reached camp at 5.30 a.m. Weighing 135 pounds, the breech block was carried back by eight men from 'E' Squadron on the orders of Karri-Davies. In the post war years the trophy graced the dinner table at Imperial Light Horse functions. Karri-Davies later presented it to field-Marshal Smuts. The sighting rod was presented to General Hunter by Karri-Davies.

In the raid on Gun. Hill the Light Horse lost five men wounded. Lieutenant-Surgeon Ligertwood stayed behind with the wounded men. Trooper R. Nicol died from wounds on 10th December.

While searching in a tent on Gun Hill for a candle or something to give more light for the engineers attaching the explosives to the guns, Karri-Davies found a letter.

Ladysmith. Natal.

7th December, 1899.

To My Dear Sister,

It is with pleasure I inform you that I am well and in good health through the blessing of God. It is my hearty wish that the letter will find you the same. I have already written two letters to my father and one to Jacobus and I am longing to hear from you all. It appears there must be something wrong as I do not receive any letters and I don't think you forget to write. I will try again and if I do not get an answer, then there must be something wrong here.

It is one month and three days since we besieged Ladysmith and I don't know what will happen further. The English we see every day walking about the town and we are bombarding the town every day with our cannon. They have erected plenty of breastworks outside the town. It is very dangerous to attack the town. Near the town they have naval guns, from which we receive very heavy fire which we cannot stand. I think there will be much blood spilt before they surrender, as Mr Englishman fights hard and well and our own burghers seem a bit frightened.

So, my dear Sister, write soon and say how you are getting on. You will not believe how hard it is not to hear from my brother and relatives. I would like to write more, but the sun is very hot and still further the flies are so troublesome that I don't get a chance of sitting still. You may send me letters without stamps by writing on the envelope, 'field Service'. Write me if Pieter is still on the Basutoland Border. I will close now with dearest love and thousands of greetings to all the people. My address is, 'Gunner W.J. Groenewald, Head Laager, c/o Major Erasmus, Ladysmith'.

I Remain, Your Affectionate Brother,
Wessel Groenewald

"At daylight on 8th December[21] 11th Surgeon-Major W.F. Davies left the Light Horse camp with his ambulance wagon and six mules and a servant. Major Davies passed our outposts and reached the foot of Gun Hill now held by the Boers. He stopped the wagon and advanced with a servant under a Red Cross flag, closely scrutinized by the Boers. Lieutenant Ligertwood who had remained on the ground at Gun Hill during the night, came out of the bush on the left and met Major Davies. At the same time a party of Boers moved forward also. The medical party was taken up the nek between Gun Hill and Bulwana, behind the Boer lines of wire entanglement.

"The Boers drove the wagon off to get the wounded. Permission to accompany them was refused. When the wagon returned with the wounded the journey was continued through the Boer lines towards a small hospital 2½ miles in the rear of the enemy lines. Major Davies rode his own horse and gave his servant's horse to Lieutenant Ligertwood. It was found by the Boers that the servant's saddle wallets were full of cartridges. The servant had carelessly kept them, although he had left his rifle and bandolier behind. He had placed his Medical Officer in a position of being liable to arrest – 'stuffed with cartridges'.

"Feeling they might be virtual prisoners, Davies asked for the Commandant and told him of the discovery. At the hospital the Boer doctors entertained the party with a good meal, while helping the wounded from the wagon. When the Commandant came, Davies put the case to him on the hospital stoep. The party was summoned for examination by General Schalk Burger, who said they would be detained as prisoners of war.

"The General also asked: 'How is it that arms are frequently found in your ambulance wagons?' Major Davies replied: 'Because when a wounded man is picked up on the field, his rifle and accoutrements were put in with him. It is not allowed, but it is sometimes done.' The Major pointed out that in the matter of the cartridges in the wallets: 'Without arms the cartridges cannot be of use to us.'

"The General also asked: 'Why do your ambulance wagons go so far forward during an action?' Major Davies replied: 'Excessive zeal'."

General Schalk Burger also accused Major Davies of having been a member of the Reform Committee and this Major Davies did not deny. In the end, the entire medical party was allowed to return to Ladysmith with the wounded.

On 10th December, Lieutenant-Colonel C. Metcalfe, commanding 2nd Battalion, Rifle Brigade, led a night raid against a howitzer position on Surprise Hill, north-west of the town. Surprise Hill was reached by passing between two kopjes held by the Boers. A special detachment led by Lieutenant Digby-Jones, a Royal Engineer, succeeded in destroying the howitzer. In the meantime, burghers converging from Thornhill's Kopje and from Bell's Kopje, barred the way back to the supporting lines. In a confused running fight in the dark, often at close quarters and the point of the bayonet, the troops lost 17 killed, 40 wounded and six missing.

In manning the vital posts on Wagon Hill, two squadrons of Light Horse were continuously on guard in support of the King's Royal Rifles. In rotation, the squadrons alternated the Wagon Hill picket duty with spells of duty back at the Light Horse camp near Ladysmith. Trooper Phillip Tucker, 'B' Squadron, referred in his Diary[22] to picket duty on Wagon Hill: "Up at 3 a.m. and marched out to Wagon Hill again. I don't know why they always make us march on foot to our pickets now. There is no shelter in the rain, except what we can make by piling up a few stones and lying down behind them. There is a Boer gun on the hill opposite us – Mounted Infantry Hill. I only wish we had more fine weather, less flies and more clean water. I am huddled up behind a rock with a mackintosh over my head, kept up by my rifle to keep the rain off while I write. Sniper shot is coming through in the mist.

"I often go three or four days without washing and twice went for 10 days without changing clothing. I am quite used to tea and coffee without milk now. The flies are fearful, nearly driving everybody mad. All the drinking water has to be boiled. Only 33 men in the Squadron are fit for duty out of 72." The temperature alternated between 100° Fahrenheit in the shade and at other times, especially at night, the troops felt the cold and were glad to rug up.

Nevertheless, the troops on Wagon Hill did enjoy a certain diversion. In his Diary, Trooper Tucker recorded: "On the night of 6th December, 13 of us went to Bester's Farm and looted 40 ducks, fowls and turkeys at 2 a.m., before marching into town on foot." The farm was in the valley below the southern crest of the Caesar's Camp-Wagon Hill ridge, in the no-man's land between the Boer and British perimeters. The farm was one of the richest in the district, but the family was suspected of supplying information to the commandos and regarded as rebels. One member of the family was placed under arrest. An 'F' Squadron Diarist recorded:[23] "Bester was a Natal rebel."

On Christmas Day, Lieutenant P. Normand, 'C' Squadron, recorded:[24] "The Boers filled several shells with Plum Pudding. Using a nail they scratched on the shell in English: 'With Christmas Greetings,' and fired them into the town." On New Year's Day a challenge to 'Mr Franchise' to turn out and fight arrived enclosed in a plugged shell. Sugar, raisins and sand were also sent over in shells. Trooper Tucker reported having fried goat for Christmas Dinner. Tucker also helped to fill the bags for the children's Christmas tree. "I was one of the six told off to help with the Christmas Tree and we had a high old time of it. We had to do all the climbing on ladders to reach the presents." Major Karri-Davies gave an account[25] of how the "Ladysmith Siege Christmas Tree" came about: "Colonel Dartnell and I were discussing how we could give the little ones of Ladysmith, most of whom had been living for the past two months in holes by the river bank, as happy a time as might be possible under the novel circumstances. Owing to the shelling which the town was subject to, it was quite out of the question to gather the young people together during the day time, so we decided that the best thing to do was to have a Christmas Tree Party.

"We accordingly searched the town and persuaded the proprietors of some of the shops to open up and sell us all sorts of suitable goods to hang on the tree. Then we called in Mr George Tatham who very kindly agreed to lend us his hall, while his wife volunteered to assist in the decoration of the tree and to look after the supper if we could procure the ingredients and materials for the feast. Archdeacon Barker whom we next visited to ensure that our arrangements for a party on Christmas night did not interfere with his arrangements, also volunteered his help, with that of his wife and daughter.

"While looking for a suitable tree, I found the orthodox English Christmas tree growing side by side with the bluegum of Australia and the mimosa of South Africa. It immediately struck me that Mother Earth's suggestion was the right one and that since the soldiers of all parts of the Empire were fighting side by side, it would be appropriate to have the Empire botanically represented by Christmas trees grown on South African soil. With the assistance of the officers and men of the Natal Mounted Police and the Imperial Light Horse, we placed the trees in position in the hall.

"Major Doveton arrived and immediately said: 'Where's Canada? She must be represented.' Off he went to return later with a huge Canadian fir tree. Colonel Dartnell and Miss Olive Barker, the daughter of the Anglican Archdeacon Barker, took charge of the South African tree and the rest of us dressed the other trees. We felt that with the valuable assistance of 120 pounds of sweets, together with mountains of cakes, lemonade and ginger beer, we were ready to welcome as many young guests as Ladysmith could provide. Of course, there were many sick children, but they were not forgotten and presents were put aside for them.

"At half past seven the door of the hall was opened. As they entered each child was given a ticket to present at the Tree for gifts. In less than an hour all of the children – about 250 – had received three or four presents each. The General and his Staff were good enough to come and join in the fun. After refreshments had been served the hall was cleared and dancing was kept up until eleven o'clock, when we all joined in singing God Save the Queen."

Corporal Wickham and Trooper Godfrey volunteered to take special food and medical supplies from Pietermaritzburg to Major Woolls-Sampson who was recovering from wounds in Ladysmith. The two were Light Horsemen. After being wounded at Elandslaagte they had been sent to Pietermaritzburg from Ladysmith before the beginning of the siege. Both Wickham and Godfrey spoke Zulu and Afrikaans fluently. Crossing the Tugela River from the direction of Greytown, and leaving the horses at the drift, they proceeded on foot. When within only six miles of Ladysmith at dusk and about to begin a final dash into the town, they bumped into a black wagon driver at the service of a commando. Over the next six days, spend in hiding and keeping clear of the Boers searching right on their heels, the two men were forced to live on the convalescent food intended for Woolls-Sampson. By making their way in through the Boer lines, Wickham and Godfrey gathered much valuable information.

The year ended quietly. The Republican forces were still camped on the surrounding hills, after several months of trying to capture Ladysmith by bombardment and siege. Numbers of burghers were joined by their wives and families travelling across the borders to be with the men. The women enjoyed the spectacle of the guns bombarding the town while the men were occupied in guard duties and sniping. On 5th December the Ladysmith Lyre, a special siege news sheet, advertised cheap train excursions from Pretoria to Mount Bulwana: "Where to Spend a Happy Day. To the Ladies of Pretoria. Messrs. Kook and Son, beg to announce a personally conducted tour – Saturday to Monday – to witness the siege of Ladysmith. Full view of enemy guaranteed. Tea and Shrimps on train direct from Durban. Four in hand or ox wagon from Modder Spruit to Bulwana. Fare 15/- return. One guinea if Long Tom is in action. Lovers half price."

By 31st December, no less than 1,588 of the garrison and townspeople were ill with either enteric fever or dysentery.

[1] In his diary in the Karri-Davies Collection
[2] 23rd March 1900
[3] A Preacher in the Dutch Reformed Church
[4] *Through Shot and flame* J.D. Kestell
[5] Later Field-Marshal Earl Haig. The Commander of British Forces in France, December 1915
[6] A report in the Karri-Davies Papers
[7] The typed 'F' Squadron Diary
[8] From part of a diary in the Karri-Davies Collection
[9] From part of a diary in the Karri-Davies Collection
[10] L.S. Amery, Editor of the *Times History of the War in South Africa*
[11] From a short diary in the Karri-Davies Collection
[12] In despatches from Cape Town, 23rd March. 1900
[13] The typed 'F' Squadron diary
[14] *Pictures of the War* John Stuart
[15] *Besieged in Ladysmith* H. Watkins-Pilchford
[16] In the Karri-Davies Collection of Papers
[17] Presently Lieutenant-General
[18] From Imperial Light Horse typed Regimental Diary of Engagements in the Karri-Davies Collection
[19] Donga – a surface cutting caused by erosion and action of water
[20] From the account in the Imperial Light Horse Regimental typed diary
[21] From an account in the Karri-Davies Collection of Papers
[22] The diary in the Karri-Davies Collection
[23] In the Karri-Davies Collection of Papers
[24] From a Diary in the Karri-Davies Collection
[25] In the Karri-Davies Papers

CHAPTER 5

THE DEFENCE OF WAGON HILL AND CAESAR'S CAMP ON – 6TH JANUARY 1900

From 27th to 30th December 1899, Trooper Tucker – 'B' Squadron served a spell of picket duty on Wagon Hill. Upon being relieved the Squadron returned to Ladysmith. From 3.30 a.m. on 2nd January, 'B' Squadron was on duty on Wagon Hill for a day and a half, marching back to the Ladysmith camp on the morning of the 3rd. Of those particular days Trooper Tucker recorded in his Diary: "On the Hill nothing of excitement took place."

In common with his comrades, Phillip Tucker was completely unaware that the great assault, the outcome of which would decide the fate of Ladysmith was about to take place. The defence of - Caesar's Camp depended on 560 men of the Manchester Regiment in five sand-bagged and stone redoubts with thick 12 feet walls up to seven feet high, capable of holding 400 men. Shellproof, with underground magazines, they were connected to headquarters in Ladysmith by telephone. The guns and redoubts were ranged up along the northern crest of the plateau, six 15-pounder guns of the 42nd Royal field Artillery and a 12-pounder naval gun with a detachment of Natal Naval Volunteers.

A line of pickets held small rifle pits along the southern crest. A bare plateau lay between the redoubts and the picket line. One picket with a Hotchkiss machine gun was covered in the rear by a 9-pounder gun. To the east, the Manchester's left flank linked up with the Natal Volunteers under Colonel Royston, whose line extended from the south-eastern slopes of Caesar's Camp for three miles along an open plain dotted with thorn bush and dongas as far as the Helpmekaar road.

Without guns, the Wagon Hill plateau was less strongly defended by 150 men from three companies of the King's Royal Rifles behind small rifle pits and a sangar of loose stones facing the southern crest. The Rifles had the support of 'C' Squadron Light Horse, based on a rough redoubt of sandbags and loose stones on the north-west high corner of the plateau, overlooking the nek and Wagon Point. 'C' Squadron had two advanced pickets posted along the southern crest, one overlooking Bester's Farm in the valley and the other in the nek, adjoining Wagon Hill near the old howitzer positions. On Wagon Point 'D' Squadron Light Horse posted pickets facing the southern crest and in the nek opposite the abandoned howitzer positions. On the slope in the nek a Natal Naval Volunteer 3-pounder Hotchkiss machine gun was placed in position on the night of 5th January.

The entire Wagon Hill-Caesar's Camp ridge formed part of the defence section under the command of Colonel Ian Hamilton, who had just 1,000 men to defend the entire ridge with a crest-line of four and a half miles: "The extreme west end of Wagon Hill is separated from the main hill by a nek running into a gully on the north and west sides. This portion is called Wagon Point, or Wagon Post. The top of the hill slopes from north to south slightly and then into the valley where Bester's Farm is situated. From the hill there is a fine view of the road to Van Reenen's Pass and of the country around Bester's Farm.

"The 'C' and 'D' Squadrons Light Horse had been on picket duty on Wagon Hill and Wagon Point from Wednesday, 3rd January and were to have been relieved on the morning of the 6th by 'E' and 'F' Squadrons. 'C' Squadron, 18 officers and men under Lieutenant Mathias and Lieutenant Normand were posted on Wagon Hill. Normand was one of the Jameson Raiders. 'D' Squadron, made up of 41 officers and men under Lieutenant James Richardson[1] and Lieutenant Adams, held the extreme edge and corner of the ridge known as Wagon Point. Both squadrons posted pickets on the night of 5th January and officers found everything to be in order during the night.

"Early that night Lieutenant Richardson and Sergeant Winthorpe of 'D' Squadron penetrated the enemy lines to Middle Hill to find out whether the enemy gun rested in the sangar all night. They got within 15 yards of the gun and found it was moved at night into an embrasure just behind the sangar. They met no pickets. Although so close to the enemy, the two saw no evidence of impending preparations for attack. The sentries were warned of the absence of the officers."[2] It was hoped to establish that a night raid like the successful raid on Gun Hill might also be undertaken against the gun on Middle Hill.

During the night of 5th – 6th January, an unusual number of men were active on Wagon Point. Shortly after 7 p.m., Lieutenant R. Digby Jones arrived with a party of 25 sappers and Royal Engineers from the 23rd field Company and 15 naval men from HMS *Powerful*, to work on a 15-pounder naval gun emplacement. A platform for a 4.7 naval gun mounting was also hauled up on an ox-wagon to the end of Wagon Point. The 4.7 gun was left on a wagon below the northern crest. A detachment of 50 men from the Manchester Regiment working with the parties returned to Caesar's Camp at about 2 a.m. At the same time half a company of Gordon Highlanders arrived to work, having come from fly Kraal, behind the northern crest of Caesar's Camp. The working parties carried lanterns and altogether made a great deal of noise.

Commandant-General Piet Joubert decided to mount a strong assault against the Ladysmith defences. Detailing 4,000 burghers to attack the Wagon Hill-Caesar's Camp ridge, he aimed to dominate the town from the broad flat plateau on Caesar's Camp with artillery and rifle fire. On the night of 5th January the commandos assembled in the hills south of the British position. The main laager was behind Middle Hill, 2,000 yards from Wagon Point. Under General J. De Villiers, 2,000 Free State burghers gathered behind Mounted infantry Hill, working around from there into Bester's Valley below Wagon Hill. Another 2,000 Transvaal burghers marched along the valley to Fourie's Spruit, lying beneath the southern crest of Caesar's Camp.

Sometime after 1 a.m. on the 6th, picked men from the Harrismith commando began to make their way up the steep southern side of the nek between Wagon Point and Wagon Hill. Corporal Arthur Dunne, 'C' Squadron, in charge of a picket in the nek, heard sounds in the valley below. Realising that the burghers were on the move, Corporal Dunne sent Trooper Frank Rogers to warn Lieutenant Mathias, in command of the Light Horse redoubt on Wagon Hill. At 2.30 a.m., Dunne decided to warn the other pickets by firing down the slope. The combined volleys of Corporal Dunne and Troopers Goddard and Plunkett provoked a strong outburst of fire from the burghers coming up the hillside.

Trooper Rodgers arrived to find Lieutenant Mathias away fixing a guard over the 4.7 gun, still loaded on a wagon under the northern crest. In the absence of Mathias, at about 2.45 a.m. Lieutenant Normand sent the off duty men forward to support the pickets who by now were outnumbered and being pressed back. Corporal Arthur Robbins was shot dead. He was the first man to fall.

Sergeant J. Laing who had gone with Lieutenant Mathias to the 4.7 gun on the wagon wrote:[3] "After seeing that everything was in order, Lieutenant Mathias and I were slowly walking up the hill when an excited voice shouted: 'sergeant Laing, come quickly, we are being attacked.' On hearing this we started running. On the way up the Lieutenant instructed me to call the five or six men we had in reserve to proceed at once to the front to support our pickets. This we did and started firing down the hill. At this point I lost sight of Lieutenant Mathias, who went too far over the hill and got amongst the attacking Boers. After some time we were joined by No. 2 Troop Pickets, who had been forced back after heavy loss. While we were still firing, Lieutenant Normand arrived and gave the order for everyone to retire to the sangar."

At this point, something more than half an hour after the outbreak of firing, Lieutenant E. Walker, an auctioneer from Pietermaritzburg, brought the Natal Naval Volunteers 3-pounder Hotchkiss quick firing gun into action from the slope on the nek beneath the redoubt. The gun had arrived on Wagon Hill only about an hour before the alarm. At break of dawn the gun crew fired in the direction of the burghers, steadying the advance. After several of the men were either shot or wounded, Walker fired a few more rounds himself. A number of the Light Horse were hit in the half light in the scramble up the slope from the nek.

"Now 'C' Squadron lost many in casualties as the men had to expose themselves to reach the top of the ridge. Corporal George Ferrand, formerly correspondent in Johannesburg for the *Morning Post* and in command of one of the pickets in the nek and Trooper Richard Dawson were killed on the edge of the ridge. Trooper Henry Gorton and Sergeant Laing were wounded and fell among the rocks. They remained where they were all day, exposed to the sun and a thunder storm. 'Dickie' Gorton, the more exposed was found to have seven different wounds as he lay between the fire of both parties. Gorton had not long before recovered from wounds received at Elandslaagte. Sergeant Laing, being in some shelter, received a second wound from a ricocheting bullet. Trooper Rodgers, went out to look for the extra ammunition which had been brought up but left behind at the time of the order to retire. He called out to Trooper Thomas Chadwick to help him carry it in. Just as Rodgers stooped to lift the box he fell without a word with a bullet in the head. Chadwick had just reached him, when he also fell, mortally wounded. in trying to stop Rodgers from falling. The ammunition was left where it lay. On the top of the ridge the men got behind boulders. Corporal Dunne was shot dead inside the redoubt."[4]

Lieutenant Mathias and Corporal Webb, who in the darkness and the confusion separately found themselves among the Boers, were luckily not detected. For a while Mathias pretended to be one of their number. When the Hotchkiss gun opened fire for the second time, just after being dragged up the slope into the redoubt and narrowly escaping being captured, both men took advantage of the brief unsettling effect the gun fire had on the enemy to make good their escape. Soon afterwards the gun stopped firing and went out of action for the rest of the day.

Having gained the nek between Wagon Point and Wagon Hill, the storming burghers pushed back the pickets lining the southern corner of the crest immediately above and below the nek, thus completely isolating 'D' Squadron and the working parties on Wagon Point. The burghers established themselves in the loose rocky outcrops near the south-eastern edge of the main Wagon Hill plateau and along the ledge running along the top of the nek. From these positions they kept up a heavy short range fire upon the Light Horse in the redoubt and on the men settled down among the boulders on the east slope away from the redoubt.

Lieutenant Mathias sent Corporal Webb to the King's Royal Rifle fort, a well-constructed post on the northern crest between the Light Horse redoubt and the nek linking with Caesar's Camp. The Rifles could spare few reinforcements, no more than a corporal and eight men. About 12

Gordon Highlanders, after scattering in the confusion in the dark on Wagon Point, managed to reach the redoubt. A party of brave burghers crept up almost to the Light Horse lying in the rocks. At the closest point scarcely more than a rifle's length separated the parties. The most forward burghers were soon forced to give ground from what proved to be the most forward point reached on Wagon Hill by the attacking parties that day.

Soon after daybreak the situation was that, in addition to holding the nek, about 250 Boers had established themselves in rocks above the nek on the main plateau of Wagon Hill.

Many of the Boers had brought two rifles with them, allowing the one to cool while the other became hot.[5] The thin line of 'C' Squadron Light Horse was all that stood in the way of the Boers extending forward and over-running the plateau. The sangar near the southern crest held by two companies of the King's Royal Rifles was also fully engaged and held firm against the Boers.

As a result of the warning received by the outbreak of the firing on Wagon Hill, the change of pickets on Caesar's Camp carried instructions from Lieutenant-Colonel A. Curran for the incoming pickets to remain at their posts, so the entire crestline was doubly manned. The attack by the Transvaalers on Caesar's Camp began almost an hour after the beginning of the fighting on Wagon Hill, the picket line opening fire just before 4 a.m. For the remainder of the day the southern crest on Caesar's Camp was held without difficulty. The Boers never succeeded in reaching the summit at any point. On the lower south-eastern flank of Caesar's Camp, the Transvaalers drove in the Natal Volunteer pickets. Half an hour later they reached the upper slopes and almost wiped out the No. 5. Manchester picket. The picket post of 16 men fought on until the end of the day. Privates J. Pitts and R. Scott were the only survivors. Pitts was unwounded. Both men were awarded the Victoria Cross. By 5 a.m. the burghers held the whole of the east and south east slopes of Caesar's Camp.

Colonel Ian Hamilton had bivouacked below the northern crest of Caesar's Camp. At the first sound of firing he ordered the 2nd Gordon Highland Battalion, held in reserve at fly Kraal, on the northern underfeature of Caesar's Camp called Maiden's Castle, to reinforce the Manchesters. The arrival of the Gordons on the eastern flank effectively stopped any possibility of a burgher advance towards the Manchester Forts. By 6 a.m., the 53rd Battery Royal field Artillery, firing from a range of 2,200 yards in the thorn bush flats near the Klip River, in the section held by the Natal Volunteers, had completely nullified any initial advantage gained by the Transvaalers.

Salvo after salvo landed on the eastern extremity of their ridge. The burghers took whatever cover they could find among the rocks and in the thorn bushes. The shelling also had the effect of halting the advance of Boer reserves, confining them to the valley below. The 53rd Battery withstood all attempts from guns on Mount Bulwana and the neighbourhood of Lombard's Kop to put it out of action. By 10 o'clock the Manchesters and Gordons under Captain R. Carnegie had made safe the sangars on the eastern crest. Completely isolated, the burghers on the eastern slopes were still hanging on after it was clear that the attack on Caesar's Camp had ended in failure.

As soon as Colonel Hamilton was satisfied that the prompt arrival of the Gordons and a small detachment of Natal Volunteers had removed any immediate threat to Caesar's Camp, he hurried across to Wagon Hill where the sound of violent rifle fire continued. At the King's Royal Rifle Fort he found Major Gore-Browne with a handful of men and was apprised of the general situation. Hamilton immediately telephoned headquarters for reinforcements.

On 6th January, General White was indisposed and the command was in the hands of his Chief of staff, Major-General Sir Archibald Hunter. For the remainder of the day, while Hamilton concentrated on the more serious situation at Wagon Hill, the command at Caesar's Camp was held by Lieutenant-Colonel A. Curran of the Manchester Regiment. Answering to the bugle call of "Boots and Saddle" at 4.15 a.m. the three Light Horse Squadrons under Colonel Edwards galloped fast out of town by 4.30 a.m. and arrived at Wagon Hiil by 5.10 a.m. The remainder of the Gordons from fly Kraal followed and three companies of King's Royal Rifles from Observation Hill under Major Campbell were called and arrived after 7 a.m. The 18th Hussars galloped up at 9 a.m. and waited in reserve below the Hill near the 4.7 gun. During the morning a party of Boers, working around to the west side made an attempt to capture the gun but were beaten off. The 21st Battery entered the valley to the west of Wagon Hill under orders to subdue the rate of gun and rifle fire falling on Wagon Point from Middle Hill. The 42nd Battery on Caesar's Camp and the 12-pounder were also in action against Middle Hill and the riflemen in the nearby dongas and scrub.

A troop from 'E' Squadron, the first of the Light Horse squadrons to arrive at the Hill, was sent around to Wagon Point. The Gordon Highlanders were also sent to reinforce the extreme end of Wagon Point, followed at 8 a.m. by a company of the Rifles. Led by Captain W. Codrington, 'E' Squadron went straight up the Hill to the point where hard pressed 'C' Squadron, still holding on gamely after fully two hours' fighting and more than three hours from the first alarm, still clung to the position that was the key to the entire Wagon Hill plateau. Lieutenant Normand wrote: "Whenever anyone moved he would be sure to get plugged. I took 36 men up the Hill three nights earlier and 17 were killed or wounded." Mr John Stuart, a besieged *Morning Post* correspondent wrote: "The fire was so hot and continuous that to be hit once, meant unless you were killed outright, to be hit again and again, so long as you could be seen." Ammunition was brought up to some of the Boers in nosebags.

The newly arrived Light Horse squadrons ran up through a re-entrant to the right of the Rifles fort, extending to the right and to the left over open ground sloping gradually up to where the burgher marksmen were established under cover of rocks. 'B' Squadron under Major Doveton veered away far to the left in the direction of where the Rifles were. The men suffered heavily crossing the open space to reach the cover of a few rocks. At one time only 30 yards separated the extreme left of 'B' Squadron from the Boer right.

Trooper Phillip Tucker was shot in the chest while placing a field dressing on the arm of Lance-Corporal Walter Jago. Tucker fell dead by the side of Jago. Only a few days before Phillip Tucker had written to assure his mother in Pietermaritzburg that so far he had come through unscathed. In the event of something happening to him Tucker wrote:[6] "But if it should be so, I want you not to trouble too much about it and to remember that it is far and away the death I would soonest have. I only wish I could see you again to say a proper goodbye. I only wish we were in Johannesburg again. I would never have forgiven myself if I had not been in it."

Major Doveton fell mortally wounded and died in Ladysmith on 14th February. He failed to respond after his arm was amputated. General Joubert allowed Mrs Doveton to pass through the lines with special food and medicines and to return to Pietermaritzburg. Major Doveton was 54 years of age and well known in Johannesburg. Corporal Moore and Lance-Corporal Greathead were both shot in the head from a distance of 50 yards. Sergeant Major Greenall was shot in the arm and lay out in the cross fire unable to move until nightfall.

Lieutenant John Pakeman led 'F' Squadron slightly to the right, veering in the direction of the redoubt. Pakeman fell facing the enemy and lay in the line of fire for some hours, unattended except for water carried out to him. He died before noon, his body riddled with bullets. Lieutenant Pakeman was about 40 years of age and was the Editor of the *Transvaal Leader*. In September 1899, he was arrested on a charge of treason. The charge was presently reduced to one of contravening the Press Law of 1896. Pakeman was released on bail and in common with many other prominent Uitlanders escaped from the Transvaal. About the same time a warrant went out for the arrest of Mr Moneypenny, the Editor of the Johannesburg *Star*, who escaped over the border by eluding the guards on a train.

Lord Ava, the eldest son of the Marquis of Dufferin was also shot. Ava was acting as galloper to Colonel Hamilton and had pushed up into the firing line to reconnoitre. As soon as he lifted his head above a stone he met a hail of bullets. On raising himself a second time he was shot. Colonel Rhodes went out under fire to where Ava lay, mortally wounded. Trooper Stoughton crawled up and applied a field dressing to his side. Without gaining consciousness Lord Ava died, in Ladysmith, and was buried in the town cemetery. He had previously been in action with the Devons at Elandslaagte and took part in the raid on Gun Hill. Despite wounds in the buttock and the shoulder, Colonel Edwards lead the men to the redoubt. From then on 'F' Squadron suffered few losses, due no doubt to the protection of the redoubt.

'E' Squadron under Captain W. Codrington of the 11th Hussars occupied the intermediate ground. Trooper Ernest Mocatta, shot through the head, was the first to fall. Amid the din and clatter of firearms, Captain Codrington's call to rush the Boer position went almost unheard. Only one trooper followed him. Within a few yards the Captain fell wounded. Corporal Weir rendered assistance to Captain Codrington who fell as they dashed across an open 80 yard space. When the hot sun beat down on the Captain's bare head as he lay in the open, Weir crept back and got water for the fainting Captain under heavy fire all the time. Weir stayed with the Captain until 2 p.m. Trooper Clement Keen attempted to follow to give assistance, but was wounded within a space of 20 yards.[7] For his gallant action, Corporal W.A. Weir was awarded the D.C.M.

Four companies of King's Royal Rifles under Major Campbell occupied ground above the re-entrant between the Rifle's Fort and the Light Horse redoubt. On Colonel Hamilton's orders, the Rifles made three unsuccessful charges by 8.45 a.m., rushing the Boers in the rocks across the grassy no-man's land between the main groups of opposing riflemen. Each rush brought heavy losses. Major Robert Bowen, Major Digby Mackworth and Lieutenant Noel Todd were among those killed. Colonel Hamilton decided against any further attempts. By 1.45 p.m., three squadrons of 5th Lancers had extended in support across the summit of Wagon Hill.

The Diarist from 'F' Squadron wrote: "The writer was told off to remain with those to hold the horses and the others were ordered to the top of the Hill. The horses were taken into a donga or dry watercourse for protection. firing slackened a little about 10 a.m. In the lull some food was got up and handed around. The heat was tremendous in the full power of the sun and all suffered from thirst. Some men were sent down to get spare ammunition from the saddle wallets. Soon afterwards we were ordered to ride the horses back to camp as quickly as possible. Not an easy task to take four horses along, especially if one hangs back and nearly pulls you off the saddle.

"All available men were then ordered back to Wagon Hill on foot. After a hot dusty walk we arrived back at the foot of the Hill. The ambulance wagons and dhoolies were collected there and a shell burst close to one of the wagons. We clambered up at about noon, passing a party of 18th Hussars in reserve. Bullets were whistling around everywhere and the situation seemed peculiar."

When Captain Richardson of the 11th Hussars in command of the 40 troopers comprising 'D' Squadron Light Horse on Wagon Point heard the firing before dawn, he at once regrouped his pickets and in the dark formed as best he could a line facing the sound of the firing. Captain Richardson had positioned 22 men on the south-east flank of the Point along a fairly open slope overlooking the nek. In the light of dawn the men found themselves open to fire from across the nek. Before the morning was out the detachment was almost wiped out, with 17 of the 22 either killed or wounded. Captain Richardson was among the wounded. Lieutenant W. Adams, well-known in Johannesburg as "Coffee" Adams took rover command, but was shot in a position behind a small boulder. Towards noon, Trooper Linscott crept around the rocks to get water, carrying some down the hill to the wounded. A bullet passed through his hat. By about 2.30 p.m., Troopers Wilson and Nolan and three other unwounded men, succeeded in getting back to the detachments further down the Point.

At the first sound of firing Lieutenant Digby Jones collected a mixed detachment of sappers and naval blue jackets behind the 12-pounder gun emplacement. The working lamps were extinguished and the men returned fire as the burghers spread into the nek. Another party of sappers and Light Horse at the lower 4.7 emplacement, also coming under fire, beat off a Boer spearhead. A party of Gordons working with Digby Jones went looking for the rifles stacked up some distance away. Scrambling about in the dark they found themselves mixed up with the Boers in the nek and suffered losses. Eventually, a number came upon the pickets. A few managed to reach the Light Horse redoubt on Wagon Hill. Some were taken prisoner and not released until late in the day. Digby Jones led a sortie up the slope and momentarily stopped the Boers from coming further down the hill.

Soon after his arrival with the first reinforcements from Ladysmith, Major Karri-Davies became the senior Light Horse officer on Wagon Hill when Colonel Edwards was wounded. About noon Karri-Davies arrived at Wagon Point and directed fire against burghers in the valley below the brink of the southern crest. When a group of burghers threatened from a flank position only a few hundred yards off, Karri-Davies, Sergeant Burnett and one other, crept around the rocks to warn a group of Gordons of the danger and of the need to be wary of hitting their own men. In rising from cover to check the Boer position, Karri-Davies was wounded slightly in the upper part of the leg, which for the time being put him out of the firing line. At this stage the Light Horse had scarcely 20 fit men on Wagon Point. Major C. Miller-Wallnutt with a party of Gordons endeavoured to work around the western side of the Point, but rifle and gun fire from Middle Hill and Mounted Infantry Hill thwarted any such movement.

By mid-morning the various detachments held Wagon Point from the southern rim to a line reaching up the Point beyond the gun emplacements. By the time Colonel Hamilton arrived at the Point soon after noon, the position had quietened and the firing seemed to have exhausted itself. Hamilton and Miller-Wallnutt at once set about planning a counter-attack, but unbeknown to them a new Boer attack was already under way.

General De Villiers detailed Field-Cornets Jacob De Villiers and Zacharias de Jager to leave the position in the rocks on Wagon Hill with about 20 other sharpshooters. Collecting more men from the slopes below, the Field-Cornets proceeded along a lower level beneath the crestline to

Wagon Point. Appearing unexpectedly on the skyline, they sent the Gordons and the Rifles back almost on sight. From about 1 p.m. they commenced to move rapidly down the Point.

The front on Wagon Point had been quiet for an hour. The flare up of Mauser fire behind the retreating soldiers from the advancing burghers, attracted volleys from the Light Horse Redoubt on Wagon Hill, causing the burghers to falter in their stride. Only Gert Wessels continued to follow the Field-Cornets in the dash down the slope to seize the naval gun emplacement. From the bottom of the slope along the inner rim of the Point, sappers and blue jackets, resting after being relieved from up in front by the regular soldiers, dashed back up the slope with a handful of Light Horse. Sergeant Lindsay, Troopers McKenzie, Smart and Albrecht of the Light Horse, 2nd Lieutenant G. Dennis Royal Engineers, Gunner W Sims and Petty Officer H. Lee of the Royal Navy, Lieutenant P. Fitzgerald 11th Hussars – serving as Adjutant with the Light Horse, Major Miller-Wallnutt of the Gordon Highlanders and Colonel Hamilton all took part in the sortie. Lieutenant Fitzgerald was Australian born.

As soon as he reached the 4.7 gun emplacement, Miller-Wallnutt was killed. Hamilton steadied himself against the sandbagged parapet and continued to fire with his revolver. Albrecht, Lindsay and Lee, well up with Hamilton, also fired from the emplacement. Both de Jager and De Villiers died within a few yards of the parapet. Digby Jones, Dennis and Corporal Hockaday, also an Engineer, defended from the 12-pounder gun pit. Gert Wessels was shot close up against the gun pit. Digby Jones and Albrecht led a counter-attack further up the Point where the burghers were still hanging back. The attack was supported by the 18th Hussars, the Gordons and the Rifles who by now had rallied. Digby Jones died from a bullet in the throat as he set about straightening up the line. Lieutenant Dennis was also killed when he left cover and ran out to where Digby Jones had fallen. Trooper Albrecht died instantly with a bullet in the head. Gunner Sims received a wound in the face from a shrapnel burst.

In the short convulsive action the hill leading to the extremity of Wagon Point was held at a time when, but for the hesitation of the burghers in failing to give the expected support to field-Cornets De Jager and De Villiers, the British might have been swept from the Point. Lieutenant Robert Digby Jones, 23rd Field Company Royal Engineers, and Trooper Herman Albrecht, 'E' Squadron, Imperial Light Horse, who so gallantly led the counter-attack, were posthumously awarded the Victoria Cross. Trooper Albrecht was a South African born in Aliwal North. Lieutenant Fitzgerald was mentioned in despatches and later awarded the D.S.O. Lieutenant Dennis and Gunner Sims were mentioned in despatches.

At about four o'clock in the afternoon a violent storm, working up from the west, broke over the battlefield, drenching the contestants. Pea shaped marbles of hail fell for about 20 minutes and angled rain swept down for an hour. In some rifle pits the men found themselves up to the waist in water: "In nine years it was the heaviest storm I have ever experienced in South Africa. It was impossible to see a yard in front and there was no shelter anywhere. Down below on the veldt the country was like a vast lake – a great sheet of water. The Boers seemed to fire faster than ever."[8]

At the height of the storm the rifle and gun fire increased. On the eastern slopes of Caesar's Camp the burghers, previously without hope of getting away before dark, took the opportunity to escape across the rapidly swelling waters of Fourie's Spruit. On the slopes bordering the Spruit many were cut down by the Lee-Metfords and the guns of the 42nd Battery. On Wagon Hill, where the situation had been stationary for some hours, the defenders with the wind and the rain in their faces, found the burghers creeping closer and firing faster, before they were beaten off with difficulty. On Wagon Point, the Boers made a last unsuccessful assault behind a curtain of rain. When Colonel Hamilton returned to Wagon Hill from Wagon Point, he took fresh stock of the position. The burgher sharpshooters lay where they had been since early morning, in the rocks along the ledge above the nek. They looked out over the grassy slope across which charging soldiers had more than once failed to advance. Hamilton telephoned Headquarters and General Hunter decided that the enemy must be driven from the Wagon Hill Plateau before dark. Moreover, that it was not the job for battle weary troops.

At 4 p.m. three companies of the 1st Devonshire Regiment left the camp near the Klip River just outside the town. An hour later Colonel Park reported to Hamilton, the troops resting for the time being below the northern crest of Wagon Hill, between the King's Royal Rifle fort and the Light Horse redoubt. Hamilton and Park moved quietly up the slope to roughly the position where Lord Ava and Lieutenant Pakeman had been hit. Hamilton pointed out the position held by the burghers beyond 130 yards of open ground.

Making their appearance above the crest with 180 bayonets, the Devons charged across the open space between the 5th Lancers and the Light Horse. After a brief pause when the right wing went to ground firing, as the left came into line having veered too wide, the Devons advanced directly in the face of the considerable Mauser fire and in the full view of the enemy. Some of the burghers, rising from the cover of the rocks stood openly to fire. The irresistible charge made by the Devons took them to the fringe of the rocky outcrop, but the fighting went on for some time around the crest before the burghers finally relinquished the hold on Wagon Hill.

The losses of the Devons amounted to 70 killed and wounded. Colonel Park was the only officer to get through unscathed. Lieutenant I. Masterson, running back from the rocks with orders to direct the fire from the Light Horse, managed to stagger in with three bullets in the thigh. For his gallantry, he was awarded the Victoria Cross.

By dark the firing had stopped everywhere. The great assault directed chiefly at the flanks of the long ridge called by the Boers the Platrand, had ended in defeat. A defeat due in large measure to the reluctant support of the second wave of burghers to the pre-dawn storming parties. The British losses were 424 killed and wounded. Many of the wounded lay where they had fallen for 13 hours, exposed to the hot sun and the torrential rain. The Imperial Light Horse losses were 23 killed and 36 wounded. Lieutenant Brooking, 'E' Squadron, who went into action with his troop on Wagon Point wrote:[9] "Every stone had a pool of blood on one side and the other side pasted grey with Bullets." Four Light Horse Officers specially mentioned in despatches were awarded the D.S.O.; Surgeon-Major W Davies, Captain c. Fowler, Lieutenant G. Mathias and Lieutenant P. Normand.

The 'F' Squadron Diarist wrote: "As the storm gradually abated the firing slackened. When we joined the Squadron in their Redoubt the men were huddled up behind the shelter of sand bags and stones. Everyone was wet through and shivering with cold. About an hour previously the weather had been semi-tropical and sultry. It was now nearly dark. The Boers kept up a vigorous fire for about five minutes and then retired down the Hill.

"Some food and drink was brought to us and we lay down to sleep among the rocks on wet ground. When we awoke in the morning we saw some of our dead had been brought up and laid in two rows close to where we were sleeping. It was a gruesome sight not soon forgotten. We were ordered to man the outside slope of the Hill and put up piles of stonework for protection in case of attack. The graves at the foot of the Hill were dug by natives supervised by the Public Works Department."

Trooper c. Mann wrote:[10] "At daybreak we saw no Boers except on the far hills. They sent the ambulance wagons to collect their dead and wounded. We had the job of carrying them down the Hill as we would not allow their people up on the Hill. I since found out that it was the old men of the Heilbron and Harrismith commando who attacked us."

The Reverend J.D. Kestell with the Harrismith commando on Wagon Hill wrote:[11] "It was a fearful day – a day no one who was there ever forgot. The heat too, was unbearable, the sun shot down his pitiless rays upon us and the higher he rose the hotter it became. It was terrible to see the dead lying uncovered in the scorching rays and our poor wounded suffered indescribable tortures from thirst.

"How glad I was that I could do something for the wounded. I bandaged those within reach. I also rendered first aid to the British wounded; one Tommy said to me after I had bandaged him: 'I feel easier now.' A sergeant of the Imperial Light Horse who had discovered that I was a minister remarked: 'You are preaching a good sermon today.'

"How the wounded suffered from thirst. Long before midday there was not a drop of water left in our flasks. So intolerable was the thirst, that there were burghers who went down to the dongas below in search of water where there was none and where they knew that almost certain death awaited them."

Sergeant J. Laing, 'C' Squadron, who lay wounded in the nek between Wagon Hill and Wagon Point from about daybreak wrote:[12] "As the sun rose, the heat became intense and my wound gave me anxiety and pain and I could not stop the bleeding. I took the puttee off my right leg and tied it tightly above the left knee and tried to stop the dripping, but without avail as I was in such a cramped position. However, I found that the blood on the ground had congealed with the intense Heat. As a last resort, on seeing this, I undid my puttee and boot and put my foot in the sun and to my great relief my ankle became one clot of blood – the bleeding had ceased.

"By this time the heat was so intense and my thirst more so; in fact it became so bad that I had to place my finger on my tongue to hold it down to get my breath. Before this I had appealed to the two Boers who were firing over my head to give me a drink of water. At last, one of them who had a very short beard handed me his water bottle – which was a British one – what relief I got from that drink. To my intense sorrow, which I feel to this day, on handing back the bottle and while he was putting the strap round his neck, my unknown benefactor was shot through the face and disappeared from my sight with the blood gushing from his mouth. This he got for his kind and humane action which I shall never forget.

"Later on in the afternoon a very heavy rain fell, when I was able to lick the water on the rock. Shortly after this, the firing became very severe from both sides. I tucked my head well under the rock; it was then that I got shot through the back from a ricocheting bullet. I might mention here within a few yards of where I lay my old friend 'Dickie' Gorton received eight bullet wounds, Trooper Atley lay dead and Trooper R. Dawson. Also two others whose names I cannot remember except George Blair our cook, who had deserted his pots and pans and joining in the defence was shot through the thigh.

"During the evening I was found by Dr Ligertwood and others, had my wound dressed and was given some brandy and a blanket to lie on. As it was now dark it was impossible to remove all the wounded so I lay there all night. The first thing I remembered in the morning was being carried to the foot of the Hill on a stretcher to await the ambulance. My next experience was that I awoke suddenly and to my intense horror, found myself among the dead who had been carried off the Hill for the purpose of burial. I recovered my senses and kept shouting, when a lieutenant from 'E' Squadron heard and rushed over. He recognised me immediately and said: 'Good God, Sergeant Laing, what are you doing here? Why haven't they taken you to hospital?' He gave me some brandy from his flask and within a few minutes he had a Scotch cart with two bullocks and a leader, who was none other than Trooper Ginger Wilson of No. 2 Troop, 'C' Squadron.

"Another wounded man was laid alongside me who had been shot through the head. We then proceeded to the Light Horse camp in Ladysmith. One moment my wounded pal, who was unconscious, would be on top of me and with another few jolts, I'd be on top of him. However, we duly arrived at the camp. Everyone rushed out. Sergeant Macgregor of the Light Horse Ambulance Staff, came out and informed Ginger Wilson that we should not have been there at all, but taken to the church in Ladysmith. He gave me a drink of brandy and I asked him to give my pal a drink also. To my great surprise, I found that my wounded comrade was not a Gordon Highlander as I thought, but a Dutchman named Harold Schultz, of the Harrismith commando. I heard later that he recovered and was exchanged for one of our prisoners.

"To cut a long story short, we arrived at the church and my wounds were dressed. I lay on a mattress on the floor with a blanket over me. In the afternoon at 5 o'clock, one of the R.A.M.C. doctors was walking through the hospital looking at the wounded. He spotted my foot sticking out from under the blanket; he immediately asked where I was shot and what regiment I belonged to. After my reply he sent an orderly to Surgeon-Major Davies at the Light Horse camp, saying that he might send someone down as one of his men required attention. Shortly afterwards Dr Ligertwood arrived. On seeing my foot which had turned a bluish colour, he got a pair of scissors and ripped off the bandages. He got two orderlies to massage my foot and leg. This evidently was useless, so they tied a temporary bandage round my foot and before leaving me, he said that I would be quite alright and that I would be in Intombi Hospital before 7 o'clock next morning.

"Another little incident. Next morning I was put on a dhooley[13] consisting of a bamboo pole carried on the shoulders of two Indians. L was left swinging in the centre on a kind of a hammock. I had only a grey shirt on and before reaching the station I was upset three times in the street. On arrival at the station I was dumped into a luggage van. To my surprise the next man to me was my dear pal 'Dickie' Gorton. Poor old Dick. He had terrible hiccoughs and could not stop. When I arrived at Intombi Hospital the first man to greet me was Lieutenant Cresswell of the Light Horse, who gave me a cup of tea. The next thing I remember was when I was on a table in the operating theatre. I was surrounded by doctors and a lecture was being given by Major Bruce. My last memory was Dr Howarden telling me I had to lose part of my leg. Then he administered the anaesthetic. A very long while after, I woke up in a hospital tent. I understand I went through a very rough time and had a narrow squeak. I would like to mention that my poor old pal 'Dickie' Gorton hiccoughed himself to death in the bed next to me."

On 9th January, Colonel Hamilton wrote to Lieutenant-Colonel Edwards: "I write this line just to let you and your brave fellows know that in my despatch it will be made quite clear that the

Imperial Light Horse were second to none. No one realises more clearly than I do that they were the backbone of the defence during the long day's fighting. Hence, make this clear to the men. To have been associated with them I have always felt to be the highest privilege and honour."[14]

In his despatches General White reported:[15] "I desire to draw attention to the gallantry displayed by the ranks of the Imperial Light Horse, some of whom were within 100 yards of the enemy for 15 hours exposed to a deadly fire. Their losses were terribly heavy, but never for one moment did any of them waver, or cease to show a firm example of courage and determination to all who came in contact with them."

The outcome of the day on 6th January was partly due to every post on the Ladysmith perimeter being connected to a telephone exchange at the cottage Headquarters in the town. General Hunter stated:[16] "It was, I suppose, the first instance on record of a fight over a considerable area, ever having been directed by telephone."

In September 1899, the Natal Government supplied Colonel Scott Chisholme in Pietermaritzburg with 475 Martini-Metford rifles, the service weapon of the Natal Carbineers. On 8th January 1900, the Martini-Metford rifles with which the Light Horse had fought on Wagon Hill were replaced with Lee-Metford magazine rifles. Up to this stage the Light Horse had been at a disadvantage with the single loading rifle. The burghers generally had magazine rifles, giving them time to fire several shots against one from the Light Horse. Bayonets were also issued to the Light Horse. The men were concerned that by the issue of bayonets they were likely to become "foot-sloggers," as the infantry were called.

---

[1] 11th Hussars attached
[2] From the typewritten Regimental Light Horse Diary of Engagements
[3] From *The Story of the Imperial Light Horse* G.F. Gibson
[4] From the Regimental Typed Diary of Engagements
[5] *Pictures of the War* J. Stuart
[6] In his Diary in the Karri-Davies Collection
[7] In the Light Horse Typed Diary of Engagements
[8] In the 'F' Squadron Typed Diary
[9] In a diary in the Karri-Davies Collection
[10] From a Diary in the Karri-Davies Collection
[11] *Through Shot and flame* J.D. Kestell
[12] From *The Story of the Imperial Light Horse* G.F. Gibson
[13] A swinging litter borne on men's shoulders
[14] In the Imperial Light Horse Typewritten Diary of Engagements in the Karri-Davies Collection
[15] Despatches, 23rd March, 1900
[16] From the Typewritten Regimental Light Horse diary of Engagements

CHAPTER 6
THE ACTIVITIES OF 'A' SQUADRON, IMPERIAL LIGHT HORSE
OCTOBER 1899 – APRIL 1900

'A' Squadron was the first of the Imperial Light Horse Squadrons to leave Pietermaritzburg. With Major Doveton in command, the Squadron reached Estcourt on 12th October 1899. Orders were received to remain at Estcourt for the defence of the town and to keep in cheek certain Boer farmers in the district of Weenen who were thought likely to give trouble. There was much disappointment in the Squadron at not going forward with the other Light Horse squadrons to Ladysmith. 'A' Squadron camped just south of the town alongside the Natal Volunteers. The British force at Estcourt was under the command of Colonel C.J. Long, Royal Artillery. Soon after the battle of Elandslaagte on 21st October, when Colonel Scott Chisholme was killed and Major Woolls-Sampson was wounded, Major Doveton was ordered to Ladysmith by train on 24th October.

Lieutenant H. Bottomley, the next senior officer, was appointed to command 'A' Squadron. Shortly afterwards, he was made a captain by Major-General H. Hildyard. About the same time, Lieutenant Tom Bridges, Royal field Artillery was attached to 'A' Squadron. The strength of the Squadron was 81 officers and men, including Lieutenants D. Gilfillan, H. Campbell and Ross. The Squadron patrolled the district for 25 miles around. On the afternoon of 24th October, a Boer detachment was reported near Highlands in the direction of Mooi River. Lieutenant Gilfillan with 10 men and a sergeant was sent to investigate. Gilfillan returned at 8 p.m. and reported all quiet. On the afternoon of 1st November, information was received of Boers scouting from Colenso. British patrols advanced as far as Frere and beyond, along the road to Colenso. The Light Horse was ordered to march to Colenso, the order being withdrawn when news came through that the small garrison at Colenso was about to fall back 24 miles along the railway to Estcourt.

The Colenso garrison was made up of small detachments of the Dublin Fusiliers, Durban Light Infantry and the Natal Field Battery. With the cutting of the telegraph and the railway between Ladysmith and the south on 3rd November, it was not long before the small force based at the railway village near the southern bank of the Tugela River came under artillery fire, against which the short-ranged Natal Battery had no effective reply.

At this time the British troops in the region immediately south of Ladysmith amounted to no more than 2,300 men. A Composite Regiment of about 450 troopers was formed, made up of a company of the 2nd Battalion King's Royal Rifles Mounted infantry, 2nd Battalion Royal Dublin Fusiliers Mounted Infantry Section, a squadron of the Natal Carbineers, a detachment of Natal Mounted Police and 'A' Squadron Imperial Light Horse.

After much patrolling on the outskirts of Estcourt, 'A' Squadron was in action for the first time on 15th November after heavy gun fire was heard from the direction of Frere, 12 miles along the road to Colenso. 'A' Squadron – 57 men strong – was ordered out. Major D McKenzie, Natal Carbineers, followed with 40 men and took over command of the column. Beyond Frere, the column engaged a detachment of the commando that only a few hours before had wrecked an armoured train steaming towards Colenso. Mr Winston Churchill was among those captured.

Taking cover, the Light Horse shot six Boers from 800 yards. The others rode off at full gallop to a kopje. Trooper Hillhouse was wounded in the thigh. Under cover of a heavy rainstorm the column retired in good order from a situation that was becoming dangerous after the commando was reinforced up to 2,000 strong. Riding back in heavy rain the Squadron covered the retirement of the walking and the wounded from the armoured train. The Light Horse returned to camp at 3.30

By delaying the advance from Colenso and patrolling so cautiously towards Estcourt, the commandos under Louis Botha and Joubert ceded precious time to the British allowing breathing space before the arrival at the front of the troops hastily disembarking in Durban. Leaving the containing force still around Ladysmith, commandos numbering 4,000 advanced along both sides of the railway as far as Nottingham Road, only 40 miles from Pietermaritzburg. Some patrols ranged up to within 10 miles of the town.

On 16th November, Major-Gen6eral Hildyard arrived at Estcourt, just ahead of the slowly approaching commandos, bringing with him considerable reinforcements. Also on 16th November and again on 20th, the Light Horse joined in reconnaissances from Estcourt in the direction of Highlands and Mooi River, locating the enemy on each occasion but returning without firing shots. By 20th November the Boer forces advancing east and west of the railway formed a junction between Willow Grange and Highlands, leaving Estcourt encircled.

The Boers placed a big gun on Brynbella, a two mile long ridge commanding Willow Grange from the west. General Hildyard decided to make a night assault and capture the gun threatening Estcourt.

On the afternoon of 22nd November, the infantry marched five miles6 through heavy rain from Estcourt to Beacon Hill, a cone shaped hill 5,000 yards north of Brynbella. Guided by Mr Chapman a local farmer, two battalions of infantry, the West Yorkshire and East Surrey, marching before midnight, reached the north-east corner of Brynbella by 3.30 a.m. The hill was taken without loss the burghers having withdrawn along the ridge for almost a mile. The gun had been withdrawn some hours before. Meanwhile, the troops came under heavy rifle fire from the burghers along the ridge and from gun and pom pom[1] fire.

The Light Horse under Captain Bottomley advanced to cover the infantry after orders had been given for the soldiers to withdraw. Dismounting at the foot of the hill the men in making their way up passed the retiring infantry and the walking wounded. On the summit the Light Horse took cover behind a wall in an abandoned laager. A small company of about 10 West Yorkshiremen, without officers and unaware of the order to retire, were keeping up a steady rate of fire. The dead and wounded lay all around them. Nevertheless, they had no thought of retiring until a junior officer reached them bearing the specific order to do so.

The Light Horse kept the Boers in check for nearly an hour until the soldiers were off the hill. Unfortunately the field artillery covering the retreat ceased firing just as the last of the infantry and wounded were leaving the base of the ridge. The Light Horse moved swiftly down the hill without the benefit of covering fire from the guns. Before the horses could be reached, the Boers were in position on the hill, firing down on the men as they ran.[2]

The rapid build-up of British troops, guns and supplies by rail from Durban to Mooi River continued on the 24th and the following days. General Joubert decided to contract his extended lines back to Colenso. On Sunday, 26th November, a British mounted column advanced from Estcourt along the road to Frere and established that the Boer army was in retreat. On the left flank the Light Horse killed two Boers near Ennersdale. Marching over rain-sodden country, Joubert's army arrived at Colenso by nightfall on 27th November. In the retreat over a wide front they drove before them thousands of sheep, cattle and wagons looted from the farms of southern Natal. A German serving with the commandos described the appearance of the Boer army as something like a Tramp's Crusade.

Major-General D. Dundonald,[3] commanding the mounted corps, advanced along the line of the railway on 28th November with a column of 900 troopers and a battery of field artillery. The Light

Horse scattered enemy outposts near Chieveley. The column halted within 1,500 yards of Colenso village, while the guns shelled the positions on the Heights across the Tugela River, forcing the Boer gunners to reply. Returning to Estcourt, the column heard the explosion when the Boers blew up the railway bridge spanning the river.

On 30th November a detachment of 30 Light Horse and the Natal Carbineers joined in a demonstration by marching to Weenen, a village some distance to the east from Frere. The detachment camped overnight at Weenen after a singsong in the hotel. Captain Bottomley wrote:[4] "From one of the high hills on the road to Weenen we saw no less than six Boer camps behind Colenso, extending as far as Bulwana mountain. Colenso itself is strongly fortified, guns bristling on every kopje behind the village. They have a long range gun there too, as they sent a shell after us at 9,000 yards and nearly dropped Captain Gough who was signalling me to retire. It would be absolutely impossible to take Colenso from the front. We cannot charge into the place as we will have the Tugela River to cross right under their guns. Naturally, both the railway and the foot bridges will be blown up by that time."

General Sir Redvers Buller, appointed Commander-in-Chief in South Africa, arrived in Cape Town on 31st October, when the Army was on the defensive on every front. General Buller decided to split up the divisions then disembarking from Britain. Accordingly, he despatched Lieutenant-General P. Methuen[5] along the western railway to relieve Kimberley. Major-General Sir W. Gatacre was given a small force and the task of holding the Cape Midlands in the face of invasion, in the wake of commando crossings of the Orange River at Norval's Pont and Bethulie. Embarking for Durban from Cape Town, General Buller took the biggest part of the available force to relieve Ladysmith.

By the end of November 1899 the British had 52,000 troops in South Africa.

On 30th November illness forced General Joubert to retire from the Natal front, leaving Louis Botha in command of the Republican forces along the Tugela River. Botha proceeded to dig in along the river Heights over a front several miles long. Botha had about 8,000 burghers, with four guns and a pom pom, plus a number of deceptive dummy gun emplacements built of corrugated iron. From the Heights behind the Colenso road and rail bridges, the burghers looked out from invisible sandbagged trenches to the plain beyond the river, over an unrestricted field of fire.

General Butler arrived in Chievely on 5th December. Over the next few days he made two reconnaissances with a mounted column across open ground slightly to the left of Colenso village and in full view of the Boer positions on the Heights across the river. On 6th December, Captain Bottomley wrote: "We are going to escort General Buller to Colenso this afternoon in force. I cannot find out what his intention is, or whether the guns are going with us. He will have the whole of the cavalry brigade with him, which now means about 1,800 horse." On these reconnaissances the mounted brigade acted as escort to a Field Battery, shelling the Heights with the object of drawing the fire and spotting the Boer dispositions, but unlike 28th November, there was no reply from the Boer occupied bank of the river.

On 13th December, in another show of force, several batteries from Buller's 44 gun armament and a brigade of infantry paraded on the open veldt in full view of the entrenched Boers on the Heights across the river, without provoking the slightest response from the Boer gunners.

Hlangwane Hill, about two miles east of the Colenso railway bridge was the one position along the south bank from which raking fire could render untenable the defences on the Colenso Heights. Hlangwane was also the only outpost south of the river retained by the Boers. Yet the Hill was only of secondary importance in the strategy by General Buller.

On the night of 13th-14th December, a commando numbering about 800 burghers on Hlangwane Hill panicked. Disregarding orders, the burghers retired across the river, leaving the Hill undefended. That the Hill on the Boer left flank was so lightly held was indicative of the degree of certainty in the mind of the Boer leader that the British were about to launch a frontal attack against the Colenso Heights. With great difficulty and after a lot of negotiation on the 14th, General Botha succeeded in getting the Wakkerstroom commando to occupy the Hill, but only after the drawing of lots. In common with the general lack of information on the disposition of the Boer forces, General Buller was unaware that for some time, up to within a few hours before his Army advanced to give battle, Hlangwane Hill was undefended.

Early on the morning of 15th December, Buller advanced in a frontal attack against the Colenso kopjes. Covered by an artillery barrage, four brigades of infantry marched up the open plain towards the river. General Botha's plan was to allow the leading infantry column to cross by the road bridge unopposed, by which time all the brigades were expected to be within rifle range of the burghers entrenched on the Heights.

The left infantry flank under Major-General A. Hart, marching in a line just to the west of the road bridge and mislead by a faulty sketch, unwittingly entered deep into the centre, of a large loop in the river. Without knowing exactly where they were in relation to the drift for which they were heading, the men extended and lay as close to the ground as possible. In this situation the Brigade became bogged down without any plan. After an hour spent under heavy fire from three sides without much cover, Hart's Brigade received the order to retire. By the time the Brigade had disengaged and withdrawn, the casualties had reached 550.

The centre column of marching infantry under General Hildyard and the eastern or right flanking brigade under Major-General G. Barton, moved towards the river along the line of the railway, behind the guns of the 14th and 66th Royal field Artillery under Colonel Long. By 6 a.m. the guns were about a mile ahead of the infantry, when Colonel Long fixed on a firing position for the batteries in a slight depression on the veldt east of the railway station, only 1,300 yards from the closest Boer trenches at Fort Wylie,[6] on the Heights across the river.

Colonel Long's guns were well within Mauser range, being much nearer to the river than he intended, a mistake due to the thick mist rising from the river. After the systematic drawing up of the guns, the ammunition teams retired to the shelter of a donga about 50 yards back. Long's guns may have been advanced too far, nevertheless, the losses of the gun crews were not great and inside an hour the guns had effectively silenced the Mauser fire from Fort Wylie. The supply of ammunition gave Long his greatest concern and was the cause of the gunners retiring to the donga with the wounded, leaving the 12 guns standing undamaged in the slight depression on the open veldt. The lifting of the restraining fire from the batteries heralded a resurgence of gun and rifle fire from over the river.

When General Buller realised that Long's batteries were no longer firing, he came to the conclusion that the guns had been put out of action and he decided that they should be withdrawn. General Hildyard with infantry drawn up out of rifle range, was ordered to advance two battalions to take part in the withdrawal of the guns. Under cover of shells from the long range naval guns well in the rear, the infantry approached the line of the railway station and the road bridge. At this point they faced a hail of bullets and were forced to take cover behind the few village buildings and railway sheds and in small shelter trenches dug by the Durban Light Infantry in the first week in November before the evacuation. From these positions the soldiers put out a strong rifle fire that effectively drove some of the burghers from the lower trenches on the far side of the river.

General Buller was badly shaken and bruised by a bursting shell. A shell also killed a Staff officer. About the same time the ammunition wagons for Long's guns were ready to go forward. The gunners were still in the donga waiting for the arrival of the wagons. Halting the wagons, Buller called for volunteers to retrieve the guns. Limber teams dashed forward in a disastrous but gallant effort to turn the guns around and haul them back. Only two guns of the 66th Battery were saved, one almost miraculously without the loss of a single man or horse in the limber team. The other teams were cut up, with loss of life among officers and men. No less than six Victoria Crosses were awarded for gallantry in the attempt to save the batteries.

Having been an onlooker at the unsuccessful attempt to save the guns and with the infantry defeat suffered by Hart's Brigade well in mind, General Buller decided to abandon the guns and to call off the battle everywhere. At 10.30 a.m., Hildyard received orders to withdraw from Colenso village. By 2.30 p.m. the entire infantry force had withdrawn from the field. From the 18,000 men in the early morning advance, there were 1,127 casualties, including 145 killed, 220 taken prisoner and 762 wounded. The Boer casualties were only 38.

General Hildyard reported:[7] "I sent the Regiment up to get between the railway and the guns and cover the guns with fire. What had really happened was this. Colonel Long went forward to this position. When they got the guns into action they swept the kopjes – those red kopjes – and the Boer was unable to fire. And when Long finished his ammunition, he could not get any more and the Boers got into action again and put the guns out of action. I believe from all enquiries I made that it was at 1,300 yards. Of course, the guns were lying out under sight of the kopje. At 5 p.m. the Boers crossed the river by the narrow road bridge. Without in any way being molested they hitched up the 10 guns still standing undamaged with the breech blocks intact. They also drove off with six ammunition wagons."

General Dundonald's Mounted Brigade had orders to cover the right flank of the frontal movement against the Colenso kopjes. Dundonald's effective force after allowing for baggage and horseholders was something less than a 1,000 men, supported by the 7th Field Battery. The size of the force and the weight of armaments signalled the concept of a secondary operation against Hlangwane Hill. In any event, the strength of the force indicated that Buller contemplated the infiltration of the.Colenso kopjes from Halangwane as something less than of the foremost importance.

Dundonald's column dismounted at 7.15 a.m. more than a mile south of Hlangwane Hill. The newly raised South African units, Thorneycroft's Mounted Infantry and the South African Light Horse, covered the right and left flanks. The Light Horse marched in the centre along with the units known as the Composite Regiment. The strength of the dismounted troopers was about two thirds the strength of the burghers on the Hill. Whereas the troops on the flanks found cover at the foot of the Hill among scattered boulders and thick groves of low bush, the Composite Regiment much less well off, found itself in the centre of a ploughed field. The men were forced to lie low under pom pom and rifle fire, unable to raise their heads from the level of the dark soil offering no amount of camouflage against the khaki tunics. Unable to get infantry support and lacking the backing of artillery other than the 7th Battery, the fire of which at one period was diverted to the Colenso kopjes, the troops remained pinned down around the foot of Hlangwane for four hours until the arrival on the scene of General Buller with the order to withdraw. By 5 p.m. the Light Horse was back in Chieveley.

Trooper A. Duirs,[8] 'A' Squadron Imperial Light Horse, described the battle of Colenso: "On 15th December we marched at 3 a.m. and rode through lines of infantry. Soon there was one continuous roar of rifles with a lull now and then when our shells dropped amongst them. I never could have imagined rifle fire to have made such a noise. No smoke or flash to enable one to locate the enemy, only one infernal rattle.

"We arrived opposite Hlangwane Hill with Thorneycroft's Mounted Infantry on our right and the South African Light Horse on our left. We left our horses under cover of a ridge out of the rifle fire. The South African Light Horse took their horses too close to the Boers and lost heavily in both men and horses and prisoners. We advanced over the donga and through bush that was growing pretty thick. Towards the foot of the Hill we halted right in the middle of a ploughed field. There we lay like so many dead men. I thought all our men were dead, they lay so still. I strained my eyes looking for a Boer, but it was impossible to see one. They were shooting from between rocks. After lying in the boiling sun for what seemed hours, we at last got the order to retire.

"Much to my astonishment nearly all the men jumped up and ran back to the donga. While resting and talking we discovered that the orders had not been carried on to the Carbineers who were in a donga on our right, so I volunteered to carry the order back. I got to the donga in which the Carbineers were, guided by the sound of firing. I also found to my joy a big pool of water. I had a long drink and filled my water bottle. We brought all our wounded back with us and never lost a rifle. Later I helped carry our wounded up to the ambulance wagon, where I found Dr McLean hard at work. The heat was awful and the thirst worse than anything I had ever experienced. How the infantry stood the heat and thirst down on that awful plain I can't imagine.

"On the way back we heard of the loss of the guns and could see them on the plain in front of Fort Wylie. We came back to Chieveley station and arrived back in camp after dark at the end of one of the thirstiest days I have ever spent. Out of our Squadron of about 55 men, we had three killed and six wounded. The Carbineers lost about the same."

Troopers W. Longdon, N. Blakeway and A. Jackson were left dead on the field. During the armistice on 16th December, the three Light Horsemen were picked up from the field and buried alongside the railway station at Chieveley.

Captain Bottomley[9] described the action at Hlangwane: "We advanced on foot, Natal Carbineers on the right and a company of Mounted Infantry composed of King's Royal Rifles on our left. On reaching an open ploughed field about 600 yards from the foot of Hlangwane, we encountered a heavy cross fire from our right, which was probably intended for Thorneycroft's Mounted Infantry.

"The Regiment was commanded by Major Walters of the 7th Hussars, who instead of allowing us to double forward, blew his whistle which was a signal to lie down. While in this position we were subjected to a hot fire until the order to retire was passed down from the left. On reaching our horses the feeling of the Squadron was so strong against Major Walters, that the matter was reported to Lord Dundonald. We requested permission to act independently or to have another officer to command the Composite Regiment. The consequence was that for some weeks 'A' Squadron as well as the other two units acted independently under their own officers."

A Light Horse Diarist[10] wrote: "Major Walters halted us in ploughed land that made us good marks for the Boers. Longdon, Jackson and Blakeway were shot dead. Freshney shot through the eye. In retreat McGill, Nelson, Crawley, Rawstorne, Stone and Clarke were wounded. Shepherd got sunstroke." Lieutenant T. Bridges wrote:[11] "I made up my mind, orders or no orders, never to let my men be put in such a foolish position again."

When the Light Horse retired, Trooper Freshney was left behind, believed to be dead. One of the men ran back under fire and placed a hat over his face. On the following morning Freshney was found alive, although close to death. The bullet had penetrated from the left eye to almost the full length of the spinal cord. At the first opportunity Freshney was invalided to England. His survival was due to the protection the hat gave to his bared head in the sun. Trooper Crawley was also invalided to England.

On 16th December, General Buller informed the War Office that in his opinion it would be better to entrench the Army at Chieveley rather than try to relieve Ladysmith. A despatch from Buller to General White on the same day contained the suggestion that White should make the best terms he could get from the enemy. The immediate reaction of the British Government resulted in the appointment of field-Marshal Lord Roberts as Commander-in-Chief in South Africa, with Major-General Lord Kitchener as Chief-of-Staff. General Buller retained the command in Natal. On 22nd December the Light Horse joined in a reconnaissance towards the Tugela, west from Chieveley beyond Pretorius Farm. Trooper Duirs and Trooper Walter Francis received praise for volunteering and successfully carrying out hazardous scouting. Cattle and horses were herded and driven in under the eyes of the Boers firing at long range.

At Chieveley on Christmas Day the Light Horse attended church parade in the morning and took part in sports in the afternoon. On Boxing Day the Squadron struck camp. Marching to Frere the men were detailed to an outpost west of the town.

Relaxing over the New Year weekend, the men played cricket when not on duty. Lieutenant A Shore and Lieutenant R. Barnes, 4th Hussars, and 20 men wounded at Elandslaagte rejoined the Squadron. Four Colt machine guns were allotted to the Composite Regiment. On Tuesday 9th January, a day of heavy rain, General Dundonald gave orders to be ready to march by 6 a.m. The next morning.

By 9th January with the arrival of the 5th Infantry Division under Lieutenant-General Sir Charles Warren, the Natal army was built tip to 30,000 men. Leaving a containing force in front of the Colenso kopjes, Buller marched on the 10th with Warren and 23,000 men from Pretorius Farm to Potgieter's Drift on the Tugela about 16 miles in a direct line west from the railway at Colenso. The slow moving army, with 650 animal-drawn vehicles stretched out for miles over the rain sodden tracks across the veldt.

Spearheading the advance on 10th January, Dundonald's Mounted column of 1,500 men, occupied the village of Springfield without a fight and camped for the night at nearby Mount Alice, opposite Potgieter's Drift. Mount Alice, 700 feet high overlooked the drift and it provided a commanding view of the Heights to the east and to the west. The march to Potgieter's was the opening round in the second attempt to relieve Ladysmith. The strategy was to find the Boer right flank and turn the whole position. General Buller recorded in despatches on 14th January: "I find the enemy's position covering Potgieter's Drift so strong that I shall have to turn it."

Acting on a good report from Trichardt's Drift four miles upstream, Buller decided that a turning movement could be launched from the drift around a long ridge known as Thabanyama, or Rangeworthy Heights. On 16th January, General Warren – second in command in Natal – advanced with three infantry brigades and six batteries on a night march to Tricliardt's Drift. General Buller stayed at Potgieter's Drift where the balance of the force under Major-General N. Lyttelton was to provide diversionary moves.

The Light Horse paraded soon after 5 p.m. on the 16th and half an hour after midnight established a camp opposite Trichardt's Drift. At dawn on the 17th a start was made to construct pontoon bridges across the river on the upstream side of the drift. The pontoons were completed by the engineers at a time when only a few hundred burghers manned the Heights three miles back from the river. Before the pontoons were in position a Light Horse patrol – Lieutenant Bridges and Troopers Savory, Duirs and Metcalfe – forded the river with the water coming half-way up to the saddle flaps. Cautiously examining the ground on the far bank, the patrol came under fire when only a few hundred yards from a farm house a mile or two from the river. The patrol escaped without casualties and the farm house was shelled. By late afternoon all the mounted corps were across. Two British regular troopers were drowned.

In France in 1917, Trooper Harry Savory was killed, shot by a sniper from a village church tower.

General Warren declined to make any advance on the far side of the river before every one of the regiments had filed over. Keeping the infantry close to the pontoon head, the General personally supervised in detail the crossing of the entire supply column. Meanwhile, behind the interior lines, the Boers were busy mobilising and digging in on Rangeworthy Heights; overlooking the British bridgehead.

Early on the morning of the 18th, Dundonald's mounted corps, engaged in covering the left flank between the river and the Heights, received information from Africans. They told of a small commando advancing west on the main road running from Ladysmith behind Rangeworthy Heights in the direction of Acton Homes farm. Dundonald's horsemen, 1,500 strong, passed Bastion Hill west of the bridgehead and veering north-west advanced about 10 miles to the junction of the Acton Homes–Ladysmith road. Dundonald had been given special orders from Buller to protect the left flank and "to act according to circumstances." General Warren's orders from Buller were to "refuse the right" while probing beyond Bastion Hill to the Ladysmith road.

When General Warren heard that Dundonald had left the precincts of the bridgehead he at once ordered the return of 500 Royal Dragoons to give support to the main force at the bridgehead camp. Captain Bottomley, 'A' Squadron wrote: "Galloping some miles up the bank, keeping well under cover, we made for kopjes through which the road ran, Carbineers on right and Imperial Light Horse on left. Under cover of rocks we saw the Boers galloping up, the two scouts 50 yards ahead did not see us and waved their men on. firing began from less than 300 yards. The Boers were completely surprised and before long hoisted white flags in all directions. Lieutenant Shore was shot in the shoulder by some of the enemy as they were galloping away. Dr Briscoe was on the spot and gave attention. Some of the King's Royal Rifles coming up in support as the enemy retired lost two wounded."

The ambush set up on the side of the Acton Homes road had routed a commando of about 250 under Commandant Opperman. About 50 Boers were either killed, wounded or taken prisoner. Field-Cornet Metz was among those killed.

Captain Bottomley wrote: "Shortly after, General Dundonald and Staff rode up and ordered us to hold the position while he sent for reinforcements. He explained that the surrounding country was such, that an entry into Ladysmith was possible and easy from this point, as it was not well defended. On being referred to Sir Charles Warren the request was refused."

The refusal to send either guns or infantry was followed by the recall on the 19th of Dundonald's column to the point where Warren was, with infantry and baggage, about two miles west of the pontoon, for not until that morning had Warren made up his mind to get moving. Once on the road Warren quickly decided that the track was too narrow and difficult for the heavily laden wagons. The slow progress of the wagons made them particularly vulnerable to the enemy content to watch from the Heights. By late afternoon, the entire column was back where it had started from in the morning.

For the next three days Warren's force attacked Rangeworthy Heights lying directly in front of the Drift, with the objective of gaining control of the road passing over the range at a point the British called Three Tree Hill. Warren's long delay at the bridgehead gave the Boers time to occupy the section of the range in strength and to dig in along the crest of the Heights. From the trenches they looked down over 1,000 yards of open bare slope, beyond which projected a spurred and rocky underfeature. Warren's infantry, attacking under cover of artillery up through the lower features was confronted with 1,000 yards of bullet swept glacis. After four hours of trying to advance and the loss of 300 men, the troops slept that night among the boulders and small scrubby bushes in the kloofs.[12]

The Light Horse became involved when Dundonald's column seized Bastion Hill, a prominence on the Boer right. When at length two battalions of infantry arrived to exploit the position won by the dismounted troopers, the Boers in the meantime had strengthened the sector, so the attack on Bastion Hill came to nothing. By the morning of 22nd, repeated bombardment and infantry assaults at the cost of 500 casualties had failed to make a dent in the Boer line. By this time, General Buller had become heartily dissatisfied with Warren's performance in the field. A heated discussion between the two ended in a snap decision to attack Spion Kop, the 1470 feet summit of a high ridge almost three miles long. Spion Kop dominated the skyline to the right, alongside where the infantry attack had been directed over several days and where the troops were holding the positions they had gained. From the summit of Spion Kop several saddles ran off throwing up somewhat lesser peaks with intervening gullies.

A mixed force of 1750 regulars and volunteers made a night march up a long south-western spur of Spion Kop on 23rd January, scattering a Boer patrol on the mist covered summit at dawn. The men entrenched as best they could on the rocky plateau capped with only a light thickness of topsoil. The lifting of the mist revealed the actual position of the main trench. Nothing better than a shallow ditch, it had been unwittingly scooped out under the veil of mist right in the centre of the plateau. As soon as the mist lifted the Boer artillery found the range and for the rest of the day plastered the British position.

From the short range of nearby peaks, riflemen poured in a devastating fire. Others much more daring, moved right up to the rim of the northern crest of the plateau, sniping at close range from the cover of rocks. In strong efforts to dislodge the burghers, the troops made several unsuccessful rushes to the rim in front of the trenches. By noon the rushes were spent and the soldiers were confined to the trenches. The British gunners could not silence the Boer artillery and the pressure from the rifle fire was unremitting until dark. The dead piled up in and around the congested trenches and lay spread over the small area. The shortage of water also caused much suffering. Reinforcements arriving on or near the summit at intervals during the day increased the number on or near the battle area to about 4,000 troops. By the end of the day, the British losses were 1,205 killed, wounded and taken prisoner. The British lost more men either killed or died from wounds on Spion Kop on 24th January 1900, than on any other single day in the war.

Major-General E. Woodgate in command on Spion Kop was mortally wounded before midday. The responsibility of command fell to Lieutenant-Colonel A. Thorneycroft. Soon after sunset, in the absence of information relating to plans for the next day, Colonel Thorneycroft decided that the men, in particular those who had been on the Kop since early morning, were in no condition to face the ordeal again on the following day. By the order of Thorneycroft, but unknown to Warren until it was too late to reverse the decision, the Kop was evacuated overnight. One notable aspect of the battle of Spion Kop was the tardy and often non-existent line of communication between General Warren and the command on the summit.

Nearly all the Boer riflemen also left the scene of the battle overnight. Wagons and horsemen retired along the road to Ladysmith. Only a handful of burghers were left and found themselves unexpectedly alone on the battlefield at dawn with the dead and the wounded.

In describing the scene on Spion Kop on the day after the battle, the Reverend JD Kestell wrote:[13] "General Buller obtained leave from General Botha to bury his dead. It was heartrending to see how many were there. Many of them were flung into the long trenches that had served as breastworks and so great was the number that the earth did not sufficiently cover them all. Some even remained unburied. We did not know what the exact number was, but we saw the dead lying in heaps."

Early on the very night that the march up Spion Kop took place, Lieutenant T. Bridges, 'A' Squadron, was sent with a patrol in the rear of the Boer lines. Lieutenant Bridges wrote:[14] "I was sent to try and work round the rear of the Boers and find out what was going on. I left camp at dark with a patrol and made for a well-marked conical hill outside our left flank. Here we left our horses and I took with me one man, a red headed colonial lad named Stanley London who knew the ground and could speak Kaffir and the Taal and could hold his own in a scrap. Travelling as light as possible and armed only with revolvers, we walked most of the night and found our way to a pass in the Drakensberg Range called Van Reenan's, where we concealed ourselves and waited for day-break.

"As soon as it got light we were able to see several laagers behind Spion Kop and also one below us. The route we had taken during the night was now well marked by a ribbon of track across the dewy grass. To our left was the road through the rocky pass, the line of communications for the Free State commandos engaged at Ladysmith. The laager below us was already being struck and moving to the north. During the day we could see horsemen and wagons from behind Spion Kop following suit. This was important news, but there was no hope of getting it back as the Boers were everywhere. Even if we succeeded in crossing the open valley in daylight we were some 20 miles from camp and the horses were not to meet us until 10 p.m. that night. So we camouflaged our hideout and ate our emergency rations while I made a sketch and took notes.

"Two Boers rode towards us at about nine o'clock in the morning, following our tracks. When they arrived at the foot of the hill they held a consultation. Then one dismounted and proceeded to follow our spoor on foot, while the other remained with the two horses. This required action. London suggested that he should move round and ambush the stalker and either capture or shoot him. So he disappeared and I went on with my observations. A quarter of an hour later I heard his whistle. On my answering it he appeared with a Mauser slung on his shoulder and preceded by a middle-aged nervous looking Boer dressed in moleskins. London had hidden near our tracks. As soon as the Boer passed he held him up from behind. All day our prisoner stayed and we became quite matey and swopped information and rations.

"He said he had no stomach for the war and would not be sorry to go to a prison camp. He looked on Ladysmith as already relieved and pointed out to me the long line of wagons moving north. But still Boer shells were bursting accurately on Spion Kop and there was evidence of a stubborn struggle there. After an hour or so our prisoner's companion got tired of waiting and shouting down below rode off, taking both horses with him. We could see the conical hill where the patrol was to meet us. Our prisoner volunteered to take us there by a shorter route as soon as it got dark enough to move.

"At sundown we moved off, negotiating the rough hillside before dark and then walked across the open veldt in single file. The Boer walked between us, myself leading and London, pistol in hand, behind. Our captive was as good as his word and we arrived at our rendezvous two hours before the horses. London and I agreed to keep half hour watch and ward on our prisoner. However, having been awake for 24 hours, on the very first watch I went off to sleep and was only aroused by the patrol with our horses. But the Boer had gone, although London still had his rifle slung on his shoulder. It was lucky for us that he was not a tough customer. We hurried back to camp. I sent in my report, but the abandonment of Spion Kop had already been decided upon. It had been ordered at 7.30 on the evening and Buller only knew of it next morning.

"It was galling to learn that the Boers had also abandoned the position, leaving only a few die-hards on the hill."

Trooper Stanley London was killed in France in 1917.

On 25th January the engineers threw another bridge across the Tugela. From daylight on the 26th, right through until 2.30 p.m. on the 27th, the long line of retiring transport wagons wheeled and sloshed back to the bridgehead. The entire operation took place in heavy rain. On the drenching night of 26th January, the infantry withdrew in rain and pitch black darkness.

Trooper T. Sulivan, an Australian serving in the Natal Mounted Police detachment attached to Dundonald's Composite Regiment recorded:[16] "After the battle of Spion Kop I had to act as guide to Sir Charles Warren and his Army to retire across the Tugela. This was one of the many awkward positions I had been in through the war."

Captain Bottomley wrote: "On the 26th we took part in the retirement across the Tugela. Biscuit tins were placed along the route across the veldt, which were plainly visible in darkness and mist. On 5th February we saddled up and marched down to Vaal Krantz where we were held in reserve immediately behind Buller's camp."

Within a few days of the withdrawal from Spion Kop, General Buller was ready to make another attempt to breach the Boer defences, by forcing a break in the hills a few miles downstream from Potgieter's Drift. With guns drawn up on Swaartz Kop, a hill in a deep loop formed in the river a few miles from Mount Alice, the British shelled Vaal Krantz, a flat-topped ridge 3,500 yards across the river. East from Vaal Krantz, a road passed over a strip of flat ground and wound through a narrow defile in the hills to the Ladysmith plain. As General Buller contemplated it seemed to be a weak point in the Boer line of defences.

On 5th February the infantry crossed the river by pontoon bridge, marched over mealie[16] fields and overcoming resistance gained a firm footing on Vaal Krantz. Overnight General Botha reinforced the threatened section of his defences so well, that by the next morning he was able to counter-attack effectively and prevent the British advance. General Buller used every one of his 66 guns but because of his unwillingness to be involved in further heavy infantry losses made no attempt to seize either Green Hill or Doornkop, both necessary steps to gain control of the defile through the Heights. Instead, the infantry was ordered to retire on the 7th back across the river. Once again the slow moving pace of Buller's Army allowed the Boers to overcome an initial element of surprise by drawing on reinforcements within their interior lines. The British casualties at Vaal Krantz were 34 killed and 335 wounded.

Captain Bottomley reported: "On the 7th, Boer shells were dropping on our lines. We saddled up and retired up the steep side of Swaartz Kop and camped on the other side."

On the 8th February the Light Horse returned to Springfield near Mount Alice. On the 10th the Regiment marched towards Chieveley, moving in to the old camp there on 11th February. Light Horseman, Sergeant F.W. Swift commented:[17] "Buller has no dash and does not think quickly enough."

General Buller directed the fourth and final attempt to breach the Heights along the northern bank of the Tugela, by attacking Boer positions situated along the southern bank east of the Colenso bridges. Whereas when the battle of Colenso was fought, the Boers held only Hlangwane Hill south of the river, the lines now extended further east to include two other hills.

On 12th February, Dundonald marched with a mixed force of infantry, artillery and a mounted column to Hussar Hill, a low elevation of bushy ground leading up to Hlangwane Hill. Hussar Hill was taken without much opposition. Captain Bottomley recorded: "On 12th February we took part in fighting on Hussar Hill on the right flank. It was the first of a series of battles lasting 14 days."

General Buller stayed on Hussar Hill for an hour, contemplating the position before him, then retired with the entire column to Chieveley. On the 14th, Dundonald again occupied Hussar Hill. Because of the extreme heat, Buller preferred not to march the infantry again without a rest, so no further advance took place until the morning of the 17th, when more than 40 guns on Hussar Hill shelled burghers on the high ridges of Monte Christo and Cingolo. Captain Bottomley led the Light Horse and the Natal Police to the eastern extremity of Monte Cristo. Captain Bottomley reported:[18] "Duirs, Metcalfe and Walter Francis were ordered to the front to reconnoitre. They returned at the double after having found the enemy only 200 yards ahead in dense bush. We advanced in extended order, firing point blank into the bush. The enemy broke and retired along the crest which was a mile long. About half way along the ridge the Light Horse was joined by the Natal Carbineers. On nearing the western extremity of the plateau, 300 Boers galloped down the slopes and made towards a drift on the junction of the Tugela and Klip Rivers. The Light Horse was relieved in the afternoon by a regular unit."

The operation south of the river continued on the 18th and 19th, when the Light Horse joined in a flank move along the bank of the Tugela. The last of the Republican forces retired overnight from Hlangwane Hill and vacated the south bank.

From Hlangwane Hill artillery raked the enemy, holding positions on the Colenso Kopjes and the neighbouring heights. On the 21st the infantry crossed by a 98 yard pontoon spanning the river. The positions overlooking Colenso fell after heavy fighting against entrenched defences in rugged hills over 72 hours. General Buller reported in despatches:[19] "On the 25th – Sunday – I directed my guns not to fire unless attacked and proposed to the enemy a cessation of hostilities to bury the dead and bring in the wounded, many of whom on both sides had been left lying unattended for 40 hours or more. This the Commandants, who were, I believe, Botha and Meyer, at length assented to, but they insisted on taking prisoners all the men not very badly wounded."

Buller constructed another pontoon bridge downstream over which a large body of infantry crossed on the 27th, a date acknowledged with thanksgiving as Majuba Day in the South African Republic. For the first time in the campaign, Buller was sending into action at one time the full weight of his infantry and artillery. Bitter fighting followed until the weight of numbers overwhelmed the defence in the last range of hills forming the Boer line centred on Pieter's Hill. Kept in reserve, the Light Horse watched from a kopje. The demoralized commandos fled back across the Klip River drifts around Ladysmith, where the siege commandos were already beginning a hurried retreat towards Elandslaagte.

On the morning of the 28th the Light Horse received orders to advance by the pontoon bridge. After a brief skirmish with a commando 150 strong near Nelthorpe, the Squadron pressed on in a leading position to within sight of Ladysmith, when they were joined by the Natal Carbineers. The column of volunteers rode on, passing through the valley between Mount Bulwana and the Caesar's Camp–Wagon Hill ridge. From Wagon Hill at about 5 p.m. some officers of Colonel Hamilton's staff and men on outpost duty spotted khaki-clad horsemen riding down the valley. From Caesar's Camp the Manchester garrison cheered wildly when the column passed close by Intombi Hospital.

Captain Bottomley reported: "On the morning of 28th February, General Dundonald led his Brigade through the advanced infantry who were fatigued after the fighting at Pieter's Hill and halted on the ridge overlooking Pieter's station. After a slight skirmish we reached a ridge overlooking Onderbroek Spruit and held it until the remainder of the Brigade came up.

"To maintain our leading position the Squadron extended to the right and cautiously reconnoitered the steep hill on our front. We climbed it and found ourselves on a plateau of some extent, which gave us a view of Intombi Hospital and in the distance Ladysmith. Here we halted for our comrades the Natal Carbineers and were joined by our officer commanding, Major Gough,[20] who had commanded us since Spion Kop. Verbal orders had been received to return to Onderbroek Spruit to camp for the night, as Buller did not intend to move that day. A consultation on the spot resulted in sanctioning our riding into Ladysmith.

"We started off in something like order, but under a great excitement the ride developed into a wild gallop down the rocky slopes of the hill, the fastest horse of the party leading. As this could only lead to serious consequences to our horses, it was finally agreed that the entry should be made in column of fours, each four to consist of two Imperial Light Horsemen and two Carbineers, with all officers in front. This was the manner of our entry into Ladysmith on the afternoon of 28th February at 5 p.m. Dundonald and staff entered the town four hours later."

In the Light Horse camp in Ladysmith the news of a relief column sighted coming over the hills was received with great excitement. There was further excitement when horsemen were seen coming in not far from the town. Major Woolls-Sampson greeted the column from a rickshaw near the drift over the Klip River at the end of the main street. Along the main street the column was met by General White, General Hunter and Colonel Hamilton. A Light Horse Diarist[21] wrote: "The scene in the Imperial Light Horse Camp that night will live forever in the memory of those present."

That night 'A' Squadron slept in the tents of the Regiment. On the following morning the Squadron received orders to return to Onderbroek Spruit. On the way across, Lieutenant Bridges, No. 1 troop, climbed the slopes of Mount Bulwana. He was the first of the British force to enter the Boer Laager. Wagons were sent from Ladysmith to the laagers for provisions and a convoy came through from the Tugela with comforts for the sick and wounded. General Buller rode informally into Ladysmith before setting up headquarters at Nelthorpe. On 3rd March, Buller and his Staff made a formal entry into Ladysmith at the head of the troops. From 10 o'clock in the morning the Army took more than five hours to march through the town. In his report to the War Office General Buller wrote: "It was the men who did it. Danger and hardship meant nothing to them and their courage, tenacity and their endurance, were beyond all praise."

The final phase of the operation to relieve Ladysmith had cost the British 1,893 in men killed, wounded and missing.

General White despatched a column with the pick of the weakened horses in an attempt to pursue the fleeing commandos. The column had advanced no more than a few miles beyond Modder Spruit, when Buller called off the pursuit.

The Army rested in Ladysmith until 7th May, when the drive began that ended in the Boers being pushed right out of Natal and with the linking up of Buller's Army with Lord Roberts in the eastern Transvaal. After the raising of the siege, Ladysmith was never again in the forefront of the war, reverting rather to something like its old role of a garrison town. To some like Nevinson, the correspondent of the London *Daily Chronicle*, who went through the siege, Ladysmith would never be the same again.

After a visit to the town in 1903, Nevinson wrote:[22] "I was like one of the dead who return. I remembered so much more than the people then walking up and down the familiar streets. The stones and trees and turns of the road were to me full of hidden significance which no history could record. Who knew or cared of that scooped hollow in the river bank, now overgrown with saplings, where Maude and I hid Steevens from the sun and shells a few days before he died. History passes such things in silent ignorance. They were no longer remembered and that was why I felt like the dead who return, for I alone remembered them all. I said a last farewell to Ladysmith."

On 3rd March, Major Karri-Davies and Lieutenant J. Cresswell left for Pietermaritzburg on horseback by way of Colenso. On Sunday, 4th March, a Church Parade attended by General Buller and staff, by General White and staff and all the troops who went through the siege, was held on the old Light Horse camping ground. Wagons arrived in the afternoon bringing the first letters and parcels for the Light Horse in four months. The following telegram[23] was received from the Uitlander Committee on the 1st March:

"Am directed by the Uitlander Committee to convey the heartiest congratulations on successful relief of Ladysmith, towards which event your force has so nobly contributed, while deploring the heavy loss your Regiment has sustained in the campaign. The Committee are moved by a sense of admiration for the spirit of duty and patriotism displayed by the Imperial Light Horse."

Leaving 'A' Squadron camped at Star Hill with the Composite Regiment, the Light Horse rode out from Ladysmith on the afternoon of the 7th March, moving by easy stages towards Colenso. Because of the weakened horses and men a camp was made along the Colenso road. The Regiment entered Colenso on the afternoon of the 8th and camped close to the Tugela. Half of the men were granted 10 days leave. The Squadrons arrived in Pietermaritzburg on 22nd March, to be re-equipped and the strength increased to 600. On 2nd April the Regiment entrained for Ladysmith. Seven trains were needed to take men, horses and equipment to Ladysmith by 3rd April. 'A' Squadron ended its association with the Composite Regiment, marking the occasion with a smoking concert on the eve of returning to the Light Horse.

The Light Horse contributed to a presentation, by the combined mounted regiments in Ladysmith, of gold medals in the form of brooches, to 19 nursing sisters at the Intombi Hospital. The names of the regiments were inscribed on the back of the medals.

The Imperial Light Horse left Ladysmith on the 7th April for Elandslaagte. Because of the non-arrival of the wagons the men slept in the open without blankets. On 11th April the Light Horse was detached from General Buller's force at Elandslaagte, with only the vaguest rumours of a destination. The Regiment passed through Ladysmith before proceeding to Durban and by ship to Cape Town.

[1] A one-pounder Automatic Vickers gun, with 25 shells on a belt
[2] From a diary in the Karri-Davies Collection
[3] Lord Dundonald
[4] From the diary in the Karri-Davies Collection
[5] Lord Methuen
[6] The fortified Colenso Kopjes
[7] Before the Royal Commission in London 1902–03
[8] In his diary in the Karri-Davies Collection
[9] in his diary in the Karri-Davies Collection
[10] In the Karri-Davies Collection
[11] *Alarms and Excursions* Lieutenant-General Sir T. Bridges
[12] Kloof – a ravine or a cleft
[13] *Through Shot and flame* J.D. Kestell
[14] *Alarms and Excursions* Lieutenant-General Sir T. Bridges
[15] In his diary in the Karri-Davies Collection
[16] maize fields
[17] From notes in the Karri-Davies Papers
[18] In his diary in the Karri-Davies Collection
[19] 14th March, 1900 at Ladysmith
[20] In World War I, as General Sir Hubert Gough, he commanded 5th Army in France
[21] In the Imperial Light Horse Typed Diary of Engagements in the Karri-Davies Collection
[22] *Ladysmith, the Diary of a Siege 1900* H.W. Nevinson
[23] In the Karri-Davies Collection of Papers

CHAPTER 7
A SUMMARY OF THE MARCHES UNDERTAKEN BY THE BRITISH ARMY TO THE FALL OF PRETORIA
5TH JUNE 1900

When Field-Marshal Lord Roberts landed in South Africa as Commander-in-Chief on 10th January 1900, British forces on the three fronts had met with serious setbacks. On not one front was the Army strong enough to force the enemy position. Apart from General Buller on the Tugela, General Gatacre suffered a reverse at the end of a night march to Stormberg Junction in the northern Cape Midlands. In the region around Colesberg and the Orange River, General French was content to hold the enemy over an extended front. In the advance to Kimberley, after pushing the Republican forces from defensive positions at Belmont, Graspan and Modder River, General Methuen suffered a heavy defeat a few miles east of the railway at Magersfontein ridge, only 12 miles from Kimberley.

The British Army suffered from a number of disabilities. In a country where the European population was small and towns and villages few and widely spaced, there was difficulty in procuring supplies to feed the troops and transport animals. Everything had to be carried over the narrow gauged single track railways. There was also the need for more mounted troops. The artillery had an advantage in numbers but was generally outranged: "There could be no doubt about it," Roberts said,[1] "when we could not reach the Boer guns at the range when they were effective against us." Roberts also found that: "Even so late as the 10th January 1900, when I landed in South Africa, maps of the theatre of war on a scale suitable for military operations were practically non-existent." Roberts also said: "Detailed information of the enemy's territory was scanty in the extreme and details of our own frontiers had not been surveyed except the northern corner of Natal."

By this time also, there had been changes in the style of some of the equipment worn in the field. Swords and everything bright had been replaced by leather on dull khaki.

Lord Roberts moved up by the western railway, beyond Orange River Station, 600 miles from Cape Town and 75 miles from Kimberley. Orange River Station was the only remaining bridgehead spanning the Orange River. After the battle of Magersfontein, General Methuen retained his position on the railway near Modder River Station. The Republican Army under General Piet Cronje continued to bar the way to Kimberley from entrenched positions along the Magersfontein ridge. The intention of Lord Roberts was:[2] "To enter the Orange Free State from the neighbourhood of Methuen's camp and by turning the enemy's flanks effect the relief of Kimberley."

Beginning from a point just south of Methuen's camp the army, under Roberts, marched east and then north-west in a great flanking movement around Cronje's position. In the hottest month of the year, by a swift flanking movement across roadless veldt – waterless between widely spaced rivers – Kimberley was relieved without much fighting by the cavalry column under Lieutenant-General French. Meanwhile, infantry with mounted escorts was left holding the drifts on the Modder and Riet Rivers, between Cronje at Magersfontein and his line of communication with Bloemfontein. Completely deceived, Cronje made a belated attempt to retire towards Bloemfontein along several miles of the Modder just beyond Paardeberg Drift. Near Paardeberg the Boers formed a laager within the deep river banks sunk below the level of the plain and in dongas near – the river. A line of thick scrubby bushes along the plain outlined the course of the winding river. For 10 days the laager withstood heavy bombardment and infantry attacks.

Firing out over river flats, Boer riflemen took heavy toll of infantry charging across in frontal assaults. In the absence of Roberts who was indisposed, General Kitchener launched a number of unsuccessful infantry attacks across open ground on 18th February with the intention of defeating the laager quickly before the expected arrival of Boer reinforcements to the rescue. On that one day the British casualties were 1,270. In deciding to lay siege to the laager rather than take it by assault, Roberts drew up all the available artillery and shelled the two miles of the river continuously. The riverside siege ended on 27th February when General Cronje surrendered unconditionally with 4,000 burghers.

Four months had passed since the sending of the Boer ultimatum and the British had at last succeeded in carrying the war into the territories of the Republics.

Lord Roberts remained at Paardeberg for a week, because of the poor condition of the horses, boggy roads and the need for supplies. Meanwhile, the Army was built up to 30,000. From Paardeberg, in actions along the Modder at Poplar Grove and Driefontein, the Republican forces were swept across the Free State plains. By the time Roberts entered Bloemfontein on 13th March, the troops were exhausted from marching in heat and rain, from fighting and, of necessity, reduced to short rations.

The defeat of the Republican forces on the plains of the Free State weakened the position of the commandos south of the Orange River, allowing the British to enter Colesberg and advance along the railway between the Orange River and Bloemfontein. Roberts rested the Army at Bloemfontein, waiting on the arrival by rail of supplies, remounts and reinforcements through Colesberg from the southern ports. Meanwhile the troops suffered from an outbreak of enteric fever caused by the drinking of polluted water in the march across the Free State, especially from the river at Paardeberg.

The advance from Bloemfontein through the Free State to the Vaal River began on 3rd May 1900 in three parallel columns on a wide front. The outnumbered Republican forces fought delaying actions at river crossings, resisting only long enough to escape from flanking mounted columns whose down or upstream movements accompanied by clouds of dust could be seen for miles in the open country. Foot-weary infantry, marching resolutely forward, scarcely sighted the enemy before the Vaal River. The main Army crossed the Vaal without opposition on 27th May.

Within a few days the British formed a 20 mile front along the Klip River only 11 miles from Johannesburg and about 250 miles from Bloemfontein. General Louis Botha, Commander-in-Chief of the Republican forces, placed guns and several thousand burghers along the heights on the southern outskirts of Johannesburg. After a day of patrolling forward beyond the drifts, under fire from guns on the heights, the British withdrew to the river. On the next morning French crossed the river on the extreme left and pressed on to Doornkop. Close to the right of French, the Gordon Highlanders, under Ian Hamilton, completed an assault on the heights with a bayonet charge, opening up the Boer right. From the Klip River the British enveloped Johannesburg from the east and the west, but not until Botha had succeeded in retiring north with his forces. Johannesburg fell on 31st May. Roberts wasted little time in marching to Pretoria.

President Kruger left Pretoria by the Lourenco Marques railway for the safety of the eastern Transvaal and subsequently to exile in Europe. Botha made only a token resistance before withdrawing from Pretoria. On 5th June 1900, the Union Jack was hoisted over the capital of the South African Republic.

---

[1] Before the Royal Commission in London 1902–03
[2] Stated to the Royal Commission in London 1902–03

CHAPTER 8
The Relief of Mafeking, 17th May 1900
The Light Horse enters Johannesburg 23rd June and Camps outside Pretoria, 27th June.

General Hunter arrived in Kimberley on 21st April 1900. Hunter had instructions from Lord Roberts to build up a flying column to march to the relief of Colonel R.S. Baden-Powell's[1] garrison at Mafeking. The Imperial Light Horse arrived in Kimberley by train on 24th April and camped at Dronfield. The Regiment was about to join Colonel B. Mahon's flying column to relieve Mafeking. On the 2nd May, at the end of a long hot and dusty day's march with the Kimberley Mounted Corps, the Light Horse made contact with Colonel Mahon's column at Barkly West.

Colonel Mahon, an officer in the Irish Hussars, was provided with a column made up of 900 mounted troops of the Light Horse and the Kimberley Mounted Corps, 100 picked infantry from General Barton's Fusilier Brigade, comprised four troops, one each representing either England, Scotland, Wales or Ireland. The column had the support of four guns from 'M' Battery, Royal field Artillery, two pom poms and carried provisions for 16 days. Skirting to the west from the railway, the column arrived at Taungs, 75 miles from Kimberley in three days, having left on 7th May: "The men obtained good supplies of fowls, turkeys and vegetables, nearly every saddle had something hanging from it of an edible nature."[2]

The troops entered Vryburg on 9th May after the Boers had occupied the village for six months. Major Karri-Davies and a troop from 'B' Squadron were the first to enter. Meeting with no resistance the column found the village decorated in red, white and blue. At the same time, those storekeepers with well-stocked shops took the opportunity to mark up their wares. An unexpected stock of good forage for the horses was discovered.

On the march, over the next two days, no water at all was found in the bushveldt. The column covered 15 miles on the first day and 20 miles on the second day. Most of the farms passed displayed white flags in the form of table cloths and sheets. Although the white flag was hoisted as a sign of neutrality, a search of a farm house often resulted in a haul of ammunition. The column halted for four hours on the 13th near Brodie's Farm where Karri-Davies scrounged milk and butter for the Regiment. Leaving the farm early on the same afternoon, the column advanced five miles and watered at Wright's Farm.

Colonel Mahon received information that a commando under Commandant P. Liebenberg, with a gun and a pom pom, was astride the road in a nek at Koedoesrand. Unwilling to risk the possibility of being delayed, Colonel Mahon left the road and veering west skirted around Koedoesrand and continued to advance north. Mahon hoped that Liebenberg had been avoided altogether.

Commandant Liebenberg's commando, however, appeared on the right of the column, by partly surprising and clashing with scouts about 15 miles west of the railway. 'D' Squadron under Lieutenant Bridges, dismounting in thick bush, returned fire at only 200 yards. Without knowing the strength of the Boers, 'D' Squadron in giving ground retired and joined 'C' and 'B' Squadrons. Opinion was divided among the officers whether to retire or advance without calling for assistance. Meanwhile, Mauser fire was coming from three directions.

"'A' Squadron on the left flank came in for heavy firing while still mounted from the enemy concealed in bush. All the Squadrons retired to the rear, followed by the enemy until they were out of range. As the enemy advanced through the bush the men went forward on foot to meet them. Artillery and pom poms arrived, but were delayed in going into action because of the ammunition not coming up. The guns were firing until 5 p.m., the pom poms causing great destruction to the enemy. In reality it was a short fight, most of the engagement being borne by the Light Horse, after we were taken by surprise."[3]

Corporal A. Duirs, 'A' Squadron, received a flesh wound in the upper part of the leg. Duirs rested himself against a tree and kept firing. With three successive shots he accounted for three Boers. The Light Horse casualties for the day were five killed, 15 wounded and two missing. Corporal Walter Francis, one of the best shots in the Regiment, was killed. Troopers H. Taylor, C. Davis, G. Bonsey and H. Boone were also killed. Sergeant A. Haynes died of wounds the next day. Major Mullins was severely wounded. Trooper Elliot and Corporal King were among those wounded. The missing men were two advanced scouts, Lance-Corporal Clifford Hill and Trooper Clement Gardner, both of 'C' Squadron. A long search at the end of the day failed to find them.

After the surrender of Pretoria, Hill was released from the prisoner of war camp at Waterval, some miles north of the capital. Several months later, he returned to the scene of the fight. He located Gardner's skeleton, just where he had fallen near his dead horse, where he buried the remains, not far from Wright's Farm near Kraaipan.

The fight took place about six miles west of Brodie's Farm. That night the men slept behind saddled horses in readiness for a second attack. On the following day, the 14th, the column remained at arms all day. Few miles were covered. The wounded were left at Wright's Farm in the care of Lieutenant Ligertwood. On the 15th, because of the sandy nature of the ground, the men walked most of the way leading the horses. Water could only be found by digging holes in the sand. The Boers dogged the rear all the way. In the afternoon, the column linked up with a column led by Lieutenant-Colonel H. Plumer[4] at Jan Massibi on the Molopo River, 18 miles west of Mafeking. Colonel Plumer operated from a base in Rhodesia. Colonel Mahon, as the senior officer assumed command of the combined column.

Colonel Plumer's column had also reached Jan Massibi at the end of a night march. His column of 800 men, together with 100 Queensland Mounted Infantry acted as escort to a battery of Royal Canadian Artillery. Both columns of men and animals rested on the 15th after the tiring marches. Some prisoners, taken by Mahon on the march from Kimberley, were sent on to Bulawayo. Early on the morning of the 16th the columns moved off, divided into two Brigades.

Colonel Mahon reported in despatches:[5] "We advanced 6.30 a.m. towards Mafeking along the north or right bank of the Molopo River in two parallel columns at half a mile interval, the convoy on the centre slightly in rear. I formed the force into two brigades, the 1st Brigade under Lieutenant-Colonel Plumer and the 2nd Brigade under Lieutenant-Colonel Edwards, "with Plumer's Brigade on the right and Edwards on the left. At 12.30 p.m., firing was heard on the left front and I advanced Edwards's Brigade. As we advanced I found the Boers had taken up positions all around us and had five guns and two pom poms. I continued my advance to Mafeking, the Boers retiring from our front and keeping up with us on our flanks.

"At 4.40 p.m., I had a message from Colonel Plumer to say his advance was checked on the right by a gun and pom pom fire from the White House called Israel's Farm. I ordered the Horse Artillery to shell the house. They soon silenced the gun but not the pom pom. I ordered the infantry to take the house which they did and captured a lot of ammunition.

"By 4.45 p.m., all firing ceased and the Boers retired from all parts. I advanced two miles nearer Mafeking and left the infantry holding the house. The smallness of our casualties was due to our very wide front and loose formation. After ascertaining by patrol that the road was open, I ordered an advance to Mafeking. We started at 12:30 a.m. and marched seven miles to Mafeking, which place we entered at 3.30 a.m. on the 17th May.

"I cannot speak too highly of the behaviour of all ranks, more especially the Royal Horse Artillery and the Imperial Light Horse, both during the march which was long and tiring and during the engagement. The march was rendered more fatiguing by having an enemy on our flanks and always looking for an opportunity to delay and harass us and thus rendering scouting more necessary and extra work on men and horses."

A picked patrol from 'A' Squadron led by Major Karri-Davies left the main column at 5.45 p.m. on the 16th and finding the road open rode straight into Mafeking. In an exciting ride on a dark night along a strange road, some of the horses actually stumbled into the trenches on the outskirts of the town. The patrol was guided from the outposts to the centre of the town, where the men were literally pulled off their horses by the townspeople. Major Karri-Davies met Colonel Baden-Powell at Headquarters.

Corporal Duirs and Trooper Ernest Warby volunteered to ride back to the main column with despatches. Trooper Warby wrote to his family in Australia: "Then our Major Karri-Davies called for volunteers to ride with him to the town, a distance of about five miles. You can bet I was in that lot. We galloped all the way, striking across country. We could hear the Boers racing about in all directions and calling to each other, but we were not noticed. The first challenge we got was from a good old English voice: 'Halt, who goes there?' We yelled out: 'The Imperial Light Horse.'

"It was a Mafeking picket stationed outside the town. It was a grand meeting. We were nearly pulled off our horses. The cheering was heard from the town and soon we were met by men galloping out to learn what was up. When we got to Headquarters the crowd swarmed around us, everyone wanting to shake hands with us at once. Then they struck up Rule Britannia and the National Anthem. After the excitement had died down, two of us answered the call for volunteers to ride back to the camp and let them know we had got through safely. We got two fresh horses and after having a cup of coffee and a ship's biscuit, being the first mouthful we had touched that day, we started back.

"We had a narrow squeak or two on the way, but we got through and after we had reported, the whole column started forward. We landed in the town about 3.30 a.m. on the 17th May. At daybreak we finished the job by shelling the enemy out of their main camp, capturing a number of their wagons and one nine-pounder gun. Our horses were knocked up, so we could not follow up our victory."

Surgeon-Major Davies returned to Wright's Farm for the wounded, who suffered greatly from the rough shaking up they received in the ambulance wagons on the way to the Victoria Hospital.

The Queen's Birthday on 24th May was celebrated in Mafeking with a combined parade in the morning of garrison and relief forces. An inspection by Baden-Powell was followed by Royal Salutes and three cheers for the Queen. The Light Horse took a full share of the prizes in the sports meeting held on the Recreation Ground in the afternoon. At night a united smoking concert was held in the Market Square. The railway to Bulawayo was repaired and the first train from that town steamed in with provisions, mainly grain for the horses.

On 27th May a Light Horse working party under Karri-Davies repaired telegraph lines outside Mafeking. A detachment with two pom poms under Major Karri-Davies and Captain Gilfillan left Louw's Farm on the 28th and took formal possession of Ottoshoop, a village just inside the Transvaal border. Lieutenant E Kirk was wounded in the shoulder on patrol along the Lichtenburg road. Colonel Edwards and Major Karri-Davies led a detachment of Light Horse to Jacobsdal on the 31st May, to read a Proclamation. They visited Zeerust also for the same purpose. By this time, telegraphic communication between Mafeking and Zeerust had been restored.

The Light Horse set up Regimental Headquarters at Ottoshoop, using the village as an advance supply depot, until the 6th June. The Regiment was engaged in patrolling and bringing in forage, cattle, sheep and horses, all of which were sent on to Mafeking. Considerable numbers of burghers came in to surrender arms and take the oath of neutrality in return for Protection Certificates.

Captain Normand took 'C' Squadron along the road to Lichtenburg on 1st June, arriving on the 2nd, the same day as a squadron of British Yeomanry from General Hunter's Division rode in from Vryburg in the south-west. The Light Horse Squadrons continued to leave Ottoshoop for Lichtenburg, where General Hunter's cavalry brigade was also assembling. All arms in the town were given up and the Union Jack hoisted. On 3rd June, 'C' Squadron rode out to a group of farms at Manana, about five miles from the village: "All the farmers," wrote Captain Normand[6] "were very pleased to see us and were much relieved to hear that the war is almost over." At Manana, Dr Davies obtained milk for the small military hospital established in the school-house in Lichtenburg.

On 3rd June, by taking over the command from Colonel Edwards, Major Woolls-Sampson became Colonel of the Imperial Light Horse. Although still lame, Colonel Woolls-Sampson had recovered sufficiently from the wound received at Elandslaagte. The Regiment camped at Lichtenburg for a week and then marched to Ventersdorp, joining General Hunter's 10th Division on 10th June. The Division set out to march to Potchefstroom on the following day.

General Hunter's orders were to carry out the pacification of the Ventersdorp, Potchefstroom, Klerksdorp area of the western Transvaal. The mounted column entered Potchefstroom on the 11th and waited for the arrival of the infantry. Away from the town the Light Horse was engaged in patrolling. Under Major Karri-Davies the men also worked at repairing the railways and over-hauling rolling stock, in an effort to get the communications with Klerksdorp and Krugersdorp cleared.

The Union Jack hoisted at Potchefstroom was the same flag that had flown over Pretoria in 1881 and was the object of a mock burial. Ever since that time the flag had been carefully preserved by the 2nd Royal Scots Fusiliers. Along the road to Klerksdorp, 'C' Squadron marched with the infantry, scouting and acting as advance guard. Captain Normand wrote in his Diary: "Potchefstroom to Klerksdorp about 28 miles, the country being very difficult and rocky and hilly. Bluffed the town into surrender. Over 1,000 rifles were handed in on the 14th June." Lieutenant Kirk took a 'B' Squadron patrol along the railway towards Krugersdorp and found the bridge near Bank had been blown up. The patrol returned to Potchefstroom.

Cavalry and a battalion of infantry occupied Frederickstad on the railway to Krugersdorp. Leaving the infantry to garrison Frederickstad, the Light Horse marched with the cavalry to Randfontein before entering Krugersdorp at 5 p.m. on 18th June. The Landrost and officials of the town were arrested. The Court House, the Railway station and the Telegraph were seized. The Light Horse was active in patrolling and protecting the tracks under repair by railway working gangs. Outposts were fired on by the enemy. The Union Jack was officially flown at Krugersdorp on 20th June. Major Karri-Davies and Surgeon-Major Davies left for Johannesburg on a rail trolley, returning two days later. Caches of arms were found in Krugersdorp and from the surrounding district many burghers came in to surrender arms. The Light Horse was engaged in destroying the arms.

General Hunter received orders to march to Springs and Heidelberg, leaving small garrisons in the occupied towns. Hunter joined Hamilton's column at Heidelberg on 25th June.

On 13th June 1900, the strength of the Imperial Light Horse was 558, made up of 466 men and 32 officers fit and 60 sick or recovering from wounds.

The Light Horse marched from Krugersdorp on 23rd June, halting at florida and Fordsburg to water the horses. The Regiment marched along Commissioner Street in Johannesburg to the Market Square: "Cheering was the order of the march and all were in high spirits."[7] There was much disappointment when, after marching through the streets to the racecourse, the Regiment camped for the night on Meyer's Farm, at the southern outskirts of the town. The men formed a deputation of three to meet Colonel Woolls-Sampson and put the case for the men with homes and interests in Johannesburg and who had been away for so long. The Colonel gave full reasons for the Regiment not staying in the town, without in any way allaying the disappointment of the men.

On 24th June the Regiment marched for Heidelberg, guarding a convoy going to General Ian Hamilton. On the 25th, the Light Horse was detached from Hunter's Division, camping overnight at Boksburg, where Colonel Edwards, appointed Commissioner at Krugersdorp, said farewell to the Regiment.

Still attached to Colonel Mahon's Brigade, the Light Horse arrived at Erasmus Farm outside Pretoria on 27th June. 'C' Squadron reached the Light Horse camp from Klerksdorp on the afternoon of 2nd July, just two months after the Regiment left Dronfield. Accompanied by General Kitchener, Lord Roberts shook hands with Colonel Woolls-Sampson and congratulated him on the excellent record of the Regiment in the field. Roberts reported in despatches on 5th July 1900: "I have recently inspected Mahon's small force which did such excellent work in the relief of the Mafeking garrison. The Imperial Light Horse which I purposely brought from Natal to take part in the expedition are a most soldierly and workmanlike body of men."

---

[1] Subsequently Major-General
[2] In the typewritten diary of Engagements in the Karri-Davies Collection
[3] In the typewritten diary of Engagements in the Karri-Davies Collection
[4] Subsequently Brigadier-General. In May 1915, assumed command of the 2nd Army in France. In 1919 he was made a Field-Marshal
[5] 23rd May 1910, to General Hunter commanding 10th Division
[6] In the typewritten diary of Engagements in the Karri-Davies Collection
[7] in the typewritten diary of Engagements in the Karri-Davies Collection

CHAPTER 9
THE CAMPAIGN IN JUNE–JULY 1900 – WITKLIP 7TH JULY – THE DRIVE THROUGH EASTERN TRANSVAAL THE LIGHT HORSE MARCHES WITH GENERAL FRENCH TO BARBERTON

Within two days after the entry into Pretoria of Roberts with the main Army, General Hunter in conjunction with Colonel Baden-Powell and Colonel Plumer, had commenced to penetrate deeply into the western Transvaal. On 11th June, Colonel Mahon's mounted column entered Potchefstroom and Colonel Plumer reached Ventersdorp, only 86 miles from Johannesburg. On 12th June, in a battle extending over two days and centred on a range of hills about 16 miles north-east of Pretoria, General Botha was defeated at Diamond Hill by the Army led by Lord Roberts. As the result of the break-through on Diamond Hill, Botha was forced to abandon positions extending over 30 miles along a curved range. The force of 6,000 burghers and guns dispersed along' the Delagoa Bay railway in the direction of Middleburg.

Lord Roberts returned to Pretoria from Diamond Hill, faced with the problem of providing urgently needed remounts for the mounted corps and with the Army suffering all the disadvantages arising from the need to secure the long line of communication so loosely held between Bloemfontein and Pretoria. To keep open the line of communications over which his supplies must come, Roberts was forced to detail large bodies of troops along the length of the railway. Raiding commandos ably led by General Christian De Wet, seized every opportunity to destroy the track and the bridges and to intercept and wreck the supply trains.

Meanwhile, General Buller, fighting up through northern Natal from Ladysmith, entered the Transvaal from Laing's Nek. By 12th July, Buller reached Volksrust, just inside the Transvaal border. Towards the end of July, General Hunter attacked and trapped strong forces under General De Wet in the Brandwater Basin on the slopes of the Drakensburg Range in the Free State. After De Wet managed to escape with 2,500 men, five guns and hundreds of wagons, General M. Prinsloo and General J. De Villiers surrendered unconditionally on 30th July with 4,000 burghers.

After the battle of Diamond Hill, until the end of June, Roberts withdrew his lines closer to Pretoria, but soon found that it was necessary to clear the outlying country where the enemy was becoming increasingly active. To this end and as a preliminary move for the main projected advance east to the Portuguese border, Roberts despatched Major-General E. Hutton with a force of 5,500 men to clear the hilly country between Tiger Poort and Springs, south-east of Pretoria. Botha had about 3,500 men in the region.

At the beginning of July, Roberts reported in despatches: "The enemy assumed an aggressive attitude towards the east of Pretoria and the following dispositions were made to prevent them from getting round our right flank and interrupting railway communications with the south. Mahon's troops, the Imperial Light Horse, one battery of Horse Artillery and two battalions from Hart's Brigade, were ordered to Rietfontein, six miles east of Irene. The column was strengthened by Hutton, who assumed the command."

On 6th July, General Hutton had reached a position south-east of Tiger Poort, towards Bapsfontein. Hutton sent Colonel Mahon forward with artillery, mounted infantry and the Imperial Light Horse to occupy high ground around Bapsfontein. Captain Normand recorded in his Diary on the 6th July: "Turned east from the road and drove in a strong Boer outpost. Caught a glimpse of Pilcher's column on our extreme left. Turned south and met General Hutton with 2,500 men and.

camped in poor positions on Prinsloo's Farm. The night was so cold that many of the men were unable to sleep and walked round all night."

On the next day, Saturday 7th July, Hutton ordered Mahon to drive east with the mounted troops in the direction of Witklip Farm beyond Bronkhorstspruit. Captain J. Donaldson, a mile in advance with 'C' Squadron, twice reported seeing Boers on a hill 1,000 yards away from the main column on the left flank. At 10 a.m., 'C' Squadron in advance was replaced by 'A' Squadron. Captain W. Currie, 'B' Squadron, was ordered by Colonel Mahon to take the hill on which the burghers were seen by Captain Donaldson. 'B' Squadron had, until then, been marching in line with 'M' Battery in the column of troops. When Captain Gilfillan, 'A' Squadron, saw 'B' Squadron advancing in the Direction of the hill from which scouts had already reported being fired on by the enemy in force, he sent a trooper to inform Mahon and Colonel Woolls-Sampson of the extent of the danger, but the message arrived too late for the advance to be stopped.

Soon after noon near the top of the hill, 'B' Squadron advance scouts, Corporal Hopley, Troopers Ben Holt, Buncombe and Scandrett came almost face to face with six Boers. Both groups opened fire at something like 60 yards. One Boer was killed and the Light Horse lost a horse killed. Before long 'B' Squadron clashed with the enemy in full force. The arrival of Boer reinforcements added to the heavy close range rifle fire from 600 yards. Trooper Hardy crawled back to warn the artillery officer of the exact position of the Light Horse, after shells had fallen dangerously near the men.

The artillery eventually silenced the Boer guns and the Mauser fire also decreased under pressure from the guns. Four unsuccessful attempts were made to take the order to retire to the troops on the hillside. Trooper Roger Sharpley and three others each had a horse shot from under them in making the attempt. At 3.30 p.m. the Light Horse retired, reaching the camp on Prinsloo's Farm at 8 p.m. An atmosphere of gloom pervaded the Light Horse camp, for many of those killed had been right through the Ladysmith actions.

Lieutenant B. Webb wrote:[1] "The order came for 'B' Squadron to dismount and extend to the left. The Squadron dismounted, extending at the double. The ground sloped upwards and from where the men were dismounted you could not see beyond a hundred yards or so. Lieutenant Kirk and his troop were the first up. No. 2 troop was almost wiped out, only two or three came back. Trooper Adrian Moodie was killed while retiring. Farrier-Sergeant Charles Woolley was killed while holding horses, the others were killed in the firing line. Captain W. Currie was killed near the spot where Lieutenant Edwin Kirk fell. Corporal Edwin Atherstone, Troopers Grahame King, George Drennan and Henry Lane were also killed. Sergeant John Marshall died next morning in a farm house." Sergeant Douglas Damant and Sergeant Ballards, Troopers Harwin, Hills. Jones and Raith, all from 'B' Squadron, received wounds. Sergeant-Major Cunningham, 'F' Squadron was also wounded. Trooper Arthur Bouchier died from wounds at the hospital in Johannesburg after having an arm amputated.

Trooper Kirk returned to the field overnight to look for the body of his brother: "In the ascent up the slope Lieutenant Kirk lost his revolver and from then on was unarmed. He took shelter behind a small ant-hill in company with Trooper Hill-Jones. The Lieutenant directed Hill-Jones where to fire. On seeing a Boer 300 yards away, Kirk told Jones to fire at him. He did so and missed. Kirk then spoke sharply to Jones for not taking more careful aim, but before he could fire, the Boer shot

Jones in the arm. Jones said: 'I wanted to shoot him, but he didn't let me.' Kirk then took up Jones's gun. While he was firing a bullet pierced the ant-hill and killed him on the spot."[2] Early the next morning volunteers accompanied Major Karri-Davies to bury the dead. Orderlies and Medical Officers, Generals Botha, Smuts and Commandant Dircksen with armed burghers stood around the open graves. Botha spoke to Karri-Davies, expressing his surprise that only 60 men had attacked the hill on the previous day. The Boer losses were 12 killed and 30 wounded.

Surgeon-Major Davies and Lieutenant-Surgeon Ligertwood and staff were on the field immediately after the retirement on the 7th to attend to the wounded. They were away from the Light Horse camp for several days: "As darkness set in on the 7th the wounded were sent to a store owned by a German near the action and made into a temporary hospital. Here the Boers had formed their laager. A request made next morning for the Boers to allow the Imperial Light Horse ambulance to come up was refused. Hutton's Brigade could be seen in the distance. The artillery commenced to shell the laager and the vicinity of the German store. Although the Red Cross flag flew from the roof of the store, it was not visible from where the British artillery was situated in a hollow. There was great anxiety for the safety of the wounded.

"Nevertheless, on the morning of the 8th the Light Horse ambulance and the New South Wales ambulance left Prinsloo's Farm and headed in the direction of the German store. Within two miles of the store the ambulance were forced to turn back by Boer fire and a number of other attempts failed for the same reason. A party with a Boer flag set out for the Boer lines. It was also forced back by enemy fire. finally, the ambulances went out under the cover of darkness and arrived at the Boer laager without opposition. In reply to a question as to why the ambulances and the parties were stopped, Commandant Dircksen said: 'Your artillery fire on farm houses containing only women and children.'

"On the morning of the 9th, Commandant Dircksen refused to allow the wounded to be moved to the Light Horse camp for proper attention. Sergeant J. Marshall of 'B' Squadron died from wounds. He was buried in the garden at the German store. Commandant Dircksen and the Boers who had drawn near stood with uncovered heads. A piece of boxwood recorded Marshall's name and regimental number. General Botha allowed the ambulance to leave with the wounded by proceeding to Springs, as going via the Light Horse camp would have entailed passing through the Boer lines. From Springs the wounded were sent by train to Johannesburg, where the Hotel Victoria had been turned over for a hospital."[3]

After the action at Wjtklip the Light Horse, the advance guard to Colonel Mahon's Brigade, left Prinsloo's Farm on 10th July, in pursuit of the Boers riding swiftly north. The Regiment camped in Pretoria from 12th to 15th. General French addressed the corps and paid a high compliment to their record. On 16th July, Light Horse scouts contacted Boers in skirmishes 10 miles north of Pretoria. Mahon's column pursued the burghers along the Delagoa Bay railway, beyond Bronkhorstspruit and Balmoral. On Saturday 21st July, 'B' Squadron was fired on towards sundown, without suffering losses. Fortunately, the Boers were too hasty in firing and so made their dispositions known. The Army under Roberts, advancing along the railway, occupied Middleburg, 86 miles from Pretoria on 27th July. In the intense cold an officer and three men of the Argyle and Sutherland Highlanders died from exposure after the baggage trains, failed to turn up. The Highlanders were forced to go on picket duty without great coats or extra warm clothing. Some of the men were revived by the Light Horsemen, who built fires, gave them warm clothing for their bare legs and provided coffee and rum.

Leaving General French in advanced positions at Middleburg, Lord Roberts turned his attention to the country north and west of Pretoria, where the Boers were increasing in numbers and boldness. Returning through Bronkhorstspruit and Prinsloo's Farm, Colonel Mahon's column passed slowly through Pienaar's Poort and entered Pretoria on 30th July. Lord Roberts inspected the column as it marched through the Market Square to the camp at Daspoort.

Marching from Pretoria with a column under Lieutenant-General Ian Hamilton, Mahon's Brigade was present at the re-taking of Zilikat's Nek on 2nd August, when the Berkshire Infantry suffered heavy losses. General Hamilton marched west of Pretoria to Rustenburg in the Magaliesberg Range, where Major-General Baden-Powell was surrounded. The Light Horse entered Rustenburg in advance of Hamilton's Brigade which stayed outside the town. The Light Horse marched further west with Baden-Powell to relieve Lieutenant-Colonel C. Hore, an Imperial Officer, who with 500 Australians and Rhodesians under his command was besieged at Elands River Post camp. Before reaching the besieged camp, Baden-Powell turned back, believing that Colonel Hore and the colonial garrison had been relieved by Major-General F. Carrington marching east from Zeerust and Marico. Baden-Powell was mistaken. Nevertheless, the camp at Elands River, with garrison and a huge quantity of stores, gallantly held out until 16th August when it was rather fortuitously relieved by General Kitchener's column at the end of a long unsuccessful chase from the Vaal River on the heels of the elusive General De Wet.

Lieutenant Webb, 'B' Squadron wrote:[4] "Sunday, 5th August. This is the second time we have relieved Baden-Powell. Monday, 6th August. Marched 6 a.m. No Transport. Halted and fed 14 miles out. Returned to Rustenburg 3 p.m. Baden-Powell was in command and no commanding officer could have had a better force under him of the same strength. We marched, and every man was well mounted – horses as hard as nails. We heard big guns firing from some distance off and we were all looking forward to a continuation of the march and a fight. But no, like the Duke of York, he marched up a hill and then he marched them down again."

After camping in Commando Nek on 9th August, Mahon's Brigade marched through the Nek to Hekpoort, crossing country made difficult at times with ploughed fields and wire farm fences. Turning west, south of Commando Nek on 13th August, the Light Horse formed part of General Hamilton's flying column with orders to head off General De Wet, who having crossed the Vaal at Schoeman's Drift, made for the Magaliesberg with a number of British columns in close chase. Despite the loss of guns and wagons, De Wet was able to make his escape to the north, eluding his pursuers by way of Olifant's Nek on 14th August.

At 6.30 a.m. on 17th August, the Light Horse forming the advance guard of Colonel Mahon's column under General Hamilton, took part in the attack on Olifant's Nek. General De Wet had left a rear-guard of 200 burghers to defend the Nek. Artillery fire forced the Boers from good cover. By the time the Light Horse came up to gallop through the Nek the burghers had got clean away, leaving behind wagons and ammunition. Late on the same afternoon the Light Horse was back in Rustenburg.

Continuing to press on after De Wet, the Regiment engaged the Boer rear-guard in bushy country. On 21st August, nine burghers were captured in a farm house, which at the time was being used as an outpost. By 24th August the Light Horse was camped at Warmbaths 62,miles north of Pretoria. De Wet was forced to split up what was left of his commando, some heading east towards the Delagoa Bay railway. De Wet turned back with a small detachment and crossed the Magaliesberg by a little known bridle track between Commando Nek and Olifant's Nek, before crossing the Vaal to the Free State. The Light Horse returned to Pretoria on 31st August, passing, along the road, the former prisoner of war camp at Waterval, where many British prisoners were held until the fall of Pretoria.

The Army for the offensive against Botha along the Delagoa Bay railway totalled 20,000 men. Operations commenced on 21st August when Roberts was still in Pretoria. Botha's main line extended for 50 miles across the railway, 20 miles east from Belfast. Roberts assumed command on 26th August. The British advance rested mainly on a front centred on the railway and extended 12 miles to the south. General Buller, having joined the main Army at the end of the march from Natal, broke through Botha's line at Bergendal, a farm south of the railway. Pursued further east to Komatipoort on the Portuguese border, about 2,500 of Botha's commandos dispersed in hilly country north and south of the border. About 700 burghers crossed the border into Portuguese territory. General Buller captured Lydenburg, north east of Belfast on the 6th September. General French entered Carolina south of the railway on the same date. On the 25th September, Lieutenant-General R Pole-Carew occupied Komatipoort.

After the fall of Pretoria, President Kruger took up residence in a railway saloon carriage at Machadodorp 140 miles from the Portuguese border. At the end of June, he moved further east to Waterval Onder where the climate was more equitable. When it became apparent that the aged President would at some time fall into the hands of the British, he moved a little further along the railway to Nelspruit and from there left by train for Delagoa Bay on 11th September. From Portuguese territory President Kruger passed to exile in Europe.

On 30th August, Colonel Mahon left Pretoria for Belfast. His mounted brigade was made up of the Queensland Mounted Infantry, the New Zealand Mounted Rifles and the Imperial Light Horse. On 3rd September, Mahon reached Belfast and received orders to join General French at Carolina. The Light Horse arrived at Carolina on 5th September.

General French left Carolina for Barberton by a mountain road on 9th September, marching with infantry, cavalry, field artillery and naval guns. Nine miles along the road, French was opposed by 500 Boers with two guns and a pom pom from a position of strength above the road. The mounted corps and artillery the burghers back before the infantry had time to come into action. On 10th September the column covered only six miles. In difficult country the Light Horse took up the advance. The column was continually troubled by snipers from positions overlooking the road. On 12th September, 'M' Battery attached to Mahon's column, silenced enemy gunners protecting a wagon convoy. 'A' Squadron under Captain Donaldson, riding wide in pursuit in broken country took 20 prisoners, wagons and rifles. The men filled their pockets and saddle flaps with flour, sugar and rice taken from the wagons. Captain Donaldson with local knowledge of the country, was of special value to General French.

Impeded by dongas and drifts in the rough mountain terrain, the wagons were unloaded, partly manhandled and reloaded more than once. Some wagons out of control, fell, overturning down mountain gorges. Although there was very little fighting, the going was in every way physically tough.

Leaving the less mobile sections of the column, French took the cavalry by a bridle track over the mountains, on a direct route to Barberton, dropping 3,000 feet in 15 miles. The cavalry occupied the town without opposition, several hundred Boers coming in from the countryside to surrender. The main column arrived in Barberton on 16th. The rear-guard escorted by 'F' Squadron Light Horse, reached Barberton on the following day. General Schoeman was found imprisoned in the Barberton gaol because of his refusal to break the oath of neutrality given to the British.

Lieutenant Webb recorded: "Arrived Barberton, 11 a.m. Sunday 16th September. Because of the activities of snipers, this notice was posted around the town:

TO THE INHABITANTS OF BARBERTON

This is to give you notice that if any shooting into the town, or sniping in its vicinity takes place, the Lieutenant-General Commanding will withdraw the troops and shell the town without further notice?

15-9-1900. Signed D. Haig, Lieutenant-Colonel,

Chief Staff Officer to Lieutenant-General French.

"The sniping stopped. The Dutch women got frightened and passed around the word. French took many locomotives and prisoners."

The Regiment remained at Barberton until 28th September. Many rifles, wagons, much ammunition and great quantities of stores were seized. One hundred locomotives were taken. The Light Horse was detached from Colonel Mahon's column and ordered to Pretoria. The Colonel had been a popular and capable commander and was cheered in farewell by the men. The Regiment reached Waterval Onder on 2nd October, on the way to Machadodorp. From there on 5th October, 'A' and 'E' Squadrons escorted General Kitchener to Pretoria. The other Light Horse squadrons entrained for Pretoria, stopping overnight at Witbank.

At the camp in Pretoria there was a particular three day period of unrest in the ranks. Whereas it was generally thought that the Regiment was about to be disbanded, because of the popular misconception held by many that the war was practically over, rumour also reported that General Kitchener proposed to disband all irregular units with the exception of the Imperial Light Horse, which was to be kept active in the field. When it became obvious that in practically every case the men were ready to exercise any offer of discharge, it was decided that the right of discharge would apply to those with service prior to 1st March 1900. For the men who decided to stay with the Regiment, one month of leave in rotations of two weeks was granted. On this basis, a discharge was taken by all except 50, who decided to see the war through to the end.

---

[1] In a diary note in the Karri-Davies Papers
[2] An account in the Karri-Davies Collection of Papers
[3] From an account in the Karri-Davies Collection of Papers
[4] In a diary in the Karri-Davies Collection

Chapter 10
WESTERN TRANSVAAL-OCTOBER 1900 – AUGUST 1901
ACTIONS AT FREDERICKSTAD – CYFERFONTEIN – GEDULD NEAR HAARTEBEESTFONTEIN
WILDFONTEIN – MARCHING WITH MAJOR-GENERAL BABINGTON

Whereas in October 1899 the commandos waited expectantly, poised on the borders of the colonies for the order to drive the British into the sea, military defeats had ordained that one year later they were destined to be harried in their own territory for another 20 months, cut off from the sea and the world beyond, while the British held most of the towns and communications. At the same time the commandos were conducting a particularly effective type of guerrilla warfare, by avoiding large bodies of troops and taking every opportunity of attacking weak detachments, isolated towns or villages, garrisons, some camp, convoy or section of the railway. By September 1900 a new pattern of warfare was established.

In the early part of 1900 many dispirited burghers left the commandos and returned to the farms, surrendering their arms in return for a British pass accepted upon an undertaking on oath to remain neutral. In October 1900, Roberts reported in despatches: "Subsequent to the occupation of Johannesburg, the organised forces of the enemy were materially reduced in numbers, many of the burghers in arms surrendering their rifles and voluntarily taking the oath of neutrality, but the submission only proved real when the burghers were protected from outside interference." Operations by resourceful and elusive guerrilla leaders like De la Rey, De Wet, Ben Viljoen and Louis Botha rekindled the spirit of resistance: "I conceived," wrote General De Wet,[1] "a great plan of bringing under arms all burghers who had laid down their arms and taken the oath of Neutrality and of sending them to operate in every State."

The British operated in a hostile countryside, where almost every farmhouse was a source of supply, of intelligence, a refuge or even a small arsenal. Roberts ordered the burning of farm houses, crops, the seizure of wagons and livestock, particularly on farms situated close to uprooted sections of the railway, either known or suspected of having assisted the enemy.

The Light Horse remained in Pretoria engaged in camp duties until 15th October, when the Under-strength squadrons marched to entrain at Elandsfontein for Krugersdorp, before going onto Frederickstad. Early in October, General De Wet crossed the Vaal River at Schoeman's Drift from the Free State with 1,000 burghers and fours guns. Under orders to head him off, Major-General G Barton marched on 17th October through Bank and Welverdiend to Frederickstad Station. Frederickstad, on the Krugersdorp–Klerksdorp railway, was encircled by low hills. The Mooi River, on a course almost parallel with the station, flowed only a mile or so away. The British force camped near the station and on a low circle of hills.

On 18th October, General Barton was strengthened by the arrival of a mounted corps of about 500 strong made up of Light Horse and Imperial Yeomanry. Barton's column of about 2,000 men, consisted mainly of infantry of the Royal Scots Fusiliers and the Royal Welsh Fusiliers, 40 Australian Mounted Bushmen, six field guns, a 4.7 gun and three pom poms. The Light Horse was still in the middle of reorganising and recruiting, following the acceptance of the discharges in Pretoria. Under Colonel Woolls-Sampson, the corps could only muster two under strength squadrons each of 60 men. 'B' Squadron under Captain T. Yockney was made up mainly of veterans and 'D' Squadron under Captain Evans consisted mainly of new recruits.

With a force increased to 1500 burghers by the addition of Commandant Liebenberg's commando, General De Wet moved up from the Vaal through the hilly country of the Gatsrand with six guns and a pom pom. On the morning of 20th October, a British detachment on reconnaissance from Frederickstad moved out at about 8.15 am. along the Potchefstroom road. The detachment was made up of both squadrons of Light Horse with three companies of Welsh Fusiliers and two guns. Three or four miles along the road the detachment was attacked and remained under fire all the way back to camp. Casualties amounted to 15. The Light Horse lost Trooper Isidor Simpson killed and Trooper H. Bowden wounded.

General De Wet attacked the British positions with gun and rifle fire from the south and from the east. General Barton withdrew overnight from low ground around the station and disposed the troops on hills in the east, with the main base on Gun Hill, two miles east of the station. On this hill Barton placed a 4.7 gun and two companies of Royal Scots Fusiliers. Slightly further to the east, on the northern slopes of a hill overlooking the railway, three companies of Royal Welsh Fusiliers, some mounted men and a pom pom were positioned.

Two miles south of the railway, six companies of Royal Scots, with two field guns and a pom pom were on South Hill. Altogether, Barton's force occupied good defensive positions with access to water. The Light Horse, entrenched in sangars on a slope between the Welsh in the east and the railway, sniped continually at burghers in cover at farm buildings adjoining the railway. Unaccountably, the telegraph wire extending to Welverdiend and beyond had not been tampered with, permitting Barton to communicate with Headquarters in Pretoria.

On the 22nd a shell from the 4.7 gun destroyed a pom pom gun and its crew. This gun concealed near the river, had shelled and killed a large number of transport animals. On the 24th the Light Horse was alerted to be ready to escort into camp an ammunition convoy expected from Welverdiend. Knowing that the British were running short of ammunition, General De Wet sent 300 burghers over the Mooi River on the night of 24th–25th. Leaving the horses on the far side of the river, the burghers made their way across the river flat to positions near the railway. On the night of 24th an unsuccessful attack was launched against South Hill.

British positions again came under fire on the morning of the 25th. Overnight, De Wet again despatched burghers over the Mooi River in the direction of the railway. An advanced party took up a position in a donga in front of an embankment near the railway bridge. The intention was to lie concealed during the day and rush the posts on Gun Hill under cover of darkness. A Light Horse escort of 10 men with a water cart unwittingly uncovered the burghers who promptly seized the cart. This escort became the target for close fire from the Mausers. Without realising the full strength of the burgher force, Barton despatched a company of Scots Fusiliers and a squadron of Light Horse to dislodge them. The attack failed. Captain W. Bailie and four Fusiliers were killed.

General Barton ordered a general attack against the Boer front along the railway. Infantry from South Hill and Gun Hill converged in extended lines in a frontal attack, the Light Horse covering the right flank between the river and the railway. The Boers fought stubbornly until almost midday, when the infantry moved up with fixed bayonets. They then turned and fled on foot across the open ground extending for a mile and a half to the river, throwing down bandoliers and rifles as they ran. Twenty-six burghers were found dead on the field, 30 wounded and 26 unwounded prisoners were taken. Under a hail of rifle and shell fire, the others managed to get safely over the river.

The Light Horse left the horses in the care of black horseholders, so that every man would be free to take part in the attack. After a close fight against Boers in a donga, the enemy were forced from cover with hands up. Sergeant George Wileman led his troop to a branch of the donga to receive the surrender of three burghers, who after throwing down their rifles, emerged with hands up. Sergeant Wileman then went forward at the head of the troop, whereupon a burgher quickly dropped his hands, picked up a rifle and shot him in the head. He died the next day. For the cold blooded and treacherous murder of Sergeant Wileman, three Boers were tried by court martial and shot.

Trooper J. Cherry, 'B' Squadron wrote:[2] "Sergeant Wileman died after being severely wounded. Trooper Beal and another man were wounded. Poor Sergeant Wileman was simply murdered. He was acting as troop leader this day. He was leading his troop on a trench with three Boers in it, who threw down their rifles and held up their hands. On Wileman's approach, one of the three stooped down, picked up his rifle and shot poor Wileman in the head. The Boers were made prisoners, tried by court-martial for murder, found guilty and shot.

"A somewhat similar incident happened to Captain Yockney, commanding 'B' Squadron. Several of the enemy surrendered to him and on his approach one raised his rifle and pointed straight at Yockney's breast, pulling the trigger, but then thank goodness, it did not go off, for it jammed or something. Yockney saved the burgher's life from the anger of the Light Horsemen." Before the fighting ended the advance of a relief column from Welverdiend under Colonel Hickey was reported. General De Wet withdrew his force, moving away in the direction of Lindeque's Drift. As a precautionary measure the Light Horse was ordered to guard Buffelsdoorn Pass, east of the Mooi River.

The Light Horse marched from Frederickstad to Potchefstroom on 3rd November and for some time patrolled between Potchefstroom and Klerksdorp, Potchefstroom and Frederickstad. The chief duties were keeping the railway clear of Boers trying to cut the line and bringing in families from the farms, with their furniture and household goods.

Lord Roberts returned to England at the end of November, the command passing to General Kitchener. The new Commander-in-Chief took immediate steps to intensify the war of attrition against the guerrilla forces and called for more mounted troops. The burning of farm houses and the removal of women and children into camps, together with the removal of black families attached to the farms into similar camps, became more general.

To protect the families of the surrendered burghers on the farms, Roberts had been forced to establish camps at sites along the railways. Under Kitchener, the burning of farm houses and the removal to the camps of the families of fighting burghers also became general practice. The British Commander-in-Chief regarded the farm houses as sources of sustenance and of Intelligence for the commandos. The policy was designed to hasten the end of the war, the outcome of which was no longer in doubt.

In a report made to the War Office in March 1901, Kitchener stated: "I some time ago took measures for the establishment of properly organized camps at certain selected sites on the lines of the railway, at which surrendered burghers were permitted to live with their families under our effective protection. The families of all burghers still under arms, are as far as possible brought in from the adjacent districts and similarly lodged in these camps."

At Potchefstroom the drilling and instruction took place of recruits necessary to bring the Light Horse up to strength. Some training had begun several weeks before at Irene, outside Pretoria. Sergeant-Major T. Sulivan, 'A' Squadron transferred to the Light Horse, having served from the beginning of the war with the Natal Police. He wrote from Potchefstroom that he "drilled recruits daily for the field."[3] Meanwhile, the squadrons engaged in patrolling south to the Vaal from Potchefstroom and north from Potchefstroom along the course of the Mooi River towards Naauwport.

After having taken discharges in Pretoria, a good number of former Light Horsemen held commissions in different colonial raised corps. In almost every case the men returned to the front in some capacity. Some of these former Light Horsemen – about 80 – returned to the Regiment. At the same time about 40 men from the 79th company, Imperial Yeomanry, accepted the opportunity of enlisting in the Light Horse, after being for some time attached to the Regiment. The Imperial Light Horse spent Christmas 1900 – the first Christmas since Ladysmith – at the Potchefstroom base. Late on Christmas night, Light Horse squadrons escorting a convoy, set out on a slippery rain-damaged road to Ventersdorp.

The Regiment had become very split up. 'B' and 'C' Squadrons became attached to Major-General J. Babington's column after he had replaced General Barton. The Light Horse was never entirely happy under General Barton, whose reputation was one of being not too favourably disposed towards mounted corps. 'A' Squadron remained at the Potchefstroom base, patrolling south of the Vaal, with spells of convoy work to Ventersdorp every 10 to 14 days, gathering in flocks of sheep and cattle and taking prisoners 'D' Squadron patrolled from Ventersdorp, across to Krugersdorp and along the railway from Krugersdorp to Potchefstroom. Major Codrington, having by this time recovered from the wound received on Wagon Hill, returned to take command of 'E' and 'F' Squadrons attached to a mobile column under Lieutenant-Colonel G. Benson.

Colonel Benson was the artillery officer who so ably guided the Highland Brigade across the veldt to Magersfontein. He had a mixed column of mounted troops – Australian Bushmen, Kitchener's Horse, Imperial Yeomanry, infantry and artillery. In February the two Light Horse Squadrons under Benson patrolled the Gatsrand country east of Frederickstad and in March the country between the Vaal and the Gatsrand, clearing farms and constantly in touch with the enemy. The column was disbanded in Krugersdorp early in April 1900.

In December 1900, General French organized four columns of troops in the western Transvaal, south of the Magaliesberg, where, following a successful attack on Major-General R Clement's camp in the lee of a southern spur of the Magaliesberg at Nooitgedacht, De la Rey and Beyers operated with 3,000 burghers. French had between 5,000 and 6,000 men and 40 guns. The columns converged on Ventersdorp at the end of a swath made on a wide front in a line from Commando Nek and Hekpoort Valley to Ventersdorp. Leaving a garrison at Ventersdorp, the four columns under General Babington swung back on 2nd January 1901, in a north-eastern direction towards the Magaliesberg Valley, in another attempt to corner De la Rey and Beyers who were both still roving at large.

General Babington had about 1,600 men, made up of three British mounted squadrons, 'B' and 'C' Squadrons Light Horse, 1st Royal Welsh Fusiliers, four guns of the 78th Field Battery and two pom poms. The column entered the valley on the morning of the 5th January when mist limited visibility to 50 yards. The enemy was also known to be in the neighbourhood. At about 9 a.m. some Boers were seen moving along a bare ridge away to the left, advancing from the direction of Olifant's Nek. General Babington ordered the Light Horse under Colonel Woolls-Sampson to occupy a bare hill to the left rear, on the lands of a farm called Cyferfontein. A scouting party of 14th Hussars had been over the hill an hour before and reported all clear. Riding fast on the heels of four advanced scouts – rather belatedly sent forward – Woolls-Sampson advanced the Light Horse at such a pace that two pom poms under Captain G Brierley, Royal Horse Artillery, were unable to keep up. Meanwhile, the Boers had moved swiftly across the valley from the hill where they were first seen by General Babington and his officers. The burghers lay concealed in 18 inch long grass at the top of the very hillside that the Light Horse was heading for and only 1,600 yards from Babington's infantry and convoy. A troop of 14th Hussars passed close to the hill, on the left flank of the Light Horse, without drawing fire.

Colonel Woolls-Sampson veered north-west, increasing the distance from the scouts who continued to advance on a more north-easterly line. The squadrons started up the hill, riding straight for the crest. Major C.J. Briggs, 1st King's Dragoon Guards leading 'C' Squadron, had deployed and 'B' Squadron was about to deploy, when the enemy opened fire at anything from 50 to 100 yards range "almost like machine gun fire."[4] The Boers were so close that some of the men actually picked out General De la Rey, but the wounded horses galloping madly around out in front and the furious hazardness of the situation, made the exact shooting required to cut the General down too difficult. All those who could, took cover behind the nearest dead horse.

After about 10 minutes, Woolls-Sampson gave the order to retire. Major A Hurst, 5th Dragoon Guards, attached to the Light Horse, spread the order in a dangerous manner, by galloping the full length of the scattered position, waving his hat and shouting out, "Retire." As more than half the horses were lost, many of the men had to return on foot for about half a mile to where the pom poms were.

Colonel Woolls-Sampson, Major Briggs and Captain Normand were among those whose mounts had not been hit, although bullets cut into saddles and equipment. Galloping down the hill with the remnant of his squadrons, Woolls-Sampson ordered Captain Brierley on the lower slopes to retire with the pom poms. Some of the Boers, firing from the saddle, also came galloping down the hill. Completely unaware of the proximity of the guns, the Boers stopped to strip the dead and the wounded. Appreciating the benefit of not being under direct attack, Captain Brierley took one gun and Briggs and Normand the other. Taking no notice of Woolls-Sampson's order to retire from the field, they disposed the guns in better cover commanding a good field of fire. From a range of 800 yards the gunners were successful in protecting Babington's convoy from Boers riding around from the western side of the ridge. Babington's mounted force chased De la Rey for four miles over the same valley by which the Boers had earlier approached from Olifant's Nek.

The losses of the Light Horse at Cyferfontein were 18 killed and 32 wounded. Squadron-Sergeant-Major Sandys, 5th Lancers attached and Corporal T. Gollan, Imperial Yeomanry were among the fallen. five of the wounded died, including Trooper C. Rex, Imperial Yeomanry. On the right flank in the action and caught in the heaviest fire from as close as 50 yards, 'B' Squadron suffered the most casualties. 'C' Squadron lost four killed and 14 wounded. Not one of the Light Horsemen were made prisoner by the Boers. Lieutenant Arthur Ormond, 'B' Squadron, was among those killed. Captain Adjutant B.M. Glossop, 5th Dragoon Guards attached, was wounded and had his horse shot from under him. The Boers then rode down and took his spurs and field glasses, offering in return refreshment from a water bottle. Some of the wounded died overnight and were buried next morning on top of the hill, alongside their comrades, the fallen of the previous day. The surviving wounded were taken through Krugersdorp and arrived at the hospital in Johannesburg towards evening on the day after the action.

Trooper R. Vernon, 'B' Squadron, gave an account of the fight at Cyferfontein: "We were dismounted and lying down when Colonel Woolls-Sampson got the order to occupy a ridge about a mile to our left flank. Captain Yockney said: 'see your magazines are charged, as we might get it hot,' and in a few minutes we did. We broke into a hard gallop. I was out on the extreme right hand with Maxwell, Green, Kipping and Anderson, in order named, on my left. Then Lieutenant Ormond told me to bring the right wing round, which we did. Then, on getting the order to dismount and fire, we knelt down and fired. I had three shots lying down on Lieutenant Ormond's orders, when I was hit on the left arm which was broken. Maxwell ran over and tried to get me behind a dead horse, but I would not go and I said Mac, lie down or they will kill you.' He said: 'No. I will give it to them.' He fired two shots and fell on me. I said: 'Where are you shot Mac?' He said: 'Through the heart,' and I said, 'poor old beggar.' He got up and walked about eight yards and fell down dead. A braver man never lived.

"Then I could see the havoc the Boers had made on us. Captain Yockney was wounded. I was in the ambulance when he died. We had over 40 casualties that day. The Colonel at last gave the order to retire, so those that could, got back to the column. Then the Boers came over and relieved us of our arms. I saved my revolver by sitting on it."[5]

On 11th January 1901, Colonel Woolls-Sampson ended his association with the Imperial Light Horse. Major Briggs assumed temporary command. General Kitchener appointed Major Herbert Bottomley, one of the original officers, Lieutenant-Colonel of the Regiment, an offer that Major Bottomley preferred to decline, being of the opinion that in the best interests of the Regiment, a regular officer should command. Meanwhile, Major Briggs retained temporary command.

In September 1901, Woolls-Sampson joined Colonel Benson's column as an Intelligence Officer. It was then that his great knowledge of the Boers, together with the facility of getting the maximum value from reports by the blacks, was turned to such good account. As an intelligence Officer, Woolls-Sampson performed his best service in the war. On 8th September 1901, Kitchener recorded in despatches: "In this as in other enterprises undertaken by Colonel Benson, the greatest credit was due to Lieutenant-Colonel Woolls-Sampson, whose careful leading across the veld for 34 miles on a dark night contributed materially to the success achieved." Kitchener also reported on 8th September: "General Bruce Hamilton brings to my notice the excellent work done by Colonel Woolls-Sampson, his Intelligence Officer, upon this occasion in locating the enemy and guiding the force to its objective."

In camp with the Light Horse, Colonel Woolls-Sampson sometimes noticeably failed to get the best results from the men. In the field, where in courage he was second to none, his very excitable reactions sometimes rather diminished the effectiveness of the operation in which he was engaged.

On 23rd January 1901, news was received in the field of the death of Queen Victoria on the previous day. All flags were flown at half-mast.

On 23rd February, 50 recruits were taken into 'B' and 'C' Squadrons. The Regiment was kept fully up to strength by means of selective recruiting. Major Karri-Davies, the chief recruiting officer had a roving commission to supervise recruiting from nine Light Horse offices spread over the main towns. The greatest care was taken in the selection of recruits. Captain Harbord wrote:[6] "While recruiting in Cape Town I accepted only 400 out of 1,500 applicants, knowing from experience how essential it was to have good men. I refused all who could not pass the necessary tests in riding, shooting and so on."

On 3rd March 1901, Generals De la Rey and J.C. Smuts attacked the garrison at Lichtenburg which was commanded by Lieutenant-Colonel C. Money. General Babington marched from the vicinity of Naauwpoort, north-west of Krugersdorp, to the relief of Lichtenburg. Captain Normand reported: "Wagons moved with great difficulty. Rain in torrents and had to load and off-load wagons over bad spots, until the General ordered that any wagon stuck for more than 15 minutes had to be left after the kits were destroyed as it was essential to reach Ventersdorp. Soaked through and tired and sleepless reached Ventersdorp 5 p.m. 8th March in heavy rain. News came that the Boers had withdrawn from Lichtenburg on 12th March. Most of the wagons still struck 12 miles out and 20 extra wagons to load. Rain and foggy and raw."

At Lichtenburg General De la Rey was repulsed after a day of severe fighting. General Babington reached Lichtenburg on 17th March. Marching south in pursuit of De la Rey in the direction of Klerksdorp, Babington reached Hartebeestfontein on 20th March, only one day after

1,200 Boers had left the village. During the march south, Babington took wagons and teams as well as accounting for 70 of the enemy, including 62 prisoners.

On 22nd March, 'A', 'B' and 'C' Squadrons, Light Horse, 180 men altogether, formed a detachment sent to reconnoitre the country towards Kaffirkraal. From a ridge two miles west of the farm Geduld, about seven miles north of Hartebeestfontein and north-west of Klerksdorp, No. 1 troop of 'A' Squadron, scouting in advance, spotted a party of eight Boers. By 6.30 a.m. and hotly engaged by a stronger commando, the detachment was defending itself in the cover of an empty kraal. Squadron Major Sulivan reported:[7] "The whole of our little force rallied there and awaited the advance of the Boers who galloped and fired as they came. One came as close as yards to the wall and was shot, one of them being killed after demanding a hands-up surrender. They came on pretty thick, then they retreated, leaving five killed and three wounded."

Reinforcements arrived about 8 a.m. and the entire force began to retire back to camp. Half a mile along the road, 'A' Squadron in the rear, was attacked by about 50 burghers. A running fight developed when 800 Boers with two guns and a pom pom came riding down hard on the right flank. 'C' Squadron was hard pressed and got assistance from 'B' Squadron. The only pom pom kept jamming and could not be made to fire for more than short bursts. More than once the flanks were driven in to within a few hundred yards of the gun in the centre of the column. Fortunately, none of the horses in the gun teams went down. The squadrons were able to retire in line and just managed to race the Boers to good positions on the ridges near the outskirts of the camp. Reinforced by troops and a pom pom from the camp there followed shelling from both sides before the forces retired.

Captain Normand reported: "We all had to retire, squadron after squadron covering one another's retirement and pouring volley after volley into the advancing Boers. When we reached the ridge overlooking the camp, the Boers went back and were shelled by our guns. The fight was over at 2 p.m., having started at 9.30 a.m."

The Light Horse lost five killed and 16 wounded. Those killed were Lieutenant J. Ralston, Regimental-Sergeant-Major A. Hurst, Troopers P. Jones, D. Paterson and P. Kennedy. Lieutenant A. Halling died from his wounds. Captain J Donaldson, 'A' Squadron was severely wounded. The losses of the Boers were 24 killed and wounded.

General Babington congratulated the Imperial Light Horse in the following terms:[8] "Your engagement at Haartebeestfontein on the 22nd instant, when 180 of you successfully repulsed at least 800 Boers was such that I congratulate all who took part in it. A rear-guard action is always a difficult one and it was only the excellent way you fought that saved you from annihilation. You averted a disaster for yourselves and for every man in camp. I have no hesitation in saying that no troops in South Africa could have done it better. I am only sorry you found yourselves in a tight corner."

On 23rd March the Light Horse again made contact with the enemy, with the result that four men from 'C' Squadron were wounded while escorting a convoy to Klerksdorp. On 24th March the Light Horse, marching with General Babington left camp at dawn. Moving rapidly without wagons the column pursued De la Rey towards Ventersdorp in the north. About a mile from camp the column met with heavy rifle fire from De la Rey's rear-guard on a hill in front. Babington brought up guns and the shelling forced the burghers to retire at a gallop. Babington sent Australian Bushmen and New Zealand Rough Riders riding pell mell for the Boer rear-guard. With the Light Horse in first support, the Australians and New Zealanders closed in on the convoy and the by now panic-stricken escort at Wildfontein. No less than two guns and a pom pom, five maxims and 54 wagons, cattle and 150 prisoners were taken. Captain Normand wrote:[9] "As we came up fast Boers were panic-stricken and never stood. We took two commandants and a lieutenant in the Staats Artillerie and a North Lancashire Regiment infantryman who had deserted."

The *Times History*[10] said the victory over De la Rey was: "Gained by a good tactical initiative with good mounted troops."

Sir John Maurice wrote:[11] "Babington came up next day and drove the Boers still further northward and on the 24th completed the rout by overtaking and capturing the whole of their guns – Nine – and the escort of 140 men on the banks of Taaibosch Spruit. The enemy continually took up rear-guard positions, out of which Babington continually manoeuvred them, by vigorous threats from the flanks and a menacing front, until the defence dissolved into hasty retreats under pressure and became a rout and disorder in the field."

That night the Light Horse bivouacked at Putfontein, without blankets and very short on rations, proceeding on the following day with the main column to Ventersdorp.

Within the area bounded by Klerksdorp, Ventersdorp and Lichtenburg, De la Rey's commandos were split up into small groups. The whole area was in a constant state of flux as the columns made every effort to catch up with them. On 29th March, the enemy was dispersed from farm houses only four miles from Ventersdorp.

Captain Normand noted in his Diary for April and for early May 1901: "2nd April. Marched all night to Rietpan, arriving 4 a.m., 3rd. Proceeded at a hard trot to ridges south of Tafel Kop, captured a wagon, but 200 Boers got on top of a strong position on rocky kopjes. They were reinforced by 400 from De la Rey's laager a few miles back. Shelled the ridges and the Boers cleared out to a stronger position. As our horses were done, our General decided to pull back to Rietpan. The horses had done over 25 miles.

"6th April. Rode to the top of Tafel Kop and had a grand view, seeing our old friend Naauwpoort and also Ventersdorp. Convoying and patrolling, Ventersdorp, Klerksdorp and Potchefstroom.

"14th April. Reached the flats below the hills at Kaffirs Kraal just at daylight, marching with Brigadier-General H Rawlinson's[12] column. Crossing the first line of hills, came upon the Boer laager, the Boers having no pickets out and our scouts got within 400 yards before being seen. The Boers cleared out, jumping on to horses bare backed and the whole camp fell into our hands. Killed 5 Boers, 12 wounded, 30 prisoners, one Krupp gun and two Nordenfeldt maxims taken, 12 wagons and 6 Cape carts. Numerous rifles, saddles and 30 to 40 horses.

"Three hundred Boers had taken to the hills and we shelled them. In kloofs around the laager we got 400 cattle and sheep. The laager belonged to Smuts, but he was absent with 400 men when we came snooping down. Arrived back at camp at 7.30 p.m. both horses and men dead beat. General Rawlinson was taken prisoner for about two hours when his horse was shot, but he was released, the Boers evidently not realising he was a General. He was dressed without any sign of rank.

"17th April. The Light Horse advance guard to Rawlinson's column.

"18th April. Found the Boers in the hills overlooking Haartebeestfontein in large numbers under De la Rey, Smuts and Liebenberg. Shelled them and pom pommed the ridges all day. A squadron of Roberts' Horse met with heavy fire at the Nek outside the town. Babington gave them an hour to get out before he shelled the town.

"26th April. A flag of truce came in from De la, Rey, asking for their ambulance back, which we took from them a time ago. General Babington replied, that as the ambulance was one which they had taken from us, he did not think they were entitled to have it back. "1st May. Three hundred Imperial Yeomen – Scottish and Warwickshire men are attached – they are fearful horsemen.

"8th May. Near Leeufontein, captured a Boer convoy of 28 prisoners, 25 wagons and carts, the remainder of the Boers driven towards Dixon's column, between Lichtenburg and Ventersdorp, 200 cattle and 300 sheep taken after a chase from Tafel Kop."

Lieutenant Bryon Noel, a Light Horseman, was scouting more than a mile from Babington's main column when he came almost face to face with two Boers in a hollow. The Boers were dismounted and armed. For some unexplained reason Noel was unarmed. Nevertheless, he rode straight up to the Boers, demanding "hands-up." The Boers shot his horse, but Noel kept striding on towards them, holding his pipe in position in the same manner as a revolver and continuing to call out "hands-up." In this way Noel bluffed the burghers who were both taken into camp, together with the riding horses and two pack horses.

Not more than a week later, Lieutenant Noel marched with two squadrons advancing under cover of guns. His troop got so far forward that it came within the range of the falling shells. Standing to wave his hat as a signal to the gunners, he was shot in the stomach. The men carried him a great distance, rather than subject him to the severe jolting of an ambulance. Lieutenant Noel died on the morning the column entered Zeerust. Only the day before, shortly after the camp was pitched, at his request, he was taken close to the front of the tent by his comrades, so that he could take one more look at the setting sun.

During the next few months the Light Horse continued to take part in rounding up expeditions and in providing screens for convoys. In the Lichtenburg–Schweizer–Renecke area, 'B' Squadron under Captain Harbord operated with a column led by Colonel Hickey. The Squadron at this time was down to 50 men, holding a position on the march nine miles to the right of the main column. Harbord was under instructions to be wary of engaging the enemy suspected of being in the region in superior numbers.

Acting on information received from a black man that a commando of about a 1,000 strong was only a few hours ahead of the column, Harbord ordered Lieutenant Lionel Sanders to ride after an advanced patrol, to take command of the patrol, and to be particularly on the alert for the reported commando. On the following day a scout reported to Captain Harbord that after contacting the patrol, Sanders went on ahead until he sighted another patrol in British uniform and riding in formation in a manner similar to a British patrol.

Lieutenant Sanders continued to advance, without realising until too late, that the riders in British uniform were in fact Boers. Sanders tried to shoot the leader with his revolver, then turned and rode for his life. Within a very short distance, both horse and rider were shot down. Lieutenant Sanders was carried to a farm house by the Boers where he died during the night without regaining consciousness. He was born in the Cape Province and as one of the originals in the Light Horse had been through the fighting in Natal and in the relief of Mafeking.

In August 1901, General Babington's column was disbanded. The Light Horse left Klerksdorp for Potchefstroom by train on 24th August. About this time, Major Briggs was promoted to lieutenant-colonel and appointed to command the Regiment. This appointment was received by all ranks with great satisfaction.

On the morning of 25th August, the Light Horse left Johannesburg in open trucks in the rain via Elandsfontein, reaching Ladysmith in the early afternoon. Entraining from there, the Regiment arrived in Harrismith at 9 a.m. on 26th August. That afternoon the Light Horse marched 10 miles along the Albertina River and for the first time camped with the 2nd Light Horse. The 2nd Light Horse was under the command of Lieutenant-Colonel Duncan McKenzie, a Natal farmer. The command of both Light Horse Regiments was held by Brigadier-General Sir John Dartnell, a former Commissioner of Police in Natal and commandant of the Natal Volunteers.

---

[1] *Three Years War, 1899-1902* General C. De Wet
[2] In a statement in the Karri-Davies Collection of Papers
[3] From the Diary in the Karri-Davies Collection
[4] *The Story of the Imperial Light Horse* G.F. Gibson
[5] An account in the Karri-Davies Collection of Papers
[6] From *Froth and Bubble* Captain Harbord
[7] From his diary in the Karri-Davies collection
[8] From the diary of Captain Normand, in the Karri-Davies Collection
[9] In the diary in the Karri-Davies Collection
[10] *The Times History of the War in South Africa* L. Amery
[11] *Official History of the War in South Africa* Major-General Sir J. Maurice
[12] Local rank only Colonel Sir Henry Rawlinson, later General Rawlinson, commander of 4th Army in France in World War I. Commander-in-Chief Army in India 1920

CHAPTER 11
THE ESTABLISHMENT OF THE 2ND IMPERIAL LIGHT HORSE
WITH SMITH-DORRIEN IN EASTERN TRANSVAAL
CHASING DE WET ALONG THE ORANGE RIVER IN THE CAPE COLONY

The establishment of the 2nd Imperial Light Horse was approved by General Kitchener towards the end of 1900. By December recruiting was well under way. Many of the officers were discharged men from the 1st Imperial Light Horse or from the Natal Carbineers.

On 18th December, Lieutenant-Colonel Duncan McKenzie arrived in Volksrust to take up the command from Captain Bottomley, the officer in charge. On 19th January 1901, the Regiment left Volkrust and on the following day arrived in Pretoria where General Kitchener inspected the troops. Kitchener expressed the hope that they would be as good as the 1st Imperial Light Horse.

On Monday, 21st January, the 2nd Light Horse, six squadrons 400 strong with horses and the West Yorkshire Regiment entrained for Wonderfontein, between Middleburg and Belfast. The train stopped overnight at Elands River station. Beyond Balmoral there was a long delay for railway gangs to arrive and repair sections of the track. This had been blown up by the enemy who could be seen riding away in the distance. After four days and 114 miles covered in the train, the Light Horse marched with Major-General H. Smith-Dorrien's column for Carolina. General Smith-Dorrien had the 5th Lancers, the 18th Hussars and 300 mounted infantry in his force of 3,000 men and 12 guns.

General Smith-Dorrien's column formed part of the force under General French, who with 15,000 men and 63 guns was about to engage in a great drive through the eastern Transvaal south of the Delagoa Bay Railway, in a region where General Botha has assembled 5,000 commandos with the intention of re-entering northern Natal in force.

The column soon made contact with the enemy who for most of the way sniped and hung around the flanks. At Twyfelaar on the 25th near the headwaters of the Komati River the enemy attacked with a pom pom. The column also brought a pom pom into action. Lieutenant Dr Briscoe was wounded. In a heavy storm one man was killed and two others injured by lightning. The rain was so thick that visibility was down to a few hundred yards, allowing the Boers to get the pom pom away. Three squadrons of Light Horse with mounted infantry supported by 5th Lancers drove the Boers back in a flanking movement. On 26th January the column entered Carolina.

On the following day outside Carolina, the Light Horse was engaged with a column in bringing in families and stock from the farms, when the enemy attacked strongly under cover of a heavy storm. Wet through to the skin, the men fought their way back in the dark. Two men were badly struck by lightning. Next morning General Smith-Dorrien sent four ambulances into the Boer lines to pick up the dead and the wounded. The Boers kept three of the ambulances and allowed only one to return with the wounded.

For the next nine days the Light Horse was occupied in conveying and patrolling between Carolina and Wonderfontein. There were days with little action and other trying days of skirmishing with snipers and getting wet through to the skin. The Regiment lost one man killed and five wounded. Trooper Harvey was made prisoner and presently released on the open veldt after his horse and boots were taken. Harvey sheltered in a kraal where he was eventually picked up. On the 5th February the Regiment formed the rear-guard of a convoy to Lake Chrissie. All through the day there was a continuous exchange of rifle fire with the enemy. On the same day Botha moved out of Ermelo with a force of 2,000. On 6th February General French entered Ermelo behind him.

Botha decided to attack Smith-Dorrien whose column at Lake Chrissie was rather isolated. In dry weather over most of the year the lake was nothing more than a large pan.[1] General Smith-Dorrien camped on the north shore of the lake near the village of Bothwell. At 3 a.m. on the 6th, from behind a hail of bullets, the Boers charged through the pickets and wrought great confusion by galloping through the camp. Placed forward on the west side, the West Yorkshire pickets bore the brunt of the attack, losing 20 killed. On the northern picket line the Suffolks were also strongly attacked. The mounted corps, positioned with the Highlanders near the Royal Artillery at the rear of the camp, was unable to stop several hundred horses stampeding through the lines. The Light Horse shot eight Boers, including Field-Cornets Bickaers and Spruit. By 4.30 a.m. the Boers, in the face of a spirited resistance, were retiring in several directions. Although Botha had failed in his objective of overwhelming Smith-Dorrien's camp, he had succeeded in breaking through the wide cordon spread for him by French.

At 6 a.m. the mounted corps set out in a thick mist in pursuit of the commandos. Colonel McKenzie reported:[2] "Went along the Ermelo road for four miles and then turned up the ridge to the right. When the mist lifted we saw the Boers, some on the same ridge as ourselves and some on a higher ridge directly in front of us. I could not get the Officer-Commanding to open on them with the big guns. He thought they were one of our other columns and of course all the military backed him up in this opinion.

"I told him that I could lay my life they were Boers. We did some smart work in a flank move that worked the Boers off the high ground which we took without losing a man. The Boers opened fire on us with two guns and a pom pom and we had an artillery duel. About 1,000 Boers were opposed to us. We captured a wounded Boer in a farm house."

In making a getaway through the cordon, Botha outstripped his transport. The Light Horse, riding for 20 miles along clogged roads, drove the escort off and seized wagons, 18,000 livestock and 21 prisoners.

Colonel McKenzie reported[3] on the capture of the convoy: "9th February. Marched from Lake Chrissie along the Barberton road and cut a Boer convoy in two. Some got on to the Warmbaths road, the remainder went down the Bremersdorp road and we galloped after that lot for about 12 miles, taking 100 wagons. Smith-Dorrien congratulated the Imperial Light Horse on their feat. General French wired a telegram of praise to communicate to the Regiment."

Colonel McKenzie recorded in his Diary: "11th February. Cameron Highlanders under orders killed thousands of sheep; all the sheep we captured. We took 20 wagons and a lot of women and children from the farms. Made an offer to a senior staff officer in charge of transport who was in difficulties. Got over a lot of wagons at a different drift we found for him. Took about 50 wagons across. Got all the transport across although the stream was pretty full and very swift. General Smith-Dorrien came and watched us crossing the wagons and seemed very pleased at us helping and amused at Light Horse Officers directing the wagons across. They are very pleased to get us to help them when we are not otherwise employed. For they know we understand far more of the work than they do. The Provost Marshal asked me if would allow 12 of my men to be attached to him permanently as the mounted infantry and cavalry were useless. I could only get him four. On 14th February the convoy came straight into Amsterdam."

The column operated from Amsterdam towards the apex of Natal, where heavy and at one time incessant rain for eight days, saturated the roads, the veldt and all the streams, so that even the smallest spruits were running overfull. Trooper Hanks was swept away and drowned. The conditions were such that supply wagons were unable to pass on the roads. Without even biscuits, the troops were forced to pick up what they could from the farms. In many cases they had nothing more to eat than mealies: "For the men were starving. We had been without food for about a month, only having quarter rations and very often nothing."[4]

In thick mist and rain, the troops collected families and wagons from the farms. "Smith-Dorrien sends all cattle and Boer families to Piet Retief by General French's order." Also under orders from French to Smith-Dorrien: "Wagons in places of easy access will be brought in by spans of oxen to be sent out next day, but if far off or difficult, they will be burnt."

Between 9th February and 11th March, the column took 644 horses, 50 mules, 9,500 cattle, over 31,000 sheep, 192 wagons, 51 carts, 20,000 pounds of mealies, 8,500 pounds of hay. 39 Boers were killed and 113 wounded were taken, 119 unwounded Boers captured with rifles and ammunition. After 12th March when the weather began to clear, 70 wagons came through from Volskrust. From then on the rations were not such a problem.

On 14th April, Smith-Dorrien's column left Piet Retief for Wonderfontein. The plans that Botha made to re-enter Natal had been completely foiled, even though Botha remained at large with the main part of his force. By 19th April the column reached the junction of the Ermelo and Lake Chrissie roads. Posted with the rear-guard, the Light Horse had a number of trying days, in particular the days when the wagons were delayed and caught in boggy ground. The men were also getting sick and being hospitalised at the rate of two and three a day. The number of fit men in the Light Horse was down to somewhere near 200. The column arrived at Wonderfontein on 24th April. Before he left for Pretoria, General Smith-Dorrien stated:[5] "Success was entirely due to the 2nd Imperial Light Horse and that if we had not been with them, we would not have made so many captures." He also went on to say that he would rather have had a hundred Imperial Light Horse than the 5th Lancers Regiment.

The Light Horse marched from Wonderfontein to Middleburg. Under the command of Major-General Walter Kitchener, the Regiment obtained remounts and joined Lieutenant-General Sir Bindon Blood's column, marching with the 5th Queenslanders, 6th New Zealanders, the Royal Munster Regiment and artillery, for operations in the eastern Transvaal in May and June 1901. Following his unsuccessful attempt at fording the Orange River in December 1900, General de Wet, early in February headed through the Free State. Plumer's troops (Australian Bushmen and New Zealand Rough Riders were rushed by train from Pretoria to Naauwpoort, beyond Colesberg. De Wet had succeeded in fording, undetected, the swollen Orange River into the Cape Colony on 10th February. Attached to Plumer's column the Light Horse made the first contact with him on 12th February.

Under the most trying conditions in rain and sloppy roads and on short rations, Plumer's mounted column followed De Wet as he headed west, south of the Orange River. They fought skirmishing actions with the rear-guard over several hundred miles in a great chase. Confronted by a number of encroaching columns, manoeuvring under the supreme command of General Kitchener, the raiding General De Wet was compelled to seek a passage over the flooded Orange River to return to the comparative safety of the Free State. He raced for more than 200 miles, desperately trying the flooded drifts along the course of a swollen river. On 23rd February, after at chase of 44 miles since morning, Lt. Col. A. Hennicker's column of Australian Bushmen and Royal Dragoon Guards and the Light Horse, rode down De Wet's rear-guard at sunset. The escort fled. Two guns, a 15-pounder and a pom pom were taken. A bare three miles ahead, De Wet was secure from blown horses pulling up in the gathering darkness.

General de Wet crossed the Orange River just west of Norval's Pont on 28th February. The invasion and attempted rebellion in the Cape Colony had failed. In the attempt, De Wet lost the biggest part of his commando and all of his transport and guns. On the 23rd the Light Horse lost Lieutenant Farquarson and two men wounded. Trooper J. flanegan died from wounds and was buried at Norval's Pont.

---

[1] A saucer-like depression
[2] In a Diary in the Karri-Davies Collection
[3] In a Diary in the Karri-Davies Collection
[4] From Lieutenant-Colonel McKenzie's diary in the Kerri-Davies Collection
[5] From the diary of Lieutenant-Colonel Duncan McKenzie

We Rest Here Content

Chapter 12
SEPTEMBER 1901 – FEBRUARY 1902
THE IMPERIAL LIGHT HORSE BRIGADE ACTION IN THE
HARRISMITH – BETHLEHEM – REITZ REGION, IN THE ORANGE FREE STATE

In despatches on 8th September 1901, Kitchener referred to: "A third column which will work from Bethlehem–Orange River Colony as a centre, has just been organized at Harrismith. It will be under the command of Brigadier-General Sir John Dartnell and will consist of two regiments of Imperial Light Horse specially equipped with a view to securing increased mobility." The Light Horse Brigade was one of a number of columns under the supreme command of Lieutenant-General L. Rundle. Based at Bethlehem, the Light Horse was opposed in the area by General De Wet. With a force of up to 3,000 burghers usually split up into small parties, De Wet used the village of Reitz, 32 miles north of Bethlehem, as the centre of operations. Bethlehem was a small village on the eastern approaches to the Drakensberg range in the north-east corner of the Free State. It was dependent for supplies on Harrismith, the terminal of the railway from Natal, 57 miles further east.

As a special mobile force, the Light Horse Brigade with almost 1,000 troopers made several night marches every week, based on information occasionally obtained from farmers but usually from Basuto guides under an Intelligence Officer. Ranging for 20 to 30 miles, the guides collected information from kraals concerning the movements of the Boers. At night, with the assistance of guides, the squadrons searched as many farm houses as time would allow while marching to attack a laager in the early hours of the morning. The return to camp was frequently harassed by snipers and often turned into a fighting rear-guard action.

The Light Horse transport officer, Lieutenant Bill Adams, provided fresh transport at Harrismith of two wagons to each squadron. With 10 mules per wagon it was possible to cover 35 miles a day, loaded. At the end of several days spent in breaking in remounts at Bloomfield outside Harrismith, the Brigade struck camp on 1st September and marched into Harrismith. At 8 a.m. on the morning of 5th, the Brigade marched with General Rundle's column along the line of communications to Bethlehem, the 1st Light Horse on the right and the 2nd on the left of the march, covering a front of 10 miles.

'A' Squadron Light Horse, in advance of the column came under fire from a Boer patrol and was engaged in a skirmish. Colonel Briggs sent two squadrons in support but the burghers got away. When General Dartnell heard of the attempt to capture the Boers, he expressed displeasure that his permission had not been sought. That night the column camped at Daer's Farm near Elands River. On the 7th, Trooper C. Bremner, 'A' Squadron, 2nd Light Horse was killed in a skirmish. Sergeant-Major T. Sulivan, 'A' Squadron, 1st Light Horse reported:[1] "This part of the country is splendidly adapted for Boer fighting and I must say the average Boer here seems to be a better class than the Transvalers."

By the night of the 7th the Brigade was camped inside the picket posts within a mile of Bethlehem. Sergeant-Major Sulivan wrote: "Sunday today and the old General thinks it beneficial to all in camp to attend divine service. Some were making a religious reason for the occasion to try and avoid going."

Sergeant-Major Sulivan continued in his Diary on 9th September: "Left camp at 2 a.m. for the purpose of surprising a Boer laager. We found the Boers had got into a kraal. We rushed them soon after daylight under a heavy fire. At first they maintained their position, but at last they gave way and we took 150 horses and 150 cattle, 6 wagons and a cape cart. In the cart was Commandant

Boshoff and in one of the wagons was his wife and family. After two hours we returned to Bethlehem.

"10th. In Bethlehem, a very nice little town situated on the banks of the river Jordan. Most of the people have been sent to Harrismith owing to the scarcity of supplies. The General is quartered in a house in the town and seems to be having a good time. Trust old Jack.

"11th September. 'A' Squadron was occupied in camp duties, bringing in wood for the Brigade under heavy rain and a hail storm. The cold and windy night affected the horses.

"12th All the farriers are hard at it shoeing horses, as we are going to march tomorrow towards Senekal.

"13th. Marched from Bethlehem at 8 a.m., taking three days rations. Off Slabbert's Nek we came into communication with Campbell's[2] column coming across from Brandwater Basin. Our operations at Slabbert's Nek resulted in the capture of 19 wagons, six families brought in, one Boer killed and one wounded, 1,342 rounds of ammunition, cattle, sheep and grain.

"14th. In camp today we learned this morning that we are here for the purpose of holding the Nek while General Elliot's[3] Division drove the Boers towards us.

"16th. 'A' 'B' and 'C' Squadrons marched towards Reitz for about 12 miles. We came upon a party of Boers trying to make their escape from Elliot's column. We gave chase and drove them into the ranks of Elliot's column. 40 Boers with cattle and wagons taken. We pursued 150 men which we took for Boers and succeeded in surrounding them. They turned out to be British mounted infantry – a part of Bethune's column. They looked very small when they found they had surrendered to a few Imperial Light Horse.

"On the way back to the camp the rain came down in torrents and we were all busily engaged driving cattle and horses and sheep. Soon the rain turned to hail and a worse day I never had the bad luck to experience. Everyone was wet to the skin. We got back to our lines, but having no tents or any dry change, it did not matter much whether we were in camp or not.

"18th September. Joined General Dartnell and the 2nd Light Horse who were camped at Retief's Nek. The 2nd had a night march towards the Caledon Valley, where they met some Boers with a convoy. About noon we got in touch with the 2nd and they fired on our advance, taking us for the enemy. Whilst they were thus engaged a party of Boers came charging through to within 800 yards of them. We were in a commanding position and could see every move, with two squadrons of Light Horse between us and the enemy, which prevented us from taking action. Colonel McKenzie in charge of the 2nd Light Horse was in a terrible rage. It was whilst in this rage that old McKenzie was heard to say, 'that the 1st Light Horse would eat the Boers' while the 2nd was looking at them. The 2nd lost seven horses killed. Returned Bethlehem at 5 p.m."

On 21st September, General Dartnell and the 2nd Light Horse received orders from General Kitchener to proceed immediately from Harrismith to Natal, for General Botha was known to be again preparing to invade the colony from the eastern Transvaal. Thereafter the 1st Light Horse became an independent column based at Bethlehem, where the Regiment also celebrated the second anniversary of its birth in Pietermaritzburg.

Captain Normand, 'C' Squadron reported in his Diary: "1st Regiment continued rounding up sheep and cattle, wagons and fire wood and burning large quantities of mealies. Captain Harbord cleared the Boers out of a farm and found it full of preserved bacon, candles, matches etc, in fact a regular depot. Captain Harbord burnt the farm."

After dusk on the night of 26th September, the Light Horse under Colonel Briggs, with 450 men with one 15-pounder and a pom pom, began a rather circuitous march to Reitz, a village much used by De Wet. Near the drift closest to the town they surprised Boer outposts, discovered sheltering in a farm house. Four burghers were taken from a double bed.

S.-M. Sulivan described the march: "To Reitz to take it unawares. Rushed several farms on the way and always found a few Boers. In one found Kritzinger and son, both perfect curios, being dressed up in sheep skin garments. Just before reaching the town of Reitz, when we entered a house looking for burghers, two young women in their beds gave a man who struck a match a crack on the jaw. Then they began to scream like mad. This looked suspicious and soon there was a crowd of men in the room. They found a wily burgher hiding under a mattress in a bed. We hurried on as it was soon daylight. We surrounded the town at 5 a.m. and waited until daylight before going in. "The poor unsuspecting Boers who were still in bed, rushed from their lairs and made for the open. They were doomed to disappointment as they rushed into our ranks as we lay waiting for them at the end of each street. They came on riding bareback and in their bare feet. The Light Horse on seeing them coming never moved until they got within 30 yards of us, when we opened fire. Some of them stopped and held their hands up, but one of them being a little more daring than the others kept on. He was literally riddled with bullets.

"The bag for the march was 23 prisoners and among the prisoners was Commandant De Villiers. We camped on the hill overlooking the town without lights for we knew that the Boers were closing down on us. They kept making things unpleasant by firing at us." De Wet had gathered his burghers and was preparing to harry the column on the way back to Bethlehem.

Captain Normand also recorded the raid on Reitz: "Completely surrounded Reitz at dawn, 32 miles away. Marched rapidly the whole night, capturing Boers sleeping at some farms en route. No one got out of the town as it was completely surrounded. We moved out and camped near the town water supply. In the morning a cape cart with the Landdrost of Reitz and another Boer unsuspectedly drove into town and were collared by our outposts. Heard from them that De Wet slept soundly overnight eight miles away. They had just left him."

With 23 prisoners in a mule wagon under threat of being shot if they attempted to escape, the Light Horse moved out of Reitz along the Bethlehem road at about 1 a.m. on the 28th. A few miles out the enemy set the veldt grass afire in the rear of the column, the flames burning down a slope on the left flank. In two columns 500 burghers galloped out of the dark through the glow and smoke of the burning grass to within 75 yards of the left flank. Steadiness in the confusion by 'A' and 'F' Squadrons, stopped the charge and the shouting of the exultant burghers. More good volleys were aimed at the retiring riders, silhouetted as they rode up the high ground in the light of the still burning grass.

Further along the road at Tyger Kloof Drift, De Wet's burghers waited at dawn on a commanding hill. As soon as the shells from the 15-pounder and the pom pom commenced to land on the hill the rifle fire died away and the burghers rode off. The open country to Bethlehem invited several more attacks on the rear-guard, repelled in each case with the support of the pom pom. The Regiment reached Bethlehem late in the afternoon after 48 hours' activity, riding and fighting without sleep. The casualties were light with only one man was killed and one wounded.

S.-M. Sulivan[4] gave an account of the return march from Reitz to Bethlehem: "About two miles out, 'B' Squadron in the rear broke in disorder, leaving us entirely at the mercy of De Wet and his men. The Colonel sent a message to 'A' to keep them in check, that is to Captain Donaldson. We galloped back to meet the onward charge of the Boers who were shouting as they came. When they saw us coming they seemed to waver a little. We dismounted and raked them with volleys and so silenced their shouting. The Boer prisoners in our wagon were certain their release was near and

Commandant De Villiers told the guard that in a few minutes he would be free. But due to the determination of the Light Horse he was doomed to disappointment. The Boers, seeing they had no Imperial Yeomanry against them gave us a wide berth and got away to take up a new position at a Nek they knew we had to pass through.

"Just as day was breaking, our advance guard came on to a hill overlooking the Nek. They opened fire in what was the beginning of a sharp engagement. When we got two guns on the flanks they became alarmed and broke in all directions. Our prisoners again became very despondent. Seeing his men break and pursued by us, Commandant De Villiers was heard to remark to the prisoners that the Imperial Light Horse were the most daring and reckless lot of men he ever came across. We got into Bethlehem at 5 p.m., losing one man killed, after covering a distance of 75 miles, fighting through half the way. Kitchener sent a message congratulating us on our success."

"1st October. A Boer doctor came into camp for medical aid for the men who had been wounded in the engagement with us outside Reitz. He said they had 20 killed and 30 wounded.

"3rd Made a night march along the Lindley road starting at midnight. Raided all the farms along the way until daylight, capturing Boers in all of them.

"6th There was a service in the village today, but the Light Horse apparently think that a game of football is more beneficial than going to church. These night marches are becoming a bit thick now, in fact it's a strange sight to see the Light Horse in bed now.

"10th It never rains in Bethlehem unless it pours. Still raining and we are all the more pleased. If it rains so much there will be no night marches.

"16th At a place called Slabbert's Vlei[5] we commenced operations by raiding farm houses, taking prisoners, some of whom we ran down as they attempted to gallop away.

"22nd Snow all along the Basuto border.

"27th Today we marched out along the Senekal road with the objective of getting firewood and forage on the wagons. We took 12 dismounted men for the purpose of setting a trap for the Boers. When nearing a place called Muller's Rust, we could see some Boers in front and on our flanks. In a conversation with some Kaffirs we learned there was a meeting held by Boers at a farm in the vicinity the previous night. Here we loaded up our wagons and before retiring the foot men concealed themselves in a kraal. Then we all turned homewards and as usual the Boers came up to this kraal where we had left the men. Four of them galloped up in front of our men, dismounted and commenced firing at the retiring party.

"After the first rifle report was heard, our men sprang from cover and fired into the four Boers, killing two and wounding one. The other got away, but was badly hit. We brought the wounded man into Bethlehem but he died the same night. The dead were left where they fell. The three were aged between 14 and 16 years. This was the first time we had set a trap since our arrival in this neighbourhood. No doubt it will have a very soothing effect on our friends the Boers."

On 3rd November the 2nd Light Horse returned to Harrismith after six weeks in Natal and Zululand. The Regiment formed part of the force stationed near the border above the lower Tugela, at the time when Botha's advance to the south was in process of being repulsed. The official records of the movement of troops to "Repel the invasion of Natal", show that[6] the 2nd Light Horse, made up of 485 officers and men, left Harrismith in five trains on 25th September. By the early hours of 26th, the Regiment, together with 443 horses, 250 mules and 23 wagons had arrived at Glencoe Junction. On the next day the Regiment entrained for Pietermaritzburg and Durban. From Durban three train loads of men, horses, wagons and mules left for Tugela, en route for Eshowe in Zululand.

We Rest Here Content

In despatches on 8th November 1901, General Kitchener reported: "The 2nd Imperial Light Horse which has been temporarily detached to the Zulu frontier at the end of September, returned to Harrismith by march route, on the 3rd November."

By mid-November the Light Horse Regiments were once again operating together under General Dartnell. During the combined months of September and November the Brigade carried out as many as 40 night raids, breaking up laagers and capturing live stock. Based at Harrismith on 15th November, the Brigade operated in conjunction with columns led by General Elliot and Lieutenant-Colonel H. De Lisle, in convoy and patrol duties, between Harrismith and Bethlehem and in clearing out valleys and kloofs.

S.-M. Sulivan recorded in his Diary: "24th November. 2nd Light Horse surprised Lauren's commando between Elands River Bridge and Bethlehem, surrounding a farm at night and capturing 11 Boers and killing two."

"26th Along the road to Elands River we surrounded a farm at 3 a.m. Boers on a hill overlooking the house opened fire and a man from 'D' Squadron got detached from the squadron and was spotted by a Boer concealed in rocks. The Boer ran forward on foot, shouting 'hands up,' at the same time firing at point blank range. When the Boer missed his mark, the trooper shot him in the stomach. His name was Brinsburg. He lived on the farm where he was shot. We carried him in to his mother in the house. The old lady was almost mad with grief. Her husband had been shot a year ago and two sons made prisoner. This was the last son left with her. Camped at Elands River Bridge for the night."

With the Wilge River running high between Harrismith and Bethlehem on 30th November, a combined force of 1st and 2nd Light Horse, converging from the two villages took 24 prisoners, 150 horses and 800 cattle. Along the Lindley road, north-west of Bethlehem, a flying column made up of Light Horse and Yeomanry searched for, without finding any of, De Wet's commando. Returning to Bethlehem, the rain was so heavy that the men camped overnight in a church.

General Kitchener despatched 15,000 men to the eastern Free State, to hunt systematically for De Wet and his commando over an area of 100 by 75 miles. Aided by local reports flashed by heliograph from kopje to kopje and by the excellent local "bush telegraph", De Wet evaded all efforts directed against him, often by slipping away to a different laager overnight. On the morning of 18th December, the Light Horse Brigade under General Dartnell, marching from Bethlehem to Harrismith, was heavily attacked at 11 a.m. in the valley formed by the Tyger Kloof Spruit, eight miles from Bethlehem. The advance party of 2nd Light Horse came under fire from a pom pom on a hill, an outcrop of the rugged Langberg Range away to the left. This seemed to be a signal for a concerted outbreak of Mauser fire and for a wave of burghers to come charging out of a kloof across flat land. The 2nd Light Horse dismounting, found cover in grass on a slight ridge.

The burghers manoeuvred around towards the rear of the column where the 1st Light Horse was in cover in the long grass from rifle fire coming from almost every direction. Each trooper carried three full bandoliers and the Light Horse fire was so rapid that after half an hour the burghers, without the expected support from reluctant waverers hanging back in the kloofs, began to falter before the tough resistance put up by the Light Horsemen. At the end of four hours and the arrival of a relief column from Bethlehem, De Wet's commando retired gradually to the cover of kloofs in spurs of the Langberg. The commando had more than met its match.

In despatches on 8th January 1902, General Kitchener reported: "After leaving Bethlehem on 18th. December, General Dartnell found himself opposed by a large force of Boers under De Wet who, occupying a position along the Tyger Kloof Spruit, disputed his advance, while he vigorously assailed General Dannell's flanks and rear-guard; sharp fighting was maintained throughout the day. "Every successive attack was gallantly repulsed by the two regiments of the Light Horse, until the approach from Bethlehem of the column under Major-General B. Campbell, who had established signalling communication with General Dartnell during the progress of the fight, finally compelled the enemy about 3 p.m. to beat a hurried retreat in the direction of Langberg."

Trooper A Eraser, 2nd Light Horse was killed. Surgeon-Captain T.J. Crean, Captain G. Brierley, Captain W. Jardine, Lieutenant J. O'Hara and seven men were wounded.

While attending the wounded under fire within 150 yards of the enemy, Surgeon-Captain Tom Crean was severely wounded in the stomach. Captain Crean was a six foot tall Irishman. In pre-war days he had a medical practice in Johannesburg. He joined the Light Horse when it was first founded in Pietermaritzburg and served, at first, as a trooper. He fought as a trooper at Elandslaagte and at Wagon Hill. After Wagon Hill he transferred to the Intombi Hospital medical staff. When Ladysmith was relieved he once again served as a combatant and commanded a troop until the middle of 1901.

For gallantry in the action at Tyger Kloof, Surgeon-Captain T.J. Crean was awarded the Victoria Cross. The citation read: "During the action with De Wet at Tyger Kloof 18th December 1901, this officer continued to attend the wounded in the firing line under a heavy fire at only 150 yard range, after he had himself been wounded and only desisted when he was hit a second time and as it was first thought he was mortally wounded."

In Harrismith on 23rd December, General Dartnell and his staff resigned from the Imperial Light Horse Brigade command. The *Times History* commented:[7] "The effective power of the column was somewhat impaired by the strained relations existing between Dartnell and the officers in command of the Imperial Light Horse. Accustomed for some time to act independently they seem to have given to their Brigadier less loyal support than he deserved. Dartnell who was strongly of opinion that a large column was needed for operating against De Wet, appealed to Kitchener in this sense and having been met with a refusal, resigned his command. The two regiments henceforth acted independently under Briggs and McKenzie."

From the beginning there had been a feeling in the Brigade that at 63 years of age, General Dartnell was not quite the ideal commander required for such a mobile force, which was so often under movement orders necessitating hard riding by day and by night, sometimes almost without rest over 48 hours.

On 24th December 1901, a covering force for the construction of the Harrismith–Bethlehem blockhouse line was made up of four squadrons of Imperial Yeomanry, with the gun of the 79th Battery and a pom pom. Under the temporary command of Major G. Williams, 1st Staffordshire Regiment, this force camped on a hill near Tweefontein, north-west of Elands River Bridge, a couple of miles ahead of the construction party. After a careful reconnaissance of the British camp, De Wet made a night march, approaching from the north-west. The hill called "Groen Kop" stood 250 feet above the veldt. A 250 yard plateau surmounted the steep sides, except to the east where the steepness gave way to a gradual slope.

In the early hours of Christmas morning, 800 Boers charged across the summit from the western crest, scattering the troops as they slept around the guns on the plateau and overwhelming the camp situated on the eastern slope of the hill. By 3 a.m. one hour after the firing of the first shots, the entire camp was left a shambles, with the triumphant Boers riding off with the two guns and wagons towards their favourite haven in the Langberg.

Two and a half miles east of Tweefontein, General Rundle was camped with a small detachment. When he heard that the covering force had met with disaster, General Rundle despatched a galloper to the Light Horse camp at Elands River Bridge, about 13 miles from Tweefontein. By the time the Light Horse arrived at Groen Kop, De Wet had already made off, but the work of destruction was only too evident, with officers lying around in pyjamas just where they were shot, hurriedly emerging from tents, and pickets lying dead in blankets. For being caught as they slept they had paid full penalty for such a dereliction of duty. No less than 57 officers and men were killed and 88 wounded. Among the 14 Boers found dead was Gert De Wet, a nephew of General De Wet.

Amidst the scene of death and desolation and camp debris, the Light Horse was specially saddened to find an old comrade, in Captain Crawley, lying mortally wounded. Captain Crawley had served in Natal with 'A' Squadron and had been wounded at the battle of Colenso. Invalided to England, he recovered and returned to South Africa as an officer in the Imperial Yeomanry. Between Christmas and the New Year the Light Horse Brigade became attached to strengthen General Rundle's position near Tweefontein. On a reconnaissance in the Langberg on 10th January 1901, ten prisoners were taken. From farms in the district the Brigade took 800 pounds of mealies, 200 pounds of flour and 800 pounds of wheat.

At dawn at the end of a night march near the Langberg on 11th January, Trooper Humphrey Osmond was allowed by his troop leader to reconnoitre where three Boer horses were grazing loose on the veldt. The horses were near a donga and just as Osmond was preparing to place a lead on the horses, he noticed a second group of horses and some Boers in a depression not far away. Trooper Osmond opened fire and the burghers quickly moved into the long grass. After some time and an exchange of rifle fire, Osmond decided to try and outwit the burghers by leaving his hat placed rather conspicuously on a boulder. Osmond then crawled around through the grass to outflank them. As soon as he reached a favourable position he rose in the grass and pointing his rifle caught the Boers by surprise and forced them to surrender.

Meanwhile, Osmond's horse had galloped away, but the capture was made complete by the arrival of Sergeant-Major Garnham with the troop. Nine Boers and 14 horses were taken. They comprised one of De Wet's signalling parties suitably equipped with a British heliograph outfit. Colonel McKenzie reported to Kitchener the capture of the nine Boers by Trooper Osmond and recommended him for the D.C.M. Although the capture was mentioned in despatches, the D.C.M. was not awarded. Trooper Osmond was less than 20 years of age.

Colonel Briggs reported on 26th January from the Langberg area: "Escorted the baggage of Colonel J. Dawkins' column into camp at Steyl Drift at 4 p.m. Sniping from the rear. Lieutenant Bamford slightly wounded.

"27th January. To Newmarket Farm, opposed by 200 Boers. Casualties, Sergeant Percy Cawood and Corporal John Davies. Both men were shot by Boers in khaki.

"29th January. Doing escort to the baggage.

"30th January. A night march to a small Boer laager at dawn, galloped after escaping Boers for seven miles – chase abandoned – one man slightly wounded.

"4th February. Across the Wilge River, took four hours to get baggage across.

"5th Marched, getting into position for the drive."

In 1901 Kitchener called for the construction of chains of blockhouses, at first along the railways and later extended in lines across the country. No less than 10,000 blockhouses were constructed, spaced at intervals of about half a mile. Without much fear of enemy artillery, which by this time was practically non-existent, these fortified buildings had a decided effect on restricting the free movement of the commandos.

By the end of January 1902, the blockhouse lines in the north-east of the Free State were complete. The lines extended from Kroonstad on the main railway going north-east through Heilbron and Frankfort to Vrede and Botha's Pass on the Drakensberg Range. From Kroonstad east to Lindley, Bethlehem, Harrismith and the Drakensberg, where the mountains and fortified passes formed a continuous line north to Botha's Pass. Altogether, a huge rectangle of 65 miles 140 miles.

On the 5th February, Kitchener drew up a continuous cordon of 9,000 men stretching between Frankfort in the north and Bethlehem in the south. Another 8,000 men manned the blockhouse lines of the rectangle and along the main railway going north from Kroonstad. Of the 1,500 burghers with De Wet, 300 were lost when they were either shot or captured facing the guns and searchlights of the armoured trains on the main railway, or as they came up against the northern blockhouse line between Frankfort and Heilbron where a few got through. De Wet and his followers escaped by slipping past the blockhouse lines between Lindley and Kroonstad. In his Diary on 6th February, Colonel Briggs wrote[8] from near Heilbron: "During the night at about 1.15 a.m. the Boers made a determined bid to break through the line, driving cattle through the pickets and they themselves came through the middle of them. About 20 got through with cattle, the rest being driven back. The Imperial Light Horse casualties were four killed and four wounded. The Boers had one killed, four wounded and nine taken prisoner." Two of the Light Horse wounded died. Wagons and horses were taken.

S.-M. Sulivan wrote:[9] "The firing during the night was the heaviest since Colenso."

Colonel Briggs recorded, 17th February: "Some Boers tried to pass through the line at Lieuwkuil at 1 a.m. and all through the night small parties continually tried to break through, but were easily driven back. There was firing most of the night."

S.-M. Sulivan recorded, 8th February: "Camped live miles out of Heilbron, took 60 prisoners during the day."

The number of unwounded Boers captured in the drive was 300. A total of 82 were either killed or wounded.

Colonel Briggs recorded: "9th February. The drive being over the column marched to Heilbron.

"13th Marched and crossed the Vaal to Haartebeestfontein."

S.-M. Sulivan said that it took all day to get the convoy across the Vaal River.

Colonel Briggs: "14 February. To Meyerton station this night."

S.-M. Sulivan: "17th Marched towards Standerton. Halted and bathed in the Vaal, getting ready for the drive to the Natal border."

Within a week Kitchener ordered another great drive in the rectangle between the blockhouse lines, working towards the Drakensberg mountain passes. De Wet in the meantime, turned back to re-enter the rectangle and join President Steyn at Reitz. In front of the cordons moving east were 3,000 burghers. S.-M. Sulivan recorded that the Light Horse Brigade re-crossed the Vaal from Standerton on 20th and on 21st February camped on the Kllp River at Steeles Drift. Two hundred burghers were seen on the south bank. On the 22nd the Brigade camped at Bothasberg and then marched along the blockhouse line to Vrede and beyond to the Natal border.

On 23rd February, De Wet and Steyn approached the blockhouse line at a point 20 miles south of Vrede with 900 burghers and many camp followers, women, children and old men. This particular section of the line was held by Australians and New Zealanders. Advancing at night behind a mob of cattle, De Wet broke through the cordon with about half of his force and the loss of guns and supplies. 31 burghers were taken prisoner, 14 killed and 20 wounded. The New Zealand detachment of 76 men bore the brunt of the assault, losing 23 killed and 43 wounded in an hour and a half.

Over 12 days the cordon systematically pressed forward towards the Drakensberg mountains, compressing and constricting the space between the troops and the fortified mountain passes. On successive nights the confined burghers made frantic but unavailing fierce rushes against the advancing line of troops.

In describing the events of 27th February, Sir Frederick Maurice wrote:[10] "Next morning as Briggs took his Imperial Light Horse forward, in advance of Sir Henry Rawlinson,[11] he was met by two envoys who prayed for terms on behalf of the entrapped commandos. No conditions were granted, only the retention of personal belongings and one hour to consider. Under the white flag, 648 burghers surrendered with 1,078 horses, 47 carts and wagons and 40,700 rounds of ammunition."

So it came about that the Light Horse played a prominent part in the surrender of their former Free State adversaries, the Harrismith and Heilbron commandos under Commandant Truter near Albertinia station on the blockhouse line between Harrismith and Van Reenen's Pass. More than two years had passed since the attack on Wagon Hill, when Trooper Mann, 'E' Squadron, wrote on 7th January 1900: "I have since found out that it was the old men of the Heilbron and Harrismith commandos who attacked us."

The entire drive over 12 days netted 778 prisoners, 2,500 head of stock, 2,000 horses and 2,000 wagons.

---

[1] In the Diary in the Karri-Davies Collection
[2] Major-General B. Campbell
[3] Major-General E. Elliot
[4] In his Diary in the Karri-Davies Collection
[5] Vlei – marshy ground with pools formed in the wet season
[6] Given in the Official *History of the War in South Africa* Major-General Sir J. Maurice
[7] *The Times History of the War in South Africa* L. Amery. Vol-5. Page 431
[8] In diary notes in the Karri-Davies Collection
[9] In the Diary in the Karri-Davies Collection
[10] Major-General Sir J. Maurice in the Official *History of the War in South Africa*
[11] In the 1914–18 War, General Lord Rawlinson, commanded the 4th Army and was Commander-in-Chief, Army in India, 1920

CHAPTER 13
MARCH 1902, THE 1ST LIGHT HORSE RETURNS TO THE WESTERN TRANSVAAL
PEACE PROPOSALS AND THE LAST GREAT DRIVES OF THE WAR

In the New Year of 1902, General De la Rey became very active in the western Transvaal. On 25th February, with 1,200 burghers from dense scrub in the country outside Klerksdorp he ambushed a convoy. The smashed convoy was supplying one of the few columns based away from the vicinity of the blockhouse lines. British casualties were 178 killed and wounded. Five hundred prisoners were released and left to find their way to the nearest British camp.

On 7th March a mounted column under General Methuen 1,600 strong, made up of men from 14 different units, started out from Vryburg with a section of the 38th battery, a wagon convoy and 300 infantry. The column was attacked and overwhelmed at Tweebosch, south-west of Lichtenburg. British losses were 200 killed and wounded and 600 prisoners. Methuen and De la Rey, well-tried adversaries all through the war years, met for the first time in a tent where Methuen lay wounded. De la Rey made arrangements for him to be sent to a British hospital. Once again the prisoners were released on the order of De la Rey and allowed to find their way back to the British lines.

To deal with the growing aggression of General De la Rey and his commandos, Kitchener built up a concentration of troops at Klerksdorp.

Meanwhile, at Harrismith, Kitchener paid the Imperial Light Horse the compliment of visiting their camp. S.-M. Sulivan wrote: "He paid the unusual honour to the Imperial Light Horse, in fact, we were the only regiment he spoke to."

On 12th March 1902, Kitchener ordered the 1st Light Horse to Klerksdorp and the western Transvaal. The end of the war was not far away and from this time it is not possible to trace the activities of the 2nd Light Horse.

Passing through Bethlehem and Lindley, "not a house was left standing in Lindley," the Light Horse crossed the flooded Rhenoster River to join a convoy at Vredefort and camped there for the night. At 6 a.m. on 18th March, the Regiment crossed the Vaal at Schoeman's Drift and marched to Potchefstroom, reaching Klerksdorp on 21st March.

General De la Rey was reported in the area west of the Ventersdorp–Klerksdorp blockhouse line. Kitchener organized a great drive to the main western railway, bounded by the Vaal in the south and the Lichtenburg–Ventersdorp blockhouse line in the north. During the operation the columns of 11,000 mounted troops marching without baggage, covered 70 to 80 miles within 26 hours, but De la Rey and the greater part of his force still managed to find gaps to slip through. Kitchener reported in despatches on 8th April: "Several parties broke through, one of 300 men, who were materially assisted by wearing khaki clothing, escaping between the columns." In the drive the Light Horse was attached to Colonel Henry Rawlinson's column. Colonel Briggs recorded in his Diary on 23rd March: "Night march of 35 miles with Haartebeestfontein on the right, where the Boers opened fire on our right flank. The drive started by a general advance ordered by Colonel Rawlinson. The Boers were gradually driven on to Geduld Farm, where they abandoned their guns and wagons and broke up, about 200 breaking across our front south of Hartebeestfontein. We got into camp north of Hartebeestfontein at about 8.30 a.m., having covered 75 miles."

S.-M. Sulivan reported the taking of four guns and transport, two pom poms and 138 prisoners, the result of 26 hours without off-saddling. The column returned to Klerksdorp on 26th March.

On 31st March the Light Horse marched to Korannafontein with Rawlinson. Korannafontein was situated about midway between Klerksdorp and Vryburg. In the first week in April the Regiment engaged in convoying around Klerksdorp. Also in April, Lieutenant-General Ian Hamilton assumed command of the considerable body of troops at Klerksdorp. Four columns totalling 16,000 men commenced a drive on a 100 mile front across south-west Transvaal towards the Bechuanaland border.

On the morning of 11th April the column led by Colonel R.G. Kekewich faced a determined attack from General Kemp's commando along the line of march close to the course of the Brakspruit, only a few miles from the junction of the Spruit with the Harts River, about 58 miles from Klerksdorp. Riding at full gallop from the south-west up a slight rise into a clear field of fire in broad daylight, 800 Boers charged into volleys from 1,500 rifles and six guns. At 300 yards out, most had already faltered in the gallop, although a few got to within 100 yards of the British line of defence. In despatches on 8th April 1902, Kitchener reported: "The enemy advanced rapidly to close quarters in a very compact formation, the Boers riding knee to knee in many places in two ranks, whilst their attack was supported by a heavy fire from skirmishes on both flanks. Many of the men of our advanced screen in forward positions were ridden over by the enemy, who pressed on rapidly to within 700 yards of the main body and convoy, keeping up an incessant magazine rifle fire from their horses as they approached."

The Boers were checked by mounted troops dismounting and moving steadily forward on foot to meet the oncoming charge. Commandant Potgieter fell within 90 yards of the position. General Kitchener reported on 8th April: "So far it was only a repulse, but the arrival of Lieutenant-Colonel Briggs with the imperial Light Horse, detached from the enemy's right flank from Colonel Sir Henry Rawlinson's force, turned the repulse into a rout."

On hearing the heavy firing the Light Horse galloped from a point seven miles eastward and arrived on the scene of the action at 8 a.m. The Boers lost 51 killed and 41 wounded, all of them picked up on the field by the British. The troops pursued the burghers for 20 miles along the road to Schweizer-Reneke. Wagons, 75 prisoners, two 15-pounder guns and pom poms were taken. That night the Light Horse camped on the Harts River.

Marching east, the Light Horse captured 15 Boers near Haartebeestefontein, before arriving at Klerksdorp on 16th April. In Klerksdorp they were inspected by General Kitchener, who said that the Regiment had the finest horses that he had seen in any column in South Africa. Kitchener also told the troops that the war was drawing to a close. He promised that the Light Horse would be represented in a contingent presently to be sent to England to take part in the ceremonies connected with the coronation of King Edward VII.

S.-M. Sulivan recorded on 19th April: "At a general parade to see Captain Normand – 'C' Squadron – get his D.S.O., General Hamilton informed us that the war was practically over. We all think that it is just about time."

About this time Sulivan also wrote: "Daybreak march. We were all making ready and saddled, then came the order to 'stand-To,' till further orders as there were real prospects of peace."

General Hamilton mustered his columns for a second drive to the main western railway on the wide front between the line in the north. S.-M. Sulivan described the last great drive of the war beginning with the march from Klerksdorp.

"23rd April. Marched and camped for the night at Witpoort.

"24th Marched destroying crops, camped at Brakpan.

"25th Strong force of mounted troops with empty wagons to collect mealies.

"26th Camped Palmietfontein. Not so many snipers here as a year ago.

"29th Collecting mealies in the surrounding Palmietfontein country.

30th Reconnaissance. More prisoners towards Boschpoort. All they seem to do is to try and escape from our clutches.

"2nd May. All hands destroying thousands of mealies in the district.

"4th May. One Light Horseman wounded when Boers tried to break through the blockhouse line.

"5th May. Arrived Kalk-Kraal. Not a Boer in sight.

"6th May. Struck camp at 6.30 a.m. and marched due west. Kekewich on the right and the Federal Australians on the left. Camped the night at Nooitverwacht and received orders to form a line for a drive to the Bechuanaland border. All are very eager for a fight as we have had none for some time now. A larger number of the enemy are reported in front.

"7th May. We were the centre of a line stretching from Mafeking to the Vaal. Marched towards the Hart's River which was crossed at a place called Nuids Hulp. Here we camped for the night. During the day 'A' Squadron was in advance. On our right were the Mounted Infantry and one of them was killed by the enemy.

"8th May. Marched. Terrible country. No water, but innumerable salt pans, camped Rondepan.

"9th May. Marched. Still the drive on. At noon found abandoned enemy wagons and at 3 p.m., met the border fence with British Bechuanaland. Camped 2 a.m. The enemy made a dash for our line but were repulsed at dawn. Six Boers killed.

"10th May. Marched through British territory. News of 105 captured and eight killed as a result of the drive. We came on the line at Devondale, 20 miles north of Vryburg. Not a bad haul at this stage of the game. The country we had to come through was very difficult owing to the scarcity of water and sand up to our knees.

"14th Left Devondale at 8 a.m., on the backward trek and camped at Tarantaal Kraal.
Awaiting orders from Pretoria.

"16th The full result of drive was 860 prisoners, 19 killed. A telegram from Kitchener complimenting the Imperial Light Horse for the magnificent way in which they worked. This is the fourth time he has paid us such a compliment.

"17th May. Marched 6 a.m. 'A' Squadron in advance. When approaching a farm we saw some wagons at the farm, each one flying the Red Cross. On closer examination we discovered that the wagons were the property of Mrs De la Rey who was living in a tent close by a pan near the wagons. We all pricked up our ears at the sound of such a very important personage, so we put on our best looks and approached the tent. I cannot explain the looks on the men's faces when we beheld the usual form of Vrouw[1] as is seen every day.

"The same old Kappie[2] and same genteel waist measuring the usual 53 inches round. Also three girls all of age. If I'm a judge, posing as hospital nurses. Further on we came on a salt lake. There we beheld the nicest sight we have seen for some time. In the lake there were hundreds of pink flamingos. When they took off to the wing, the brilliant pink colour dazzled in the sun, presenting one of the prettiest sights I have seen. We camped at a place called Kapolie.

"18th May. Several columns in line for Klerksdorp. The country we traversed today was a perfect desert, not a drop of water in the country and only very little where we camp tonight.

"20th May. Marched at 7 a.m. 'A' Squadron in advance. When through Kolfontein, the right flank of 'B' Squadron came on some Boers dressed in khaki. Our men took them for mounted infantry. Rode up to them and found 15 Boers in some bush. They took them prisoners and deprived them of their horses etc. We camped the night and Trooper Doval 'A' Squadron was sentenced to 14 days and discharged as useless for being asleep at his post.

"22nd. Camped north of Klerksdorp."

The Light Horse remained in Klerksdorp on camp duties and taking part in sports events. The announcement was made on 1st June of the Declaration of Peace signed in Pretoria on the night of 31st May.

On 2nd June, Kitchener telegraphed to say that a detachment of Imperial Light Horse should proceed to England to take part in the Coronation Celebrations. S.-M. Snlivan wrote: Every man thought that he had more right to go than the other. However, we got 25 N.C.O.'s and men and two officers to go to represent the Regiment. We had to be in Cape Town on the 6th to sail by the troopship "Bavarian".

"3rd June. Left Klerksdorp by train via Elandsfontein and from there by special train to the Cape. At the Cape there were representatives from all parts of the world and every regiment in the British Army, 2200 officers and men, the flower of the British Army."

Squadron-Sergeant-Major T. Sulivan No. 905, 'A' Squadron, 1st Imperial Light Horse, sailed by the troopship *Bavarian* at 5.30 p.m. on 6th June 1902.

---

[1] Housewife
[2] a sun bonnet

We Rest Here Content

CHAPTER 14
The Peace Treaty of 31st May 1902

The preliminary discussions between the Boer leaders that led up to the Peace Proposals began at Klerksdorp, the Boers travelling to the town on British passes from various regional bases. General J.C. Smuts was the last to arrive, travelling by British troopship, battleship and then by train, over a long journey from the furthest extent of his operations in the north-west Cape Colony. The discussions in Klerksdorp took place in a tent in the British camp, at the very time General Hamilton was beginning his operations from Klerksdorp to the western railway.

After discussions lasting two days, the Boer leaders agreed to negotiate with the British, journeying by train to Pretoria for talks with Kitchener. The leaders told Kitchener that they were not prepared to forego the independence of the Republics, an objective which the British Government advised the leaders through Kitchener that it was not willing to concede. After some discussion the leaders were granted facilities by the British to travel throughout the country for the purpose of conferring with the commandos. Time was allowed for the election of 60 delegates to attend a conference at Vereeniging on the Vaal River at the border of the Transvaal and the Free State on 15th May.

The delegates met in the sombre background of a countryside laid waste for the effects of the British policy of attrition. About 22,000 burghers remained in the field, spread over both Republics and the Cape Colony. The mobility of the commandos was greatly hampered and their effectiveness much reduced by the restrictions resulting from the blockhouse system. Lacking supplies of food and clothing, they depended for arms and ammunition on whatever was seized from British columns or the residue from abandoned British camps. The greatest privations were suffered by the women and children attached to the commandos in the field. Botha told the assembly of delegates: "One is only too thankful nowadays to know that our wives are under British protection." Botha made the statement with the knowledge that about 20,000 interned burghers, mostly women and children had died from disease.

It is estimated that at least 18,000 people were taken from the farms and held in what became known as concentration camps situated throughout the country. At one stage 43,000 Africans were also held in similar camps. The calamitous record of deaths in the camps was partly caused by the unsuitability of some of the first sites, by mismanagement in the early stages, by the poor health of the people arriving at the camps and because of the real difficulty in persuading people accustomed to a life of more or less isolation in the countryside to accept normal practices necessary to maintain hygiene in the close community of camp life. Although in the beginning the camps were managed by the Army, they were afterwards administered by a civil authority. Doctors, nurses and teachers were brought out from England. Children, but also many adults, attended the schools.

A Commission appointed by the delegates at Vereeniging made the journey to Pretoria for more talks with Kitchener. The discussions dragged on for nine days until the Commission returned to the delegates at Vereeniging bearing the final British terms. In the discussion that followed the Boer delegates were sharply divided, for the British Government insisted on the laying down of arms, together with the complete surrender of the independence of the Republics and the recognition of King Edward VII as the lawful Sovereign. It was not until the third day that the delegates reluctantly accepted the terms which also included the promise of financial assistance for the re-establishment of the ravaged farms and that responsible Government would be granted to the new British colonies at some early date.

The Peace Treaty was signed at Pretoria within one hour of the deadline imposed by the British Government; midnight on 31st May 1902. Over the following weeks the commandos came in from the field to lay down their arms before British officers and give an oath of allegiance to the British Sovereign.

The Declaration of Peace was signed on the threshold of the third winter of the war, almost two years and eight months after the outbreak of hostilities. The decision of the Boer leaders to sign away the independence of the Republics was taken in the full knowledge of the hopelessness of their cause after military defeats, of the pressing need for the rehabilitation of the country and in the future interests of the race.

The Imperial Light Horse Brigade was prepared to fight on indefinitely. The Brigade wanted the enforcement of unconditional surrender, rather than any form of negotiated peace, especially when it was considered that the end of all resistance with the complete collapse of the Boers was not far away.

On 16 June 1902, on the eve of the official entry into Johannesburg, the Imperial Light Horse Brigade was camped at Booysens on the southern outskirts of the town. In a parade on the following day, the Light Horse Brigade 1,200 strong, marched through the streets to the Market Square, led by Colonel Briggs and Colonel McKenzie. Very few of the original 500 were left. In the Market Square, General Kitchener took the salute on the site where the City Hall now stands. The parade took place in the presence of the towns people who made the afternoon a public holiday.

In his address of welcome to the Imperial Light Horse, Mr St John Carr, Chairman of the Johannesburg Town Council said: "You have arrived here with all honours it is possible for a regiment to have gained during the period of this campaign. We are proud that you have so well defended the honour and vindicated the character of the people of Johannesburg."

Lt.-Gen. Sir A. Hunter had inspected the Imperial Light Horse at first parade in Pietermaritzburg in 1899. Before the Royal Commission examining aspects of the war in London 1903, he said in evidence, "I had not long come from a tour abroad, where I had seen nothing but the picked guards of Sweden, Denmark, Russia, Prussia and Saxony and there was nothing I have ever seen here except the Irish Constabulary that could put a patch on them. Every man was a picture of manhood, he was beaming with intelligence. Their morale and their knowledge of the country were all excellent. Amongst them were men who talked Dutch, Kaffir and Basuto and they all had every element of success in them and they were a great success, a most undoubted success. They were the finest corps I have ever seen anywhere in my life."

We Rest Here Content

NAMES OF THE FALLEN
IMPERIAL LIGHT HORSE
ANGLO-BOER WAR 1899–1902
IMPERIUM E LIBERTAS (FOR EMPIRE & LIBERTY)

Scott Chisholme J.J. Colonel.
Doyeton D.E. Major.
Currie M.W. Captain.
Knapp J.C. Captain.
Yockney T. Captain.
Adams W.F. Lieutenant.
Brabant E.A. Lieutenant.
Halling A.R. Lieutenant.
Kirk E.E. Lieutenant.
Noel B.C. Lieutenant.
Ormond A. Lieutenant.
Pakeman J.E. Lieutenant.
Ralston. J. Lieutenant.
Sanders L.S. Lieutenant.
Hurst A.E. Reg. S.M.
Cuthbert E.H. Squad. S.M.
Lang A.J. Squad S.M.
Sandys G. Squad S.M.
Benson H.C. Sergeant.
Gawood P. Sergeant.
Melville A. Sergeant.
Haynes A.J. Sergeant.
Hendley C.H. Sergeant.
Howard G. Sergeant.
Marshall J. Sergeant.
Parkin H. Sergeant.
Wellsteed H.E. Sergeant.
Wileman G. Sergeant.
Burrows W. Far-Sergeant.
Woolley S. Farrier-Sergeant.
Atherstone E.O. Corporal.
Connell F. Corporal.
Davies J.E. Corporal.
Dickinson E. de C. Corporal.
Downer W.G. Corporal.
Dunn A.S. Corporal.
Ferrand G.A. Corporal.
Francis W. Corporal.
Gabriel W. Corporal.
Gollan T. Corporal.
Haddon J. Corporal.
James F. Corporal.
MacKenzie G. Corporal.
MacKenzie W. Corporal.
Moore G.H. Corporal.
Nash H. Corporal.
Renouf H. Corporal.
Robins Corporal.
Twange A. Corporal.
Cameron G. Lance-Corporal.
Dixon I.G. Lance-Corporal.
Greathead M. Lance-Corp.
Nettleship G.W. Lance-Corp.
Ritchie D. Lance-Corporal.
Abercrombie H. Trooper.
Ager W. Trooper.
Albrecht-H. V.C. Trooper
Anderson P. Trooper.
Ashman J. Trooper.
Atlay C.C. Trooper.
Bailey I.J. Trooper.
Bain W. Trooper.
Barrett I.R. Trooper.
Barry J. Trooper.
Belcher C. Trooper.
Bremmer G. Trooper.
Bentley H. Trooper.
Bewsher J. Trooper.
Blake J. Trooper.
Blackeway N.C. Trooper.
Bonsey G. Trooper.
Boome H.S. Trooper.
Bouchier A. Trooper.
Brady P. Trooper.
Bristol B.L. Trooper.
Bromham L. Trooper.
Brown A.C. Trooper.
Butler R.O. Trooper.
Bywater A. Trooper.
Burgers D. Trooper.
Cairns A. Trooper.
Campbell J. Trooper.
Cashman T.S. Trooper.
Carter J. Trooper.
Chadwick T.C. Trooper.
Chinnock W.W. Trooper.
Clark E. Trooper.
Clarke T. Trooper.
Coltart C. Trooper.
Cox H. Trooper.
Cribb D.H. Trooper.
Cunningham J.P. Trooper.
Dawson R.M. Trooper.
Davis C. Trooper.
Davies R.J. Trooper.
Davies W. Trooper.
Dearlove F. Trooper.
Drennan G.W. Trooper.
Downing J.E. Trooper.
Edmondson H. Trooper.
Erasmus J. Trooper.
Evans W. Trooper.
Falconer D. Trooper.
fisher F. Trooper.
Fitzpatrick G. Trooper.
flanegan J. Trooper.
Foley R.A. Trooper.
Farren R. Trooper.
Fraser A. Trooper.
Gardner C.T. Trooper.
Goddard S. Trooper.
Gorton H.C. Trooper.
Guthrie-Smith D. Trooper.
Hanks G. Trooper.
Harding C. Trooper.
Harding H. Trooper.
Hooper C. Trooper.
Howell C. Trooper.
Hervey L. Trooper.

Hunt F. Trooper.
Hutchison F. Trooper.
Hogg W.S. Trooper.
Jackson A.P. Trooper.
Johnson T. Trooper.
Johnson A. Trooper.
Jones P. Trooper.
Kennedy P. Trooper.
King G. Trooper.
Knowles T. Trooper.
Ledingham J. Trooper.
Lawrence W. Trooper.
Langley M. Trooper.
Lane H. Trooper.
Leak R. Trooper.
Lee J. Trooper.
Longden W.H. Trooper.
Lind G. Trooper.
Manning C. Trooper.
Marsden C. Trooper.
Maxwell J. Trooper.
MacKenzie R. Trooper.
McCabe A. Trooper.
McClintock K. Trooper.
McChesney E. Trooper.
Melville W. Trooper.
Miller V. Trooper.
Moodie A.P. Trooper.

Macatta E. Trooper.
Murray B. Trooper.
Murray W. Trooper.
Mapleston H. Trooper.
Norwood M. Trooper.
Nicol R. Trooper.
Ochse H. Trooper.
Ogston F. Trooper.
O'Hagen H. Trooper.
O'Shea M. Trooper.
Paterson D. Trooper.
Parmenter H. Trooper.
Pearce F. Trooper.
Preston T. Trooper.
Pierce W. Trooper.
Pinnick A. Trooper.
Raynor G. Trooper.
Rex C.H. Trooper.
Robinson C. Trooper.
Rogers F. Trooper.
Saunders W. Trooper.
Sillery A. Trooper.
Simpson G. Trooper.
Simpson I. Trooper.
Shortt A. Trooper.
Smallwood F. Trooper.
Stewart B. Trooper.
Swanson A. Trooper.

Smith T. Trooper.
Taylor J.G. Trooper.
Taylor A. Trooper.
Taylor H.E. Trooper.
Tennant S. Trooper.
Thomas I. Trooper.
Thirlwall H. Trooper.
Tucker P.Y. Trooper.
Tute R. Trooper.
Torgins S. Trooper.
Townsend J.W. Trooper.
Upton C. Trooper.
Wallace E.H. Trooper.
Walshlaager E.H. Trooper.
Wingate J. Trooper.
Williams N. Trooper.
Winter E. Trooper.
Weid E. Trooper.
Wilkes W. Trooper.
White C. Trooper.
Whitaker H. Trooper.
Whittaker C. Trooper.
Whittle R. Trooper.
Wheeler F. Trooper.
Wright A. Trooper.
Woollcott C. Trooper.
Wolseley H. Trooper.

We Rest Here Content

THE IMPERIAL LIGHT HORSE HONOURS
AWARDS ANGLO-BOER WAR 1899–1902
LMPERIUM ET LIBERTAS (FOR EMPIRE AND LIBERTY)

VICTORIA CROSS

Trooper Herman Albrecht
Surgeon-Captain Thomas J. Crean
Captain Robert Johnstone
Captain Charles H. Mullins

K.C.B.

Colonel Sir Aubrey Woolls-Sampson

C.M.G.

Major H. Bottomley
Major H. Mullins

D.S.O.

Davies, Surgeon-Major, W.T.F.
Donaldson, Lieutenant-Colonel J.
Fowler, Captain C.H.
Jardine, Captain W.
Mathias, Lieutenant G.M.
Normand, Captain P.H.

D.C.M.

Francis, Trooper W.
Harrison Reg-Serg-Major R.
Latham, Trooper S.F.
London, Trooper S.F.

C.M.G., C.B.

McKenzie, Lieutenant-Colonel D. D.S.O.
Fitzgerald, Lieutenant P.D.
Royston, Lieutenant-Colonel J.
MacKay, Major D.W.
Pollack, Captain J.C.

D.C.M.

Sutherland, Reg.-Serg.-Major
Miller, Sergeant H.
Mansen, Trooper A.
McKenzie, Trooper C.K.
Metcalfe, Trooper F.H.
Norton, Corporal W.H.
Osborne, Sergeant
Russell, Corporal C.H.
Savory, Corporal H.
Warby Corporal E.W.
Weir, Corporal W.A.

MENTIONED IN DESPATCHES

Bombal, S.-S.-Major R.
Bottomley, Captain H. (Twice)
Bridges, Lieutenant G.T.
Brierley, Captain G.T. (Twice)
Briggs, Lieutenant-Colonel C.J. (Twice)
Brown, Corporal D.
Codrington, Captain W.R.
Cranna, Sergeant W.
Curry, Sergeant T.
Curry, Captain W.M.
Davies, Surgeon-Major W.T.F. (Twice)
Despard, Corporal G.W.B.
Donaldson, Lieutenant-Colonel J. (Twice)
Doveton, Major D.E.
Dryden, Lieutenant I.H.
Duirs, Lance-Corporal A.B.
Edwards, Lieutenant-Colonel A.H.M. (Twice)
Fitzgerald, Lieutenant P.D.
Fowler, Captain C.H. (Twice)
Francis, Trooper W. (Twice)
Halling, Lieutenant A.R.
Harrison, Reg.-Serg.-Major R.
Hughes, Corporal W.G.
I-luntly, Lieutenant D.H.
Jardine, Captain W. (Twice)
Johnston, Corporal D.
Kelly, Trooper T.
Kirk, Captain E.E.
Knapp, Captain J.C.
Latham, Trooper D.W.
London, Trooper S.F. (Twice)
Loveland, Corporal W.G.
Matheson, Corporal R.F.
Mathias, Lieutenant
Maxwell, Lieutenant D.L.
Metcalfe, Trooper F.I.-I. (Twice)
Mullins, Captain C.H. (Twice)
Normand, Captain P.H. (Twice)
Norton, Corporal W.H. (Twice)
Orr, Captain J.E.
Osborne, Sergeant
Osmond, Corporal H.D.
Phillips, Corporal A.J.
Rogers, Major H.A.
Rowell, Corporal J.B.

Russell, Corporal C. (Twice)
Savory, Corporal H. (Twice)
Scott Chisholme, Colonel J.J.
Search, Trooper R.E.
Smith, Trooper J.P.
Sulivan, Sq.-S.-Major T.
Symonds, Corporal M.I.
Tyron, Lieutenant S.K
Warby, Corporal E.W. (Twice)
Webb, Lieutenant B.F.
Weir, Corporal W.A.
Woolls-Sampson, Major A. (Twice)
Nicholson Lieutenant B.
Belton, Sergeant E.A.

MENTIONS IN DESPATCHES

General Buller's Despatch, The Convent, Ladysmith, 14th March 1900:
"Lance-Corporal A.B. Duirs, conspicuous gallantry on several occasions, in carrying out dangerous reconnaissances."

General Buller's Despatch, The Convent, Ladysmith, 30th March 1900:
"Captain H. Bottomley and Lieutenant T. Bridges – Royal Artillery attached – recommended for good work."

General Kitchener's Despatch, 8th May 1901:
"Sergeant Osborne, went back under fire and took out of action Trooper Law who would otherwise have been captured." This took place when De la Rey's convoy and guns were captured near Vaal Bank – 24th March 1901. D.C.M. awarded 23rd April 1901.

General Kitchener's Despatch, 8th May 1901:
"Captain W.R. Codrington – 11th Hussars, attached Imperial Light Horse – an officer of great promise. Has several times done good work when placed in command of detached parties." This was with Colonel Benson in operations in the Gatsrand, 16th March to 3rd April 1901.

General Kitchener's Despatch, 8th May 1901:
"Captain P.H. Normand, Lieutenant Dryden, Lieutenant Holling, Captain G.F. Brierley, Captain J. Donaldson, brought to notice in the capture of De la Rey's guns, 24th March 1901." Captain Normand was awarded the D.S.O. by the War Office by telegram 9, dated 23rd April 1901.

General Kitchener's Despatch, 8th May 1901:
"Trooper D. Brown, carried Sergeant Currie whose horse had been shot, out of close range under fire. Promoted to Corporal by Order of the Commander-in-Chief."

General Kitchener's Despatch, 8th July 1901:
"Lieutenant D.L. Maxwell, on 31st December 1901, at Hartebeestfontein, though wounded, remained with his patrol till he fainted from loss of blood."

General Kitchener's Despatch, 8th July 1901.
"Sergeant E.A. Belton, for good service in Eastern Transvaal, during Lieutenant-General French's operations, February, March, April 1901."

General Kitchener's Despatch, 8th August 1901:
"Lieutenant B.F. Webb, for on 17th July 1901, at Bultfontein, charging a Boer position with only 12 men and taking it, shooting two Boers himself with his pistol."

General Kitchener's Despatch, 8th August 1901.
"Corporal W.G. Hughes, Troopers T. Kelly, M. Symonds, D. Johnston, the first men up in a charge on a position held by a strong force of the enemy at Doornbult, western Transvaal, 17th July 1901. Corporal Hughes promoted to Sergeant and Troopers Kelly, Symonds and Johnston to Corporal by The Order of the Commander-in Chief."

General Kitchener's Despatch, 8th August 1901:
"Trooper J.P. Smith, at Doornbult, western Transvaal on 17th July 1901, a party retiring and one man being dismounted, he at great personal risk, returned and took him out of action on his own horse, the enemy at the time being within 400 yards."

General Kitchener's Despatch, 8th August 1901.
"Trooper B. Rowell, in charge of a pack horse with ammunition and accidentally left behind when the patrol retired, though hotly pursued by the enemy, who at one time got within 50 yards of him and heavily fired on, stuck to his pack horse and brought it out to safety. Promoted to Corporal by order of the Commander-in-Chief."

General Kitchener's Despatches, 8th December 1901.
"Captain W. Jardine and Captain J. Donaldson on 27th September were conspicuous for their coolness and promptitude in fighting in the Reitz district."

General Kitchener's Despatches, 8th December 1901:
"Trooper R.E. Search, in action near Reitz 28th September 1901, seeing the enemy making for an important position, galloped alone across their front and then continued to fight though wounded. Promoted to Corporal by the order of the Commander-in Chief."

General Kitchener's Despatches, 8th December 1901.
"Corporal R.F. Matheson, Trooper A. Phillips for good capture of three armed Boers, 22nd September 1901. Corporal Matheson promoted to Sergeant and Trooper Phillips promoted to Corporal by orders of the Commander-in-Chief."

General Kitchener's Despatches, 8th March 1902:
"Trooper H.D. Osmond for single handed capture of 8 armed Boers in the Langberg, 11th January 1902. Promoted to Corporal by order of the Commander-in-Chief."

General Kitchener's Despatches, 8th March 1902:
"Captains G.T. Brierley and W. Jardine for good work in holding their position against an attack at Langberg, 18th December 1901."

General Kitchener's Despatches, 1st June 1902:
"Lieutenant B. Nicholson, with three men captured 18 Boers on 15th April 1902 at Yserspruit, after a long chase."

General Kitchener's Despatches, 1st June i902:
"Troopers W.G. F. order, W.A. Allen and E. Eldridge at Yserspruit on 15th April 1902, captured 18 Boers after a long chase. Promoted to Corporal by the order of the Commander-in-Chief."

THE POSTHUMOUS AWARD OF THE VICTORIA CROSS TO TROOPER HERMANN ALBRECHT NO. 459 1st IMPERIAL LIGHT HORSE

The following has been extracted from *The History of the Victoria Cross* by Phillip A. Wilkins.
The following announcement appeared in the *London Gazette*, 8th August 1902:
"The King has been graciously pleased to approve of the Decoration of the Victoria Cross being delivered to the representatives of the undermentioned officers, non-commissioned officers and men who fell during the recent operations in South Africa in the performance of acts of valour, which would in the opinion of the Commander-in-Chief of the Forces in the field, have entitled them to be recommended for that distinction had they survived.
H. Albrecht, Trooper 459 Imperial Light Horse. On 6th January 1900 at Wagon Hill, during the great assault on Ladysmith by the Boers, Albrecht behaved with the greatest bravery in leading a party of men who were dashing for the top of the hill to seize the position before the enemy could do so. Lieutenant Digby-Jones shot the leading Boer, the next two being disposed of by Albrecht, who during the stubborn fight which took place, unfortunately met his death."

MANUSCRIPT SOURCES

THE KARRI-DAVIES COLLECTION OF PAPERS IN THE AFRICANA LIBRARY, JOHANNESBURG

The principal Manuscripts in the Karri-Davies Collection used are the following:

Lieutenant-Colonel C.J. Briggs – 1st Imperial Light Horse – A diary.
Lieutenant-Colonel D. McKenzie – 2nd Imperial Light Horse – A diary.
'F' Squadron 1st Imperial Light Horse: A diary.
Captain H. Bottomley 1st Imperial Light Horse:- Diary and letter.
Squadron-Sergeant-Major T. Sulivan: 'A' Squadron 1st Imperial Light Horse: A diary.
Trooper C.S. Mann 1st Imperial Light Horse: A diary.
Trooper P.Y. Tucker 1st Imperial Light Horse: A diary.
Trooper F.R. Vernon 1st Imperial Light Horse: A diary.

PRINTED SOURCES

The Johannesburg *Star* – 16 June 1902.

Amery, L.S. *Times History of the War in South Africa*. London. Sampson Low, Marston, 1902-5.

Bridges, Lieutenant-General Sir T. *Alarms and Excursions* Longmans Green and Co. London, New York, Toronto. 1938.

De Wet, C. General. *Three Years War October 1899-June 1902* Westminster. Archibald Constable and Co. Ltd. 1902.

Creswicke, L. *South Africa and the Transvaal War* Edinburgh, T.C. and E.C. Jack. 1900.

Garibaldi, G.A. *Toast To Rebellion* London John Lane. The Bodley Head. 1936.

Kestell, J.D. *Through Shot and flame* London. Methuen & Co. 1903.

Harbord, Captain. *Froth and Bubble* London. Edward Arnold and Co. 1915.

Gibson, George F. *The Story of the Imperial Light Horse* G.D. & Co. 1937. All Rights Reserved.

Ian Hamilton & Mr Justice Woolls-Sampson. *Anti-Commando* London. Faber & Faber, 24 Russell Square.

Nevinson, H.W. *Fire of Life* London. James Nisbet & Co. Ltd., in association with Victor Gollanz.

Maurice, Major-General Sir F. *Official History of the War in South Africa* London. Hurst & Blackett. 1907.

Stirling, J. *The Colonials in South Africa, 1899-1902* William Backwood & Sons. Edinburgh & London, 1907.

Stuart, John. *Pictures of the War* Westminster. Archibald Constable & Co. Ltd. 1902.

Watkins-Pitchford, H. *Besieged in Ladysmith* Pietermaritzburg. Shuter and Shooter. 1964.

Her Majesty's Stationery Office, London. 1899.

Further Correspondence Relating to Political Affairs in the South African Republic. His Majesty's Stationery Office, London. South African Despatches 1900-1902.

Willkins, Philip A. *The History of the Victoria Cross* London. Archibald Constable and Co. Ltd. 1904.

The Imperial Light Horse Regiment

Accounts of their actions and

other incidents by

various authors

JOHN JAMES SCOTT-CHISHOLME

JOHN JAMES SCOTT-CHISHOLME, of the ancient Border family of Chisholmes of Stirches in Hawick, was born at Stirches on 1st August, 1851. His earlier services were with the 9th Lancers, with which Regiment he served in the Afghan War 1876–80. On the 13th December while attending the burial of killed in an action near Kila Kasi, the 9th Lancers were suddenly ordered to turn out. With the 5th Punjab Cavalry and some of the 14th Bengal Lancers and Guides Cavalry, the 9th fell in with the enemy near the Siah Sing heights, and catching them on both flanks scattered them over the plain. In the charge of the 9th Lancers the Commanding Officer, Captain Butson was killed and Captain Scott-Chisholme was shot through the thigh, the flash of the rifle burning his clothes, so close was the discharge. In spite of his very severe wound, Scott-Chisholme remained in the saddle and brought the regiment out of action. For this gallant conduct he was promoted Brevet Major.

For some years Scott-Chisholme was Military Secretary to the Governor of Madras, and on May the 8th, 1889, he exchanged into the 5th Lancers and took his regiment from India to Natal in 1898. After being granted an extension of a year in command, he left the regiment in August 1899.

In September of that year the assent of the Imperial Government was received and authority granted for the formation of a corps of 500 mounted riflemen for service in the event of hostilities. Colonel Scott-Chisholme was given the task of organising and commanding tbe Corps, and Her Majesty the Queen granted to it the title of the "Imperial Light Horse." In its first action at Elandslaagte Hill, the regiment lost its gallant Colonel in the moment of victory. Twice wounded he still struggled on at their head until a third bullet gave him the death he always desired.

His example and d6evotion to duty was never forgotten by his Light Horsemen, whose doings during the long war were ever in keeping with their early training.

The ideal of a "Beau sabreur," a splendid horseman, one of the best Colonels who ever commanded a Cavalry Regiment and a sympathetic friend, he was beloved by the officers and men of his regiment. The memory of "Jabber" Chisholme will live long in the 5th Lancers. A monument has been erected on the spot where he fell, on Elandslaagte Hill, by his comrades in the 5th Lancers and the Imperial Light Horse, and another in his native place of Stirches at Wilton Parish Church. He was the last in the male line of the Chisholmes of Stirches.

(Extract from G.F. Gibson *The Story of the Imperial Light Horse* G.D. & Co 1937)

Major A.H.M. Edwards's appointment to command

Major-General Sir A.H.M. Edwards has written as follows:

"On the 25th October I was detailed to command the troops ordered to escort the remains of Colonel Scott-Chisholme for the purpose of burial.

"The funeral took place after dark and for some reason the customary salute of three volleys was not given, probably the Authorities thought it might draw the enemy's gun-fire.

"Scott-Chisholme's death, and the fact that the second-in-command, Major A. Woolls-Sampson had been very severely wounded, left the command of the Imperial Light Horse vacant.

"Friends suggested that I should apply for it, but I did not do so. I thought no more of the subject until the day after 'Black Monday' (30th October), when I was sent for by General French, who asked me whether I would accept the Command if it were offered me. This I agreed to do. He held out very little hope of my receiving such an offer, as he explained, there was considerable opposition to be expected on the part of some of the senior officers of the Regiment to the appointment of an officer from another Regiment.

"A couple of days later General French left Ladysmith, and, having heard nothing more on the subject from him I concluded that someone else had received the appointment.

"On the 4th November, I was sent for by the Commander-in-Chief, Sir George White, who offered me the Command, which I accepted there and then. He asked me if he could do anything for me, and I said I would like to be granted the temporary rank of Lieutenant-Colonel, which would enable me to exercise command without let or hindrance. This he agreed to do. He had evidently seen Karri-Davies on the subject, and I shall always remember how anxious he was to soften the blow that my appointment might be to the senior officers, because he sat down and wrote the draft of the order which eventually was promulgated in the Field Force Order.

"To the best of my recollection it read as follows:-
"At the request of Major Karri-Davies and the officers of the I.L.H., Major A.H.M. Edwards, 5th Dragoon Guards, is appointed to the command of the I.L.H. during the absence of Lieutenant-Colonel A. Woolls-Sampson, and is granted the local rank of Lieutenant-Colonel, while so employed.
"It appeared that on the previous day the I.L.H. had suffered heavily in action, losing two of their best officers, Captain Knapp and Lieutenant Brabant, and it is possible that influenced Sir George in coming to his decision. The next day I transferred my belongings from the 5th Dragoon Guards to the I.L.H.

"I took over from Major Karri-Davies who explained to me that he did not feel justified in retaining command as he had had no military experience, and it would not be fair to the Regiment, if he did. He promised me that he would give me every assistance and support. This I have no hesitation in saying he always did. As I got to know him, I found him to be a straight-forward, warm-hearted, generous man. A most extraordinary character, at times petulant as a spoilt boy, and at others blazing out into the role of a very high order of imperialist. I was assured by all that the greatest care had been taken in the raising of the Regiment."

(Extract from G.F. Gibson *The Story of the Imperial Light Horse* G.D. & Co 1937)

We Rest Here Content

THE BATTLE OF ELANDSLAAGTE

"They thought themselves worthy of great things — being worthy"
Aristotle ("Great Souled Man.")

About 4.30 p.m. the infantry attack had commenced. The Devons, under Major Park, advancing across the open in very extended order, made a frontal attack upon the Boer position, while the Gordons and Manchesters were working round to the right against the Boer left flank. The Devons advanced steadily through the artillery and Mauser fire to within 800 yards of the summit of the hill occupied by the Boers. Here they lay under an appalling fire for over half-an-hour waiting for the flank attack to develop and the order to advance. Considering the circumstances their casualties were not heavy, owing chiefly to the efficient handling of the men, and to the fact that their khaki uniforms blended well with the ground over which they operated.

Let it be recorded here, that the Devons, that day, set a magnificent example of courage and determination, in keeping with the best traditions of the Army.

As the Infantry began their advance, Scott-Chisholme, full of zeal and enthusiasm, refused to accept the passive role of spectator and approached General French, who said to him: "Well Chisholme, what do you want to do ?" – he replied: "I want to take that hill!" French answered: "Very well, take it!"

On the right flank the Manchesters and Gordons were pressing on to the attack where they were joined by the I.L.H. who dismounting, doubled out and extended on their right – they were eager to kill and willing to be killed. Still further on the right, 'B' Squadron of the 5th Lancers awaited their opportunity.

The two batteries, which had advanced straight to their front, following in the wake of the Devons and Manchesters, silenced, though only temporarily, the plucky Boer gunners on the hill. As the infantry reached the foot of the hill a violent storm, dramatic in its intensity, which had been threatening for some time, burst, and in a few moments had drenched everyone to the skin. In the failing light, no enemy was visible, but all could feel that the kopje was bristling with small bore rifles; as indeed it was, for a hail of bullets met the troops as they rose to the order for the final phase of the attack. Stumbling forward among the stones, jumping over the bodies of their comrades who had fallen before them, the line pressed on. A barbed wired fence partially checked the attack and men and officers fell in numbers as they crowded towards the gaps. More than half way was won, but there was no slackening of fire from the summit of the kopje although shrapnel rained upon it continuously.

Colonel Schiel and a handful of Germans came up from a farm behind the Boer position and made a gallant and well-timed attempt at a flank attack. The I.L.H., though hotly engaged towards their front, met this dangerous diversion with such promptness and resolution that it was soon defeated, the Germans being shot down to a man.

> Describing the fight, the Adjutant of the Regiment, Captain Barnes, writes:-
> "The enemy were strongly posted on their left flank end of the ridge, which the Imperial Light Horse attacked, not realising the opposition in front of them, and the increasing and unexpected severity of the Boer fire as they advanced by rushes up the hill. I must express my admiration for the coolness and determination of the men amongst whom I advanced to this day I can see vividly the men shooting deliberately in the halts between rushes-and my fear as a Regular, lest these dashing Colonials should out-distance me!
> The tenacity of the Boers was admirable in sticking it, I was hit by a Boer within ten yards of me at the top of the hill."

At last, from the valley below, the Devon bugles rang out the "Charge." The call spread along the line, and with a cheer and a great rush the frontal and flank attacks were pressed over the remaining murderous yards and the hill was taken, while the Boers either surrendered or went streaming down the reverse slopes. The "Cease fire" now sounded and the action was apparently over.

Suddenly, however, a party of Boers headed by General Kock (decorously garbed in frock coat and top hat), delivered a counter attack against the soldiers crowded on the ridge which came very near to being successful. Men, perplexed by the "Cease fire," and staggered by the sudden fury of the attack, fell back, uncovering the captured guns, which the leading Boers seized, and again opened fire.

Bewildered and angered by what seemed to them to be plain treachery, the I.L.H. leapt forward and re-attacking went berserk, the infantry rallied and again advanced. The Devons stormed a detached conical hill on the left of the position; for another mad minute the fight raged anew and the attack swept on, until Devons, Manchesters, Highlanders and Light Horse, fighting hand-to-hand with wild fury, using bayonet or clubbed rifle, recaptured the crest of the hill and pursued the retreating Burghers.

During the final charge the I.L.H. on the extreme right flank, swinging round the enemy's left, surrounded a farm house, "a strong point," and after a short encounter, stormed it, capturing 21 prisoners.

Immediately prior to the renewed attack the I.L.H. were able to assist their Regular comrades, whose casualties had been severe, particularly among the officers. Captain Charles Herbert Mullins, Lieutenant Robert Johnstone and Lieutenant A.E. Brabant, seeing for themselves the predicament in which some of the Regulars found themselves for lack of command, instantly rushed across to their aid, assumed their leadership, rallied them and reformed their line. For this singular act of leadership at a critical moment of the fight, all three of these officers were recommended for the Victoria Cross, which was awarded to two of them (related later).[1] During the Infantry attack, the Cavalry had taken up a favourable position, in anticipation of an opportunity of charging the enemy, on their line of retreat, when driven off the hill. Very ably led, they did valuable work. The moral effect of the charge which turned the Boer retreat into a stampede was great and lasting.

It was about 5.30 p.m. and under the stormy weather conditions prevailing, becoming dark, when their chance came.

The stubborn Boer defence broke, under the gallant and determined Infantry attack, the Burghers retiring northwards singly and in batches. It was then that the 5th Royal Irish Lancer Squadron under Captain Oakes, on the right and the 5th Dragoon Guards Squadron under Major Gore on the left, extended and charged. It was one of the Cavalry's few chances in the war. The effect was instantaneous. The sullen Boer retreat became a wild stampede, as the big English horses and the Australian walers on which the Cavalry were mounted charged down on the now desperately fleeing Burghers. Some of them fired from the saddle, but the Cavalry rode through and through the fugitives, doing severe execution. The Boers who had held the hill so stoutly were either scrambling wildly for safety, trusting in the handiness of their ponies to get them away, or surrendered.

The "Cease fire" again sounded and the scattered troops were rallied. The men fell in and cheered madly and the Gordon Highlanders Pipers played "The Cock of the North." The victory was complete. The enemy had been driven off a strong position of their own choosing and their retreat converted into a rout.

An added benefit was that in defeating the enemy so signally, a serious menace to the retreat of the Dundee force was removed.

Time does not efface from memory the dreadful night of the battle, searching for and succouring the wounded, collecting the dead in the pitch dark, rain and bitter cold over the extended area covered by the regiment during the battle. A farm house below the Elandslaagte Hill was requisitioned to receive the wounded. The Regimental Medical Officer, Surgeon-Major W.T. F. (Billy) Davies, tireless, cheerful, cheering and swiftly efficient, with his assistants, toiled during the whole of the night tending the wounded. Fires were made, food was prepared and all possible help and attention were given to friend and foe without distinction.

Trooper J. Hills-Jones, I.L.H., son of Major-General Hills-Jones, V.C., was one of the last of the wounded to be found, still wearing his monocle as though it were a permanent fixture. His comrades feared that he was in extremis as he had been shot through the throat and bled freely, but he relieved their anxiety by croaking thankfully that he preferred drowning in his own blood, to doing "those damned fatigues." He recovered from his wounds and returned to duty, but was again wounded at Witklip on the 7th July, 1900.

Then came the counting of the cost, and the price was high :--

    Killed and died of wounds ………………………….. 14
    Wounded Officers ………………………………..……… 8
    Wounded N.C.O.'s and men ………………….…… 26
    Total casualties …………………………………………… 48

The Regiment had lost its Leader, the beloved Scott-Chisholme. It would appear that he gave his life as an example, so that the name of the Imperial Light Horse might live. They had known him for only a few short weeks, but in the freemasonry of fighting men brought together by those tragic times, a week counted as a year in familiarising men with each other. The I.L.H. had found the leader they had wished for, a man whose patriotism, courage and dash fired their own. The last of a fighting line, he died knowing that victory was in sight, his young regiment he had trained and from which he had hoped and expected so much, had acquitted itself well.

The Colonel was bandaging a wounded trooper, during the lull just prior to the unexpected Boer counter attack, and was shot in the ankle. Waving his men on with his old Regimental scarf (the 5th Lancers) he called out: "My boys are doing well! MY BOYS ARE FIRST!"

"To see that little red rag going on and on and on without a falter, was the very bravest sight I have ever seen in my life. Marvellous to relate, he carried on untouched until the very last stage of the assault— the Boer counter attack."

"He had lived his short life and died his swift death like a hero. One moment leading five magnificent squadrons, every eye on him: the next he fall. all is over he feels it, dying sees it in the hurried side glance of those who press onwards following already a new leader."[2]

He was carried to cover by Trooper Clifford (Dick) Turpin, (a son of the the Rev. W.H. Turpin of Grahamstown), who survived Siege of Ladysmith only to be killed later in the war (in Marshall's Horse) and by Trooper C. Lamb who was severely wounded, losing a leg. The rescue was however to no purpose for the Colonel received two more bullets which killed him.

Colonel Willcox (5th Lancers) has recently written:-

"The silk scarf is in my possession. It is in a frame together with Colonel Scott-Chisholme's portrait and a plate bears the following inscription:-

    "This handkerchief was used as a flag by the late
    Colonel-Scott-Chisholme,
    Who was killed at Elandslaaqte
    when leading the I.L.H.

Presented by Lieutenant G. Palmer, 2nd Devon Regiment, by whom it was found, to the 5th Lancers."

Other officers wounded were Major Woolls-Sampson, Captain R. Barnes, Captain C.H. Mullins, Captain J.E. Orr, Lieutenants M.W. Currie, P.H. Normand, A.D. Shore and W.L. Forbes.

Major Woolls-Sampson was severely wounded in the thigh from which wound he never really recovered, it crippled him partially for the remainder of his life.

Notwithstanding this tremendous physical handicap he remained in the field to the end of the war. The day after the battle it was found that his leg had been roughly spliced, on the field, to a rifle as a splint and that this rifle was still loaded, the muzzle pointing to his armpit!

The Adjutant, Captain R. Barnes was also severely wounded in the thigh, and has a decided limp to this day, but fortunately it did not prevent his continued service in the Boer War and later in the Great War. The loss particularly in officers was severe.

Among the killed were Trooper W.T.H. Wolseley, I.L.H., a nephew of the Commander-in-Chief, and another very: promising well-known young man, Trooper Castell White, I.L.H., of Table Farm, Grahamstown. Trooper Greathead, I.L.H. (killed later at Wagon Hill) was the first to get up to Colonel Schiel — badly wounded who said to him: "Hello! You are one of the I.L.H.! Please give my regards to Woolls-Sampson and Karri-Davies;" and then as an after-thought he handed his rifle to Greathead adding: "You might care to keep this as a memento of this occasion."

Two Victoria Crosses were awarded to the regiment, a unique distinction, The responsibility of deciding on whom these greatly prized decorations should be conferred was placed on the shoulders of Captain Barnes, the Adjutant, who has written:-

"It was months after the battle that the two V.C.'s were given to the Regiment. As Adjutant I was told to make enquiries in the regiment to find out to whom in general opinion they should be given. We no doubt selected the two right men in Captain C.H. Mullins and Lieut. Robert Johnstone, but they were in fact given to the Regiment."

This was no doubt an unusual method of bestowing the greatly coveted Cross,[3] but in this case its value was, if possible, enhanced because all, who saw the splendid act of leadership, were in accord that the Crosses were rightly bestowed, the only regret being that the equally courageous action of Lieutenant Brabant was not similarly rewarded."

Charles Herbert Mullins, a son of the Manse, was born in Grahamstown, Cape Province, a product of St Andrew's College there and Keble College, Oxford, Barrister-at-Law (Inner Temple), temperamentally inclined to peace rather than war, yet in action sternly purposeful and a born leader of men, and in all things a very perfect knight *sans peur et sans reproche*. He was wounded at Elandslaagte and again most grievously on the march to the relief of Mafeking, which wound hastened his untimely death some years later.

Robert Johnstone, a very gallant Irishman, and International Rugby player was wounded in Ladysmith. He survived the war and is now living in Ireland.

A.E. Brabant, a son of Major-General Brabant, born in Cape Colony, brave and unassuming, with striking natural military gifts which had no chance to develop. He died from wounds received at Long Valley (Ladysmith) on the 3rd November, 1899.

Major-General Ian Hamilton, whose masterly handling of the Infantry contributed so materially to the victory, was recommended for the Victoria Cross; Major Woolls-Sampson was also recommended for the Cross, for his determined leadership. In regard to these recommendations a communication was received from the War Office, from which the following has been extracted:-

"With regard to Colonel (Local Major-General) Ian Hamilton, I am to observe that the act for which he was recommended was performed when he was commanding a Brigade, i.e. in the position of a General Officer. The Victoria Cross has never been conferred upon an Officer so high in rank. The Commander-in-Chief thinks this limitation a wise one, and that it would not be desirable to establish a precedent opposed to it. He is unable, therefore, to submit Major-General Hamilton's name to the Queen."

"I am to add that while Colonel Woolls-Sampson evidently led his men with much gallantry, Lord Wolseley does not feel that his conduct was sufficiently exceptional to call for the bestowal of the great favour of the Victoria Cross."

The Boers had fought with valour and determination holding their position to the very last:-
"During the most tense moment of the counter-attack the Boers had fought with an enthusiasm of fury, and an utter contempt of death which I never saw them equal again during the campaign."[4]

The Boer Artillery, under Major Hall, and Adjutants Smit and Erasmus, though outnumbered by six to one was served with skill and resolution. Though often temporarily silenced, they continued to serve their guns at shortening ranges up to the very last, even returning with the counter charge to fire case shot at the Devons. In most subsequent engagements, in which the Boers were defeated, they removed their artillery long before an assault was pushed home. It may be that at Elandslaagte the Boer Gunners were confident that the position could not be carried by assault so late in the evening – especially as from their position they hardly realised how close the flank attack had come or that, as one of their prisoner officers remarked; "Daar was nie plek om te vlug." ("There was no room for retreat.") The extending files of the Regulars and the Imperial Light Horse overlapped the reverse of the kopje and their fire swept the northern footpaths, while the rain of shrapnel destroyed every living thing on the western slopes.

The Boer losses were severe. Some 60 were killed; 150 wounded and 250 captured. Among the Boer dead were found Dr Coster, whose death was regretted by many of the I.L.H. who had known him personally and liked and esteemed him, Count Zeppelin, Landrost Bodenstein of Krugersdorp, Landrost Maré of Boksburg and Major Hall of the State Artillery. Lying wounded upon the hillside were General Kock, Colonel Schiel, Captain de Witt Hamer, of the Hollander contingent, Van Leggelo, the Public Prosecutor and other prominent Hollander and Boer officials.

"The Boer General Kock was mortally wounded. He was a man of gravity and distinction, dressed in a black frock-coat and tall hat, bearing himself during the ordeal of that dreadful night with complete self-command. No ancient Roman could have shown greater dignity and calm in the way he took the loss of his own life as well as of the battle." "I saw him once more before he died in Ladysmith, being tended exactly in every way as if he had been one of our own Generals."[5] The War Correspondents of the great London Dailies all wrote very appreciative accounts of the regiment in this battle, two of which are here quoted:—

THE MORNING POST:
"The Imperial Light Horse behaved with splendid recklessness. The final charge was magnificent. I was behind the Gordons and Imperials and saw it all. I consider it was the finest close fighting the world has ever known."

STANDARD:
"Colonel Scott-Chisholme commanding the I.L.H. obtained leave to join the infantry advance with his dismounted men, recruited from former residents of Johannesburg. They went forward with the Gordons and bore themselves with the coolness and courage of seasoned veterans. That is to say they fought side by side, foot by foot with a Regiment which owns no superiors in the world, and it does not appear that the Gordons had need to feel ashamed of their company."

A letter also appeared in *The Times* signed "South African":-

"There is a strange — a weird — trace of Nemesis in the fight at Elandslaagte, in that at the first fight in which the Reformers got their chance, there should fall before them — killed or wounded — General Kock, a member of the Executive; Dr Coster, who prosecuted them; Captain Schiel who was Superintendent of Prisons, while they were in jail; and Commandant Ben Viljoen, who represented Johannesburg in the Volksraad and persistently advocated that the Reformers should be shot without form of trial as rebels, and who was most largely responsible for the Boer order that in the case of the Johannesburg men no quarter must be given and no prisoners must be taken. They have had their fight and have taken, as one confidently expected, a soldier's revenge, if one may judge by the experience of one Reformer — Colonel Frank Rhodes who was able to give up his bed and blankets to the wounded Boer General Kock on the night of the battle, Truly a poetic revenge!"

It is a pleasure to record that Commandant Viljoen's fulminations must have fallen on deaf ears. The I.L.H. wounded, who later fell into enemy hands, were always treated with humanity and generally with the greatest kindness. The few unwounded I.L.H. prisoners who were captured (never more than a Corporal's command, but more or this anon) were treated fairly and any animosity shown towards them was rather because they could speak Dutch than that they were members of the I.L.H.

Any soldier reader will appreciate the illuminating significance of the following incident, but, for the benefit of those not initiated, let it be said that, to the lovable Tommy Atkins of that period, Beer was an Article of Faith, and of all in his bright calendar none was more devoutly worshipped than Saint John-Barleycorn. On the day after the battle the I.L.H. reached camp weary and worn and dismounted alongside the Gordon's lines as that Regiment was on the point of drawing a beer ration. Spontaneously as each Gordon received his measure he carried it across and gave it to a comrade in the I.L.H. — a generous self-denying tribute from a great fighting regiment to its younger brother-in-arms.

The foregoing account of the Battle of Elandslaagte (excluding the actual part played by the I.L.H. and those portions specially acknowledged) is based on:

"The History of the War in S.A., 1899-02," by Major-General Sir F. Maurice,

"The Times History," by Amery, "The History of the 5th R.I. Lancers," by Col. Wilcox,

and "The S.A. and Transvaal War," by Louis Creswicke.

(Extract from *The Story of the Imperial Light Horse* by G.F. Gibson.)

---

[1] Captain Mullins, VC, CMG the senior ILH officer present at the final charge, was instructed to make a written report of the the battle for official purposes. He did so, but before submitting the report, he forwarded it to Colonel Dick-Cunyngham, the officer commanding the Gordon Highlanders (who was also wounded) for his approval. His approval having been obtained, the report was sent on to Headquarters.

[2] *Anti-Commando*, by General Ian Hamilton and Victor Sampson.

[3] It had been done before in the Indian Mutiny in the 78th Highlanders.

[4] *Anti-Commando*, by General Ian Hamilton and Victor Sampson.

[5] *Anti-Commando*, by General Ian Hamilton and Victor Sampson.

A NIGHT SORTIE

On the evening of the 7th December, the Colonel, on returning to camp from Wagon Hill found the following letter from the Chief of Staff waiting:-

"General Howard and Colonel Knox are both to be allowed to carry out schemes tonight. These schemes will, if they do nothing else, put the Boers on their guard against night enterprises. I am trying to persuade Sir George that tonight is, therefore, the very last chance to take a gun, I believe it is possible for a small party of men to rush Gun Hill."

"If Sir George says YES, I will advise him to call tonight for 100 volunteers from the I.L.H. ..."

"Sir George will be back at 7.30 and I will let you know; not a word to anybody."

"We would leave by 11.30 from Colonel Knox's defence. I would arrange the demolition party apart from the I.L.H. I hope to go as a spectator. We would want bayonets."

"Yours sincerely,
(Signed) ARCHIBALD HUNTER."

This was followed a short while later by the order; "Urgent."

"100 men to rendezvous on the Helpmakaar Road below Devonshire Hill at 10.45 p.m. this evening for work under General Hunter; the men to be dismounted."

(Signed) RAWLINSON, Lt.-Col,
D.A.A.G., for C.S.O.

The Colonel reported at Headquarters for further instructions and was told to see General Hunter at a certain house in the Natal Volunteers camp, who would give him further instructions and details connected with the enterprise; he then returned to the I.L.H. camp.

While there would be no trouble or difficulty in getting 100 men of the best type, a minor difficulty did present itself, in that, on this very night the I.L.H. had arranged an open air smoking concert in their camp to which quite a number of people had been invited. To carry out secret instructions under these circumstances was not easy, and when the Colonel got back to camp the concert was in full swing.

No one had the slightest idea what the night had in store for them. They were all enjoying the relaxation, and had forgotten their grievances for the time being, while the beauty of a starlit night added to the peace of mind and contentment of all.

However, at 9.30 p.m. before the entertainment was any way near the conclusion of its programme, the Colonel was obliged to get up and say it was getting late and it was time to sing "The Queen."

Polite protests, "Not yet, Colonel," and the like met his remark.

It was all, however, of no avail; the entertainment came to an end and everybody dispersed. Fitzgerald (Acting Adjutant) hastily called together the squadron leaders remaining in camp, and the Colonel told them that 100 men were required immediately for a risky adventure – time, place, and nature being secret. Each squadron in camp had to provide its quota to be selected without delay, each man to carry 150 rounds of ammunition. Every Light Horseman volunteered, but time pressed and the officers had to make a quick selection. There was some heartburning among those not selected, but circumstances did not permit of niceties of precedence being weighed. Without fuss the lucky 100 were marched silently to the secret rendezvous, while the squadron leaders accompanied the Colonel to meet the Chief of Staff at a house occupied by Colonel Royston of the Natal Carbineers.

When the officers were assembled they were told by General Hunter that their objective was Gun Hill which was to be assaulted, the heavy guns on its summit captured and destroyed. (The original idea that 100 I.L.H. were to rush the Hill had been altered). Five hundred Colonial troops

were to be employed to carry out this enterprise. Of this number the Natal troops were to furnish 400 and the I.L.H. 100. The distribution of the force was to be as follows:-
(a) ASSAULTING COLUMNS.
100 Natal Troops (Right).
100 I.L.H. (Left).
General Hunter would accompany the Right section and the Left section would be led by, and be under the command of Colonel Edwards.
(b) FLANK GUARDS.
Right 100, Left 100 were to be supplied by the Natal troops.

The Right flank guard was to move along the Helpmekaar Road, while the Left was to move in the direction of Limit Hill, where they would take up selected positions from which they would be able to protect the assaulting columns going to and from Gun Hill, and prevent their being cut off from Ladysmith. Pre-concerted signals were arranged between the flanking guards and the assaulting columns.

The troops were to be led to their respective positions by Natal guides, under Major David Henderson, of the Argyll and Sutherland Highlanders (later Lieutenant-General Sir David Henderson, K.C.B., K.C.V.O., D.S.O., etc., etc., Director-General of Military Aeronautics). The guides had on more than one occasion carefully reconnoitred, by night, the whole area embraced by the operations, and, from the knowledge they had thus gained, were most sanguine of success.

In the meantime the troops detailed to carry out the sortie had arrived at the rendezvous which was on the Helpmekaar Road, where the defence terminated in what was known as Devonshire Post, and it was here that the I.L.H. joined them.

The men were very keen to know what was up, and this their officers, who had rejoined them, soon told them. After the scheme of the sortie had been explained and all necessary instructions given, the I.L.H. led the assaulting columns, under the personal guidance of Major Henderson, accompanied by one or two of the guides.

Night marching is difficult at the best of times, and under favourable conditions, but this advance over broken ground, covered with thorn bush and cactus, through dongas and over boulders, was infinitely trying and a severe test of march discipline. The pace was necessarily slow. Stealthiness had been sternly enjoined upon everybody, but every stumble seemed to raise an ear-splitting din which one feared was bound to be heard by the enemy. After what appeared an interminable scramble, the guides halted the assaulting columns at the points where, after deploying, they would commence their attack. It was now 2:30 a.m. Up above could be seen the crest line of Gun Hill, silhouetted black and hard against the starlit sky. Not a sound was to be heard. So far so well! The guides had done their share. It was now for the I.L.H. and their Natal and other comrades to add another illustrious chapter to the History of the Siege.

A few minutes later General Hunter came along and the I.L.H. deployed. They had been warned by the guides of a Boer picket which nightly occupied a position in the Nek between Gun Hill and Gun Kopje, to their left rear as they climbed the hill. To protect their left flank Captain Charles Mullins, V.C., with his quota, was detailed to deal with any trouble arising from that quarter.

The ascent was to be made with all possible speed and in silence; not a shot was to be fired.

The stage was now fully set, at 2.40 a.m. the order was whispered to advance. To many of the I.L.H. the moment of their lives had come. What was in store only heaven knew. Afterwards the Colonel was told that he led the attack up the hill too quickly. All he knew or cared for was that everyone seemed able to keep up with him. He had with him Major Karri-Davies and Lieutenant Pakeman, closely followed by Captain Fowler and the men of 'F' Squadron. It was so dark, when climbing the almost perpendicular hill that they were compelled to use their hands to feel the way and to haul themselves up over the boulders.

They must have made some noise, but still there was no sign of anyone having heard or detected them — it seemed providential.

At last, when they had scrambled about a quarter of the way up, loud shouting was heard from the direction of the Boer picket, which Captain Mullins had under his special care, evidently an attempt to awaken those on top of the hill. Yells of "Hans! Hans!" and "Skiet! Skiet" ("Shoot! Shoot!") rang through the night. Yelling and firing broke out on the right; from above a volley of orders was shouted in Dutch, followed by a single shot and then a ragged rifle fire directed towards the I.L.H. which passed overhead and struck with vicious splashes on the boulders below and behind; luckily for the I.L.H. they were in dead ground.

They were halted for a moment to enable them to recover breath and to regain formation. The firing above increased in intensity and in consequence the advance was resumed with less speed and greater caution. Up and up they scrambled. When nearing the crest line Colonel Edwards was inspired to shout "fix Bayonets." (The I.L.H. had not a bayonet between them!) The panting line enjoyed this *ruse de guerre*, and, with the breath remaining to them, also joyfully bellowed "fix Bayonets," and Karri-Davies, continuing the good work, boomed blood thirstily: "Give them the cold Steel".

Evidently the defenders of the guns had no taste for cold steel. Their firing ceased, and when the crest of the hill was gained it was found that the defenders had disappeared into the night.

Accurate guiding, possibly also a wonderful piece of good luck, brought the Colonel exactly to the emplacement of the big 6in. "Creusot" gun. Closely followed by Major Karri-Davies, Lieutenant Pakeman and by Captain Fowler, R.S.M. (Bill) Perrin, Sergeant finch-Smith and the 'F' Squadron quota, the Colonel was the first to enter the emplacement. Be rapidly assured himself- that no defenders lurked behind, by personally investigating its darkest recesses and by firing his revolver into the more likely hiding places. Without waste of time he then ordered the men still further forward and placed them in extended order on the flat top of the hill, where they lay down forming a covering party for the Sappers. Captain Fowke, R.E. (now General Sir George Fowke, K.C.B., etc.), at once set about preparing the gun for destruction. While this work was afoot the Colonel heard the good news that the I.L.H. had not only taken the 6in. "Creusot," but had also captured a 4.7 Howitzer and a machine gun. All the guns were, as a matter of fact, on the portion of the hill which had been allotted to the I.L.H. to attack.

The minutes dragged on in almost complete silence, while the covering party strained eyes and ears to discover the anticipated counter-attack. It was a tremendous relief when two explosions in succession announced the fact that the guns had been rendered useless and the night's adventure had been successful.

Major Karri-Davies, to make doubly sure that the "Creusot" should not be used again, obtained leave to carry away its breech-block. Sometime later the 6in. gun was repaired by the enemy and was once again in action, having been converted into a Howitzer. A new breech-block was made for it by the artisans in the Netherlands Railway Workshops in Pretoria and the gun was sent to the Kimberley front.

The 4.7 Howitzer was beyond repair, but Mr Uggla, of the Pretoria Railway Works, succeeded in making a facsimile of it. As the breech-block weighed nearly 180lbs., its removal, considering the steepness of the hillside, was a tremendous undertaking, and as it was now pitch dark it all took time. At last the withdrawal began, the I.L.H. forming the rear guard.

It was impossible for anyone to see where to place his feet and the men could not feel their way with their hands as they did on the way up. Though the ascent had been rough and extremely difficult, it was an easy task compared with the descent.

The withdrawal was orderly and was carried out deliberately. Had there been any sort of hurry or panic, lives might have been lost, and assuredly limbs would have been broken. As it turned out, there was not a fracture or even a sprain to be attended to on the troops' return to camp. When the I.L.H. got down to the bottom of the hill, they formed up and cheered wildly for Her Majesty the Queen.

The flanking parties were warned by a pre-arranged bugle call that the work was done and that they, the assaulting columns were about to return to Ladysmith, the flanks automatically covering their retreat. While out on the flanks the troops had not been called upon to take any action, and had not seen any sign of the enemy. It was getting light as the troops found their way through the bush and by the time they got back to the Helpmekaar Road it was light enough for them to see. There was nothing out of the common to be seen or heard. As a matter of fact, not a shot had been fired at them during their retirement.

The casualties were one man of Captain Mullin's party, incidentally the tallest man in the Regiment, Trooper R.G. Nicol, his height being 6ft. 5in., mortally wounded, four others slightly wounded; while the guides had three men slightly wounded, one of them being their leader, Major Henderson.

As they, a dishevelled and sweaty crowd, were nearing the Cemetery they were met by Sir George White and some of his Staff, to whom the men gave a rousing cheer as they passed. The General greeted them warmly, almost emotionally, with "Splendidly done men, gallantly done lads."

The I.L.H. were back in camp at 5.30 to find their comrades "Standing to."

A tremendous gun-fire now opened on the cavalry brigade which, under General Brocklehurst, was carrying out a reconnaissance in force up the Newcastle Road, in which they suffered several casualties.

About midday Sir George White, accompanied by General Hunter, came round to the I.L.H. camp and addressed the Regiment, which paraded dismounted. He told them how pleased he was at the success of the "sortie" and how delighted he was that it had been carried out by Colonial troops. Before the two Generals left they were both given three hearty cheers by the Regiment, and the men spontaneously gave another rousing cheer for their own gallant Colonel. The official despatch in which the episode is referred to was dated Cape Town, 3rd March, 1900, and addressed by Sir George White to field-Marshal Lord Roberts, commanding the troops in South Africa, and reads as follows:-

"On the night of the 7th December, Major-General Sir A. Hunter, K.C.B., D..S.O., made a sortie for the purpose of destroying the Boer Guns on Gun Hill, which had been giving us much annoyance. "His force consisted of 400 Natal Volunteers under Colonel Royston and 100 men of the Imperial Light Horse, under Lieutenant-Colonel A.H.M. Edwards, with 11 men of the Corps of Guides, under Major D. Henderson, D.A.A.G. for Intelligence.,to direct the column and four men Royal Engineers and 10 men No. 10 Mountain Battery Royal Garrison Artillery, under Captain Fowke, and Lieutenant Turner, Royal Engineers, with explosives and sledge hammers for destruction of the guns when captured. Sir A. Hunter's arrangements were excellent throughout, and he was most gallantly supported by his small force. Gun Hill was taken, a 6in. Creusot and a 4.7 Howitzer destroyed and a Maxim captured and brought into camp. Our loss was only one man mortally wounded, one officer and seven men wounded. I consider that Major-General Sir A. Hunter deserves the greatest credit for this very valuable exploit for which he volunteered. He brings to my notice specially the gallant behaviour of Colonel W. Royston, Commanding Volunteers, Natal; Lieutenant-Colonel A.H.M. Edwards (5th Dragoon Guards) Commanding Imperial Light Horse, Major D. Henderson, D.A.A.G. for Intelligence (wounded); Major A.J. King, Royal Lancaster Regiment; Major Karri-Davies, Imperial Light Horse; Captain G.H. Fowke, R.E.; and Lieutenant E.-V.

Turner, R.E., whose names I have much pleasure in bringing forward for favourable Consideration."

Colonel Woolls-Sampson, who had been a patient in the great hospital camp at Intombi since the commencement of the Siege, wrote the following letter to the Colonel:-

"I wish you to convey to the officers, non-commissioned officers and men of the Imperial Light Horse my sincere congratulations on their splendid achievement on Gun Hill. I am not able to write at length, but trust that all ranks will understand that I feel fully compensated for the many sacrifices it was necessary for me to make when first it was proposed to Sir Alfred Milner to raise a mounted corps for service against the Transvaal, by the gallant bearing of the Regiment in their recent exploit. It is a source of great pleasure to me and will conduce more than anything else to hasten my recovery so that I may be able to take part in equally successful operations at the Siege of Pretoria."

"With every good wish for the continued success to yourself and the Regiment."

Yours sincerely,

(Signed) A. WOOLLS-SAMPSON.

Intombi Camp, 11-12-99.

The breech-block which Major Karri-Davies succeeded in bringing away from the summit of Gun Hill, was, for many years placed on the table at any dinner or other function given by the Imperial Light Horse. Major Karri-Davies always looked upon it as his special loot; as he was solely instrumental in arranging for its removal, no one gainsaid him. It was characteristic of him that some time before he died he presented it to General Smuts, the then Prime Minister of the Union of South Africa, with a view to it being placed in the War Museum, Pretoria. It is now in the possession of General Smuts at his home in Irene, near Pretoria.

Several different accounts of what took place on this occasion have been published. One of the most realistic was written by the late Sir A. Conan-Doyle. He was not altogether correct in his facts. For instance he says that Major Karri-Davies gave the command "fix Bayonets" as they were nearing the summit. As previously related the order was given by Colonel Edwards.

In 1904 a dinner was given to the late Field-Marshal Lord Roberts, by the officers of the Imperial Light Horse at the Athenaeum Club, Johannesburg. "When the field-Marshal was returning thanks he turned to Major Karri-Davies, and pointing to the breech-block which was on the table, congratulated him on his timely bluff in calling to the men to "Fix Bayonets," Karri-Davies at once corrected him: "It was not me Sir, it was Colonel Edwards!"

To return to the retirement from Gun Hill, it was necessary to leave Trooper R.G. Nicol where he fell; he had been shot through the spine, high up, and it was thought it would endanger his life to move him. Ambulance Sergeant Dr Charles E. Ligertwood dressed his wounds and remained with him the whole night, doing everything he could to assist his comrade. Sergeant Ligertwood was the well-known Johannesburg Medical Practitioner, later to become the combatant Lieutenant-Colonel in command of the I.L.H. in the German South West African Campaign, 1914.

At daylight the following morning Surgeon-Major Davies proceeded to the spot with an ambulance to bring in the wounded. Nicol, however, had been removed by the enemy at daylight to their Hospital near their main camp.

Surgeon-Major Davies and Sergeant Ligertwood were arrested by the Boers and taken before General Schalk Burgher, the Vice President and second in command to General Joubert, Commandant Weilbach and Landdrost Keiser, when the following conversation took place, interpreted by Keiser:-

General: "It is my painful duty to inform you that I shall have to detain you as prisoners of war for a very long time."

Surgeon-Major Davies: "Tell the General please that, of course, I know he can do as he likes, we are in his power, he is a strong man, we are weak, but if he does do as he says, it is an unheard of and unjustifiable proceeding against which I protest in the name of humanity and the Red Cross under which I serve."

General: "It is because I am strong that I am speaking to you like this,"

Surgeon-Major Davies: "I suppose the reason of your action is because I hear from your men that one of your ambulances and six doctors were taken prisoners by the English on the western border; I do not believe it, it is foreign to the practice of the English and their nature to do this, and there must be some mistake. Were they not sent back?"

General: "Yes, they were sent back from Cape Town, and they helped with some of your wounded."

Surgeon-Major Davies: "Of course, if you like to make this an excuse to send us to Pretoria on the principle of tit-far-tat being right, you can do so, and I have nothing to say,"

General: "Now, I want to ask you some questions: How is it that arms are frequently found in your ambulance wagons?"

Surgeon-Major Davies: "Because I b-believe it is a rule that when wounded men are picked up in the field their rifles and accoutrements are put in with them."

This was wrong, but to the best of Surgeon-Major Davies' knowledge it was the proper answer, though somewhat imaginary.

General: "Why do your ambulance wagons go so far forward during an action? You continually hamper our fire, and you have no business there until you have obtained permission from the Generals, which can be obtained when an engagement is over."

Surgeon-Major Davies: "You must put that down to excess of zeal on the part of the doctors to succour the wounded and not to any idea of hampering your movements."

General: "Why are you two doctors out on an occasion like this, when so few men are out and it is so near your own camp?"

Surgeon-Major Davies: "It is a rule with us that every regiment is provided with a doctor. We have two, as most of our men are personal friends and are frequently under fire, and one of us always goes out even if only a few men are sent out on patrol."

General: "How do I know that you are a doctor, where is your permit?"

Surgeon-Major Davies: "By my uniform and many of your men know me personally and can identify me. We do not consider permits are required on these occasions."

General: "Why do the English do acts of war under the Red Cross flag?"

Surgeon-Major Davies: "I absolutely deny that."

General: "You were a member of the Reform Committee and were in gaol?"

Surgeon-Major Davies: "Yes!" (this did not look promising).

General: "You took an oath not to fight against the Transvaal again?"

Surgeon-Major Davies: "I beg your pardon! I took an oath not to interfere in politics for three years."

Landdrost to General: "That is so."

A short conversation now took place in Dutch between the three in low voices and Surgeon-Major Davies could not catch the drift of it, and then the Landdrost said:- "You may go."

Surgeon-Major Davies: "Where to, Sir?"

Landdrost: "Back to Ladysmith."

Surgeon-Major Davies: "Am I to take the wounded men?"

Landdrost: "Yes!"

Surgeon-Major Davies: "May I have my horses?"

Landdrost: "Yes!"

Surgeon-Major Davies: "Thank you. Please tell the General that I give my word of honour for myself and my men that we will not make use of any information we may have obtained." Surgeon-Major Davies then saluted and left with joy in his heart and a face as long as a fiddle.

It was very plucky of Ligertwood to remain with the wounded alone during the night, within the enemy lines after his own men had retired. He had had no sleep and was dog tired. To be taken prisoner afterwards was an unpleasant climax.

The wounded men were put into the Ambulance wagon, leaving Nicol, whom Surgeon-Major Davies was afraid to take for fear that he would die on the road, but he got the doctor there to promise to look after Nicol and off they started. The enemy did not escort the prisoners back the same way, but by a roundabout route at the back of their position, so that the doctors should not go through their camp again.

Shortly after, the enemy escort bade them a hearty goodbye and they got home without further adventure, having had a most interesting, though not altogether pleasant day. Trooper R.G. Nicol's brother, Lieutenant-Colonel A.W.J. Nicol, D.S.O., has written as follows:-

"As you know my brother was shot from arm-joint to arm-joint and the bullet in its passage injured his spine. He dictated his Will there and then to his comrade Walker and to Dr Ligertwood, before he was handed over to the Boer ambulance, who took him to their base hospital where he died next day. The Boers sent his body to Ladysmith under a white flag and they handed over £16 in cash, which my brother had on his person, and his watch, which were eventually sent to me.

"I heard two years afterwards from a member of the Boer ambulance, who had known my brother in Barberton, that everything possible was done for him, and the fact that his money and his watch were returned, tends to confirm the kind way in which he had been treated by the enemy and for which our family has always felt grateful."

One of the wounded was Trooper Robert Williamson, I.L.H., a Highlander of splendid physique; he had a weakness for playing the bagpipes which was sternly suppressed in the Regiment. He was shot in the thigh and compelled to go into hospital to have his wound attended to; on opening up the wound it was found that a Martini Henry bullet (lead) had mushroomed itself against the femoral without damaging the bone – an example of the fine quality of Highland anatomy.

An amusing and, for the two participants, an embarrassing incident took place during the attack on the hill. The password for the night was "Hunter." When the column was advancing Sergeant (later Lieutenant) Finch-Smith, I.L.H., was annoyed by someone, whom he mistook for one of his men, who would not keep in position, and moreover this particular man's outline in the starlight did not appear familiar. This combination of circumstances roused the Sergeant's suspicions who hissed at the unfamiliar figure "Keep in your place!" but the individual took no notice. The Sergeant then became more suspicious and grabbed him by the throat and said:

"Who are you?" "Oh! I'm Hunter," was the reply in a nearly strangled voice. "Well I know damned well that 'Hunter' is the password, but who the ---- are you?". "Oh! I'm Hunter, don't you know? General Hunter!" The brilliant young Chief of the Staff treated the incident merely as a humorous one.

The Sergeant did not hear the last of this incident for some years, and got very annoyed whenever the subject was mentioned (and still does). Although Irish, the Sergeant could see no humour nor incongruity in the situation. "Why should I not take him by the throat if I felt so inclined?" he protested, "I knew him personally in Ireland, we used to hunt with the same pack (the Duhallow Hounds)." So far as the Sergeant was concerned that fully explained and settled the incident and he wanted to hear no more about it.

To celebrate the capture of the guns a great dinner was given in the evening at which a number of the Staff were present; Colonel Frank Rhodes was also there. The dinner was followed by a smoking concert, wassail and other "innocent merriment."

On the 11th December Colonel Metcalfe asked and received permission to take out a party of the Rifle Brigade to destroy a particularly venomous 4.7 Howitzer which had been pounding Surprise Hill. Five Companies of the Rifle Brigade under Colonel Metcalfe and accompanied by Major Wing, R.A., and Lieutenant Digby Jones, R.E., made the sortie. They succeeded in blowing up the 4.7 gun, but suffered severely in losing fourteen men killed and fifty wounded. On their return this gallant party was attacked by some members of the Pretoria Commando consisting of young lawyers and civil servants, among who was the youthful Deneys Reitz, a son of a former President of the O.F.S. Republic. Young Reitz, an irreconcilable in those days, rather than take the oath of allegiance after the war, left South Africa and went to Madagascar, from where he returned a physical wreck. As a result of working in the fever stricken swamps of the island, he was a martyr to malaria for many years. He was persuaded to return to South Africa by General and Mrs Smuts. A romantic and adventurous type, a born soldier and an intellectual.

This South African loyalist and patriot, though still a young man, has had a remarkable career. He commanded the 1st Battalion of the Royal Scots Fusiliers on the Western Front. He was severely wounded in 1918, but returned to France in time to lead his battalion in the fierce battles that closed the great drama. After the Armistice he led his men to the Rhine. He is now a Cabinet Minister in the present Government of the Union of South Africa; but perhaps more remarkable still he is the Honorary Colonel of the- Imperial Light Horse.

Lieutenant-Colonel the Honourable Deneys Reitz, M.P., is the author of that delightful book "Commando" written in such fair and unbiased terms, without any sacrifice of facts. He describes therein very graphically the hardships undergone and the dangers he so willingly sought and the many deeds of daring and devotion to their cause of a small band of young Pretorians, including the author and his brothers. They fought to the last against the British.

The following is a quotation on the subject of sorties from *The Times History of the War in South Africa*:-

"The success of the sorties had a most inspiring effect on the garrison which was beginning to feel the depressing influence of inactive isolation. One can only regret several attempts were not made simultaneously on the first night against all the principal Boer guns, and that similar attempts on a larger or smaller scale were not constantly repeated during the opening weeks of the Siege. Quite apart from the military advantage of harassing the enemy, their effect as a stimulating influence would have saved more men from enteric than they cost the garrison in casualties. To the besiegers, who had gradually become more and more careless in carrying out those military precautions which are essential in the face of even the most inactive of opponents, the sorties were a severe shock. The indignation in Pretoria over the Gun Hill affair was intense. The Government censured General Schalk Burger, who, owing to General Joubert's illness, was in command. Burgher held a Court-Martial by which Commandant Weilbach of Heidelberg and Major Erasmus of the Artillery were for the time being suspended from their commands. The second sortie added to this indignation and lent colour to the suggestion then made that unfortunate sentries – men of English names, as it happened had been guilty of deliberate treachery. They were arrested and sent to Pretoria but eventually released."

The famous Historian (Amery), however, appears to have overlooked the fact that to have blown up more than one gun on the same night would have robbed the sorties of the essential element of surprise. The first gun having been blown up all the remaining gun escorts would have been on the *qui vive*. Many guns may possibly have been destroyed, but the cost would certainly have been heavy, as it would surely have been impossible to synchronise the many explosions.

Throughout the whole siege the naval guns were handicapped by a shortage of shells. When the gallant Naval Detachment arrived so opportunely in Ladysmith, they brought a certain quantity of shells with them, but only enough if used sparingly. A railway truckload of shells for the naval guns was held up at Pietermaritzburg for the mistaken reason that they might have been captured, although as a matter of fact they could have got through. The folly of it all is that had they been seized they would have been of no use to the Boers, as they possessed no guns of the same type and calibre. This was easily ascertainable as the Staff possessed an inventory giving full particulars of all enemy ordnance. Had these shells got through, the garrison would have had a far more peaceful and healthy time, as without doubt the naval guns could have silenced the enemy heavy ordnance permanently, had it not been felt necessary to use the shells so sparingly.

(Extract from G.F. Gibson *The Story of the Imperial Light Horse* G.D. & Co 1937.)

THE BATTLE OF WAGON HILL

"These men dared beyond their strength; they hozarded beyond their judgment; and in the utmost extremity they were of an unconquerable hope." Thucydides.

For a short while after the 7th December nothing of real importance occurred in Ladysmith to relieve the monotony of regimental routine duties.

Intense heat, alternating with terrific thunderstorms, followed by severe cold, poor rations and the torment of myriads of flies, undermined the physical resistance of the besieged and caused much sickness, such as diarrhoea, dysentery and enteric fever.

At this period the regiment had been reduced to about half the original effective strength by casualties and sickness.

On the morning of the 13th, and again on the 15th, heavy gunfire was heard from the direction of Colenso. On the 17th the garrison heard of the failure of Buller's attempt to cross the Tugela at Colenso, and that his losses, including guns, had been heavy. To men on short rations and in low condition this news was depressing indeed.

From the 30th November, the Imperial Light Horse had provided two Squadrons (dismounted) for the defence of Wagon Hill, and to act as an escort to the two Howitzers, Castor and Pollux, which, for a time, were placed in the Nek between Wagon Hill and Wagon Point. These guns had, however, been removed before the Boer attack on Wagon Hill on the 6th January. The two Squadrons on this duty were relieved by other two every 48 hours shortly before dawn, so that on alternate days four squadrons of dismounted men were on the hill, or in close proximity at a time when an attack might be expected.

Colonel Edwards rode to the salient on the hill nearly every day, and acquainted himself with both the defences and the nature of the ground across which an attack could be made. Decision had to be made between two schemes for the defence of the Hill and Wagon Point. One was to make the best use of the natural cover as it existed in abundance and to strengthen it, and the other was to construct redoubts, sangars and shelter trenches, the former reasonably well camouflaged and the latter plainly visible from the surrounding high hills on which were the enemy's "Creusot" guns.

Colonel Ian Hamilton, who commanded that section of the defences, favoured the use of the natural cover and Colonel Edwards agreed with him, particularly in view of the meagre number of troops available to man extensive fortifications. The defence of that portion of Wagon Hill (the western) and of Wagon Point, which was allotted to the Imperial Light Horse, was consequently prepared on those lines. The alternative would have created "Shell Traps" as was clearly proved on Caesar's Camp, where more formal protective works had been erected.

At the time of the Boer attack on the 6th January, 1900, two or three weak companies of the 1/60th Rifles held the eastern portion of Wagon Hill, adjoining Caesar's Camp, and two dismounted squadrons (numbering in all some 70 men) of the I.L.H. held the remainder.

At night the I.L.H. held a line of six schanzes or advanced posts a short distance below the crest line of the hill on the enemy's side, i.e. the southern and south-western ends. Each post was occupied by a Corporal and three to five men – about 35 men in all. As supports, approximately 35 men, held the two main sangars on the higher and dominating part of the hill. These supports patrolled frequently. Close at hand, at fly Kraal, three Companies of the Gordons constituted reserves. Thus organised the small force was considered sufficient not only to guard against surprise, but also to hold an attack for an appreciable period should one be made at night. The relative position of the advance posts, the main sangars and fly Kraal are shown on the sketch of Wagon Hill.

On the afternoon of the 5th January, Colonel Edwards rode to Wagon Hill as usual, where he discussed with Captain Richardson (11th Hussars), in temporary command of 'D' Squadron I.L.H., a personal reconnaissance to be made by him that night of the Boer 6in "Creusot" gun position on Middle Hill, preparatory to its destruction by another night attack – the half-famished, thinning ranks of the regiment still possessed enterprise and a strong fighting spirit. He also discussed the strengthening of the extreme western end of Wagon Point by a Naval 4.7 gun and a Hotchkiss, which were to be brought out from Ladysmith and placed in position that night.

Before returning to camp the Colonel talked with Captain Mackworth, of the Queen's, who was doing duty with the 60th on Wagon Hill. Captain Mackworth reported that his men were in a bad way owing to sickness and exposure (all their kit had been lost on the evacuation of Dundee, after Talana), and he sincerely hoped they would not be too exactly tested, as he considered they were not in a fit condition to stand too severe a strain. That was the last time the Colonel saw Captain Mackworth, who was killed early next morning.

After nightfall on the 5th, Captain Richardson, accompanied by Sergeant A. Winthrop (later promoted Lieutenant), began his hazardous task. Avoiding, successfully, Burgher pickets and hiding from the enemy's searchlight on Bulwana, which swept the ground they had to traverse, they made a detailed reconnaissance of the "Creusot" gun position on Middle Hill. On returning to Wagon Point at about 11:30 p.m., they found considerable activity there, consequent upon the arrival from Ladysmith of the 4.7 Naval gun and the Hotchkiss, with an escort of Gordon Highlanders, gun's crews of ten Naval ratings and Natal Naval Volunteers, and a party of about 30 Sappers to build the 4.7 emplacement on Wagon Point. Work was at once begun and the Hotchkiss was placed on Howitzer Nek, that is, between Wagon Hill and Wagon Point, on the north side.

At 3 a.m. on the 6th January 1900, the long and fateful struggle commenced. Lieutenant, acting Captain G.M. Mathias (a brother of Colonel Mathias of the Gordons of Dargaai fame), in command of 'C' Squadron, and Lieutenant Patrick Normand, one of the Jameson Raiders, each made a round of their defences, to ensure that everyone was thoroughly on the alert. The former went down the Nek on the Ladysmith side, to the guard of the four-point-seven, and the latter visited his squadron outposts on the south, or enemy side of the hill.

Normand was met by Trooper Frank Rogers, a messenger from his N.C.O., Corporal Dunn, with the report that a number of Boers could be heard at the foot of the hill, on the 'C' Squadron front. There had been some delay in reporting, because the working parties at the 4.7 gun emplacement were making considerable noise, picking and shovelling, and it was not easy to distinguish between, or to locate the various sounds. Also, the men in the forward posts were not certain whether Captain Richardson and Sergeant Winthrop had returned.

Normand, who had inherited from his Scottish ancestors courage and tenacity in a remarkable degree, was quick of decision and cool in emergency. He promptly notified Captain Mathias of the impending attack. Without awaiting further instructions he went back to the squadron main sangar to obtain and lead reinforcements in support of the outposts.

At 3.15 a.m. the first definite indication of the attack was heard. A strange voice called "Don't fire, we are the Ladysmith Town Guard!" The reply to this unconvincing ruse (the Town Guard did not browse about outside the defences at 3.15 a.m.) was a volley from the nearest Post, followed immediately by firing from the remaining Posts, which brought the attack to a temporary standstill. The enemy appeared to be led by a Commandant possessing a high tenor voice of a fine carrying capacity. He kept on singing out "Voorvaarts, julle Burghers, moenie achter die klippe lé nie!" ("Forward, you Burghers, don't lie behind the stones"), and his musical efforts served the extremely useful purpose of enabling the defenders to locate the approximate position of the attack and where to direct their fire.

From this time onwards the rifle fire from the enemy was intense, continuous and well directed and it was obvious that the Boers were pressing the assault with all the men and with all the means at their disposal.

The scattered handful of outposts doggedly hung on to their original positions, firing during approximately half-an-hour, an average of 100 rounds per man, at practically point blank range, until their rifles were too hot to hold. The majority were either killed or wounded before those who were then able to move or could be moved were ordered to retire to the sangar higher up the hill. Without question the unyielding defence made by these men was of the utmost value to their side. They held the enemy at bay sufficiently long to give their comrades, higher up the hill, ample opportunity to realise the nature, extent and direction of the attack and to make the best possible disposition to meet it. Normand had rushed up reinforcements from the main sangar in support of his outposts, and these he extended towards his left, the east, since rifle fire and shouting in Dutch were coming from that direction.

Here, about 4 a.m., we leave Normand and his handful in their tight corner while we get back to 3.15 a.m. and the fortunes of the remainder of 'C' Squadron, and, away to their right, 'D' Squadron.

Captain J.J. Richardson, 'D' Squadron, on Wagon Point, on5 hearing the outbreak of firing, proceeded to his squadron outposts. The position was thinly held but reasonably in hand. The firing having become general, he endeavoured, after consulting with his subaltern, "Coffee" Adams, to get in touch with 'C' Squadron. On nearing the Nek between 'C' and 'D' Squadrons he heard voices, and realising that the Boers had got a footing in the Nek itself, he warned Adams with a loud shout: "The Boers are here." He was promptly bowled over bleeding profusely from a wound in his right elbow joint, but in the darkness managed to struggle back to his squadron for medical attention. Meantime Captain Mathias with the remainder of 'C' Squadron had hotly engaged and repelled the enemy in the Nek. The Hotchkiss was brought into action and a number of rounds fired, with what result is not known, though the moral effect was good. The gun certainly did much to delay the Boer advance. It was then dragged by 'C' Squadron men to a comparatively safe place behind their sangar.

The line, thin but intact and fighting, withdrew slowly. The opposing sides were in such close proximity that Mathias actually got mixed up with the Boers. Breaking noisily into the Taal (Dutch), which he spoke fluently, he played the part of fire-eater until darkness and opportunity enabled him to slip ahead of the attack and rejoin the remnants of his squadron in the sangar. During his unpremeditated sojourn among the Boers, Captain Mathias heard some of the more enterprising Boers urging: "Kom kérels, laat ons die plek dadelik bestorm!" ("Come, let us storm the position at once"), while others, of greater discretion, said: "Nee! die kannone sal ons koppe afskiet, ons moet liewer wag vir meer manskappe," ("No! the cannon will blow our heads off, we had better wait for more men").

Back to Normand, still holding on determinedly. He was in an exposed position with his left "in the air." He sent to Wagon Point for reinforcements, and a Sergeant and 30 men of the Gordons joined him. These he extended to the left of 'C' Squadron, to protect his flank and to permit him to concentrate upon his immediate front. However, as he heard no firing on his left, he returned to the position allotted to the Gordons and found only the Sergeant, a resolute fellow. Presumably the others had found the place untenable and had retired. A request for additional reinforcements obtained a Sergeant and three men of the 60th.

Out-flanked and hard pressed in front, Normand decided to retire with his small force, and by direction of Captain Mathias, who had then re-joined him, he fell back to the main sangar and the

Troopers Frank Rogers (only son of Major H.A. Rogers, I.L.H.), and Chadwick were killed in a brave but vain attempt to retrieve a box of much needed ammunition from their original forward post.

In the meantime 'D' Squadron on Wagon Point were holding the attack on their front, but exposed as they were to a galling fire they suffered considerably. Captain Richardson was out of action and Lieutenant "Coffee" Adams killed. Lieutenant Tom Yockney took command.

It was dark, and the Boers with their wonderful ability to make use of any cover, had, it would seem by uncanny instinct, actually got into a position from which they could direct their fire over Wagon Point without themselves being seen from either 'C' squadron sangar close by, or against the sky line by the men of 'D' squadron extended on Wagon Point.

As the light slowly improved 'C' Squadron, now concentrated in its sangar, observed an additional number of Boers crawling up to the support of the attack on 'D' Squadron on Wagon Point. 'C' Squadron poured in an enfilading fire from their higher position which abruptly stopped this advance.

As the dawn broke Normand took four or five men to occupy a rocky outcrop to the east of 'C' Squadron main sangar, later held by 'E' Squadron, thus obtaining an extended and improved field of fire. While disposing his men he saw, to his relief, the Colonel arriving with reinforcements. From 3.15 to 5.10 a.m. two squadrons of some 70 men had held the enemy at bay. They had borne a heavy responsibility, while through the nightmare hours it seemed that the dawn and reinforcements would never come. They held the position at all costs, and fought with cool doggedness, contesting the ground inch by inch, frequently at point blank range. The officers had led their men with resolution and skill and used the meagre numbers at their disposal to the best possible advantage.

But what of the remainder of the Regiment? At 3 a.m. on the 6th January, the Colonel woke with an instinctive feeling that something was wrong and thought he heard big guns and musketry fire. As no alarm was given he dropped off to sleep again.

At about 4.30 a.m. he was awakened again by the sound of a horse splashing through the ford of the Klip River. He jumped up to meet the rider – Captain King, General Hunter's A.D.C. – who told him that the Boers were attacking Wagon Hill and had got a footing on Howitzer Nek; also that he was to take the remainder of the regiment immediately to reinforce Major Gore-Brown, 1/60th Rifles, the senior officer on the hill.

By good fortune, 'E' and 'F' Squadrons were "standing to" ready to start for the Hill on foot, in the routine course of relief duty. To these and to 'B' Squadron, which ordinarily would have remained in camp, the Colonel gave the order to mount and follow him as soon as possible. He then galloped on ahead. It was now light and a fine morning. As he approached Wagon Hill he could hear nothing except the fire of the Boer field guns in Long Valley, the shells from which were falling near some infantry moving eastwards along the northern slope of Wagon Point. Nor could he see anything except a team of oxen standing yoked, just under Howitzer Nek. Hearing no musketry fire he came to the conclusion that the attack must have been beaten off.

On arrival at the foot of Wagon Hill, the Colonel jumped off his horse, which he handed to his orderly with instructions to tell the officers commanding squadrons, now coming long at the gallop with their squadrons in extended order, to dismount and follow him up the hill.

The Colonel scrambled up the hill and on arriving at the redoubt, shown on the map found a number of the 60th assembled under its lee, Major Gore-Brown being in command.

Lieutenant Hugh Brooking and his troop of 'E' Squadron now arrived; the Colonel sent them along the northern slope of the hill towards Howitzer Nek to cover the right. He followed quickly with the remainder of 'E' Squadron under Captain W. Codrington, which the Colonel, leaving the 60th at the redoubt, led forward without delay up towards Howitzer Nek. A scrambling climb in extended order, a breather and then another scramble, brought them to Lieutenant Normand, who met them with a heartfelt "Thank God, Sir, you've come!" and, pointing to some men in slouch hats on the "hill a short distance away, said: "There they are!" While briefly explaining the position to the Colonel, Lieutenant Normand was hit in the right arm (he had been wounded in his left arm at Elandslaagte). 'E' Squadron was then rushed to the outcrop, previously held by Lieutenant Normand and his four or five men, where they threw themselves down and opened fire on the Boers who were now plainly visible. The fresh weight of fire cleared them off the top of the hill to take cover under its southern slope, whence they instantly returned the fire of 'E' Squadron, the distance being about 80 yards.

'F' Squadron, under Captain C.H. Fowler, followed hard on the heels of 'E' Squadron, and filled the gap between 'E' on the outcrop and 'C' in their sangar overlooking Howitzer Nek.

'B' Squadron galloped up shortly afterwards and were ordered to hold the outcrop southwards from, and almost at right angles to, the 'E' ridge. Major D.E. Doveton, in command, evidently not realising the proximity of the enemy, had his wrist and arm near the shoulder joint shattered whilst using his field glasses. The command of 'B' Squadron devolved upon Lieutenant Ned Kirk, (Captain Charles Mullins, V.C., being in hospital) a fine young fellow from the Eastern Province, Cape, a fearless fighter and natural leader, who had been promoted for gallantry in the field. Kirk disposed his men along the outcrop, the southern flank of which was only from 20 to 30 yards from the crest which was held by the enemy, snatches of whose conversation could be overheard. The range was so short that 'B' was able to add variety to the fighting by "bombing" their opposite numbers with rocks.

All the available members of the regiment, numbering some 200, were now in action. Sick men who had been excused duty voluntarily took part in the action, even the cooks, greasy but determined fellows, had forsaken their pots and pans and had joined in. The Regiment occupied an irregular line, conforming to the cover offering, diagonally across the hill from the end of Caesar's Camp to the main sangar and on to Wagon Point. The Colonel was in the firing line of 'E' Squadron, together with Captain Codrington, and the latter in a gallant attempt to rush forward to adjust his line to a better position, was put out of action by a gun shot through the liver. He was dragged back under cover, at terrible risk and with the greatest difficulty by Corporal W. Weir, who for his plucky action was afterwards awarded the D.C.M. Lieutenant Douglas Campbell then took command of 'E' Squadron.

As Officer Commanding, Colonel Edwards properly had no right to be in the forefront of the firing line, but perhaps strict armchair critics and pedantic interpreters of military tactics will find extenuation of his conduct in the fact that in this case he was able to make all necessary observations and dispositions personally, promptly and to the best advantage of his side; and furthermore, his presence and his cool, cheerful, soldierly bearing must have helped to sustain the good heart of his men. But he soon paid the penalty for his "transgression" of the rules, one bullet hitting him through the neck and shoulder, narrowly missing the spine, and another striking him in the buttock. Friendly hands seized his feet and pulled him back under cover of a low mound a few yards from where he had been wounded, and from that spot he continued to direct operations despite the dangerous nature of his wounds. The Regiment, as a whole, had been in action for some hours, and it was now between 8 and 9 a.m.

From his comparatively safe "headquarters" the Colonel saw a company of the Gordons pass along towards Howitzer Nek, but of other reinforcements or active and useful movements of troops in the rear he saw not a sign. No move was made to strengthen the firing line or to clear the hill by a resolute bayonet charge in force. The only attempt to advance beyond the line of the outcrops held by the I.L.H. while the Colonel remained on Wagon Hill, was the pathetically heroic and criminally wasteful dash made, under orders, by Lieutenant (or Captain) Bowen of the 60th, and his company of six men. One officer and six men to clear an immensely strong natural position held by an overwhelming number of the enemy! Bowen and his tiny band clambering on their way to their mad task encountered the Colonel who enquired their destination and orders. "Rush the open ground in front and clear the enemy off that edge of the hill, Sir," was the reply. The Colonel knew and voiced the utter impossibility of carrying out the order, but Bowen, true to his training and tradition, insisted, simply, that he must make the attempt. The Colonel then planned that such of his men whose fire could be brought to bear would cover the forward rush, and Bowen and his small party, stooping low, doubled out from behind cover, bore to the left, and then, turning right, rushed forward across the open. Lieutenant Douglas Campbell, I.L.H., and some of his men of 'E' Squadron, the more effectively to protect the rush, rose from cover and stood up to deliver their covering fire. The vain, foredoomed attempt was met with a burst of firing which lasted a minute and then died down. Bowen and his brave six fell within a few yards – dead, as was reported by Lieutenant Clem Webb, 'F' Squadron, who crawled forward to their assistance. Lieutenant Campbell was shot through the head, covered over and left for dead, and some of his men were wounded, for nothing.

The Colonel then tried to move along to Wagon Point, but could not do so, the bullet through the neck and shoulder having partially paralysed him. Otherwise he felt capable of carrying on and wished to do so. The I.L.H. Medical Officer, Major Billy Davies,[1] careless of danger, had been tirelessly tending the wounded lying on the exposed outcrop. He worked his way back to the Colonel and, after examination, ordered him to be taken to the hospital in Ladysmith, along with others who could be removed without undue risk.

At about 10.30 a.m. the Colonel handed over the command to Captain C.H. Fowler, 'F' Squadron, the senior unwounded officer present (both Majors Doveton and Karri-Davies having been wounded), and was then carried to an ambulance.

Captain Fowler remained in command and held the position intact, until the action closed at about 7 p.m., without reinforcements being sent to him and without, so far as he knew, any attempt being made to relieve him, until the Devons charged at 6 p.m.

The Colonel, while being moved to the ambulance, was astonished and furious when he saw a number of troops, snugly under cover within 50 yards of his temporary "headquarters," sitting apparently unconcerned doing nothing. Recalling Bowen's brave but futile dash, his lack of proper Support – which he now saw to be available recalling also the abandonment of his own regiment to a "lone hand" fight, his resentment will be understood and forgiven.

On taking over, Captain Fowler sent Captain P.D. Fitzgerald to Wagon Point to control the position there. He then decided upon a personal examination of the whole position, the extreme risk of which was obvious. His survey revealed to him a critical situation along the whole length of his weakly manned front. He had full need of all the coolness, resolution and resource, which the next searching, anxious eight hours proved him to possess. Some 25 percent of his all too small force had already been either killed or wounded. In places as few as nine yards separated the contestants, and the intervening space, void of cover, was watched so vigilantly that any movement of men in formation was a sheer impossibility, unless undertaken in the manner of the "Devons' Charge" described later.

During the morning there were several examples of stupid orders and gallantry of officers and men trying to carry them out. Three or four advances, in formation, by small bodies of men across the flat crest to the southern edge were ordered. It was sickening to watch these pathetically

---

[1] Billy Davies's devoted services here were of a piece with his selfless gallantry both in previous and subsequent engagements, and the Colonel, writing: (appreciatively in later years, said that at Wagon Hill he was "incidentally doing his best to be killed." Other tributes (paid by the men) less eloquent but equally true, ran "game little 'burgher' " and "five foot nothing, but all solid guts."

few but glorious men form up and "go out" without the semblance of a chance. It was futile hopeless slaughter.

Captain Fowler had crawled back for water when he came across Lieutenant Tod of the 60th getting ready for one of these futile advances; Tod asked Captain Fowler for information and was told exactly where the Boers were placed and that he would have to go through the I.L.H., who were close to the Boers. He knew he had not a chance and said so. Captain Fowler could only advise him where best to take cover as they advanced. He saw them start and saw Lieutenant Tod drop dead within half-a-dozen paces and many of his men knocked over, well behind the I.L.H., who occupied good cover. The defender's losses on Wagon Hill never should have been what they were. As long as the Boers were provided with targets like this they were happy. As a result of these advances, however, some men who had dropped unwounded crawled up to a place between the I.L.H. files where they obtained some cover and were able to get in a shot occasionally and so be usefully employed. The line across Wagon Hill from the main sangar at the nek to where it joined up with Caesar's Camp thus received a supply of men from other units who acted as reinforcements to the I.L.H.

Intermittent fire went on for hours varied with heavier bursts, as the enemy endeavoured to advance, only to be repulsed. So long as the main 'C' Squadron sangar was held, the hill could not be taken as it dominated the whole position. Captain Fowler had moved as many 'F' Squadron men to it as could be effectively used there and made it his headquarters.

The fight was now between two rough lines of men largely acting on their own initiative. Cramped behind their selected cover the men of the little force spent the long day on their bellies, the fierce Natal sun blistering their necks, the stones too hot to touch; all tortured with thirst. It was a duel between two hidden bodies of expert riflemen, adepts at making use of any cover, each side hoping to get in the first shot. The best a man could hope for, if he was able to wriggle cautiously into the shelter of a boulder a yard or two ahead, was to get a shot at the foot or elbow of an opponent. A favoured method was to fire at a slanting rock, in the hope that the bullet might be deflected to hit anyone who bad taken cover behind a boulder close by, or to cause him to change his position. In view of this state of affairs, the only possible course was to hold on. An exposed man was a dead man.

A typical example, one of many, of the tactics employed, is provided by Trooper Ogilvie Norton, 'F' Squadron, a young Natal farmer, later a Lieutenant in the 2nd I.L.H. He managed to wriggle, unperceived, into a position behind some boulders in the front line, where he was protected from the south and east, and had a view towards the west over an area not then occupied by the enemy. He anticipated that any further advance attempted by the enemy would bring some of them within his field of fire. Patiently he waited, eyes strained to detect some movement. Reward came when three of the enemy, creeping stealthily forward – screened from sight as they thought – enabled him to bring his sights to bear. He accounted for them in three successive shots and they could not have known where the shots came from.

So the long day wore on; both sides clinging obstinately to their positions, until about 3.30 p.m. a violent storm broke, fortunately with the wind from the north-east and at the backs of the defenders. The rain obliterated all vision. From the main sangar, Wagon Point could not be seen.

Taking advantage of the "cover" afforded by the storm, the Boers then made their finest move. Rushing over the stones and boulders, they made a frantic attempt to capture the main 'C' Squadron sangar; but Mathias and Normand, with the battered remnant of 'C' Squadron, reinforced by some of 'F' Squadron, continued to maintain an inflexible defence as sturdily as they had faced the earlier attacks.

Shot for shot they fought it out, courageously, but the Boers were gradually and relentlessly driven back. Nevertheless they succeeded in getting closer to the main sangar than at any time since early morning. As the rain slackened and the visibility improved, those of the attackers who had not regained their earlier cover, were in a sorry plight. Possibly to relieve the pressure upon them and to create a diversion, yet another fine move was attempted by the enemy at about 4 p.m. Daringly led by field Cornets Japie de Villiers and Zacharias de Jager, some 50 Free State Burghers, from Harrismith, hurled themselves in a reckless rush at the main gun sangar on Wagon Point. Their daredevil impetus swept a detachment of the Gordons from their path and they carried on to the very walls of the sangar. There the enemy were met by men of their own stern temper. Lieutenant Digby-Jones, R.E., pistolled the foremost leader at point blank range. Trooper Albrecht, I.L.H., shot Assistant Veld Cornet J. de Villiers of the Harrismith Commando and another Burgher. Albrecht himself was shot by J.L. de Jager of the same Commando, who in turn was shot by Lieutenant Digby-Jones, who later was himself killed. Colonel Ian Hamilton was also seen to use his revolver coolly and effectively. One stalwart sapper, whose rifle had been torn from his grasp, picked up a shovel and dealt adequately with his opponent. For a mad minute a desperate hand to hand fight raged for the possession of this important position. The steadfast handful of defenders fought doggedly, countering every thrust, until the magnificent attack faltered and broke. As the attackers withdrew, the defenders of 'C' Squadron sangar higher up the hill, who had witnessed the whole dramatic encounter, but had been compelled to hold their own fire owing to the intermingling of the enemy and defenders, opened a heavy fire, doing severe execution among the Burghers as they fell back. Unconquerable spirits who held on were Captain P.D. Fitzgerald (Acting Adjutant, I.L.H.), Lieutenant Hugh Brooking, Quarter-Master Sergeant Alexander Lindsay and some eight men of 'E' Squadron, including Trooper H. Albrecht, Lieutenant Digby-Jones, R.E., and his party of Sappers, who had been working in the sangar, all of whom had been joined in the nick of time by some Naval ratings and by Captain Miller-Wallnutt in command of the company of Gordons. Among the killed were Miller-Wallnutt, Digby-Jones and Trooper Herman Albrecht, I.L.H. A posthumous V.C. was awarded to each of the two last named.

The attack having been broken, Colonel Ian Hamilton rushed up a dismounted detachment of the 18th Hussars from the foot of the hill and security was restored.

The survivors of the I.L.H. including Fitzgerald and Brooking, now joined 'C' and 'F' Squadrons in the big sangar higher up the hill.

The long day closed; as night drew in, the fighting died away and the Boers withdrew, leaving the British still in possession of their dearly held line. But the day's work was not done and dawn had come again before the weakened, famished survivors had tended their own wounded as well as those of the enemy. The strain on the defenders had been serious; anxiety, hunger, heat, fatigue, ceaseless vigilance, had drawn many a haggard mark, the men looked twenty years older. Hushed were the customary jokes and laughter, and the elation of the victor yielded place to a profound relief and quiet pride that the Regiment had been severely tried and yet again had not been found wanting.

To summarise the action it should be recorded that the attack on the Platrand was a full dress affair from the Boer point of view. It had been long discussed by them and was well planned. Its success would have enabled the Boers to fire down from Caesar's Camp at short range into Ladysmith, taking the defences in reverse. The objections which had been raised among them were the height of the hill and the presence of some earthworks on Caesar's Camp. The objectors were ultimately over-ruled when the fact was made clear to them that the Wagon Hill portion of Platrand was not fortified, that possession of this would enable them to take Caesar's Camp, the key of the position, in reverse.

MAJUBA (a Zulu word meaning the "Place of Doves"), their classic example, was quoted as showing the superiority of the Boers against the British under conditions of snap-shooting, and in taking advantage of natural cover. The illustration of Majuba was reinforced by the recent easy victory of the Boers at Nicholson's Nek, which they had achieved with little loss to themselves by the use of similar tactics.

The leaders for the assault were carefully chosen, Vecht (fighting) General C. de Villiers, of Majuba fame, was in command.

Had the attack been delivered with determination, had the mass of Boers shown the daring and enterprise of their leaders, had they attacked Wagon Hill as the I.L.H. went up Gun Hill, they must have carried the position in the dark by weight of numbers and have crushed the small force on the hill before reinforcements could reach them. The mass of Boers went forward in the spirit of the hunter, anxious to kill in safety and not in the spirit of the soldier daring all to win an objective. This got them to the crest but no further. Would the Boer tradition of snap-shooting and making use of natural cover enable them to do, by day, what their lack of dash had caused them to fail in by Night? Their success against the British in this sort of fighting had been invariable and had passed into a tradition among them. It was not to be repeated on Wagon Hill!

With the growing light came the British reinforcements. The I.L.H., thanks to a competent leader, were not marched up to the firing line as on parade. They came independently, by squadrons, dismounted, and, as each squadron got into the danger zone, it made a dive for the position, which the experienced eye of the intrepid Edwards had selected for it, and got down under cover at once, working forward and adjusting itself to the needs of the situation. The struggle on that hill top which began before dawn to last till dusk, was to be the acid test of the Boer traditional method of fighting the method which had never before failed to give them victory.

The pick of the Boer forces fringed the southern slope of Wagon Hill. Experienced men, mingled with lads of daring, burning to live up to the feats of which they had been magnificent men, who in the last phase of the fighting and after the long day's gruelling, stood up to fire as the Devons charged. These were the men who dared all to set the seal on the Majuba tradition, by the capture of the hill to be followed by the fall of Ladysmith. The place of trial was a flat hill top with rough stones and slight outcrops. It was in the use of these stones and in snap-shooting that success or failure lay. A four-foot advance to another stone was a big gain. It could only be made after the fire, from a similar stone some 30 yards or so away, had been effectually silenced. A stone that had concealed a devastating rifle became suddenly innocuous. From one that had been harmless death came. A short scramble forward to a new stone meant a short triumph in enfilading hitherto impregnable cover. A man crawling forward to a stone had to move the body of the late defender to get cover. This was the manner of the fight throughout the whole day.

It was varied on Wagon Hill by the useless rushes of small parties in which the lives of gallant officers and men were thrown away, without a chance of achieving anything, as well as by the Boer attack in the rainstorm, and at Wagon Point on the gun emplacement. The real test, however, was the struggle between the men in the stones. As the day wore on, the British line had worked out further than it had been at the start, not greatly, but sufficiently to prove that the Boer had been more than held at his own tactics. He had met men not inferior to himself at snap-shooting, of equal value in making use of cover and of greater determination.

On Wagon Hill the Majuba tradition had been shattered, though its exponents had been the best and largest body of men, who had ever put, or tried to put, it into practice. The moral effect on the Boers was tremendous. It was their last attempt to carry any serious position by storm in the grand manner. The memory of Majuba must today be bracketed with that of Wagon Hill. Two heroic episodes in that Homeric Iliad which is the short, but heart stirring, history of South Africa.

The merits of the defence of Wagon Hill were hotly debated by all ranks in Ladysmith. Probably the best than can be said for it is that it succeeded. The obvious inadequacy of the defensive works, however, was graphically described by an officer in command of another section, when he said tersely, after examining them that "We deserved to lose."

England, realising the military and political importance of Ladysmith, waited on the details of the attack in a state of tense anxiety, occasioned by no other event in the war. Sir George White had helioed in the morning "General attack" – later "Attack repulsed." Later – "Attack renewed." Still later – "very hard pressed" – then the sun failed. This was the last news to appear in the late papers published in London on that Saturday night. England went through Sunday with the fight in a critical state, with the recent disasters of Colenso, Stormberg and Magersfontein to dwell on and with the thinly veiled hostility of an Europe hoping for the worst. Monday morning papers brought "Attack everywhere repulsed." AND THE TURN OF THE TIDE.

During that morning (Sunday, 7th January), several of the I.L.H. officers and men had talks with the Boers who had come to remove their dead. They said that some 700 of their men had attacked the southern slopes of Wagon Hill the previous day. The state of the hillside, empty cartridge cases and the like showed that there must have been a large number of men there, certainly not less than 700.

So far as can be ascertained from survivors of the I.L.H. and of the other side, 4,000 Boers took part in the attack. Perhaps not more than 2,000 actually assaulted the hill, and the remaining 2,000 acted as supports. Of the 2,000 attackers 700 or 800 actively engaged the I.L.H. on Wagon Hill and Wagon Point.

The Reverend J.D. Kestell, a prominent member of the Burgher forces, in his book "Through Shot and flame," gave an account of Wagon Hill in which their casualties are put at a very low number. (The enemy published no comprehensive official casualty lists, and semi-official and unofficial estimates of losses were usually minimised).

There has been much controversy about enemy casualties, and as there is no unanimity in the numbers recorded by the I.L.H. survivors, the writer has deemed it advisable not to make a statement in this respect other than to relate that – a short armistice having been arranged for the morning of the 7th January, 1900, the I.L.H. handed over to the enemy in the immediate vicinity of Wagon Point alone, 22 dead, including de Villiers and de Jager, their boldest leaders, who, with their party, had so gallantly rushed the gun emplacement the previous afternoon.

The I.L.H. casualties were severe – two officers, W.F. Adams and J.E. Pakeman were killed; Major Doveton died of his wounds; 25 N.C.O.s and men were killed or died of wounds; 6 officers were wounded; 24 N.C.O.s and men were wounded - making a total of:

Killed or died of wounds ………… 29
Wounded …………………………….31
    Total …………………………… 60

The officers wounded were Lieutenant—Colonel A.H.M. Edwards; Major W. Karri-Davies; Captain W.R. Codrington; Lieutenants D. Campbell, J.J. Richardson and P.H. Normand.

The loss of these officers, non-commissioned officers and men was a severe blow to the Regiment; they were of a calibre difficult to replace.

The two officers who were killed-Lieutenants Pakeman and "Coffee" Adams were buried in the cemetery; all the others were first buried in one deep grave on Wagon Hill, at the spot where the I.L.H. Monument now stands. They were later re-buried with all the honoured dead, who were killed on Wagon Hill, Regulars and Volunteers. They now sleep peacefully in a small well-cared-for cemetery on the slopes of Wagon Hill.

The wording on the Monument raised on the Hill, by their comrades, to the I.L.H. who lie
buried there, reads as follows:

"Tell England, you who pass this Monument,
We who died serving her, rest here content."

Of the seven wounded officers, Major Doveton never recovered from the shock caused by the amputation of his arm and died on the 14th February. By the kindness of General Joubert, commanding the enemy's forces, Mrs Doveton was granted permission to enter Ladysmith, which she did in time to be with her husband at the end. After the funeral she was permitted by General Joubert to pass through their lines on her return to Pietermaritzburg.

Captain Codrington lay some time between life and death but eventually lived to do many a good day's work with the I.L.H. throughout the Boer War, and again to perform meritorious service for his country in the Great War, when he commanded the 1st Motor Machine Gun Brigade.

Lieutenant Campbell made an incredibly rapid recovery and was back in mess in six weeks. He had been shot through the head, and it was thought that he was dead. Surgeon-Major Davies was perplexed at first because he could not find the wound of entrance, but, after careful examination, it was seen that the bullet had entered at the nostril and come out at the base of the skull. When surprise was expressed at his recovery, Campbell remarked: "Well it should take more than a .303 bullet through the head to kill a Scot!" Truly "A hard headed Scot!"

Karri-Davies and Normand's wounds gave them little trouble, while the Colonel's wounds did not keep him many days from his duties.

Major Karri-Davies, the ubiquitous, was of great service in many ways in the defence of Ladysmith. He evolved a dye out of permanganate of potash, which changed the colour of grey horses temporarily to a dirty yellow. The dye was also useful in dyeing uniforms – the continual washing of khaki uniforms often turned them white and sometimes offered a fine target to the enemy. Karri-Davies sought to rectify this by dyeing the uniforms. His dye at first turned them pink and after some washing it was inclined to run and turned into a light streaky pink. Karri-Davies was wearing a pair of breeches dyed with his homemade dye when crawling about the top of Wagon Hill; a certain part of his anatomy was particularly prominent and covered as it was with pink breeches, indicated his presence to the enemy almost as effectively as a helio could have done, and he was soon spotted and drilled through his buttock. He bled profusely and becoming faint was carried down the hill on a stretcher. Enraged at being out of any fight, he angrily demanded of the bearers: "Hurry up and stop this bleeding, I want to get back!" He also shouted out to some soldiers whom he saw standing about at a loose end: "Go on and give them hell". One of the stretcher bearers remarked facetiously: "The Major has tough luck – only one bullet but four wounds!"

Related by William C. Gardner, of Kingwilliamstown, Cape:

"Trooper Herman Albrecht, V.C., was first heard of at about ten years of age in the Burghersdorp–Aliwal North area (Cape). I first met him and got to know him well at Barkly East. He was an orphan and lived with a Mr. and Mrs. P. Shorten, who, I believed, had adopted him and were his next of kin. He was big for his years, tall, shy, but manly. We small boys regarded him as a champion for our rights and he always played 'cricket' a man's game. A good shot, cricketer, gymnast, swimmer and horseman, he led a happy carefree life, like so many South African youths. At about 17 he was driving a Post Cart and four horses and made good money by buying 'outlaw' horses, breaking and re-selling them. In due course, like so many more Border youths, he felt the glamour of Johannesburg calling and off he went. As you know a year or two later a more serious appeal was in the air and away he went with his new friends in Johannesburg to join the famous Imperial Light Horse, then being formed in Pietermaritzburg.

"His determination and bravery were proved at Wagon Hill, Ladysmith. He died unknown (except to a few) a hero, but left a fine legacy to the few who were privileged to know him, his tragic but gallant end acting as an inspiration and example, no doubt, to many other young Border men who played their part in the colossal upheaval of 1914-1918."

Trooper "Dicky" Gorton received no less than 13 wounds. When he was being carried away on a stretcher, he had a cheery smile left and waved a hand to his understanding comrades, in mute farewell. He died four days later. His surviving comrades like to think that:

"All the Trumpets sounded for him on the other side."

We Rest Here Content

He had been severely wounded at Elandslaagte and had only been discharged from hospital a day or two before the battle of Wagon Hill.

In many respects Gorton was typical of the Imperial Light Horseman. An Inter-Provincial Rugby player of splendid physique, he loved the rough and tumble of the game, just as he loved any other manly adventure; the keener the fight, the more his blue eyes would twinkle. To him (as to so many more of his comrades), the Empire was a Creed, and in its service his own life was of little account. Temperamentally he was good natured and easy going, but in battle a fearless and formidable opponent. Wordsworth might well have had Gorton's life and death in mind when he penned his immortal lines:

"Who is the Happy Warrior? Who is he
That every man in arms should wish to be?"

Henry Corbett Gorton was born in Burton-on-Trent, 28th October, 1871, and was educated at Burton Grammar School. A tablet was erected to his memory by a large number of his school friends in the Burton Parish Church.

On the 9th, Colonel Edwards received a delightful letter from Colonel Ian Hamilton, in which he said that the I.L.H. were the backbone of the defence and of the fighting in general that day, and that he would make this quite clear in despatches. This communication was published in regimental orders and pleased everybody.

It did much to do away with any soreness that might later have been felt by the Regiment, owing to the fact that the telegrams sent by Sir George White to General Buller and that officer's reply appeared to give the whole of the credit for the defence to the Devons alone. Let it be clearly understood, no one in the Regiment grudged the Devons the credit which was due to them; they behaved magnificently.

Later on, in his official despatch, dated Capetown, 28th March, 1900, Sir George White, referring to the part played by the I.L.H., on the 6th January, wrote as follows:

"I desire to draw special attention to the gallantry displayed by all ranks of the I.L.H., some of whom were within 100 yards of the enemy for 15 hours, exposed to deadly fire. Their losses were terribly heavy, but never for a moment did any of them waver, nor cease to show a fine example of courage and determination to all who came into contact with them."

For the gallantry which they displayed and the part they took in the action throughout the day, the following officers were specially recommended and eventually got the D.S.O.:

Surgeon-Major W.T.F. Davies.
Captain C.H. Fowler.
Lieutenant P.H. Normand.
Lieutenant (Acting Captain) Mathias.

While of the rank and file-Trooper Herman Albrecht won the Victoria Cross for his gallantry in the defence of Wagon Point, and the D.C.M. was awarded to Corporal Weir, of 'E' Squadron, for gallantry displayed under circumstances already mentioned.

Some time afterwards it was brought to the Colonel's notice that Lieutenant T. Yockney 'D' Squadron, had shown great gallantry throughout the whole attack and in attending to the wounded of his squadron who lay in exposed positions on the top of Wagon Point. Had the Colonel known of this at the time, he would certainly have been decorated.

It may be as well to have it known, that while all Regular troops were armed with magazine rifles and carried bayonets, the Imperial Light Horse at that time were armed with single loading Martini-Metfords and were not equipped with bayonets.

(Extract from G.F. Gibson *The Story of the Imperial Light Horse* G.D. & Co 1937.)

We Rest Here Content

"My experience on Wagon Hill and after," by the late Sergeant J.W. Laing

After seeing that everything was in order Captain Mathias and I were slowly walking up the hill when an excited voice shouted: "Sergeant Laing, come quickly, we are being attacked." On hearing this, we started running. On the way up Captain Mathias instructed me to call out my five or six men in reserve, to proceed at once to the front and support our pickets. This we did, and started firing down the hill.

At this point I lost sight of Captain Mathias, who went too far over the hill and got amongst the attacking Boers. However, he managed to get safely back into our lines again. After some time we were joined by No. 2 Troop Pickets, who had been forced back after heavy loss.

While we were still firing, Lieutenant Normand arrived and gave the order for everyone to retire to the sangars. It was at that moment that my ankle was shattered. Corporal Shed, who was with me, asked Lieutenant Normand if he could take me back with him, but as the firing became intense it was impossible to do so. When they left me I continued to fire down the hill. At this point the Natal Naval Brigade arrived with a gun and started firing case shot up the valley and sparks from the gun were landing all round me. They did not fire many shots when something went wrong.

A few minutes afterwards an elderly and a young Dutchman found me. The young Dutchman wanted to shoot me at sight, with the words "Jou verdomde rooinek" (you damned Redneck). I replied: "Nee nee kérel, baie seer!" (No! no! man very sore), holding up my leg with the blood dripping from it. On hearing this the old man said: "Nee! nee! moenie skiet nie!" (No! no! do not shoot). Their first question after taking my rifle and ammunition was: "Waar is die Mister White?" (Where is that Mr White) and I replied: "I have not seen him!" The kind-hearted old Dutchman, after giving me a drink from his water bottle, before proceeding, said he would return and look after me. That was the last I saw of either of them, which was to be expected.

As the morning came, firing was very heavy and two Boers were shooting over the very rock behind which I lay. I could barely raise my head, but when I did so, I saw Corporal Robbins, who was in charge of our No. 1 picket lying dead on the face of the hill.

As the sun rose, the heat became intense and my wound gave me anxiety and pain and I could not stop the bleeding. I took the puttee off my right leg and tied it tightly above the left knee and tried to stop the dripping but without avail as I was in such a cramped position. However, I found that the blood on the ground had congealed with the intense heat. As a last resource, on seeing this, I undid my puttee and boot and put my foot in the sun and to my great relief my ankle became one clot of blood – the bleeding had ceased.

By this time the heat was intense and my thirst more so; in fact, it became so bad that I had to place my finger on my tongue to hold it down to get my breath. Before this I had appealed to the two Boers who were firing over my head to give me a drink of water. At last, one of them who had a short beard handed me his water bottle – which was a British one – what relief I got from that drink! To my intense sorrow, which I feel to this day, on handing back the bottle and while he was putting the strap round his neck, my unknown benefactor was shot through the face, and disappeared from my sight with the blood gushing from his mouth. This he got for his kind and humane action which I shall never forget.

Later on in the afternoon a very heavy rain fell, when I was able to lick the water on the rock. Shortly after this, the firing became very severe from both sides. I tucked my head well under the rock. It was then that I got shot through the back by a ricocheting bullet. That was just before the famous charge was made by the Devons in which some of the I.L.H. joined and drove the Boers off the hill.

I might here mention that within a few yards of where I lay my old friend "Dickie" Gorton received thirteen bullet wounds; Trooper Atley lay dead and Trooper R. McK. Dawson (next of kin,

Admiral Seymour, R.N.), also two others whose names I cannot remember except George Blair, our cook, who had deserted his pots and pans, and joining in the defence was shot through the thigh.

During the evening I was found by Dr Ligertwood and others, had my wound dressed and was given some brandy and a blanket to lie on. As it was now dark it was impossible to remove all the wounded so I lay there all night; the first thing I remembered in the morning was being carried to the foot of the hill on a stretcher to await the ambulance. My next experience was that I awoke suddenly and to my intense horror, found myself among the dead, who had been carried off the hill for the purpose of burial. I recovered my senses and kept shouting, when a Lieutenant from 'E' Squadron heard and rushed over. He recognised me immediately and said "Good God, Sergeant Laing, what are you doing here? Why haven't they taken you to hospital?" He gave me some brandy from his flask and within a few minutes he had a Scotch Cart with two bullocks and a leader, who was none other than Trooper Ginger Wilson of No. 2 Troop, 'C' Squadron.

Another wounded man was laid alongside me who had been shot through the head. We then proceeded to the I.L.H. camp in Ladysmith. One moment my wounded pal who was unconscious, would be on top of me, and with another few jolts, I'd be on top of him. However, we duly arrived at the I.L.H. camp. Everyone rushed out, Sergeant Macgregor of the I.L.H. ambulance staff, came out and informed Ginger Wilson that we should not have been there at all, but taken to the church in Ladysmith. He gave me a drink of brandy and I asked him to give my pal a drink also. To my great surprise I found that my wounded comrade was not a Gordon Highlander as I thought, but a Dutchman, named Harold Schultz, of the Harrismith Commando. (I heard later than he recovered and was exchanged for one of our prisoners).

To cut a long story short, we arrived at the church, and my wounds were dressed and I lay on a mattress on the floor with a blanket over me. In the afternoon at 5 o'clock, one of the R.A.M.C. doctors was walking through the hospital looking at the wounded. He spotted my foot sticking out from under the blanket; he immediately asked where I was shot, and what regiment I belonged to, and after my reply he sent an orderly to Surgeon-Major Davies at the I.L.H. camp saying that he might send someone down as one of his men required immediate attention. Shortly afterwards Sergeant (otherwise Doctor) Ligertwood arrived, who, on seeing my foot, which had turned a bluish colour, got a pair of scissors and ripped off the bandages. He got two orderlies to massage my foot and leg, but this evidently was useless, so they tied a temporary bandage round my foot and before leaving me said I would be quite alright and that I would be in Intombi hospital before 7 o'clock next morning. Another little incident, next morning (Monday) I was put in a dooley consisting of a Bamboo pole, carried on the shoulders of two Indians, which left me swinging in the centre on a kind of hammock. I only had a grey back shirt on, and before reaching the station, I was upset three times on to the street. On arrival at the station I was dumped into a luggage van, and to my surprise the next man to me was my dear pal "Dickie" Gorton. Poor old "Dick," he had terrible hiccoughs and could not stop.

When I arrived at Intombi hospital the first to greet me was Lieutenant Creswell, I.L.H., who gave me a cup of tea.

The next thing I remember was when I was on a table in the operating theatre. I was surrounded by doctors and a lecture was being given by Major Bruce. My last memory was Dr Howarden telling me I had to lose part of my leg. Then he administered the anaesthetic. A very long time after I woke up in a hospital tent. I understand I went through a very rough time and had a narrow squeak. I would like again to mention that my poor old pal "Dickie" Gorton hiccoughed himself to death in the bed next to me.

(Extract from G.F. Gibson *The Story of the Imperial Light Horse* G.D. & Co 1937.)

We Rest Here Content

²Extract from "Through Shot and flame," by J.D. Kestell

The idea was that about 4,000 men should make the attack. It was decided that the Free Staters should scale the Rand from the west and south sides.

The Free Staters were drawn from Kroonstad, Heilbron, Harrismith and Winburg Commandos; and the Transvaalers from the Commandos of Vryheid, Utrecht, Wakkerstroom and Heidelberg.

The understanding was that, after the storming party had taken the hill, reinforcements would come from all sides to support them and thus carry out the attack. At about 10 o'clock we Harrismith Burghers left die laager in order to climb the hill at half-past two in accordance with the arrangements that had been made. We soon reached the Neutral Hill. Here we halted a while, and those who could, slept till one o'clock on Saturday morning, the 6th January, 1900.

At three o'clock we reached the deep dongas at the foot of the hill, and the foremost men passed through. In about twenty minutes we had climbed almost two-thirds of the hill, when we heard a beautiful voice ringing out on the morning air: "Halt! Who goes there?" No answer came from us. We continued climbing, a moment passed, and then the silence was broken by the crash of a volley; then another and another. Everywhere above, in front of us, the flashes of the rifles leapt forth into the darkness and the sharp reports followed in such swift succession as to give the impression of Maxims firing. All of a sudden I saw a great long jet of flame, and instantly the thunder of a cannon broke upon the startled air, and presently behind us I could hear the shrapnel bullets falling on the ground. Then many of those who had not yet climbed the hill, turned and fled; but others rushed upwards and rapidly approached the cornice of rocks whence the heavy firing issued. Silence was now unnecessary; and voices were heard everywhere encouraging the men. Field-Cornet Lyon and Zacharias de Jager in particular were of great assistance to the Commandant; and one constantly heard: "Come along, burghers! come along forward!" At half-past three we reached the reef of rocks and boulders, and presently I heard that two burghers had already been wounded while another lay motionless, but it was as yet too dark to see who it was. It soon transpired that it was Field-Cornet Jan van Wijk.

Before long it became light, and some of the burghers charged the Forts that were just above the ledge of rocks. They over-powered the soldiers and took them prisoners, but were forced to fall back to the escarpment of rocks immediately on account of the heavy fire directed on them from other forts. And now the roar of the cannon and rifles became terrific. This was especially the case with the ceaseless rattle of small arms; one could with difficulty distinguish separate reports: All sounded together like one continuous roar, and woke an echo from the Neutral Hill that sounded like the surging of a mighty wind.

We found ourselves under the cross cannon-fire. The shells from one of our guns flew over our heads and exploded just in front of us on the forts so that we were often in fear of being struck by our own shells; and the projectiles of the English were hurled in an opposite direction on our cannon-forts and on the burghers on Neutral Hill.

How terrible the firing was! It never ceased for a moment, for if the burghers did not rush out from time to time, to assail the forts, the English charged us. This alternate charging of each other was taking place every now and then, and it was during these attacks that the pick of our men fell. Whenever a sangar was attacked a destructive fire was directed on our men, and then some gallant fellows would always remain behind struck down. In this manner Field-Cornet Celliers of Heilbron and of Harrismith Commando, Kootze Odendaal, Mathinus Potgieter, Gert Wessels, Zacharias de lager, Jacob de Villiers and Piet Minny were killed, and Hermanus Wessels and others mortally wounded. They were mostly hit in the head, for the English as well as the Boers were on thewatch, and whenever anyone put his head from behind a stone or a fort, he was immediately fired at.

It was a fearful day – a day that no one who was there ever forgot. The heat, too, was unbearable, the sun shot down his pitiless rays upon us, and the higher he rose the hotter it became It was terrible to see the dead lying uncovered in the scorching rays and our poor wounded suffered indescribable tortures from thirst.

How glad I was that I could do something for the wounded. I bandaged those within reach. I also rendered the first help to the British wounded; one Tommy said to me after I had bandaged him: "I feel easier now," and a sergeant of the Imperial Light Horse, who had discovered that I was a minister remarked: "You are preaching a good sermon to-day."

How the wounded suffered from thirst! and there was nothing to give them – only a little Whisky which I had got from an English officer, who had been taken prisoner. I gave a little of that, only a few drops to every wounded man. Not only the wounded but all of us suffered from thirst.

Long before midday there was not a drop of water left in our flasks. So intolerable was the thirst, that there were burghers who went down to the dongas below in search of water, where there was none and where they knew that almost certain death awaited them.

How slowly, too, the time dragged! "What o'clock was it?" someone asked. It was then only ten o'clock and it seemed as if we had been fighting more than a day, for up to that moment the firing had continued unabated; and the Neutral Hill still sent back to us the echo of the firing – the echo as of a mighty soughing.

It was now asked "Where is Field-Cornet Jan Lyon?" Commandant de Villiers had known for more than an hour that that brave man had fallen; but he spoke to no one about it, for fear that the Burghers should be discouraged. It could not, however, remain a secret. Soon everyone knew what had happened and every countenance fell.[1]

At last the sun set, and as it was clear to Commandant de Villiers that no reinforcements would come and as he had already lost at least a third of his men killed and wounded, he saw that it was impossible to remain there. He, therefore, told me that he would continue there a little while longer and withdraw when it became dark.

This took place at half-past seven. We had been on the hill for sixteen hours under a most severe fire and now we retired; but we were not driven off by the Devons with levelled bayonets as I have read in an English book. We were not driven off the hill. We held it as long as it was light and when twilight fell Commandant de Villiers considered it useless to remain there. He stopped there till the last man had gone then fired some shots, not however at the Devons advancing with fixed bayonets, but in the air, in order to make the English think that we were still all in our positions. We then tramped through the water till we reached our horses, and then rode to the laager, depressed in spirits for we had left very dear ones behind us.

Of the Harrismith Commando there were 15 killed and 20 wounded; Heilbron, 4 killed and 13 wounded; Kroonstad, 3 killed and 2 wounded; Winburg, 1 wounded; altogether 22 killed and 36 wounded. Including the Transvaal, we had lost 63 killed and 145 wounded.

It is a great pleasure to record that the Reverend J.D. Kestell who moved about the hill exposed to a heavy fire, careless of his own life, succoured the wounded irrespective of their nationality. He dressed the wounds of several I.L.H. men who were too badly wounded to move from the forward posts and by stopping the flow of blood, prevented their bleeding to death. They included Sergeant A.E. O'flaherty, I.L.H. (later promoted Lieutenant, a noted classical scholar, and a talented writer and journalist).

Mr Kestell, who is still living, set a high example to all – to friend and foe alike. The I.L.H. survivors of Wagon Hill and their friends keep a grateful corner in their hearts for their chivalrous quondam enemy.

---

[1] Later on in the war, Field-Cornet Lyon's son, Jan Lyon, Jr., was appointed Commandant and was captured by the 2nd I.L.H.

Willow Grange — George Fitzpatrick

About this time, General J. Hildyard and his staff arrived in Estcourt with the 2nd Queens and the 2nd East Surreys followed closely by the 7th Battery Royal Field Artillery and the newly raised Bethune's Mounted Infantry.

The Boers were laagered on Beacon Hill near Willow Grange station, between Estcourt and Mooi River. They were within easy marching distance of the troops occupying Estcourt and Mooi River Stations. General Hildyard made up his mind to attack the enemy on the night of the 23rd November. The attack on the hill was made by the West Yorks and East Surreys, under the command of Colonel F.W. Kitchener. An unsatisfactory and inconclusive affair followed. The manoeuvring of the infantry before dark had given the enemy ample knowledge of the intended attack and, as a consequence, when the storming party reached the crest of the hill they found it evacuated. Daybreak revealed a serious position. The enemy, under the command of General Louis Botha, delivered a counter-attack. It was now a question of retiring on Estcourt fighting a rearguard action. As the infantry regiments left this very high hill, their retirement was covered by the I.L.H., some 75 mounted men to oppose 2,000 Boers and to cover the retirement of 2,000 infantrymen. Some vigorous long range firing was indulged in, but as the hill afforded the I.L.H. ample cover, there were few casualties. When the infantry were out of range the I.L.H. fell back. They had succeeded in carrying out their difficult task, probably because the enemy did not realise their insignificant numbers. Success in 1899-02 was very often achieved in this way.

Trooper George Fitzpatrick, brother of Sir Percy Fitzpatrick a popular, well-known and promising young man, was killed while assisting a wounded private in the West Yorks. Two I.L.H. men Corporals Hirst and Hayne, were wounded. The regulars suffered casualties to the extent of 16 killed and 60 wounded.

Ineffective though that night attack seemed, it, at any rate, checked the Boer advance upon Durban, which was amusingly described by a German member of the raiding force as a Lumpen Kreuzug (a Tramps' Crusade).

(Extract from G.F. Gibson *The Story of the Imperial Light Horse* G.D. & Co 1937.)

I had not discussed the battle with any of the principals or witnesses since that day; but when this tour of the battlefields under General Botha's guidance was first mentioned I determined to get from the Boer leader his own account of the battle. Botha found me a sympathetic and welcome listener. It may serve to illustrate the intimacy of our talk to explain that when my younger brother had fallen at Willow Grange in one of the fights of the Natal rail under Botha's leadership, the latter, for old acquaintances sake, had kept the lad's field glasses and carried them for more than a year to return them to me as a memento of one who was killed in the act of saving wounded comrades.

(Extract from Sir Percy Fitzpatrick *South African Memories* p196. The chapter in the book relates to a train journey with the Transvaal delegates to the Union Convention in Durban in 1908. But just when were the field glasses returned to Fitzpatrick?)

We Rest Here Content

RELIEF OF MAFEKING

How Lance-Corporal Clifford lost and found his comrade – the late Trooper Charles Gardner, both "reported missing" after the action of the 14th May, on his way to the Relief of Mafeking:-

Prior to the Relief of Mafeking, a permanent squadron of scouts were appointed to act as such during the entire trip; Lance-Corporal Clifford Hill and Trooper C. Gardner were two of those special scouts.

Instructions to the scouts were that they were, if possible to avoid engaging the enemy and that the objective of the Column was the Relief of Mafeking. Night and day, with brief halts for rest, the force pushed on; at night the route of the column could easily be followed by a listening scout; there was the intermittent raucous call of the korhaan or lesser bustard which, when disturbed, rise screaming from the ground, and the deep rumbling of the four guns and that of the wagons could be heard some distance away.

On nearing Koodoos Rand, at midday on the 13th the column had halted for a while, and 'C' Squadron Scouts, just in from a spell of duty, were busy with brushwood, preparing their billies for tea, horses standing by. Hill, coming from an interview with the squadron officer, gave an order: "Put out the fires, get mounted," mounted his horse "Billy" (No. 54, a Basuto pony, allotted to him at Pietermaritzburg, where the regiment was formed) and rode off into the bush and found a spot where a more extended view was to be had. A quick survey revealed that a Boer force was closing in from the right with a view to getting positions ahead of the British column.

He reported back to the squadrons, and the scouts began extending at intervals of from one to two hundred yards according to the density of the bush. The Column was now on the move and the scouts kept well out on the right at the same time taking care to keep in touch. Hill took up a position on the extreme right and about 50 yards on his left rode Gardner. About a mile or more on the left and somewhat in the rear was the main column. Just in front of the scouts and somewhat to the right, lay a bit of slightly higher ground with fairly extensive growth; this ran for some distance parallel with the line of march; suddenly, charging out of this in wild alarm, came seven hartebeest, with their characteristic loping bounce when going at full speed; they passed between Hill and Gardner, and "Billy," cocking his ears and straining at the bit, tried his level best to join in the chase. "No, gallant little horse, not yet."

Some movement was observed and it was now evident that the enemy were in ambush all along the ridge and that the scouts were well within range of their rifles. A message to that effect was sent back and the scouts remained halted and behaved as though they were ignorant of the proximity of the enemy. Back came a message "Push on." Forward trotted the scouts, and they had barely gone another 100 yards when the sudden crack of Mausers broke the stillness of that apparently peaceful afternoon.

Hill, lying low on "Billy's" neck, gave him his head and made for the squadron at full speed; all went well for some fifty yards when horse and man went crashing down; Hill found himself on his back with "Billy" across his legs. He lay there for some time and gradually the tumult and firing grew less; apparently the action was moving more left and away from the spot where the enemy were first encountered. All round Hill could hear the movement of horses and the voices of men, and then close by a voice in Dutch spoke "Die een lê hier en die ander daar!" (One lies here and the other there!) a party of the enemy had come up and Hill was in their hands. "He is not dead," said one as he picked up the rifle which had shot from its bucket in the fall and lay close by in the grass. Hill remembered, as he fell, instinctively flinging the field glasses which he had held in his hands, into a patch of nearby shrubbery. As the men somewhat roughly began dragging at his bandolier and haversack, Hill said in Dutch: "No, not dead, not even wounded; and what sort of darned people are you that you handle a man in this way; can't you pull the horse off one first?" "Excuse!" was the reply as they rolled the horse off and a thought struck one of them: "Jy is ook een Afrikander?" (You are also an Afrikander?) "Yes!"

was the reply, "English, not Dutch." "It was my shot that brought you down," said one. "I could have killed you, maar ek het jammer gekrij (but I took pity on you) and shot the horse instead." The horse had been shot just behind the off shoulder and the bullet, passing through the heart had come out at the point of the near shoulder; the man speaking was evidently a noted big game hunter and apparently the crack shot of that group; was it pity or hunter's instinct behind that shot? "Thanks and good luck to you!" responded Hill. As the men were busily getting the saddle and bridle off, one turned angrily to Hill. "What have you done with your field glasses? I saw them in your hand when you were looking at us a little way back; where are they now?" "Don't know!" was the reply; "I certainly had verkijkers; they must have dropped while I was racing away." A little way off another group was busy over something in the grass, while another Boer was catching Gardner's horse which had remained near his master; Hill turned to the men near him; "I am going to see how it Is with my comrade," he said, and walked off; no one hindered him. The Boers were turning my gallant comrade over, freeing him of his belt and belongings. "Is he dead?" asked Hill, "Yes!" said one, "quite-dead. He has been shot through the heart. See for yourself."

Heavy firing was still taking place somewhere to the left front, and a Boer officer rode up, giving orders to the men to hurry up and get ahead, at the same time he ordered two of them to take the prisoner back to their wagon; where those field glasses were ever found is not known, and soon that spot was left to Gardner and the dead horse, and there they remained for many months undisturbed. As the two men with their prisoner were retiring from the scene of action. A thought struck Hill: "See here, you two fellows, I have a few shillings on me, they will be of no use to me as a prisoner and will probably be taken from me at your camp, you have treated me well; if you want them you are welcome to them and nothing will be said about it." "Yes, thank you, we can do with them," and the cash promptly changed hands. Soon after, the halting place of the Boer Commando was reached, and presently it became apparent to Hill, from snatches of conversation he overheard and from the demeanour of the men, that the British column had succeeded in beating off the attack, and several dead and wounded Boers were brought in. It was now getting late when Hill was interviewed by a man who spoke very good English, and was said to be Adjutant to Commandant Liebenberg.

A. I want to ask you a few questions. Who are the I.L.H. and what do you think your column is trying to do?

H. Imperial Light Horse, we were at Elandslaagte and through the siege of Ladysmith, and have come round especially to join this column. We intend to relieve Mafeking.

A. You are late, we have already taken Mafeking.

H. You will not keep it for long, if that is so.

A. What is your particular work and what is the force?

H. I am an N.C.O. in charge of squadron scouts, and I have not much chance of judging the numbers of our column as the scouts work ahead, on the flanks, and have very little to do with the column itself.

A. In other words you are a spy?

H. Nonsense, you know well enough the difference between a spy and a scout. I work with my squadron and always wear uniform.

A. Have you ever been in this part before? Do you know the country around here?

H. Never been here in my life.

A. What do you reckon the strength of your force is?

H. At a rough guess, something like two thousand.

A. Nonsense. We have positive information that you are only nine hundred strong.

H. Nonsense. If you know anything of our column you must know the units it is composed of ourselves, the I.L.H., we consist of six squadrons, A, B, C, D, E, F. Each squadron numbers 130 men; then there are the Kimberley Horse, I do not know their strength, then the C.M.R., and Cape Police, and, as you seem to know all about us, there is the battalion of Infantry. Also guns, maxims and pom-poms.

A. Infantry! No Infantry could possibly keep up at the pace you are going.

H. They are not on foot, they ride on mule wagons.

A. You really think your column will get to Mafeking?

H. I don't think so. I *know* they will get to Mafeking; they are picked troops and you will not stop them.

Dismissed by the Adjutant, Hill saw a Cape cart in which sat a man, evidently a Britisher, and this was put in charge of the Guard. The man had been in charge of the equipment and outfit of one of the War Correspondents with the Relief Column; he had lagged behind and had been bagged.

It is an ill wind that blows nobody any good, and he provided Hill and the Guard with a good meal from his supplies and a blanket or two; the nights being extraordinarily cold. At dusk the Boer Column got under way. The prisoners were put in a wagon under guard.

Two Transvaal Police drove off with them in a Cape cart en route for Potchefstroom and Pretoria. One of the Police, named Rod, spoke English well, and as he had been in Johannesburg and struck on the names of one or two mutual acquaintances, they soon were on the best of terms. At Lichtenburg they stopped at the hotel, and Hill seized the opportunity of scribbling his name in the visitor's book. Later on, when the I.L.H. were passing through, one of them, by chance, looked through this book, and it was the first intimation they had as to the identity of the I.L.H. prisoner with the Boers (Both Hill and Gardner had been posted "missing"). They had ascertained from Boer information that one of the missing men was alive and a prisoner, but nothing more except "Hy was 'n parmantige kêrel!" ("He was a pugnacious kind of man"), and this did not help much as it did not describe either of the missing men.

On arrival at Potchefstroom the guards began to assume a distinctly military air and, for the first time, Hill, who had been treated more like an honoured guest than a prisoner, was put into a cell for the night. Next day, the journey was resumed by train and, after passing through Johannesburg, Pretoria was reached. For a few weeks Hill remained there a prisoner of war in a small enclosure, where the ground had more than a fair share of grey backed insects. He was then removed to the big camp at Waterfall and remained there about two weeks, when the entry of Lord Roberts' forces from the south brought about his release.

Hill now learned that his column, under Colonel Mahon, had successfully joined up with Colonel Plumer, and that the combined force had entered and relieved Mafeking without much difficulty, also that the information given him by the Boer Adjutant was not devoid of truth, as a few days before the relief, the Boers had attacked and actually captured one or two forts in Mafeking which they held for some time before they were themselves forced to surrender to the garrison.

At the first opportunity, Hill re-joined his Regiment in the Transvaal, and took part in the operations around Rustenburg and Warmbaths, and then on to Barberton and the mountainous country in that area.

Months had passed since the Relief of Mafeking, and reorganisation was taking place in the I.L.H. Many of the men were required for their work on the gold mines and others were returning to their normal occupations elsewhere. When Hill reported to the Orderly Room for his passport papers, one of the officers, probably the Adjutant, on duty referred to the affair at Koodoos Rand and remarked to Hill: "I see you are bound for the Cape and are detraining at Grahamstown. Gardner came from the Eastern Province; it is a sad thing for his people to realise that his body was never found." Hill let his mind wander back to that distant afternoon and place; he seemed once more to see the stampeding hartebeest, he felt "Billy" strain at the bit, he heard the outburst of rifle fire, felt the rush of the horse as he was given his head, saw the knots of Boers standing round the fallen horse and man; the whole scene was plainly before him; "If I can get near Kraaipan on the railway and find Koodoos Rand, and if any trace of the bodies remain, I will find the spots where they fell," he remarked. The matter was soon arranged, and armed with official letters and a passport, he started off by rail through the Transvaal and Free State, and up again through Kimberley, past Vryburg, and eventually reported to the military post nearest to the scene of the late engagement. The O.C. Post seemed to think the whole thing rather a wild goose chase, and that Hill would probably run into a party of Boers known to be hanging around that vicinity, when the Post would be minus a horse; however, Hill got mounted and pushed off the same afternoon on a rough track into the back country and made for a farmhouse where the owner and his wife were still in residence, as he had been informed at the Post that he could probably get some first-hand information as to direction, etc.

At Wright's farmhouse he was informed that no Boers had been around for some time, and so decided to spend the night there, and the owner said he would accompany him in the morning to the actual scene of the fight, but held out very little hope of success as the neighbourhood has been searched thoroughly. It was soon apparent to Hill that the scene of the heaviest engagement was not near the spot he wanted, and after riding through the bush for about two miles, he began to sense that the country seemed familiar; yes, surely that bit of rising ground was the line held by the Boers, and if so he must be very near to the object of his search; he would ride on a line along which he estimated he was galloping that day and had scarcely covered fifty yards when, lying in the grass, all in a heap, he came on the skeleton of a horse with hoofs intact; on the near fore-hoof, clearly visible were the letters I.L.H., No. 54.; he had found the remains of his horse "Billy", and not far away he found the complete skeleton of his dear old comrade, Gardner, in exactly the same spot. The remains were reverently taken to the farmhouse where Hill again stayed the night, and next day he returned to a somewhat anxious but much astonished Post Commandant, and handed over all that was left of his comrade for proper burial. A granite monument now marks the spot near Kraaipan."

(Extract from G.F. Gibson *The Story of the Imperial Light Horse* G.D. & Co 1937.)

RELIEF OF MAFEKING

Colonel Mahon

One afternoon, soon after they had started on the Relief, three troopers, who had been out scouting, reached camp some time before the rest of the Regiment and off-saddled; they saw a medium-sized and very alert man walking past at a smart pace obviously enjoying the exercise. That he had walked some distance was apparent from his very dusty field boots. He wore an ordinary civilian cap, a khaki tunic, cut like an officer's but obviously made from three distinct shades of drab cloth; the different colours could be seen on the pockets, sleeves and body. The troopers, who were preparing something to eat, shouted an invitation to the stranger, whom they thought must be a war correspondent, a transport conductor or other wild "civvy" fowl, to join them.

A fresh loaf of bread, fresh butter, some tea and tinned milk, and a cold chicken obtained on the previous day's foraging, provided a pleasant snack. The stranger thoroughly enjoyed his alfresco meal, listening to very frank criticisms and commendations on the conduct of the column, as far as it had gone. Opinions were freely offered and suggestions made about the manner in which operations for the remainder of the journey should be conducted. The meal over, cigarettes (already a rarity) were offered with lordly hospitality, and after a few enquiries by the visitor regarding the state of the trio's commissariat – for he had observed that army rations had not figured very largely on the menu – the "War Correspondent" resumed his walk in the direction of headquarters.

Some little time after, an orderly came along in search of the "Three Musketeers," with a substantial offering of tea, coffee, sugar, biscuits and some tinned food – "With Colonel Mahon's Compliments." Not every trooper enjoys the luxury of telling his Commander just how to do his job.

(Extract from *The Story of the Imperial Light Horse* G.F. Gibson G.D. & Co)

Officers — the relief of Mafeking:
Back row, l to r: Maj Karri-Davies (ILH), Maj Baden-Powell (Intelligence Dept), Capt Robinson R.A.,
Maj Weil (Transport), Capt Peakman (Kimberley Corps), Prince Alexander of Teck A.D.C., Capt Cobb A.S.C.
Seated, Capt Donaldson (ILH), Capt Maxwell (Kimberley Corps), Col King (Commanding Kimberley Corps), Col Mahon, Lt Col Edwards (ILH), Capt Bell-Smyth (Brigade Major), Capt Barnes (Adjutant ILH)
Front Row, Capt Ker (Commanding Infantry Detachment), Sir John Willoughby (DAAGB), Col F. Rhodes (Chief of Intelligence Department), Capt Smyth (Galloper), Capt Du Plat Taylor (RHA)

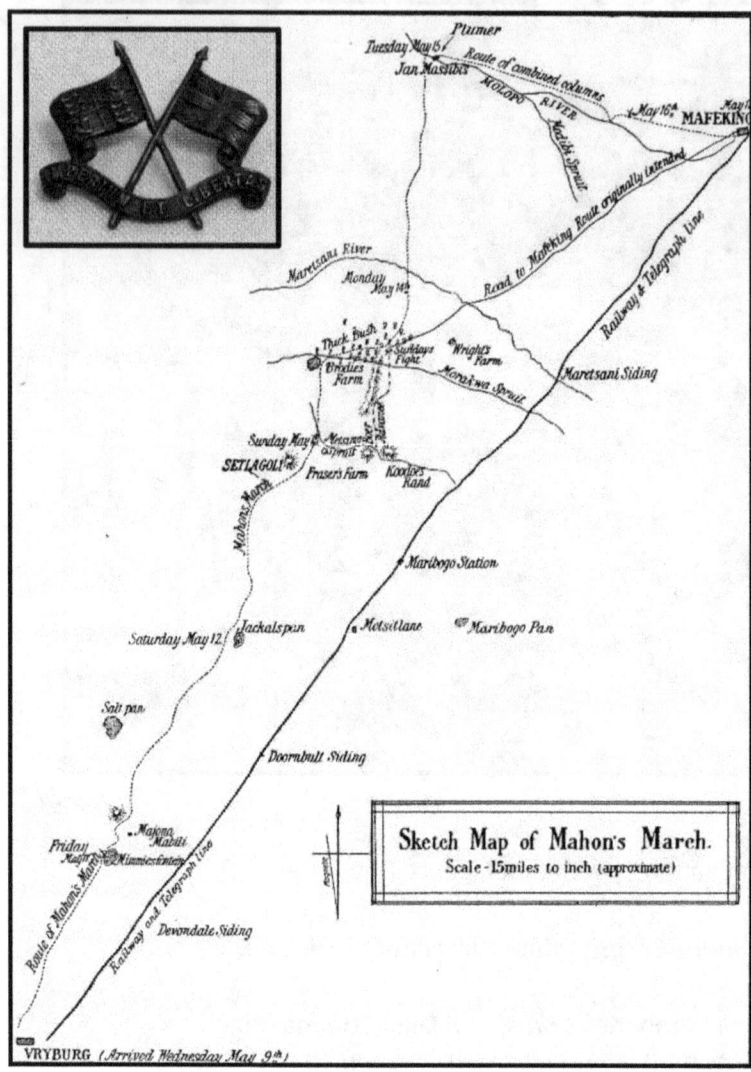

From *The Relief of Mafeking* by Filson Young

RELIEF OF MAFEKING

OFFICERS WHO SERVED WITH THE I.L.H.

Lieut-Colonel A.H.M. Edwards, 5th Dragoon Guards	Commander
Major W. Karri-Davies	Second in Command
Surgeon-Major W.T.F. Davies	Senior Medical Officer
Captain C. Ligertwood	Assistant Medical Officer
Captain J. Donaldson	Quartermaster
Captain Harber, M.R.C.V.S	Veterinary Officer
Captain R.W.R. Barnes, 4th Hussars	Adjutant

'A' Squadron — Captain H. Bottomley, Lieut. Campbell-Ross, Lieut. C.F. Rowe.

'B' Squadron – Captain C. Mullins, V.C., Lieut. D.H. Huntly, Lieut. E.E. Kirk.

'C' Squadron — Captain M.W. Currie, Lieut. F.H.P. Cresswell, Lieut. P. Normand.

'D' Squadron — Capt. T. Bridges, R.H.A., Lieut. A. Winthrop, Lieut. L. Blake.

'E' Squadron — Capt. W. Codrington, 11th Hussars, Lieut. H. Brooking, Lieut. T. Crean, Lieut Maxwell.

'F' Squadron — Capt. D. Gilfillan, Lieut. P. Greathead, Lieut. J.D. Barry.

Total of all ranks – approximately 450

We Rest Here Content

THE STORY OF SON

The following is taken from *Froth and Bubble*, by Captain M.A. Harbord, of the I.L.H.:

"That night several officers of the Relief Column dined with Baden-Powell and some of his friends, and they said afterwards that they had never eaten a better dinner, even in a first-rate London restaurant. This was followed by a sing-song in the Market Square, when Baden-Powell sang and recited and everybody looked well and happy excepting weary members of the Relief Column. They did not even give us the next day off, though being Sunday and the enemy quiet, it would not have done anybody any harm; instead of resting we had to listen to a sermon by Archdeacon Upcher, in the Square.

"I was given my commission after Mafeking, and what pleased me best about it was the fact that it enabled me to give my gallant old horse, 'Son,' an easier time, as I had a second mount as an officer. I had had 'Son' ever since we began training in Maritzburg. Colonel Scott-Chisholme was so pleased with the appearance of the horses and their condition when the Regiment was formed that he told Maxwell, Wilkinson and myself, that we could each pick one out and keep it as his own property. I chose a bay with black points as being the one that would prove most serviceable during the coming war, and I never regretted my choice for one moment, for no man was ever better served or had a better friend that I in 'Son.'

"He stood fourteen hands two, he had two white hind feet and a very small blaze. Foaled under the berg in Natal, he ranged with a big bunch of mares over the kopjes round Van Reenen's, acquiring useful knowledge of loose stones on hillsides, and ant-bear holes and jack-earths on the plains. The Dutchman who bred him broke him to rein on the neck, and to follow when his rider was on foot; taught him, too, with a sharp bit, to stay where he was on dismounting if the reins were pulled over his head.

"During the siege of Ladysmith, 'Son,' like the other horses, naturally suffered much, for there was a shortage of food for the horses as well as for the men. It did not affect his spirits much, however, for on the morning of 6th January, when the rest of the Regiment went up to the support of the others on Wagon Hill, he bolted with me from our camp to Caesar's Camp, I being too weak to hold him, as I had come out of hospital only the evening before. But several nights later, when I went out to him in the horse-lines he whinnied so piteously that I had to borrow, from various quartermasters stores, enough grain to show him that I was doing my best for him.

"On the trek to Mafeking we travelled light, taking no bedding and for extra warmth at night we carried either a cavalry cloak or British Warm, or a kaross under the saddle. I chose a duiker-skin kaross, as it could be used as a numnah during the day.

"As Sergeant I did a lot of galloping work for my troop leader as well as my own duties, and not being able to water the horses, as the little we carried in the water carts was not sufficient even for the men, 'Son' felt it much. The morning after the fight at Kraaipan (Koodoos Rand), after we had been trekking a short distance I felt him stagger several times, and finally he collapsed. I off-saddled, and waited as long as I could to give him a chance, but though he made several gallant efforts he was unable to get on his feet again. Feeling very sick about it, I was just leaving him, when up came Squadron Sergeant-Major Harrison, who had been rough-riding Sergeant of the 19th Hussars before he came to us in Ladysmith at the time Colonel Edwards took over the Regiment. He was a true horseman, and seeing what had happened, he said: "Bad luck Sergeant! You'd better put a bullet through him, or the Boers will get him if he pulls round."

"But I couldn't bear to do that so I persuaded Harrison to let me leave the old horse alive, and having poured the contents of my water bottle down his throat, we went on, I never expecting, of course, to see him again.

"We trekked all that day and night, for about seventy miles across a waterless, sandy desert. In one dry river-bed, however, we dug holes and got a little liquid of sorts to drink. Next morning at dawn we got to Plumer's camp, and halted for the day and night. In the evening Harrison came to me, and said: 'Sergeant, your old horse is in his old place alongside mine in our squadron horse-lines.'

"Feeling hurt, I told him that he might have chosen some other subject to chaff me about, but upon his declaring it was true I went down to the lines, and there, sure enough, I found 'Son.' He must have revived soon after we left him, and, following in our tracks, our halt had given him time to catch us up. I never felt more pleased about anything in my life. I rode him into Mafeking two days later."

AND THE CAPE MAIL RUSHES ON

Alongside the railway station at Frederikstad is a small cemetery beneath waving pepper trees. There lie four I.L.H. men, stout fighters and good comrades, near to the graves of their quondam enemies, who fell in the same engagement.

There they rest content, heedless of the thundering "Union Limited" as it flashes past on its thousand miles journey between Pretoria and Cape Town. Perchance they know that friendly hands still tend their graves. Some twenty years after the action of Frederikstad, a member of the I.L.H. who had taken part in the fight was making a journey from Johannesburg to Cape Town. As the train neared the scene of action, in order to get a better view of the little graveyard, he walked on to the observation platform. To his amazement he saw the conductor of the train and a coloured bed boy standing rigidly to attention.

After the train had passed the cemetery and the conductor and bed boy had relaxed, the I.L.H. man said: "Why all this ceremony?"

"I am an old I.L.H. man, Sir, and took part in the fight which occurred here, and this bed boy served at the time with the transport, so whenever we pass, we stand to attention and salute our old comrades."

(Extract from G.F. Gibson *The Story of the Imperial Light Horse* G.D. & Co 1937.)

The rear guard action at Geduld

During most of 1901 and up to the war's end, the 1st Regiment of the I.L.H. was commanded by Major Charles James Briggs, who had joined the King's Dragoon Guards in 1886 and who later, as a lieutenant-general, was to command the British forces at Salonika in the first World War. At Geduld farm, near Hartebeestfontein in the Western Transvaal, on 22 March, 1901, 175 of Briggs's men, with one Maxim, were on reconnaissance when some 400 of General Jacobus De la Rey's burghers charged down upon them. This was the second occasion in the war on which the Boers employed their new tactic of charging in close formation. They looked, according to an eye-witness, as they galloped over open ground, like "a cavalry brigade in mass".

The I.L.H. were all dismounted in a thin, extended line, but most of them speedily regained their horses. "We were all ordered to retire," wrote Captain Patrick Hill Normand, "squadron by squadron, covering one another." Thus, slowly but skilfully, pressed hard for over four miles, Briggs, whose horse was shot under him, "armed with a cigarette and a knobkerrie," fought his way back to the security of his mountain camp. From there the enemy was forced to retreat by heavy shelling.

Two officers and five men were killed and three officers and thirteen men wounded. The Boers are thought to have lost some two dozen killed and wounded. General Jan Smuts, whose commando was part of De la Rey's force, said later that "the rear guard action fought by the I.L.H. was the most brilliant one he had seen fought by either side during the whole campaign." In the course of the next two days, the column of which Briggs's men were a part, commanded by Major-General James Melville Babington, who had joined the 16th Lancers in 1873 and was to command with distinction a Corps in the first World War, gained a considerable victory over De la Rey at Wildefontein.

Lieutenant-Colonel Sir Henry Rawlinson wrote in his diary on 2 March 1901, that he had heard from Babington 'that he had got well into Delarey, had captured 2 15-pdrs, a pom-pom and 6 Maxims and 170 prisoners This,' he added, 'is a good business, the more so as it saves Babington from being stellenbosched.' (Rawlinson, 25 Mar., 1901).

(from *A History of the British Cavalry* Vol 4 1899-1913 The Marquess of Anglesey)

Hartebeestfontein 22 March 1901

Two officers of The King's Dragoon Guards achieved distinction during the war serving away from the regiment and in very different fields. Lieutenant Colonel W.H. Birbeck became the Assistant Inspector of Remounts in South Africa. The going had been so hard, and the wear and tear on horseflesh so tremendous, that the supply of remounts became crucial to the success of the campaign. Haig commented, "No one could have done this remount work as well as Birkbeck has."

Major C.J. Briggs commanded the 1st Regiment of the Imperial Light Horse from early in 1901 until the end of the war, gaining great distinction. On 22 March 1901, at Geduld Farm, near Hartebeestfontein, Briggs with 175 men was suddenly charged by 400 of De La Rey's Commando.

The ILH were dismounted, but quickly remounted and then slowly, squadron by squadron, retired over a distance of four miles, holding off the enemy and fighting their way back to their mountain camp. Briggs, whose horse had been shot under him, conducted the whole operation "armed with a cigarette and a knobkerrie". For the loss of two officers and five men killed, and some sixteen wounded, Briggs inflicted about two dozen casualties on the Boers and earned from General Jan Smuts, who was with the Boers, the verdict: "The rearguard action fought by the I.L.H. was the most brilliant one I have seen fought by either side during the whole campaign."

(Extract from *The Story of the Imperial Light Horse* G.F. Gibson)

TRANSLATION FROM THE BOOK: "FIGHTING AND FLYING OF BEYERS AND KEMP"
("Veg en Vlug met Beyers en Kemp) (By J.F. Naude).

HARTEBEESTFONTEIN AND STOMPIES

"...General Kemp then left Randfontein with 180 mounted men and the artillery. Kemp had ' guns (2 Armstrongs, 1 pom pom) and 2 hand maxims. Two smart Lieutenants, Jaap van de Venter and Odendaal were in charge of these guns. We were now on the Western Highveld in the neighbourhood of Lichtenburg. The country around was very exposed, with but a few hills here and there.

The large mealie lands which extended over the hills speak for the fertility of the area, which was watered by neither rivers, springs or wells. Here we met General de la Rey whom we accompanied to field Comet Classen's farm near Lemoenfontein. An English force had marched past there the previous day as the still-smouldering store house, in which grain and wool were stored, indicated.

On reaching Geduld, we received a message to say that the English were at Hartebeestfontein, so we marched back to Lemoenfontein, before nightfall. On the following morning at daybreak the English forces were at Geduld, which we had passed the previous evening. They were about 400 strong and had with them one pom pom. Who would have thought that these were the advance guard and that the main force was drawn up behind the nearby hill? Therefore our .scouts had to proceed to the highest points on the hills around Geduld and Hartebeestfontein so as to learn the true state of affairs. As we drew slowly near General de la Rey had General Smuts on his right flank, while General Kemp formed the left flank.

It was apparent that this English force had been sent in advance so as to draw us out and thus learn our strength.

There was a herd of cattle at Geduld which the English wished to capture, some of our men successfully prevented this scheme by reaching the herd first, therefore the enemy's pom pom started firing on our men and the cattle, in a vain endeavour to drive the beasts out. With about 80 men from the left flank, we attacked the English, General, de la Rey ordered General Smuts on his right flank to do the same. The English, on perceiving that we were planning an attack retreated. They did not fly but merely worked back to the hill where they had left their pom porn. They now bombarded us fiercely so we were forced to beat a hasty retreat. We had to charge along an open plain, and then towards a hill under the enemies shell fire. On reaching the hill we found but poor shelter against the enemy's pom pom, which was then taken and lodged behind a hill.

When we reappeared from the hill we emerged in a half circle formation. The pom pom was now gone, but from the mealie lands in front of us the Lee-Metford's commenced firing. We charged into the mealie lands, firing as we went. The English slipped out the other side and we were again subject to the pom pom's fire. Our men were not dismayed, but pressed forward with their Generals so as to capture the pom pom. The English fought in close formation around the gun to prevent its capture by us, The pom pom was shelling our front, but we would have captured it had it not been that an English officer decided that it would be better to sacrifice the lives of 50 men rather than lose the gun – and retreat in safety. Therefore, this officer of Babington's, ordered 50 men to dismount from their horses and take up their position in the thick grass, while the pompom was speedily taken back to Hartebeestfontein. On the ridges to our front and to our left were the English, whom we harassed as we drew nearer. We vigorously attacked the retreating enemy in front of us.

This was the warmest moment of the skirmish, we sprang from our horses and with the bridle over our arms we advanced firing to within 30 or 40 yards. The English bullets whined all around us. We were now among them and took those who were wounded or killed as captives. The pom pom had been saved, but at the cost of more than 20 men, those who had given their lives were of the I.L.H. Our loss was one killed (Conan-Doyle said that our losses were heavier than those of the enemy). The English returned to Hartebeestfontein where they took possession of a ridge situated in such a manner that we decided that it would be unwise to attack them."

IN THE WESTERN TRANSVAAL.

Lieutenant B.C. Noel (a son of the Manse) was a very daring I.L.H. subaltern, a splendid type of young English manhood, of good physique, with an utter disregard of death.

When the Regiment was in the Lichtenburg–Zeerust area on the 6th July, Noel was in charge of the scouts on the left flank. They were some 2,500 yards from the main body – perhaps too far – but being anxious to see what was beyond a rise, Noel told his nearest scout where he was going, and galloped off to investigate by himself. He was riding his own horse, a wonderful jumper, named Father O'flynn, which he had brought out from England with him. He had ridden some distance when he came suddenly upon two dismounted Burghers kneeling by their horses in some hollow ground. Extraordinary as it may sound, Noel had no revolver nor any weapon with him, and he could only bluff, shouting to them to "Hands up," he raced towards them. They let him ride to within thirty yards and they both fired, bringing his horse down by a shot through its off fore-knee, luckily a clean wound made by a hard-nosed bullet.

Noel jumped up and pulling out his pipe case as though handling a revolver, ran towards them, yelling to them to "hands up". They did so, and collecting their horses, rifles and bandoliers, of which they each had two, he brought them to camp.

A week later the Regiment was trekking in the lead mine area, a difficult country to operate in, containing many huge wooded valleys; and steep hills. Two squadrons, Noel's being one, were advance guard, covered by the guns. They were crossing one of the precipitous valleys, the Burghers sniping from the far side. Noel with his troop got too far in advance and was shelled by the artillery who mistook them for Boers. Noel stood up and signalled with his hat on a rifle to show who they were. As he did so he was shot through the stomach. He was brought into camp that night, and everything possible was done for him. Men of his own troop carried him on a stretcher for many long miles to spare him from the jars and jolts of a lumbering ambulance wagon, but he died after a week of agony on the morning on which the Regiment entered Zeerust. At sunset the day before, seeming to know he was going, he asked two brother officers, who were sitting with him, to move him to the entrance of his tent, so that he could have one more look at the sun. His last words were that it would be the last sunset he would ever see.

The day he was wounded he sent for Captain Harbord and said to him, "Look here, old chap, I'm fonder of Father O'flynn than of most things or people, so I want you to have him. I know I can't live long, take him now, and promise me – won't you – that you will never part with the old horse unless you are absolutely obliged to. If you must let him go, ask old Maxwell (Captain David Maxwell, I.L.H., now Colonel Maxwell, D.S.O.) to have him, and if he can't, shoot the horse. I won't ask you to look after him, because I know that you will, and I would sooner he was in your hands 'than in anybody's."

Captain Harbord relates in his book "Froth and Bubble": "I saw old Noel once more before he died, but he was in such pain that I could not stand looking on, being unable to help. Father O'flynn was a golden chestnut, an Irish hunter and a wonderful leaper. It was no effort for him to jump. At the close of a big drive once, towards the end of the war, there were about a dozen columns collected at Klerksdorp, and they had a jumping competition. There were about fifty entries, some of them well-known horses from different parts of the world, and some especially good walers brought over by the Australians and New Zealanders. But Father O'flynn beat the lot.

(Extract from G.F. Gibson *The Story of the Imperial Light Horse* G.D. & Co 1937.)

LIEUTENANT B.C. NOEL

Lieutenant B.C. Noel (a son of the Manse), was a very daring I.L.H. subaltern, a splendid type of young English manhood, of good physique, with an utter disregard of death.

When the Regiment was in the Lichtenburg–Zeerust area on the 6th July, Noel was in charge of the scouts on the left flank. They were some 2,500 yards from the main body – perhaps too far – but being anxious to see what was beyond a rise, Noel told his nearest scout where he was going, and galloped off to investigate by himself. He was riding his own horse, a wonderful jumper, named Father O'flynn, which he had brought out from England with him. He had ridden some distance when he came suddenly upon two dismounted Burghers kneeling by their horses in some hollow ground. Extraordinary as it may sound, Noel had no revolver nor any weapon with him, and he could only bluff, shouting to them to "Hands up," he raced towards them. They let him ride to within thirty yards and they both fired, bringing his horse down by a shot through its off fore-knee, luckily a clean wound made by a hard-nosed bullet.

Noel jumped up and pulling out his pipe case as though handling a revolver, ran towards them, yelling to them to "hands up." They did so, and collecting their horses, rifles and bandoliers, of which they each had two, he brought them to camp.

A week later the Regiment was trekking in the lead mine area, a difficult country to operate in, containing many huge wooded valleys; and steep hills. Two squadrons, Noel's being one, were advance guard, covered by the guns. They were crossing one of the precipitous valleys, the Burghers sniping from the far, side. Noel with his troop got too far in advance, and was shelled by the artillery who mistook, them for Boers. Noel stood up and signalled with his hat on a rifle to show who they were. As he did so he was shot through the stomach. He was brought into camp that night, and everything possible was done for him. Men of his own troop carried him on a stretcher for many long miles to spare him from the jars and jolts of a lumbering ambulance wagon, but he died after a week of agony on the morning on which the Regiment entered Zeerust. At sunset the day before, seeming to know he was going, he asked two brother officers, who were sitting with him, to move him to the entrance of his tent, so that he could have one more look at the sun. His last words were that it would be the last sunset he would ever see.

(Extract from G.F. Gibson *The Story of the Imperial Light Horse* G.D. & Co 1937.)

THE REARGUARD ACTION – HARTEBEESTFONTEIN

"One of the wounded of 'A' Squadron was a Colonial, and spoke Dutch almost as well as the Burghers. He was wearing a pair of leather breeches, and was wounded in the thigh. As the Burghers galloped up, one of them halted near him, fired a shot at him which grazed his head and then, jumping off his pony, laid hold of him and roughly began to drag off his breeches. 'A,' was in great pain, cursed him in Dutch, whereupon, the Burgher, accusing him of being a traitor, dropped him, and picking up his rifle, said that he would finish him. But before he could do so a big man with a long beard galloped up, and taking in the situation at a glance, to the fury and disgust of the despoiler, gave him two heavy cuts across the shoulders with the sjambok, telling him in Dutch what he thought of him and bidding him leave at once. 'A,' who was very faint with loss of blood and pain caused by the brutal treatment he had received, became aware, somewhat to his surprise, that the big man was holding his water bottle to his lips.

"Drink this," said the Dutchman, "it will do you good. It is good Cape dop (brandy)."

Taking a good pull, 'A' thanked him, and the kind Samaritan replied: "You are very welcome; though we fight against each other, we need not behave as brutes. If we both live through this war, I hope we may meet again."

As he rode off he turned and said: "You don't know my name; if you want me, ask for de la Rey."

(Extract from *Froth and Bubble* by Captain H.A. Harbord, of 'B' Squadron, I.L.H.)

Lieutenant L.S. Sanders

On the 31st July the Regiment, forming a portion of Colonel Hickie's Column (now Major General Sir W.B. Hickie, K.C.B., who commanded the 16th – Irish Division – Shamrock Division on the Western Front in the Great War) was marching in the Lichtenburg–Schweizer Reneke area. Colonel Hickie sent for Captain Harbord and ordered him to take his squadron out on a special mission on the right flank, a distance of about nine miles, and to keep in touch with the Column. Harbord replied that he only had fifty men in his squadron, and as he would be travelling at right angles to the direction to be followed by the column, it would be impossible for him to keep in touch. The Colonel said impatiently: "Oh, very well, if you would rather not, I'll send someone else." Harbord answered that of course he would carry out his instructions to the best of his ability. Just before he started, Colonel Briggs informed Harbord that, if he found the enemy in superior numbers, he was to avoid an engagement and return.

On his way Harbord saw a Hottentot shepherd and hailed him. After a lot of questioning and some threats the latter said that Commandant Vermaas, with about a thousand men had passed him a few hours earlier and could not be far off.

As the advance screen was getting too far ahead of the squadron, Harbord sent Lieutenant L.S. Sanders to take control, first telling him to retire on the squadron if he saw the enemy. The remainder of the squadron followed at a gallop, halting when they reached the top of a rise commanding a good view.

Harbord noticed that Sanders had not caught up with the advance party who were all galloping towards a house on the farm Vlakfontein. Among the buildings a mounted man was seen. Harbord realised from previous experience, that, when a Burgher rode as openly as this man was doing, it indicated that there were more in the immediate neighbourhood. At that moment Sanders halted and made a signal to show that he, too, had seen the mounted man. Then Harbord, looking through- his glasses, saw eight troops of mounted men in troop formation (column of troops), all in khaki uniforms, riding towards the farm buildings and wondered to which British column they belonged. He saw that Sanders had rallied some of the men and as they continued on their way, Harbord concluded that Sanders must have seen the large number of mounted men referred to. At that moment Harbord's squadron was fired on from the rear. Getting his men into squadron line, he extended, faced about and dismounted; they had no sooner done so when he saw a large body of the enemy galloping down from a kopje and another body coming out of a mealie patch below it. 'B' Squadron immediately opened fire, checking both movements; some of the enemy got off their horses and returned the fire, but others galloped round to Harbord's right and left fronts with the obvious intention of surrounding him.

Harbord ordered his senior subaltern to retire with the squadron to a hill on their left front leaving him a few men to cover their retreat. When he saw that the squadron was well on its way, he made after them.

When on the high ground, Harbord halted the squadron and waited for some time, to give Sanders and the scouts an opportunity of rejoining, him, but neither they nor the Boers appeared. Harbord then moved off in the direction which the column had taken and arrived at the camp very late.

Harbord reported to Colonel Briggs as quickly as possible what had occurred and with some of the other squadron leaders got Colonel Briggs to ask Colonel Hickie to allow the Regiment to go back and ascertain what had happened to Sanders and his scouts. Colonel Hickie refused, saying there was no time, as he had to be at a certain rendezvous by a certain date.

Next morning before dawn a scout, who had been taken prisoner by the Boers, came in: the Burghers had stripped him before releasing him. The scout brought a note from Commandant Vermaas which read:-

"The next time a British General wished to take me and my Commando of a thousand men prisoners, it would be wiser to send more than fifty men to do it."

From this scout the I.L.H. learned about Sanders' unhappy but gallant end. It appears that on seeing the mounted troops advancing in orderly formation like British troops, all dressed in khaki uniforms, Sanders went on alone to meet the members of another supposed British force. He was quite close to them before he discovered that they were Boers and not British; he then drew his Mauser pistol and fired several shots at their leader who happened to be Commandant Vermaas himself, missing him. Sanders then turned and raced for it, but both he and his horse were shot before they had covered a few lengths. The Boers took him to the farm house where he lived till nightfall, but never regained consciousness.

Lieutenant Sanders was cut off absolutely and heavily outnumbered, and he might have been justified in surrendering. Instead, he decided to fight, and if ever a man deliberately chose certain death he did. Sanders' death was in keeping with the Regimental Tradition — DEATH RATHER THAN SURRENDER.

Sanders, a young Colonial who hailed from the Eastern Province, was equally fluent in Dutch and English, was one of the original five Hundred I.L.H., and had seen a great deal of fighting. When so many of, his comrades were granted commissions, he asked an officer who had served with him as a trooper, if he thought he stood a chance of obtaining a commission. The answer was "No." Sanders was an efficient soldier; very small and, so far as appearance was concerned, not at all well favoured.

Immediately after the conversation referred to, Sanders took his discharge from the Regiment and was subsequently employed collecting cattle with another column. This column was attacked and a team and gun got away, the drivers having, no doubt, been killed or incapacitated. Sanders, without any hesitation, mounted and galloped after the runaway team and brought them back to safety. The officer commanding the column was much impressed by the gallant act and was anxious to recommend Sanders for reward. Sanders, however, said that, if his action was deserving of recognition, he would prefer to be given a Commission in his old Regiment; the I.L.H., which had been his ambition since its inception. Sanders obtained his heart's desire and was posted to 'B' Squadron under Captain Harbord, only to be killed a month or two later.

(Extract from G.F. Gibson *The Story of the Imperial Light Horse* G.D. & Co 1937.)

TYGER KLOOF SPRUIT

On the morning of 18th December, the Light Horse Brigade under General Dartnell, marching from Bethlehem to Harrismith, was heavily attacked at 11 a.m., in the valley formed by the Tyger Kloof Spruit, eight miles from Bethlehem. The advance party of 2nd Light Horse came under fire from a pom pom on a hill, an outcrop of the rugged Langberg Range away to the left. This seemed to be a signal for a concerted outbreak of Mauser fire and for a wave of burghers to come charging out of a kloof across flat land. The 2nd Light Horse dismounting, found cover in grass on a slight ridge.

The burghers manoeuvered around towards the rear of the column where the 1st Light Horse was in cover in the long grass from rifle fire coming from almost every direction. Each trooper carried three full bandoliers and the Light Horse fire was so rapid that after half an hour the burghers, without the expected support from reluctant waverers hanging back in the kloofs, began to falter before the tough resistance put up by the Light Horsemen. At the end of four hours and the arrival of a relief column from Bethlehem, De Wet's commando retired gradually to the cover of kloofs in spurs of the Langberg. The commando had more than met its match.

Trooper A. Fraser, 2nd Light Horse was killed. Surgeon-Captain T.J. Crean, Captain G.

Brierley, Captain W; Jardine, Lieutenant L. O'Hara and seven men were wounded.

While attending the wounded under fire within 150 yards of the enemy, Surgeon-Captain Tom Crean was severely wounded in the stomach. Captain Crean was a six foot tall Irishman. In pre-war days he had a medical practice in Johannesburg. He joined the Light Horse when it was first founded in Pietermaritzburg and served, at first, as a trooper. He fought as a trooper at Elandslaagte and at Wagon Hill. After Wagon Hill he transferred to Intombi Hospital medical staff. When Ladysmith was relieved he once again served as a combatant and commanded a troop until the middle of 1901.

For gallantry in the action at Tyger Kloof, Surgeon-Captain T.J. Crean was awarded the Victoria Cross. The citation read: "During the action with De Wet at Tyger Kloof 18th December 1901, this officer continued to attend the wounded in the firing line under a heavy fire at only 150 yard range, after he had himself been wounded and only desisted when he was hit a second time and as it was first thought he was mortally wounded."

(Extract from G.F. Gibson *The Story of the Imperial Light Horse* G.D. & Co 1937.)

THE KING'S COLOURS

The great honour, the presentation of the King's Colours (King Edward's) to the Regiment Johannesburg on 28th September, 1904, was conferred by HRH Princess Christian.

Addressing Lieutenant-Colonel J. Donaldson, DSO, then commanding the ILH and Lieutenant Alfred Harte, the Colour Bearer, the Princess presenting the King's Banner said:

"Yours was the first Volunteer Regiment formed at the commencement of the late war. Your record throughout the prolonged struggle was unsurpassed. I present you with this Standard, which my brother the King has been pleased to direct to be entrusted to your care. I know it will be zealously and carefully guarded, and I trust it will help those that join your Regiment to emulate and maintain unblemished name for heroism and patriotism."

Presentation of the King's Colour by Her Royal Highness Princess Christian to the Imperial Light Horse.

The monuments and headstones of the Imperial Light Horse

Transcript of the report giving details of the monuments erected between 1903 and 1905 at the sites of mass burials as well as individual headstones placed on individual graves. From G.F. Gibson *The Story of the Imperial Light Horse.*

Johannesburg,
28th July, 1905.

To the Chairman,
  Imperial Light Horse Memorial Committee,
    Johannesburg.

Sir,

I have the honour to inform you that the Imperial Light Horse Monuments have now been completed throughout Natal, the Transvaal and the Orange River Colony in accordance with the resolution passed at a meeting of the Memorial Committee held on Friday, 19th June, 1903, and I beg herewith to submit my report thereon.

NATAL.

(a) The following Headstones have been erected, in all cases enclosed by railings and suitably inscribed:—

(1) DURBAN.
  Trooper R. J. Whittle.
  Trooper C. C. Atlay.
(2) MARITZBURG.
  Sergt.-Major A. J. C. Lang.
  Corporal W. G. Downer.
  Trooper A. E. Swanson.
  Trooper C. D. B. White.
(3) HOWICK.
  Corporal A. H. Twange.
(4) MOOI RIVER.
  Trooper C. H. Robinson.
  Trooper D. Falconer.
(5) CHIEVELEY.
  Trooper H. D. Longden.
  Trooper A. R. Jackson.
  Trooper N. C. Blakeway.
  Trooper H. S. Mapleston.
(6) LADYSMITH BOROUGH CEMETERY.
  Trooper R. G. Nicol.
  Trooper J. P. F. Cunningham.
  Trooper T. C. Chadwick.
  Trooper J. E. Downing.
  Trooper F. Dearlove.
  Trooper J. F. Wingate.
(7) INTOMBI CEMETERY.
  Farrier-Sergeant W. Burrows.
  Sergt. H. C. Benson.
  Trooper J. Campbell.
  Trooper J. C. E. Carter.
  Trooper F. W. Pearse.
  Trooper W. P. Lawrence.
  Trooper R. A. Foley.
  Trooper J. G. Taylor.
  Trooper H. C. Ochse.
  Trooper W. G. B. Saunders.
(8) CHARLESTOWN.
  Trooper H. Walshlager.

(b) The following Obelisks have been erected:—

(1) ELANDSLAAGTE.

(a) Obelisk erected on the spot where Colonel Scott-Chisholme was killed.

In Memory of
Colonel JOHN JAMES SCOTT CHISHOLME
(late of the 5th Lancers)
who commanded the Imperial Light Horse, and fell while leading that Regiment at Elandslaagte, 21st October, 1899.

[4]

Erected by the Officers, Non-Commissioned Officers and Men of the 5th Lancers and Imperial Light Horse.

(b) Obelisk in Cemetery inscribed with the names of those who are buried there:—

THIS MONUMENT IS ERECTED BY THEIR COMRADES IN MEMORY OF

Sergeant-Major E. H. Cuthbert. Trooper K. McClintock.
Sergeant C. H. Hendley. Trooper R. S. Farren.
Trooper F. J. T. Hunt. Trooper H. J. Wolseley.
Trooper A. C. W. Sillery. Trooper F. C. Fisher.

who fell in action at Elandslaagte, on 21st October, 1899, and are buried on this spot.

*"Tell England, ye who pass this Monument,
We, who died serving her, rest here content."*

(2) WAGON HILL (No. 1).

Obelisk on the scene of the fighting, inscribed with the names of all those who were killed on 6th January, 1900, or who died from wounds received on that day, as follows:—

THIS MONUMENT IS ERECTED BY THEIR COMRADES IN MEMORY OF Officers, N.C.O.'s and Troopers of the Imperial Light Horse, who fell at Wagon Hill, on the 6th of January, 1900.

Lieut. W. F. Adams. Trooper H. Albrecht, v.c.
Lieut. J. E. Pakeman. Trooper J. H. Bewsher.
Sergeant G. Howard. Trooper P. Brady.
Corporal A. S. Dunn. Trooper T. C. Chadwick.
Corporal E. de C. Dickinson. Trooper R. M. Dawson.
Corporal G. A. Ferrand. Trooper W. S. Hogg.
Corporal J. Haddon. Trooper G. Lind.
Corporal A. M. Robbins. Trooper R. M. Mackenzie.
Corporal G. H. Moore. Trooper E. W. Mocatta.
Lance-Corporal G. G. Cameron. Trooper T. T. Preston.
Lance-Corporal M. Greathead. Trooper P. Y. Tucker.
Lance-Corporal G. W. R. Nettleship. Trooper F. C. Rogers.

- - - -

Died from wounds received.

Major D. E. Doveton. Trooper H. C. Gorton.
Trooper J. F. Wingate. Trooper C. C. Atlay.
Trooper J. Carter. Trooper W. G. B. Saunders.

WAGON HILL (No. 2).

Obelisk in the Cemetery inscribed with the names of those who are buried there, as follows:—

[5]

THIS MONUMENT IS ERECTED BY THEIR COMRADES IN MEMORY OF

Sergeant G. Howard.	Trooper H. Albrecht, v.c.
Corporal A. S. Dunn.	Trooper J. H. Bewsher.
Corporal E. de C. Dickinson.	Trooper P. Brady.
Corporal G. A. Ferrand.	Trooper R. M. Dawson.
Corporal J. Haddon.	Trooper W. S. Hogg.
Corporal A. M. Robbins.	Trooper G. Lind.
Corporal G. H. Moore.	Trooper R. M. Mackenzie.
Lance-Corporal G. G. Cameron.	Trooper T. T. Preston.
Lance-Corporal G. W. R. Nettleship.	Trooper P. Y. Tucker.

who fell in action at Wagon Hill, 6th January, 1900, and are buried on this spot.

"Tell England, ye who pass this Monument,
We, who died serving her, rest here content."

INTOMBI CEMETERY.

Obelisk inscribed with the names of all who are buried in the Cemetery, as follows:—

THIS MONUMENT IS ERECTED BY THEIR COMRADES IN MEMORY OF N.C.O.'s and Troopers of the Imperial Light Horse who are buried in this Cemetery.

Farrier-Sergeant W. Burrows.	Trooper F. W. Pearce.
Trooper W. P. Lawrence.	Trooper J. G. Taylor.
Trooper W. G. B. Saunders.	Trooper H. C. Gorton.
Trooper R. A. Foley.	Trooper D. Guthrie Smith.
Trooper J. C. E. Carter.	Trooper H. C. Benson.
Trooper J. Campbell.	Trooper H. C. Ochse.
Trooper A. C. Shortt.	Trooper Bernard Stewart.

"Tell England, ye who pass this Monument,
We, who died serving her, rest here content."

LADYSMITH BOROUGH CEMETERY.

(1) Obelisk inscribed with the names of all who are buried in the Cemetery, as follows:—

THIS MONUMENT IS ERECTED BY THEIR COMRADES IN MEMORY OF Officers, N.C.O.'s and Troopers of the Imperial Light Horse who are buried in this Cemetery.

Colonel J. J. Scott-Chisholme.	Trooper E. W. Mocatta.
Major D. E. Doveton.	Trooper J. P. F. Cunningham.
Captain J. C. Knapp.	Trooper F. C. Rogers.
Lieutenant A. E. Brabant.	Trooper T. C. Chadwick.
Lieutenant W. F. Adams.	Trooper J. E. Downing.
Lieutenant J. E. Pakeman.	Trooper F. Dearlove.
Corporal M. Greathead.	Trooper J. F. Wingate.
Trooper R. G. Nicol.	Trooper J. P. Powers.

"Tell England, ye who pass this Monument,
We, who died serving her, rest here content."

[6]

(2) Obelisk to the memory of Col. J. J. Scott-Chisholme, as follows:
IN MEMORY OF COLONEL JOHN JAMES SCOTT CHISHOLME
(late of the 5th Lancers)
who commanded the Imperial Light Horse and fell while leading
that Regiment at Elandslaagte, 21st October, 1899.
Erected by the Officers, Non-Commissioned Officers and Men of the
5th Lancers and Imperial Light Horse.

- - - -

LADYSMITH BOROUGH CEMETERY.
(3) Obelisk to the Memory of Lieut. A. E. Brabant, as follows:—
ERECTED BY HIS COMRADES TO THE MEMORY OF
LIEUTENANT A. E. BRABANT
who died on 5th November, 1899, from wounds received in action
in the Long Valley

- - - -

Obelisk to the Memory of Lieut. J. E. Pakeman, as follows:—
ERECTED BY HIS COMRADES TO THE MEMORY OF
LIEUTENANT J. E. PAKEMAN
who fell in action at Wagon Hill, on 6th January, 1900.

- - - -

TRANSVAAL.
The following Headstones have been erected, enclosed by railings and
suitably inscribed:—

(1) ELANDSFONTEIN CEMETERY.

Regt.-Qt.-Master Sergt. C. Belcher. Trooper W. H. Davies.
Corporal G. Mackenzie. Trooper N. Williams.
Trooper R. J. Davies. Trooper C. Coltart.
Trooper J. P. McCabe.

(2) FREDERICKSTAD.

Trooper I. D. Simpson. Trooper Aschmann.

(3) JOHANNESBURG.

Sergt. G. Wileman. Trooper M. G Norwood
Sergt. H. E. Welsteed. Trooper A. C. Brown.
Corporal W. Mackenzie. Trooper R. J. Barratt.
Trooper A. Bouchier. Trooper C. S. Manning.
Trooper A. P. D. Moodie. Trooper L. Bromham.

(4) KLERKSDORP.

Sergt. H. Parkin. Trooper S. Torgins.
Trooper E. Clark.

(5) KLIP DRIFT.

Lieut. L. S. Sanders. Trooper B. L. Bristol.

[7]

(6) LAKE CHRISSIE.

Lance-Corporal D. W. Ritchie.
Trooper J. Erasmus.
Trooper C. Marsden.
Trooper F. H. Smallwood.

(7) PRETORIA.

Sergt. A. S. Melville.
Trooper A. H. Pinnick.

(8) REITKUIL.

Trooper F. G. Ogston.

(9) STANDERTON.

Trooper H. Edmonson.
Trooper T. Knowles.

(10) VENTERSDORP.

Trooper D. S. Burgess.
Trooper J. J. Bailey.

(11) WITKLIP.

Trooper Grahame Maxwell King.

(12) PIET RETIEF.

Trooper H. J. Harding.
Trooper J. W. Lee.
Trooper G. Hanks.

(13) MAFEKING.

Trooper T. S. Cashman.

(14) NORVALS PONT.

Trooper J. Flanegan.

The following Obelisks have been erected:—

(1) WITKLIP.

Obelish erected about three miles from the scene of the fight and inscribed with the names of all who fell on 7th July, 1900, as follows:

THIS MONUMENT IS ERECTED BY THEIR COMRADES IN MEMORY OF Officers, N.C.O.'s and Troopers of the Imperial Light Horse who fell at Witklip, on the 7th July, 1900.

Captain W. M. Currie.
Lieutenant E. Kirk.
Sergeant J. Marshall.
Farrier Sergeant C. Woolley.
Corporal E. O. Atherstone.
Trooper G. W. Drennan.
Trooper Grahame M. King.
Trooper H. Lane.
Trooper A. P. D. Moodie.

Died from wounds received:—

Trooper A. Bouchier.

"Tell England, ye who pass this Monument,
We, who died serving her, rest here content."

- - - -

(2) NAAUWPOORT NEK.

Obelisk erected over the graves of those who fell on 5th January, 1901, and inscribed with their names, as follows:—

THIS MONUMENT IS ERECTED BY THEIR COMRADES IN MEMORY OF Officers, N.C.O.'s and Troopers of the Imperial Light Horse who fell at Naauwpoort Nek, on the 5th January, 1901.

[8]

Captain T. Yockney.	Lieutenant A. Ormond.
S.S.M. Sandys (5th Lancers).	Corporal T. Gollan, Imperial Yeomanry
Corporal H. Nash.	Trooper W. W. Chinnock "
Trooper P. Anderson.	Trooper A. E. Wright "
Trooper J. W. Maxwell.	Trooper T. Clarke "
Trooper C. J. Harding.	Trooper G. Raynor "
Trooper R. O. Butler.	Trooper J. Blake "
Trooper W. Melville.	Trooper A. Bywater "
Trooper W. Pierce.	Trooper M. A. Langley.

Died from wounds received:—

Trooper R. Leck.	Trooper A. C. Brown.
Trooper J. Bentley.	Trooper L. Bromham.
Trooper C. H. Rex, Imperial Yeomanry.	

"Tell England, ye who pass this Monument,
We, who died serving her, rest here content."

(3) MARITZANI.

Obelisk erected on the farm Neverset in memory of those who fell in the Relief of Mafeking, 13th May, 1900, as follows:—

THIS MONUMENT IS ERECTED BY THEIR COMRADES IN MEMORY OF N.C.O.'s and Troopers of the Imperial Light Horse, who fell at Maritzani, on the 13th May, 1900.

Corporal W. Francis.	Trooper G. Bonsey.
Trooper H. E. Taylor.	Trooper H. S. Boone.
Trooper C. Davis.	Trooper C. T. Gardner.

Died from wounds received:—

Sergeant A. J. Haynes.

"Tell England, ye who pass this Monument,
We, who died serving her, rest here content."

(4) HARTEBEESTEFONTEIN.

Obelisk erected in Hartebeestefontein Cemetery in memory of those who were killed on 22nd March, 1901, as follows:—

THIS MONUMENT IS ERECTED BY THEIR COMRADES IN MEMORY OF Officers, N.C.O.'s and Troopers of the Imperial Light Horse who fell at Hartebeestefontein on the 22nd March, 1901.

Lieutenant J. Ralston.	Trooper D. Paterson.
R.S.M. A. E. Hurst.	Trooper P. Kennedy.
Trooper P. Jones.	

Died from wounds received:—

Lieutenant A. R. Halling.

"Tell England, ye who pass this Monument,
We, who died serving her, rest here content."

(5) ZEERUST.

Obelisk in memory of Lieutenant Byron Cecil Noel.

[9]

ORANGE RIVER COLONY.

The following Headstones have been erected enclosed by railings and suitably inscribed:—

(1) BETHLEHEM.

Corporal P. Connell.
Trooper E. H. McChesney.
Trooper C. Hooper.
Trooper C. Bremer.
Trooper M. O'Shea.
Trooper W. Ager.
Trooper J. W. Townsend.
Trooper H. Abercrombie.

(2) ELANDS RIVER.

Trooper A. L. Fraser.

(3) HARRISMITH.

Corporal F. James.
Corporal W. Gabriel.
Trooper B. F. Murray.
Trooper F. Wheeler.

(4) KALKFONTEIN (District Vrede).

Sergeant P. Cawood.
Corporal J. E. Davies.

(5) LINDLEY (Craven's Rust).

Corporal J. Renouf.

(6) HEILBRON.

Trooper C. Upton.
Trooper W. Evans.
Trooper T. Johnson.
Trooper H. C. Thirlwall.

(7) VINKES.

Trooper S. Tennant.

The number of single Tombstones and Obelisks erected is as follows:

Single Tombstones	92
Obelisks	14

Officers:—

Killed and died of wounds	14
Wounded	29

N.C.O.'s and Men:—

Killed and died of wounds	107
Wounded	191
	341

In concluding this report I beg to express my opinion that all the work has been well done and cannot fail to give satisfaction to the Regiment and to the relatives of all those to whose memory the Monuments have been erected.

(Signed) C. ELLIS, *Secretary.*

We Rest Here Content

RANK		NAME		BURIED		ACTION	Hst/Mon	Yes
Tpr	H.	Abercrombie	DOW	Bethlehem	ILH	Paardeplaatz	G	X
Lt	W.F.	Adams	KIA	Ladysmith	Mon	Wagon Hill	O2 O5	
Tpr	W.	Agar	DOD	Bethlehem	ILH	Bethlehem	G	X
Tpr	H.	Albrecht	KIA	Wagon Hill	Mon	Wagon Hill	O2 O3	
Tpr	P.	Anderson	KIA	Krugersdorp	Mon	Cyferfontein	O9	
Tpr	H.L.	Aschmann	KIA	Potchefstroom	Mon	Frederickstad	G	
Cpl	E.O.	Atherstone	KIA	Braamfontein	Mon	Witklip	O8	
Tpr	C.C.	Atlay	DOW	Durban	Cross	Wagon Hill	G O2	X
Tpr	J.J.	Bailey	KIA	Ventersdorp	ILH	Elandsfontein	G	X
Tpr	W.B.	Bain	DOD			Albert Docks		
Tpr	J.R.	Barrett	DOD	Braamfontein	Mon	Johannesburg	G	
Tpr	J.H.	Barry	KIA	Heilbron		Heilbron		
Rgm Sgt	C.E.B.	Belcher	DOD	Braamfontein	Mon	Elandsfontein	G	
Sgt	H.C.	Benson	DOW	Intombi	ILH	Elandslaagte	G O4	X
Tpr	J.H.	Bentley	DOW	Krugersdorp	Mon	Cyferfontein	O9	
Tpr	J.H.	Bewsher	KIA	Wagon Hill	Mon	Wagon Hill	O2 O3	
Tpr	N.C.	Blakeway	KIA	Clouston	ILH	Hlangwane	G	X
Tpr	G.	Bonsey	KIA	Mafikeng	Metal	Neverset	O10	
Tpr	H.S.	Boome	KIA	Mafikeng	Metal	Neverset	O10	
Tpr	A.	Bouchier	DOW	Braamfontein	Mon	Witklip	G	
Lt	A.E.	Brabant	DOW	Ladysmith	Mon	Mtd Inf Hill	O5 O6	
Tpr	P.	Brady	KIA	Wagon Hill	Mon	Wagon Hill	O2 O3	
Tpr	G.	Bremer	KIA	Bethlehem	ILH	Concordia	G	X
Tpr	B.L.	Bristol	KIA	Ottosdal	Mon	Rietvlei	G	
Tpr	L.	Bromham	DOW	Braamfontein	Mon	Cyferfontein	G O9	
Tpr	A.C.	Brown	DOW	Braamfontein	Mon	Cyferfontein	G O9	
Tpr	D.S.	Burgess	KIA	Ventersdorp	ILH	Doornpan	G	X
Farr Sgt	W.	Burrows	DOD	Intombi	ILH	Ladysmith	G O4	X
Tpr	R.O.	Butler	KIA	Krugersdorp	Mon	Cyferfontein	O9	
Tpr	A.	Cairns	KIA			Rietvlei		
L Cpl	G.G.	Cameron	KIA	Wagon Hill	Mon	Wagon Hill	O2 O3	
Tpr	J.	Campbell	DOD	Intombi	ILH	Ladysmith	G O4	X
Tpr	J.C.E.	Carter	DOW	Intombi	ILH	Wagon Hill	G O2 O4	X
Tpr	T.S.	Cashman	DOD	Mafikeng	ILH	Mafikeng	G	
Sgt	P.	Cawood	KIA	Vrede	Mon	Kalkfontein	G	
Tpr	T.C.	Chadwick	DOW	Ladysmith	ILH	Wagon Hill	G O2 O5	X
Tpr	E.	Clark	KIA	Klerksdorp	ILH	Palmietfontein	G	
Tpr	T.	Clementson	DOI	Colesberg	Mon	Norval's Pont		
Tpr	C.	Coltart	D	Braamfontein	Mon	Johannesburg	G	
Cpl	F.	Connell	KIA	Bethlehem	ILH	Roodepoort	G	X
Tpr	H.J.	Cox	DOD	Braamfontein	Mon	Johannesburg		
Tpr	D.H.	Cribb	DOI	Bloemfontein	Mon	Brandkop		
Tpr	J.P.F.	Cunningham	DOW	Ladysmith	ILH	Elandslaagte	G O5	X
Capt	W.M.	Currie	KIA	Braamfontein	Mon	Witklip	O8	
Sgt Maj	E.H.	Cuthbert	KIA	Elandslaagte	Mon	Elandslaagte	O1	

Tpr	R.J.	Davies	DOD	Primrose	Mon	Elandsfontein	G	
Tpr	W.H.	Davies	DOD	Primrose	Mon	Elandsfontein	G	
Cpl	J.E.G.	Davies	KIA	Vrede	Mon	Kalkfontein	G	
Tpr	C.	Davis	KIA	Mafikeng	Metal	Neverset	O10	
Tpr	W.R.	Daws	KIA	Primrose	Mon	Elandsfontein		
Tpr	R.M.	Dawson	KIA	Wagon Hill	Mon	Wagon Hill	O2 O3	
Tpr	F.	Dearlove	KIA	Ladysmith	ILH	Mtd Inf Hill	G O5	X
Cpl	E.deC.	Dickinson	KIA	Wagon Hill	Mon	Wagon Hill	O2 O3	
L Cpl	J.G.	Dixon	DOD	Bethlehem	Metal	Bethlehem		
Maj	D.E.	Doveton	DOW	Ladysmith	Mon	Long Valley	O2 O5	
Cpl	W.G.	Downer	DOD	Fort Napier	ILH	Fort Napier	G	X
Tpr	J.E.	Downing	DOD	Ladysmith	ILH	Ladysmith	G O5	X
Tpr	G.W.	Drennan	KIA	Braamfontein	Mon	Witklip	O8	
Cpl	A.S.	Dunn	KIA	Wagon Hill	Mon	Wagon Hill	O2 O3	
Tpr	H.	Edmondson	DOW	Standerton	Mon	Lake Chrissie	G	
Tpr	J.	Erasmus	DOW	Lake Chrissie	ILH	Lake Chrissie	G	X
Tpr	W.	Evans	KIA	Heilbron	Mon	Heilbron	G	
Tpr	D.	Falconer	DOD	Mooi River	ILH	Mooi River	G	X
Tpr	R.S.	Farren	KIA	Elandslaagte	Mon	Elandslaagte	O1	
Cpl	G.A.	Ferrand	KIA	Wagon Hill	Mon	Wagon Hill	O2 O3	
Tpr	F.C.	Fisher	KIA	Elandslaagte	Mon	Elandslaagte	O1	
Tpr	G.	Fitzpatrick	KIA	Estcourt	Mon	Willow Grange		
Tpr	J.	Flanegan	DOW	Colesberg	ILH	Heilbron	G	X
Tpr	R.A.	Foley	DOD	Intombi	ILH	Ladysmith	G O4	X
Cpl	W.	Francis	KIA	Mafikeng	Metal	Neverset	O10	
Tpr Guide	A.L.	Fraser	DOW	Harrismith	ILH	Tygerskloof	G	X
Tpr	F.A.	Freshney	DOW	Lincoln, Eng		Colenso		
Cpl	W.	Gabriel	DOW	Harrismith	ILH	Newmarket Farm	G	X
Tpr		Gardner	D	Mafikeng	Metal	Neverset		
Tpr	C.T.	Gardner	KIA	Mafikeng	Mon	Neverset	O10	
Tpr	S.	Goddard	DOD	Howick	Mon	Howick		
Tpr	F.H.C.	Gorton	DOW	Intombi	Mon	Wagon Hill	O2 O4	
L Cpl	M.	Greathead	KIA	Ladysmith	Mon	Wagon Hill	O2 O5	
Tpr	D.	Guthrie-Smith	DOW	Intombi	Mon	Ladysmith	O4	
Cpl	J.	Haddon	KIA	Wagon Hill	Mon	Wagon Hill	O2 O3	
Lt	A.R.	Halling	DOW	Hartebeestfontein	Mon	Hartebeestfontein	O11	
Tpr	G.	Hanks	DRO	Wakkerstroom	ILH	Piet Retief	G	X
Tpr	H.J.	Harding	DOD	Wakkerstroom	ILH	Piet Retief	G	X
Tpr	C.J.	Harding	KIA	Krugersdorp	Mon	Cyferfontein	O9	
Sgt	A.J.	Haynes	DOW	Mafikeng	Metal	Neverset		
Sgt	C.H.	Hendley	KIA	Elandslaagte	Mon	Elandslaagte	O1	
Tpr	L.T.	Hervey	DOD	West End	Mon	Kimberley		
Tpr	W.S.	Hogg	KIA	Wagon Hill	Mon	Wagon Hill	O2 O3	
Tpr	V.G.	Hooper	KIA	Bethlehem	ILH	Vischgat	G	X
Sgt	G.	Howard	KIA	Wagon Hill	Mon	Wagon Hill	O2 O3	

We Rest Here Content

Tpr	C.	Howell	DRO	Tugela River				
Tpr	F.J.T.	Hunt	KIA	Elandslaagte	Mon	Elandslaagte	O1	
Rgt Sgt Maj	A.E.	Hurst	KIA	Hartebeestfontein	Mon	Hartebeestfontein	O11	
Tpr	F.	Hutchinson	DOD	Harrismith	Head	Harrismith		
Tpr	A.P.	Jackson	KIA	Clouston	ILH	Hlangwane	G	X
Cpl	F.	James	DOD	Harrismith	ILH	Harrismith	G	X
Tpr	A.H.	Johnson	KIA					
Tpr	T.	Johnson	KIA	Heilbron	Mon	Katkop	G	
Tpr	P.	Jones	KIA	Hartebeestfontein	Mon	Hartebeestfontein	O11	
Tpr	P.	Kennedy	KIA	Hartebeestfontein	Mon	Hartebeestfontein	O11	
Tpr	G.M.	King	KIA	Braamfontein	Mon	Witklip	G O8	
Lt	E.E.	Kirk	KIA	Braamfontein	Mon	Witklip	O8	
Capt	J.C.	Knapp	KIA	Ladysmith	Mon	Mtd Inf Hill	O5	
Tpr	T.	Knowles	DOD	Standerton	Mon	Standerton	G	
Tpr	H.	Lane	DOW	Braamfontein	Mon	Witklip	O8	
Sgt Maj	A.J.C.	Lang	DOD	Fort Napier	ILH	Victoria Hotel, Pmb	G	X
Tpr	M.A.	Langley	KIA	Krugersdorp	Mon	Cyferfontein		
Tpr	W.T.P.	Lawrence	DOD	Intombi	ILH	Ladysmith	G O4	X
Tpr	R.	Leak	DOW	Krugersdorp	Mon	Cyferfontein	O9	
Tpr	J.	Ledingham	K	Ladysmith	Mon	Ladysmith		
Tpr	J.W.	Lee	DOAB	Wakkerstroom	ILH	Piet Retief	G	X
Tpr	G.	Lind	KIA	Wagon Hill	Mon	Wagon Hill	O2 O3	
Tpr	W.H.	Longden	KIA	Clouston	ILH	Hlangwane	G	X
Cpl	W.	Mackenzie	D	Braamfontein	Mon	Johannesburg	G	
Cpl	G.	MacKenzie	DOD	Braamfontein	Mon	Elandsfontein	G	
Tpr	R.M.	MacKenzie	KIA	Wagon Hill	Mon	Wagon Hill	O2 O3	
Tpr	C.S.	Manning	DOD	Braamfontein	Mon	Johannesburg	G	
Tpr	H.S.	Mapleston	DOD	Chieveley	ILH	Colenso	G	X
Tpr	C.	Marsden	KIA	Lake Chrissie	ILH	Lake Chrissie	G	X
Sgt	J.	Marshall	KIA	Braamfontein	Mon	Witklip	O8	
Tpr	J.W.	Maxwell	KIA	Krugersdorp	Mon	Cyferfontein	O9	
Tpr	P.	McCabe	DOAL	Primrose	Mon	Elandsfontein	G	
Tpr	E.H.	McChesney	KBL	Bethlehem	ILH	Vischgat	G	X
Tpr	K.R.G.	McClintock	KIA	Elandslaagte	Mon	Elandslaagte	O1	
Tpr	J.	McIntry	D	Braamfontein	Mon	Witklip		
Sgt	A.S.	Melville	DOD	Pretoria	ILH	Pretoria	G	X
Tpr	W.	Melville	KIA	Krugersdorp	Mon	Cyferfontein		
Tpr	V.	Miller	DOD	Bethlehem	Metal	Bethlehem		
Tpr	E.W.	Mocatta	KIA	Wagon Hill	Mon	Wagon Hill	O2 O5	
Tpr	A.P.D.	Moodie	DOW	Braamfontein	Mon	Witklip	O8	
Cpl	G.H.	Moore	KIA	Wagon Hill	Mon	Wagon Hill	O2 O3	
Capt	C.H.	Mullins	DOW	Grahamstown	Cross	Maritsane		
Tpr	B.F.	Murray	DOD	Harrismith	ILH	Harrismith	G	X
Tpr	W.	Murray	DOW	Braamfontein	Mon	Witklip (Diamond Hill)		

We Rest Here Content

Tpr	H.	Muson	DOW	Standerton				
Cpl	H.	Nash	KIA	Krugersdorp	Mon	Cyferfontein	O9	
L Cpl	C.W.R.	Nettleship	KIA	Wagon Hill	Mon	Wagon Hill	O2 O3	
Tpr	R.G.	Nicol	DOW	Ladysmith	ILH	Gun Hill	G O5	X
Lt	B.C.	Noel	DOW	Zeerust	Cross	Oog van Marico	O12	
Tpr	M.G.N.	Norwood	DOD	Braamfontein	Mon	Johannesburg	G	
Tpr	H.	O'Hagan	D			Cyferfontein		
Tpr	M.	O'Shea	KIA	Bethlehem	ILH	Tygerkloof	G	X
Tpr	H.C.	Ochse	DOW	Intombi	ILH	Elandslaagte	G O4	X
Tpr	F.H.	Ogston	KIA	Klerksdorp	ILH	Rietkuil	G	X
Lt	A.	Ormond	KIA	Krugersdorp	Mon	Cyferfontein	O9	
Sgt	J.B.	Orrett	D	Maitland	Mon			
Lt	J.E.	Pakeman	KIA	Ladysmith	Mon	Wagon Hill	O2 O5 O7	
Sgt	H.	Parkin	DOD	Klerksdorp	ILH	Matjespruit	G	X
Tpr	H.	Parmenter	DOD	Braamfontein	Mon	Johannesburg		
Tpr	D.	Paterson	KIA	Hartebeestfontein	Mon	Hartebeestfontein	O11	
Tpr	F.W.	Pearce	DOD	Intombi	ILH	Ladysmith	G O4	X
Tpr	J.	Pearson	D	Ladysmith	Mon	Ladysmith		
Tpr	W.	Pierce	KIA	Krugersdorp	Mon	Cyferfontein		
Tpr	A.H.F.	Pinnick	DOD	Pretoria	ILH	Pretoria	G	X
Tpr	J.P.	Powers	D	Ladysmith	Mon	Ladysmith	O5	
Tpr	T.T.	Preston	KIA	Wagon Hill	Mon	Wagon Hill	O2 O3	
Lt	J.	Ralston	KIA	Hartebeestfontein	Mon	Hartebeestfontein	O11	
Cpl	J.H.	Renouf	KIA	Lindley	Mon	Craven's Rust	G	
L Cpl	D.W.N.	Ritchie	KIA	Lake Chrissie	ILH	Lake Chrissie	G	X
Cpl	A.M.	Robbins	KIA	Wagon Hill	Mon	Wagon Hill	O2 O3	
Tpr	C.H.	Robinson	DOD	Mooi River	ILH	Mooi River	G	X
Tpr	F.C	Rogers	KIA	Wagon Hill	Mon	Wagon Hill	O2 O5	
Lt	L.S.	Sanders	KIA	Ottosdal	Mon	Korannafontein	G	
Tpr	W.G.B.	Saunders	DOW	Intombi	ILH	Wagon Hill	G O2 O4	X
Tpr	A.C.	Shortt	DOW	Intombi	Mon	Wagon Hill	O4	
Tpr	A.C.W.	Sillery	KIA	Elandslaagte	Mon	Elandslaagte	O1	
Tpr	G.	Simpson	DOW			Hamelfontein		
Tpr	I.D.J.	Simpson	KIA	Potchefstroom	Mon	Frederickstad	G	
Tpr	F.H.	Smallwood	KBL	Ermelo	Mon	Twyfelaar	G	
Tpr	T.	Smith	DOD	Pretoria	Mon	Pretoria		
Tpr	B.	Stewart	DOD	Intombi	Mon	Ladysmith	O4	
Tpr	A.E.	Swanson	DOP	Fort Napier	ILH	Fort Napier	G	X
Tpr	A.B.	Taylor	D			Diamantuur		
Tpr	J.G.	Taylor	DOD	Intombi	ILH	Ladysmith	G O4	X
Tpr	H.E.	Taylor	KIA	Mafikeng	Metal	Neverset	O10	
Tpr	S.	Tennant	KIA	Harrismith	ILH	Klipkraal	G	X
Tpr	H.C.	Thirlwall	KIA	Heilbron	Mon	Katkop	G	
Tpr	J.I.	Thomas	DOD	Newcastle	Mon	Charlestown		
Tpr	S.	Torgins	KIA			Sterkfontein	G	

Tpr	J.W.	Townsend	KIA	Bethlehem	ILH	Naauwpoort Nek	G	X
Tpr	P.Y.	Tucker	KIA	Wagon Hill	Mon	Wagon Hill	O2 O3	
Tpr	R.S.	Tute	DOD	Ladysmith	A	Ladysmith		
Cpl	A.H.	Twange	DOD	Howick	Mon	Howick	G	
Tpr	C.	Upton	KIA	Heilbron	Mon	Katkop	G	
Tpr	E.H.	Wallace	D					
Tpr	E.H.	Walshlager	DOD	Newcastle	ILH	Charlestown	G	
Sgt	H.E.	Wellstead	DOW	Braamfontein	Mon	Frederickstad	G	
Tpr	F.	Wheeler	DOW	Harrismith	ILH	Ladysmith	G	X
Tpr	C.D.B.	White	DOW	Fort Napier	ILH	Elandslaagte	G	X
Tpr	C.	Whittaker	DOIA	Krugersdorp	ILH	Krugersdorp		X
Tpr	B.E.	Whittaker	DOIR	Colesberg	Mon	Norval's Pont		
Tpr	R.J.	Whittle	DOD	Wyatt Road	ILH	Durban	G	X
Tpr	E.	Wild	DOW	Fauresmith	Metal	Fauresmith		
Sgt	G.	Wileman	DOW	Braamfontein	Mon	Frederickstad	G	
Tpr	J.W.	Wilkes	DOW	Pretoria	Mon	Pretoria		
Tpr	W.R.	Willcocks	DOD	Wakkerstroom	Mon	Wakkerstroom		
Tpr	N.	Williams	DOD	Primrose	Mon	Elandsfontein	G	
Tpr	J.F.	Wingate	DOW	Ladysmith	ILH	Wagon Hill	G O2 O5	X
Tpr	C.W.	Winter	DRO	Compies River				
Tpr	H.J.	Wolseley	KIA	Elandslaagte	Mon	Elandslaagte	O1	
Tpr	W.	Wood	D	Pretoria	Metal	Pretoria		
Tpr	C.H.	Woolcott	KIA	Vlakfontein				
Farr Sgt	C.S.	Wooley	KIA	Braamfontein	Mon	Witklip	O8	
Capt	T.	Yockney	KIA	Krugersdorp	Mon	Cyferfontein	O9	

<u>Obelisks:</u> O1 – Elandslaagte O2 – Wagon Hill O3 – Wagon Hill cemetery O4 – Intombi O5 – Ladysmith Borough O6 – Ladysmith Borough Lt. A.E Brabant O7 – Ladysmith Borough Lt. J.E. Pakeman O8 - Witklip O9 - Naauwpoort Nek O10 – Maritzani O11 – Hartebeestfontein O12 – Zeerust

We Rest Here Content

Casualty list and monuments   *As per Steve Watt's listing from "In Memoriam"*

RANK		NAME		BURIED	*	ACTION	**	***
Tpr	E.H.	Wallace	D					N
Tpr	A.H.	Johnson	KIA					N
Tpr	C.W.	Winter	DRO	Compies River				N
Sgt	J.B.	Orrett	D	Maitland	Mon			P
Tpr	H.	Muson	DOW	Standerton				
Tpr	C.	Howell	DRO	Tugela River				
Tpr	C.H.	Woolcott	KIA	Vlakfontein				
Tpr	W.B.	Bain	DOD			Albert Docks		N
L Cpl	J.G.	Dixon	DOD	Bethlehem	Metal	Bethlehem		P
Tpr	W.	Agar	DOD	Bethlehem	ILH	Bethlehem	G	X
Tpr	V.	Miller	DOD	Bethlehem	Metal	Bethlehem		P
Tpr	D.H.	Cribb	DOI	Bloemfontein	Mon	Brandkop		
Tpr	J.I.	Thomas	DOD	Newcastle	Mon	Charlestown		P
Tpr	E.H.	Walshlager	DOD	Newcastle	ILH	Charlestown	G	P
Tpr	H.S.	Mapleston	DOD	Chieveley	ILH	Colenso	G A	X
Tpr	F.A.	Freshney	DOW	Lincoln, Eng		Colenso		
Tpr	G.	Bremer	KIA	Bethlehem	ILH	Concordia	G	X
Cpl	J.H.	Renouf	KIA	Lindley	Mon	Craven's Rust	G	P
Tpr	H.	O'Hagan	D			Cyferfontein		N
Tpr	L.	Bromham	DOW	Braamfontein	Mon	Cyferfontein	G O9	P
Tpr	A.C.	Brown	DOW	Braamfontein	Mon	Cyferfontein	G O9	P
Tpr	J.H.	Bentley	DOW	Krugersdorp	Mon	Cyferfontein	O9	P
Tpr	R.	Leak	DOW	Krugersdorp	Mon	Cyferfontein	O9	P
Capt	T.	Yockney	KIA	Krugersdorp	Mon	Cyferfontein	O9	P
Cpl	H.	Nash	KIA	Krugersdorp	Mon	Cyferfontein	O9	P
Lt	A.	Ormond	KIA	Krugersdorp	Mon	Cyferfontein	O9	P
Tpr	P.	Anderson	KIA	Krugersdorp	Mon	Cyferfontein	O9	P
Tpr	R.O.	Butler	KIA	Krugersdorp	Mon	Cyferfontein	O9	P
Tpr	C.J.	Harding	KIA	Krugersdorp	Mon	Cyferfontein	O9	P
Tpr	M.A.	Langley	KIA	Krugersdorp	Mon	Cyferfontein	O9	P
Tpr	J.W.	Maxwell	KIA	Krugersdorp	Mon	Cyferfontein	O9	P
Tpr	W.	Melville	KIA	Krugersdorp	Mon	Cyferfontein	O9	P
Tpr	W.	Pierce	KIA	Krugersdorp	Mon	Cyferfontein	O9	P
Tpr	A.B.	Taylor	D			Diamantuur		N
Tpr	D.S.	Burgess	KIA	Ventersdorp	ILH	Doornpan	G	X
Tpr	R.J.	Whittle	DOD	Wyatt Road	ILH	Durban	G A	X
Cpl	G.	MacKenzie	DOD	Braamfontein	Mon	Elandsfontein	G	P
Rgm Sgt	C.E.B.	Belcher	DOD	Braamfontein	Mon	Elandsfontein	G	P
Tpr	P.	McCabe	DOAL	Primrose	Mon	Elandsfontein	G	P
Tpr	R.J.	Davies	DOD	Primrose	Mon	Elandsfontein	G	P
Tpr	W.H.	Davies	DOD	Primrose	Mon	Elandsfontein	G	P

Rank	Initials	Surname	Cause	Place	Unit	Cemetery	Notes
Tpr	N.	Williams	DOD	Primrose	Mon	Elandsfontein	G
Tpr	W.R.	Daws	KIA	Primrose	Mon	Elandsfontein	
Tpr	J.J.	Bailey	KIA	Ventersdorp	ILH	Elandsfontein	G
Sgt	C.H.	Hendley	KIA	Elandslaagte	Mon	Elandslaagte	O1 A
Sgt Maj	E.H.	Cuthbert	KIA	Elandslaagte	Mon	Elandslaagte	O1 A
Tpr	R.S.	Farren	KIA	Elandslaagte	Mon	Elandslaagte	O1 A
Tpr	F.C.	Fisher	KIA	Elandslaagte	Mon	Elandslaagte	O1 A
Tpr	F.J.T.	Hunt	KIA	Elandslaagte	Mon	Elandslaagte	O1 A
Tpr	K.R.G.	McClintock	KIA	Elandslaagte	Mon	Elandslaagte	O1 A
Tpr	A.C.W.	Sillery	KIA	Elandslaagte	Mon	Elandslaagte	O1 A
Tpr	H.J.	Wolseley	KIA	Elandslaagte	Mon	Elandslaagte	O1 A
Tpr	C.D.B.	White	DOW	Fort Napier	ILH	Elandslaagte	G A
Sgt	H.C.	Benson	DOW	Intombi	ILH	Elandslaagte	G O4 A
Tpr	H.C.	Ochse	DOW	Intombi	ILH	Elandslaagte	G O4 A
Tpr	J.P.F.	Cunningham	DOW	Ladysmith	ILH	Elandslaagte	G O5 A
Tpr	E.	Wild	DOW	Fauresmith	Metal	Fauresmith	
Cpl	W.G.	Downer	DOD	Fort Napier	ILH	Fort Napier	G A
Tpr	A.E.	Swanson	DOP	Fort Napier	ILH	Fort Napier	G
Sgt	H.E.	Wellstead	DOW	Braamfontein	Mon	Frederickstad	G
Sgt	G.	Wileman	DOW	Braamfontein	Mon	Frederickstad	G
Tpr	H.L.	Aschmann	KIA	Potchefstroom	Mon	Frederickstad	G
Tpr	I.D.J.	Simpson	KIA	Potchefstroom	Mon	Frederickstad	G
Tpr	R.G.	Nicol	DOW	Ladysmith	ILH	Gun Hill	G O5
Tpr	G.	Simpson	DOW			Hamelfontein	
Cpl	F.	James	DOD	Harrismith	ILH	Harrismith	G
Tpr	F.	Hutchinson	DOD	Harrismith	Head	Harrismith	
Tpr	B.F.	Murray	DOD	Harrismith	ILH	Harrismith	G
Lt	A.R.	Halling	DOW	Hartebeestfontein	Mon	Hartebeestfontein	O11
Lt	J.	Ralston	KIA	Hartebeestfontein	Mon	Hartebeestfontein	O11
Rgt Sgt Maj	A.E.	Hurst	KIA	Hartebeestfontein	Mon	Hartebeestfontein	O11
Tpr	P.	Jones	KIA	Hartebeestfontein	Mon	Hartebeestfontein	O11
Tpr	P.	Kennedy	KIA	Hartebeestfontein	Mon	Hartebeestfontein	O11
Tpr	D.	Paterson	KIA	Hartebeestfontein	Mon	Hartebeestfontein	O11
Tpr	J.	Flanegan	DOW	Colesberg	ILH	Heilbron	G
Tpr	J.H.	Barry	KIA	Heilbron		Heilbron	
Tpr	W.	Evans	KIA	Heilbron	Mon	Heilbron	G
Tpr	N.C.	Blakeway	KIA	Clouston	ILH	Hlangwane	G A
Tpr	A.P.	Jackson	KIA	Clouston	ILH	Hlangwane	G A
Tpr	W.H.	Longden	KIA	Clouston	ILH	Hlangwane	G A
Cpl	A.H.	Twange	DOD	Howick	Mon	Howick	G
Tpr	S.	Goddard	DOD	Howick	Mon	Howick	
Cpl	W.	Mackenzie	D	Braamfontein	Mon	Johannesburg	G
Tpr	C.	Coltart	D	Braamfontein	Mon	Johannesburg	G
Tpr	J.R.	Barrett	DOD	Braamfontein	Mon	Johannesburg	G
Tpr	H.J.	Cox	DOD	Braamfontein	Mon	Johannesburg	
Tpr	C.S.	Manning	DOD	Braamfontein	Mon	Johannesburg	G

Tpr	M.G.N.	Norwood	DOD	Braamfontein	Mon	Johannesburg	G		P
Tpr	H.	Parmenter	DOD	Braamfontein	Mon	Johannesburg			P
Cpl	J.E.G.	Davies	KIA	Vrede	Mon	Kalkfontein	G		P
Sgt	P.	Cawood	KIA	Vrede	Mon	Kalkfontein	G		P
Tpr	T.	Johnson	KIA	Heilbron	Mon	Katkop	G		P
Tpr	H.C.	Thirlwall	KIA	Heilbron	Mon	Katkop	G		P
Tpr	C.	Upton	KIA	Heilbron	Mon	Katkop	G		P
Tpr	L.T.	Hervey	DOD	West End	Mon	Kimberley			
Tpr	S.	Tennant	KIA	Harrismith	ILH	Klipkraal	G		X
Lt	L.S.	Sanders	KIA	Ottosdal	Mon	Korannafontein	G		P
Tpr	C.	Whittaker	DOIA	Krugersdorp	ILH	Krugersdorp			X
Tpr	F.	Wheeler	DOW	Harrismith	ILH	Ladysmith	G A		X
Farr Sgt	W.	Burrows	DOD	Intombi	ILH	Ladysmith	G O4 A		X
Tpr	J.	Campbell	DOD	Intombi	ILH	Ladysmith	G O4 A		X
Tpr	R.A.	Foley	DOD	Intombi	ILH	Ladysmith	G O4 A		X
Tpr	W.T.P.	Lawrence	DOD	Intombi	ILH	Ladysmith	G O4 A		X
Tpr	F.W.	Pearce	DOD	Intombi	ILH	Ladysmith	G O4 A		X
Tpr	B.	Stewart	DOD	Intombi	Mon	Ladysmith	O4 A		P
Tpr	J.G.	Taylor	DOD	Intombi	ILH	Ladysmith	G O4 A		X
Tpr	D.	Guthrie-Smith	DOW	Intombi	Mon	Ladysmith	O4 A		P
Tpr	J.	Pearson	D	Ladysmith	Mon	Ladysmith			P
Tpr	J.P.	Powers	D	Ladysmith	Mon	Ladysmith	O5 A		P
Tpr	J.E.	Downing	DOD	Ladysmith	ILH	Ladysmith	G O5 A		X
Tpr	R.S.	Tute	DOD	Ladysmith	A	Ladysmith	A		
Tpr	J.	Ledingham	K	Ladysmith	Mon	Ladysmith	O5 A		P
Tpr	J.	Erasmus	DOW	Lake Chrissie	ILH	Lake Chrissie	G		X
L Cpl	D.W.N.	Ritchie	KIA	Lake Chrissie	ILH	Lake Chrissie	G		X
Tpr	C.	Marsden	KIA	Lake Chrissie	ILH	Lake Chrissie	G		X
Tpr	H.	Edmondson	DOW	Standerton	Mon	Lake Chrissie	G		P
Maj	D.E.	Doveton	DOW	Ladysmith	Mon	Long Valley	O2 O5 A		P
Tpr	T.S.	Cashman	DOD	Mafikeng	ILH	Mafikeng	G		P
Capt	C.H.	Mullins	DOW	Grahamstown	Cross	Maritsane			
Sgt	H.	Parkin	DOD	Klerksdorp	ILH	Matjespruit	G		X
Tpr	D.	Falconer	DOD	Mooi River	ILH	Mooi River	G		X
Tpr	C.H.	Robinson	DOD	Mooi River	ILH	Mooi River	G		X
Lt	A.E.	Brabant	DOW	Ladysmith	Mon	Mtd Inf Hill	O5 O6 A		P
Capt	J.C.	Knapp	KIA	Ladysmith	Mon	Mtd Inf Hill	O5 A		P
Tpr	F.	Dearlove	KIA	Ladysmith	ILH	Mtd Inf Hill	G O5		X
Tpr	J.W.	Townsend	KIA	Bethlehem	ILH	Naauwpoort Nek	G		X
Tpr		Gardner	D	Mafikeng	Metal	Neverset			P
Sgt	A.J.	Haynes	DOW	Mafikeng	Metal	Neverset			P
Cpl	W.	Francis	KIA	Mafikeng	Metal	Neverset	O10		P
Tpr	G.	Bonsey	KIA	Mafikeng	Metal	Neverset	O10		P
Tpr	H.S.	Boome	KIA	Mafikeng	Metal	Neverset	O10		P
Tpr	C.	Davis	KIA	Mafikeng	Metal	Neverset	O10		P

Tpr	C.T.	Gardner	KIA	Mafikeng	Mon	Neverset	O10	P
Tpr	H.E.	Taylor	KIA	Mafikeng	Metal	Neverset	O10	P
Cpl	W.	Gabriel	DOW	Harrismith	ILH	Newmarket Farm	G	X
Tpr	T.	Clementson	DOI	Colesberg	Mon	Norval's Pont		N
Tpr	B.E.	Whittaker	DOIR	Colesberg	Mon	Norval's Pont		N
Lt	B.C.	Noel	DOW	Zeerust	Cross	Oog van Marico	O12	P
Tpr	H.	Abercrombie	DOW	Bethlehem	ILH	Paardeplaatz	G	X
Tpr	E.	Clark	KIA	Treurfontein	ILH	Palmietfontein	G	P
Tpr	J.W.	Lee	DOAB	Wakkerstroom	ILH	Piet Retief	G	X
Tpr	H.J.	Harding	DOD	Wakkerstroom	ILH	Piet Retief	G	X
Tpr	G.	Hanks	DRO	Wakkerstroom	ILH	Piet Retief	G	X
Tpr	W.	Wood	D	Pretoria	Metal	Pretoria		
Sgt	A.S.	Melville	DOD	Pretoria	ILH	Pretoria	G	X
Tpr	A.H.F.	Pinnick	DOD	Pretoria	ILH	Pretoria	G	X
Tpr	T.	Smith	DOD	Pretoria	Mon	Pretoria		
Tpr	J.W.	Wilkes	DOW	Pretoria	Mon	Pretoria		
Tpr	F.H.	Ogston	KIA	Klerksdorp	ILH	Rietkuil	G	X
Tpr	A.	Cairns	KIA			Rietvlei		N
Tpr	B.L.	Bristol	KIA	Ottosdal	Mon	Rietvlei	G	P
Cpl	F.	Connell	KIA	Bethlehem	ILH	Roodepoort	G	X
Tpr	T.	Knowles	DOD	Standerton	Mon	Standerton	G	P
Tpr	S.	Torgins	KIA			Sterkfontein	G	N
Tpr	F.H.	Smallwood	KBL	Ermelo	Mon	Twyfelaar	G	
Tpr	M.	O'Shea	KIA	Bethlehem	ILH	Tygerkloof	G	X
Tpr Guide	A.L.	Fraser	DOW	Harrismith	ILH	Tygerskloof	G	X
Sgt Maj	A.J.C.	Lang	DOD	Fort Napier	ILH	Victoria Hotel, Pmb	G	X
Tpr	E.H.	McChesney	KBL	Bethlehem	ILH	Vischgat	G	X
Tpr	V.G.	Hooper	KIA	Bethlehem	ILH	Vischgat	G	X
Tpr	C.C.	Atlay	DOW	Durban	Cross	Wagon Hill	G O2 A	X
Tpr	J.C.E.	Carter	DOW	Intombi	ILH	Wagon Hill	G O2 O4 A	X
Tpr	F.H.C.	Gorton	DOW	Intombi	Mon	Wagon Hill	O2 O4 A	P
Tpr	W.G.B.	Saunders	DOW	Intombi	ILH	Wagon Hill	G O2 O4 A	X
Tpr	A.C.	Shortt	DOW	Intombi	Mon	Wagon Hill	O4 A	P
Tpr	T.C.	Chadwick	DOW	Ladysmith	ILH	Wagon Hill	G O2 O5 A	X
Tpr	J.F.	Wingate	DOW	Ladysmith	ILH	Wagon Hill	G O2 O5	X
L Cpl	M.	Greathead	KIA	Ladysmith	Mon	Wagon Hill	O2 O5 A	P
Lt	W.F.	Adams	KIA	Ladysmith	Mon	Wagon Hill	O2 O5 A	P
Lt	J.E.	Pakeman	KIA	Ladysmith	Mon	Wagon Hill	O2 O5 O7 A	P
Cpl	E.deC.	Dickinson	KIA	Wagon Hill	Mon	Wagon Hill	O2 O3 A	P
Cpl	A.S.	Dunn	KIA	Wagon Hill	Mon	Wagon Hill	O2 O3 A	P
Cpl	G.A.	Ferrand	KIA	Wagon Hill	Mon	Wagon Hill	O2 O3 A	P
Cpl	J.	Haddon	KIA	Wagon Hill	Mon	Wagon Hill	O2 O3 A	P

Cpl	G.H.	Moore	KIA	Wagon Hill	Mon	Wagon Hill	O2 O3 A	P
Cpl	A.M.	Robbins	KIA	Wagon Hill	Mon	Wagon Hill	O2 O3 A	P
L Cpl	G.G.	Cameron	KIA	Wagon Hill	Mon	Wagon Hill	O2 O3 A	P
L Cpl	C.W.R.	Nettleship	KIA	Wagon Hill	Mon	Wagon Hill	O2 O3 A	P
Sgt	G.	Howard	KIA	Wagon Hill	Mon	Wagon Hill	O2 O3 A	P
Tpr	H.	Albrecht	KIA	Wagon Hill	Mon	Wagon Hill	O2 O3 A	P
Tpr	J.H.	Bewsher	KIA	Wagon Hill	Mon	Wagon Hill	O2 O3 A	P
Tpr	P.	Brady	KIA	Wagon Hill	Mon	Wagon Hill	O2 O3 A	P
Tpr	R.M.	Dawson	KIA	Wagon Hill	Mon	Wagon Hill	O2 O3 A	P
Tpr	W.S.	Hogg	KIA	Wagon Hill	Mon	Wagon Hill	O2 O3 A	P
Tpr	G.	Lind	KIA	Wagon Hill	Mon	Wagon Hill	O2 O3 A	P
Tpr	R.M.	MacKenzie	KIA	Wagon Hill	Mon	Wagon Hill	O2 O3 A	P
Tpr	E.W.	Mocatta	KIA	Wagon Hill	Mon	Wagon Hill	O2 O5 A	P
Tpr	T.T.	Preston	KIA	Wagon Hill	Mon	Wagon Hill	O2 O3 A	P
Tpr	F.C	Rogers	KIA	Wagon Hill	Mon	Wagon Hill	O2 O5 A	P
Tpr	P.Y.	Tucker	KIA	Wagon Hill	Mon	Wagon Hill	O2 O3 A	P
Tpr	W.R.	Willcocks	DOD	Wakkerstroom	Mon	Wakkerstroom		P
Tpr	G.	Fitzpatrick	KIA	Estcourt	Mon	Willow Grange		P
Tpr	J.	McIntry	D	Braamfontein	Mon	Witklip		N
Tpr	A.	Bouchier	DOW	Braamfontein	Mon	Witklip	G	P
Tpr	H.	Lane	DOW	Braamfontein	Mon	Witklip	O8	P
Tpr	A.P.D.	Moodie	DOW	Braamfontein	Mon	Witklip	O8	P
Tpr	W.	Murray	DOW	Braamfontein		Witklip	O13	P
Capt	W.M.	Currie	KIA	Braamfontein	Mon	Witklip	O8	P
Cpl	E.O.	Atherstone	KIA	Braamfontein	Mon	Witklip	O8	P
Farr Sgt	C.S.	Wooley	KIA	Braamfontein	Mon	Witklip	O8	P
Lt	E.E.	Kirk	KIA	Braamfontein	Mon	Witklip	O8	P
Sgt	J.	Marshall	KIA	Braamfontein	Mon	Witklip	O8	P
Tpr	G.W.	Drennan	KIA	Braamfontein	Mon	Witklip	O8	P
Tpr	G.M.	King	KIA	Braamfontein	Mon	Witklip	G O8	P

*   ILH = ILH headstone on site according to "In Memoriam".
Mon = Name inscribed on War Graves Commission column at site.
Metal = Metal cross at site.   Head = Special headstone

**   G = ILH headstone erected according to ILH Memorial Committee report (Appendix I in Gibson "The Story of the Imperial Light Horse")
Ox = Name inscribed on Obelisk as numbered.

***   X = Headstone intact and photographed
P = Photograph of name on monument or obelisk   N = no information

<u>Obelisks:</u>
O1 – Elandslaagte and stone monument.
O2 – Wagon Hill
O3 – Wagon Hill cemetery
O4 – Intombi
O5 – Ladysmith Borough
O6 – Ladysmith Borough Lt. A.E Brabant
O7 – Ladysmith Borough Lt. J.E. Pakeman
O8 – Witklip
O9 – Naauwpoort Nek
O10 – Maritzani
O11 – Hartebeestfontein
O12 – Zeerust
O13 – Diamond Hill (War Graves Commission monument)
MBR – Regimental monument on Battle Ridge, Elandslaagte
M1 – War Graves Commission Monument, Ladysmith Borough
M2 – War Graves Commission Monument, Intombi Hospital
A – All Saints Church plaque

We Rest Here Content

RANK	NAME			BURIED		ACTION	Date of action	Headstone/ Monument	Yes	Other data	Died
Tpr	J.	McIniry	D	Braamfontein	Mon					CMR	
Tpr	E.H.	Wallace	D								
Tpr	J.P.	Powers	D	Ladysmith Town	Mon			O5		A	31 Oct 99
Tpr	D.	Guthrie-Smith	DOW	Intombi	Mon			O4		A Age 23	12 Nov 99
Tpr	W.T.P.	Lawrence	DODE	Intombi	ILH			G O4	X	A	04 Dec 99
Tpr	B.	Stewart	DODE	Intombi	ILH			O4		A	11 Dec 99
Tpr	J.E.	Downing	DOD	Ladysmith Town	ILH			G O5	X	A	19 Dec 99
Tpr	J.G.	Taylor	DODE	Intombi	ILH			G O4	X	A	20 Dec 99
Tpr	R.A.	Foley	DODE	Intombi	ILH			G O4	X	A	18 Jan 00
Tpr	J.	Campbell	DODD	Intombi	ILH			G O4	X	A	23 Jan 00
Farr Sgt	W.	Burrows	DODE	Intombi	ILH			G O4	X	A	30 Jan 00
Tpr	F.W.	Pearce	DODc	Intombi	ILH			G O4	X	A	01 Feb 00
Tpr	J.	Ledingham	K	Ladysmith Town	Mon					A	21 Feb 00
Tpr	R.S.	Tute	DODE	Ladysmith						A	18 Mar 00
Tpr	R.J.	Whittle	DODE	Wyatt Road	ILH			G	X	A Age 30 At sea	10 Apr 00
Cpl	W.G.	Downer	DODE	Fort Napier	ILH			G	X	A Age 26	12 Apr 00
Tpr	H.S.	Mapleston	DODE	Chieveley	ILH			G	X	A	16 Apr 00
Tpr	D.	Falconer	DODE	Mooi River	ILH			G	X	Age 23	07 May 00
Tpr	W.B.	Bain	DODD			Albert Docks					20 May 00
Tpr	T.S.	Cashman	DOD	Mafikeng	ILH			G			02 Jun 00
Tpr	J.	Pearson	D	Ladysmith Town	Mon						30 Jun 00
Tpr	A.H.	Johnson	KIA							NMR	01 Aug 00
Tpr	D.H.	Cribb	DOI	Bloemfontein	Mon	Brandkop					07 Nov 00
Cpl	W.	Mackenzie	D	Braamfontein	Mon			G			10 Dec 00
Tpr	C.S.	Manning	DOD	Braamfontein	Mon			G			12 Jan 01
Tpr	M.G.N.	Norwood	DOD	Braamfontein	Mon			G			25 Jan 01
Tpr	F.H.	Smallwood	KBL	Ermelo	Mon	Twyfelaar		G			25 Jan 01
Tpr	J.I.	Thomas	DODE	Newcastle	Mon	/Charlestown					25 Jan 01
Tpr	G.	Simpson	DOW			Hamelfontein					15 Feb 01
Tpr	A.H.F.	Pinnick	DOD	Pretoria	ILH			G	X		19 Feb 01
Tpr	G.	Hanks	DRO	Wakkerstroom	ILH	Amsterdam		G	X		22 Feb 01
Tpr	H.	Muson	DOW	Standerton							25 Feb 01
Tpr	C.W.	Winter	DRO	Compies River							25 Feb 01
Tpr	A.	Cairns	KIA			Rietvlei					02 Mar 01
Tpr	J.W.	Lee	DOAB	Wakkerstroom	ILH	Piet Retief		G	X		15 Mar 01
Tpr	J.W.	Wilkes	DOW	Pretoria	Mon						24 Mar 01
Tpr	C.	Whittaker	DOIA	Krugersdorp	ILH				X		25 Mar 01
Tpr	W.R.	Willcocks	DODE	Wakkerstroom	Mon						31 Mar 01
Tpr	H.J.	Harding	DODE	Wakkerstroom	ILH	Piet Retief		G	X		06 Apr 01
Tpr	E.H.	Walshlager	DODD	Newcastle	ILH	Charlestown		G			18 Apr 01
Tpr	T.	Smith	DOD	Pretoria	Mon						30 Apr 01
Sgt	A.S.	Melville	DODE	Pretoria	ILH			G	X		04 May 01
Tpr	H.J.	Cox	DOD	Braamfontein	Mon						02 Jun 01
Sgt Maj	A.J.C.	Lang	DOD	Fort Napier	ILH	Victoria Hotel, Pmb		G	X	Age 40	03 Jun 01
Tpr	H.	Parmenter	DODE	Braamfontein	Mon						26 Jun 01
Tpr	B.E.	Whittaker	DOIR	Colesberg	Mon	Norval's Pont					14 Jul 01
Tpr	T.	Knowles	DODH	Standerton	Mon	Standerton		G			14 Aug 01
Sgt	H.	Parkin	DODP	Klerksdorp	ILH			G	X		22 Aug 01
Tpr	L.T.	Hervey	DODE	West End	Mon	Kimberley					26 Aug 01
Tpr	W.	Agar	DODE	Bethlehem	ILH			G	X	Age 20	30 Sep 01
Cpl	G.	MacKenzie	DODT	Braamfontein	Mon			G			08 Oct 01
Tpr	C.	Howell	DRO	Tugela River						Canadian	17 Oct 01
L Cpl	J.G.	Dixon	DOD	Bethlehem	Metal					Age 42	03 Nov 01
Tpr	E.H.	McChesney	KBL	Bethlehem	ILH	Vischgat		G	X		09 Nov 01
Tpr	V.	Miller	DODE	Bethlehem	Metal						26 Dec 01
Tpr	C.H.	Robinson	DODD	Mooi River	ILH			G	X		19 Jan 02
Sgt	P.	Cawood	KIA	Vrede	Mon	Pramkop		G			27 Jan 02
Cpl	F.	James	DODE	Harrismith	ILH			G	X	Australian	07 Feb 02
Tpr	B.F.	Murray	DODE	Harrismith	ILH			G	X		17 Feb 02
Cpl	J.H.	Renouf	KA	Lindley	Mon	Craven's Rust		G			09 Mar 02
Tpr	A.E.	Swanson	DOPP	Fort Napier	ILH			G	X	Age 22	09 Mar 02
Cpl	A.H.	Twange	DODE	Howick	Mon			G			19 Mar 02
Rgm Sgt	C.E.B.	Belcher	DODE	Braamfontein	Mon			G			29 Mar 02
Tpr	S.	Goddard	DODT	Howick	Mon	Howick					02 Apr 02
Tpr	N.	Williams	DOD	Braamfontein	Mon	Elandsfontein		G			08 Apr 02
Tpr	F.	Hutchinson	DODD	Harrismith	Head	Harrismith					13 Apr 02
Tpr	W.H.	Davies	DOD	Primrose	Mon	Elandsfontein		G			29 Apr 02
Tpr	A.B.	Taylor	D			Diamantuur					08 May 02
Tpr	R.J.	Davies	DODD	Braamfontein	Mon			G			06 Jun 02
Tpr	P.	McCabe	DOAL	Braamfontein	Mon			G			25 Jun 02
Tpr	J.R.	Barrett	DODE	Braamfontein	Mon			G			26 Jun 02
Tpr	C.	Coltart	D	Braamfontein	Mon			G			13 Jul 02
Sgt	J.B.	Orrett	D	Maitland	Mon						23 Sep 02
Tpr	W.	Wood	D	Pretoria	Metal	Pretoria					21 Dec 02
Sgt Maj	E.H.	Cuthbert	KIA	Elandslaagte	Mon	Elandslaagte	21 Oct 99	O1		A	21 Oct 99
Tpr	R.S.	Farren	KIA	Elandslaagte	Mon	Elandslaagte	21 Oct 99	O1		A	21 Oct 99
Tpr	F.C.	Fisher	KIA	Elandslaagte	Mon	Elandslaagte	21 Oct 99	O1		A	21 Oct 99
Sgt	C.H.	Hendley	KIA	Elandslaagte	Mon	Elandslaagte	21 Oct 99	O1		A	21 Oct 99

<u>Obelisks:</u> O1 – Elandslaagte O2 – Wagon Hill O3 – Wagon Hill cemetery O4 – Intombi O5 – Ladysmith Borough O6 – Ladysmith Borough Lt. A.E Brabant O7 – Ladysmith Borough Lt. J.E. Pakeman O8 - Witklip O9 - Naauwpoort Nek O10 – Maritzani O11 – Hartebeestfontein O12 – Zeerust

We Rest Here Content

Rank	Initials	Surname	Status	Place	Unit	Battle	Date	Code	X	Notes	Date 2
Tpr	F.J.T.	Hunt	KIA	Elandslaagte	Mon	Elandslaagte	21 Oct 99	O1		A	21 Oct 99
Tpr	K.R.G.	McClintock	KIA	Elandslaagte	Mon	Elandslaagte	21 Oct 99	O1		A Age 32	21 Oct 99
Tpr	A.C.W.	Sillery	KIA	Elandslaagte	Mon	Elandslaagte	21 Oct 99	O1		A	21 Oct 99
Tpr	H.J.	Wolseley	KIA	Elandslaagte	Mon	Elandslaagte	21 Oct 99	O1		A	21 Oct 99
Tpr	J.P.F.	Cunningham	DOW	Ladysmith Town	ILH	Elandslaagte	21 Oct 99	G O5	X	A	24 Oct 99
Tpr	C.D.B.	White	DOW	Fort Napier	ILH	Elandslaagte	21 Oct 99	G	X	A	25 Oct 99
Sgt	H.C.	Benson	DOW	Intombi	ILH	Elandslaagte	21 Oct 99	G O4	X	A	07 Dec 99
Tpr	H.C.	Ochse	DOW	Intombi	ILH	Elandslaagte	21 Oct 99	G O4	X	A Age 20	12 Dec 99
Tpr	F.	Dearlove	KIA	Ladysmith Town	ILH	Mtd Inf Hill	03 Nov 99	G O5	X		03 Nov 99
Capt	J.C.	Knapp	KIA	Ladysmith	Mon	Mtd Inf Hill	03 Nov 99	O5		A	03 Nov 99
Lt	A.E.	Brabant	DOW	Ladysmith Town	Mon	Mtd Inf Hill	03 Nov 99	O5 O6		A	05 Nov 99
Tpr	F.	Wheeler	DOW	Harrismith	ILH	Ladysmith	04 Nov 99	G	X	A	01 Jan 00
Tpr	G.	Fitzpatrick	KIA	Estcourt	Mon	Willow Grange	23 Nov 99				23 Nov 99
Tpr	R.G.	Nicol	DOW	Ladysmith Town	ILH	Gun Hill	08 Dec 99	G O5	X		09 Dec 99
Tpr	N.C.	Blakeway	KIA	Clouston	ILH	Hlangwane	15 Dec 99	G	X	A	15 Dec 99
Tpr	A.P.	Jackson	KIA	Clouston	ILH	Hlangwane	15 Dec 99	G	X	A	15 Dec 99
Tpr	W.H.	Longden	KIA	Clouston	ILH	Hlangwane	15 Dec 99	G	X	A	15 Dec 99
Tpr		Tiver	KIA			Hlangwane	15 Dec 99				15 Dec 99
Tpr	F.A.	Freshney	DOW	Lincoln, Eng		Colenso	15 Dec 99			Age 31 Died in Lincoln, UK	20 May 06
Tpr	R.	Leak	DOW	Krugersdorp	Mon	Cyferfontein	05 Jan 00	O9			06 Jan 00
Tpr	P.	Anderson	KIA	Krugersdorp	Mon	Cyferfontein	05 Jan 00	O9		P	05 Jan 01
Lt	W.F.	Adams	KIA	Ladysmith Town	Mon	Wagon Hill	06 Jan 00	O2 O5		A	06 Jan 00
Tpr	H.	Albrecht	KIA	Wagon Hill	Mon	Wagon Hill	06 Jan 00	O2 O3		A Victoria Cross	06 Jan 00
Tpr	J.H.	Bewsher	KIA	Wagon Hill	Mon	Wagon Hill	06 Jan 00	O2 O3		A	06 Jan 00
Tpr	P.	Brady	KIA	Wagon Hill	Mon	Wagon Hill	06 Jan 00	O2 O3		A	06 Jan 00
L Cpl	G.G.	Cameron	KIA	Wagon Hill	Mon	Wagon Hill	06 Jan 00	O2 O3		A	06 Jan 00
Tpr	R.M.	Dawson	KIA	Wagon Hill	Mon	Wagon Hill	06 Jan 00	O2 O3		A	06 Jan 00
Cpl	E.deC.	Dickinson	KIA	Wagon Hill	Mon	Wagon Hill	06 Jan 00	O2 O3		A	06 Jan 00
Cpl	A.S.	Dunn	KIA	Wagon Hill	Mon	Wagon Hill	06 Jan 00	O2 O3		A	06 Jan 00
Cpl	G.A.	Ferrand	KIA	Wagon Hill	Mon	Wagon Hill	06 Jan 00	O2 O3		A	06 Jan 00
L Cpl	M.	Greathead	KIA	Ladysmith Town	Mon	Wagon Hill	06 Jan 00	O2 O5		A Age 28	06 Jan 00
Cpl	J.	Haddon	KIA	Wagon Hill	Mon	Wagon Hill	06 Jan 00	O2 O3		A	06 Jan 00
Tpr	W.S.	Hogg	KIA	Wagon Hill	Mon	Wagon Hill	06 Jan 00	O2 O3		A	06 Jan 00
Sgt	G.	Howard	KIA	Wagon Hill	Mon	Wagon Hill	06 Jan 00	O2 O3		A	06 Jan 00
Tpr	G.	Lind	KIA	Wagon Hill	Mon	Wagon Hill	06 Jan 00	O2 O3		A	06 Jan 00
Tpr	R.M.	MacKenzie	KIA	Wagon Hill	Mon	Wagon Hill	06 Jan 00	O2 O3		A	06 Jan 00
Tpr	E.W.	Mocatta	KIA	Wagon Hill	Mon	Wagon Hill	06 Jan 00	O2 O5		A	06 Jan 00
Cpl	G.H.	Moore	KIA	Wagon Hill	Mon	Wagon Hill	06 Jan 00	O2 O3		A	06 Jan 00
L Cpl	C.W.R.	Nettleship	KIA	Wagon Hill	Mon	Wagon Hill	06 Jan 00	O2 O3		A	06 Jan 00
Lt	J.E.	Pakeman	KIA	Ladysmith Town	Mon	Wagon Hill	06 Jan 00	O2 O5 O7		A	06 Jan 00
Tpr	T.T.	Preston	KIA	Wagon Hill	Mon	Wagon Hill	06 Jan 00	O2 O3		A	06 Jan 00
Cpl	A.M.	Robbins	KIA	Wagon Hill	Mon	Wagon Hill	06 Jan 00	O2 O3		A	06 Jan 00
Tpr	F.C	Rogers	KIA	Wagon Hill	Mon	Wagon Hill	06 Jan 00	O2 O5		A	06 Jan 00
Tpr	P.Y.	Tucker	KIA	Wagon Hill	Mon	Wagon Hill	06 Jan 00	O2 O3		A Maritzburg College	06 Jan 00
Tpr	W.G.B.	Saunders	DOW	Intombi	ILH	Wagon Hill	06 Jan 00	G O2 O4	X	A	08 Jan 00
Tpr	J.F.	Wingate	DOW	Ladysmith Town	ILH	Wagon Hill	06 Jan 00	G O2 O5	X	A	08 Jan 00
Tpr	T.C.	Chadwick	DOW	Ladysmith Town	ILH	Wagon Hill	06 Jan 00	G O2 O5	X	A	10 Jan 00
Tpr	F.H.C.	Gorton	DOW	Intombi	Mon	Wagon Hill	06 Jan 00	O2		A	11 Jan 00
Tpr	J.C.E.	Carter	DOW	Intombi	ILH	Wagon Hill	06 Jan 00	G O2 O4	X	A	22 Jan 00
Tpr	A.C.	Shortt	DOW	Intombi	Mon	Wagon Hill	06 Jan 00	O4		A	22 Jan 00
Maj	D.E.	Doveton	DOW	Ladysmith Town	Mon	Long Valley	06 Jan 00	O2 O5		A Age 54	14 Feb 00
Tpr	C.C.	Atlay	DOW	Durban West St	Cross	Wagon Hill	06 Jan 00	G O2		A	28 Mar 00
Tpr	H.	Edmondson	DOW	Standerton	Mon	Lake Chrissie	06 Feb 00	G			25 Feb 00
Tpr	C.	Marsden	KIA	Lake Chrissie	ILH	Lake Chrissie	06 Feb 00	G	X		06 Feb 01
Tpr	G.	Bonsey	KIA	Mafikeng	Metal	Maritsani	13 May 00	O10			13 May 00
Tpr	H.S.	Boome	KIA	Mafikeng	Metal	Maritsani	13 May 00	O10			13 May 00
Tpr	C.	Davis	KIA	Mafikeng	Metal	Maritsani	13 May 00	O10			13 May 00
Cpl	W.	Francis	KIA	Mafikeng	Metal	Maritsani	13 May 00	O10			13 May 00
Tpr	C.T.	Gardner	KIA	Mafikeng	Mon	Maritsani	13 May 00	O10			13 May 00
Tpr	H.E.	Taylor	KIA	Mafikeng	Metal	Maritsani	13 May 00	O10			13 May 00
Sgt	A.J.	Haynes	DOW	Mafikeng	Metal	Maritsani	15 May 00				16 May 00
Capt	C.H.	Mullins	DOW	Grahamstown	Cross	Maritsane	16 May 00				24 May 16
Cpl	E.O.	Atherstone	KIA	Braamfontein	Mon	Witklip	07 Jul 00	O8			07 Jul 00
Capt	W.M.	Currie	KIA	Braamfontein	Mon	Witklip	07 Jul 00	O8			07 Jul 00
Tpr	G.W.	Drennan	KIA	Braamfontein	Mon	Witklip	07 Jul 00	O8			07 Jul 00
Tpr	G.M.	King	KIA	Braamfontein	Mon	Witklip	07 Jul 00	G O8			07 Jul 00
Lt	E.E.	Kirk	KIA	Braamfontein	Mon	Witklip	07 Jul 00	O8		CMR	07 Jul 00
Sgt	J.	Marshall	KIA	Braamfontein	Mon	Witklip	07 Jul 00	O8			07 Jul 00
Farr Sgt	C.S.	Wooley	KIA	Braamfontein	Mon	Witklip	07 Jul 00	O8			07 Jul 00
Tpr	H.	Lane	DOW	Braamfontein	Mon	Witklip	07 Jul 00	O8			10 Jul 00
Tpr	A.P.D.	Moodie	DOW	Braamfontein	Mon	Witklip	07 Jul 00	G O8			10 Jul 00
Tpr	A.	Bouchier	DOW	Braamfontein	Mon	Witklip	07 Jul 00	G			14 July 00
Tpr	W.A.	Murray	DOW	Diamond Hill		Witklip	18 Jul 00			Hilton College	19 Jul 00
Tpr	H.L.	Aschmann	KIA	Potchefstroom	Mon	Frederickstad	16 Oct 00	G			16 Oct 00
Tpr	I.D.J.	Simpson	KIA	Potchefstroom	Mon	Frederickstad	20 Oct 00	G			20 Oct 00
Sgt	G.	Wileman	DOW	Braamfontein	Mon	Frederickstad	25 Oct 00	G			09 Nov 00

We Rest Here Content

Rank	Initials	Surname	Cause	Place1	Type	Place2	Date1	Obelisk	Note	Date2
Sgt	H.E.	Wellstead	DOW	Braamfontein	Mon	Frederickstad	25 Oct 00	G		24 Nov 00
Tpr	D.S.	Burgess	KIA	Ventersdorp	ILH	Doornpan	01 Jan 01	G	X	01 Jan 01
Tpr	H.	O'Hagan	D			Naauwpoort Nek	05 Jan 01		New Zealand	
Tpr	R.O.	Butler	KIA	Krugersdorp	Mon	Cyferfontein	05 Jan 01	O9	P	05 Jan 01
Tpr	C.J.	Harding	KIA	Krugersdorp	Mon	Cyferfontein	05Jan 01	O9		05 Jan 01
Tpr	M.A.	Langley	KIA	Krugersdorp	Mon	Cyferfontein	05 Jan 01		P	05 Jan 01
Tpr	J.W.	Maxwell	KIA	Krugersdorp	Mon	Cyferfontein	05 Jan 01	O9		05 Jan 01
Tpr	W.	Melville	KIA	Krugersdorp	Mon	Cyferfontein	05 Jan 01		P	05 Jan 01
Cpl	H.	Nash	KIA	Krugersdorp	Mon	Cyferfontein	05 Jan 01	O9	P	05 Jan 01
Lt	A.	Ormond	KIA	Krugersdorp	Mon	Cyferfontein	05 Jan 01	O9		05 Jan 01
Tpr	W.	Pierce	KIA	Krugersdorp	Mon	Cyferfontein	05 Jan 01		P	05 Jan 01
Capt	T.	Yockney	KIA	Krugersdorp	Mon	Cyferfontein	05 Jan 01	O9		05 Jan 01
Tpr	J.H.	Bentley	DOW	Krugersdorp	Mon	Cyferfontein	05 Jan 01	O9		06 Jan 01
Tpr	A.C.	Brown	DOW	Braamfontein	Mon	Cyferfontein	05 Jan 01	G O9		09 Jan 01
Tpr	L.	Bromham	DOW	Braamfontein	Mon	Cyferfontein	05 Jan 01	G O9		16 Jan 01
Tpr	C.H.	Woolcott	KIA	Vlakfontein			27 Jan 01			27 Jan 01
Tpr	J.	Erasmus	DOW	Lake Chrissie	ILH	Lake Chrissie	06 Feb 01	G	X	06 Feb 01
Cpl	D.W.N.	Ritchie	KIA	Lake Chrissie	ILH	Lake Chrissie	06 Feb 01	G	X	06 Feb 01
Tpr	J.J.	Bailey	KIA	Ventersdorp	ILH	Elandsfontein	15 Feb 01	G	X	WGC Potch	15 Feb 01
Tpr	E.	Wild	DOW	Fauresmith	Metal		04 Mar 01			08 Mar 01
Rgt Sgt Maj	A.E.	Hurst	KIA	Hartebeestfontein	Mon	Hartebeestfontein	22 Mar 01	O11	5 Dr Gds	22 Mar 01
Tpr	P.	Jones	KIA	Hartebeestfontein	Mon	Hartebeestfontein	22 Mar 01	O11		22 Mar 01
Tpr	P.	Kennedy	KIA	Hartebeestfontein	Mon	Hartebeestfontein	22 Mar 01	O11		22 Mar 01
Tpr	D.	Paterson	KIA	Hartebeestfontein	Mon	Hartebeestfontein	22 Mar 01	O11	IY 20	22 Mar 01
Lt	J.	Ralston	KIA	Hartebeestfontein	Mon	Hartebeestfontein	22 Mar 01	O11		22 Mar 01
Tpr	F.H.	Ogston	KIA	Klerksdorp	ILH	Rietkuil	17 Apr 01	G	X	17 Apr 01
Tpr	E.	Clark	KIA	Treurfontein	ILH	Palmietfontein	09 May 01	G		09 May 01
Tpr	T.	Clementson	DOI	Colesberg	Mon	Norval's Pont	14 Jun 01			17 Jun 01
Lt	B.C.	Noel	DOW	Zeerust	Cross	Oog van Marico	06 Jul 01	O12		10 Jul 01
Tpr	B.L.	Bristol	KIA	Ottosdal	Mon	Rietvlei	31 Jul 01	G		31 Jul 01
Lt	L.S.	Sanders	KIA	Ottosdal	Mon	Rietvlei	31 Jul 01	G		31 Jul 01
Tpr	S.	Torgins	KIA			Sterkfontein	14 Aug 01	G	Bloemhof	14 Aug 01
Tpr	G.	Bremer	KIA	Bethlehem	ILH	Concordia	07 Sep 01	G	X	Metal cross	07 Sep 01
Cpl	F.	Connell	KIA	Bethlehem	ILH	Roodepoort	24 Sep 01	G	X	24 Sep 01
Cpl	M.	O'Shea	KIA	Bethlehem	ILH	Tygerkloof	28 Sep 01	G	X	Age 22	28 Sep 01
Tpr	J.W.	Townsend	KIA	Bethlehem	ILH	Naauwpoort Nek	07 Oct 01	G	X	Age 45	07 Oct 01
Tpr	H.	Abercrombie	DOW	Bethlehem	ILH	Paardeplaatz	21Oct 01	G	X	Age 35	25 Oct 01
Tpr	V.G.	Hooper	KIA	Bethlehem	ILH	Vischgat	11 Nov 01	G	X	Canadian	11 Nov 01
Tpr Guide	A.L.	Fraser	DOW	Harrismith	ILH	Tygerskloof	15 Jan 02	G	X	16 Jan 02
Tpr	S.	Tennant	KIA	Harrismith	Mon	Klipkraal	25 Jan 02	G	X	25Jan 02
Cpl	J.E.G.	Davies	KIA	Vrede	Mon	Pramkop	27 Jan 02	G		27 Jan 02
Cpl	W.	Gabriel	DOW	Harrismith	ILH	Newmarket Farm	29 Jan 02	G	X	05 Feb 02
Tpr	J.H.	Barry	KIA	Heilbron		Katkop?	07 Feb 02			07 Feb 02
Tpr	W.	Evans	KIA	Heilbron	Mon	Katkop	07 Feb 02	G	Australian	07 Feb 02
Tpr	T.	Johnson	KIA	Heilbron	Mon	Katkop	07 Feb 02	G		07 Feb 02
Tpr	H.C.	Thirlwall	KIA	Heilbron	Mon	Katkop	07 Feb 02	G		07 Feb 02
Tpr	C.	Upton	KIA	Heilbron	Mon	Katkop	07 Feb 02	G		07 Feb 02
Tpr	J.	Flanegan	DOW	Colesberg	ILH	Botha's Drift	23 Feb 01	G	X	08 Apr 01
Lt	A.R.	Halling	DOW	Hartebeestfontein	Mon	Hartebeestfontein	22 Mar 02	O11		23 Mar 02

<u>Obelisks:</u> O1 – Elandslaagte O2 – Wagon Hill O3 – Wagon Hill cemetery O4 – Intombi O5 – Ladysmith Borough O6 – Ladysmith Borough Lt. A.E Brabant O7 – Ladysmith Borough Lt. J.E. Pakeman O8 - Witklip O9 - Naauwpoort Nek O10 – Maritzani O11 – Hartebeestfontein O12 – Zeerust

The Imperial Light Horse Regiment

The monuments and headstones:

Casualty lists and location maps.

Pictures of all graves still extant.

We Rest Here Content

Elandslaagte and Rietfontein – the battles, casualties and references.

RANK	NAME		BURIED		ACTION	Date	Hst/Mon		Died
Sgt Maj	E.H.	Cuthbert	KIA	Elandslaagte	Mon	Elandslaagte	21 Oct 99	O1 A	P	21 Oct 99
Sgt	C.H.	Hendley	KIA	Elandslaagte	Mon	Elandslaagte	21 Oct 99	O1 A	P	21 Oct 99
Tpr	R.S.	Farren	KIA	Elandslaagte	Mon	Elandslaagte	21 Oct 99	O1 A	P	21 Oct 99
Cpl	F.C.	fisher	KIA	Elandslaagte	Mon	Elandslaagte	21 Oct 99	O1 A	P	21 Oct 99
Tpr	F.J.T.	Hunt	KIA	Elandslaagte	Mon	Elandslaagte	21 Oct 99	O1 A	P	21 Oct 99
Tpr	K.R.G.	McClintock	KIA	Elandslaagte	Mon	Elandslaagte	21 Oct 99	O1 A	P	21 Oct 99
Tpr	A.C.W.	Sillery	KIA	Elandslaagte	Mon	Elandslaagte	21 Oct 99	O1 A	P	21 Oct 99
Tpr	H.J.	Wolseley	KIA	Elandslaagte	Mon	Elandslaagte	21 Oct 99	O1 A	P	21 Oct 99
Tpr	C.D.B.	White	DOW	Fort Napier	ILH	Elandslaagte	21 Oct 99	G A	X	25 Oct 1899
Sgt	H.C.	Benson	DOW	Intombi	ILH	Elandslaagte	21 Oct 99	G O4 A	X	04 Dec 1899
Tpr	H.C.	Ochse	DOW	Intombi	ILH	Elandslaagte	21 Oct 99	G O4 A	X	12 Dec 1899
Tpr	J.P.F.	Cunningham	DOW	Ladysmith	ILH	Elandslaagte	21 Oct 99	G O5 A	X	24 Oct 1899

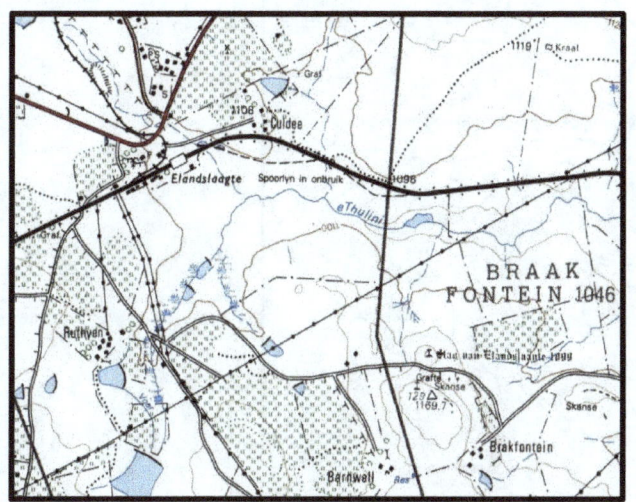

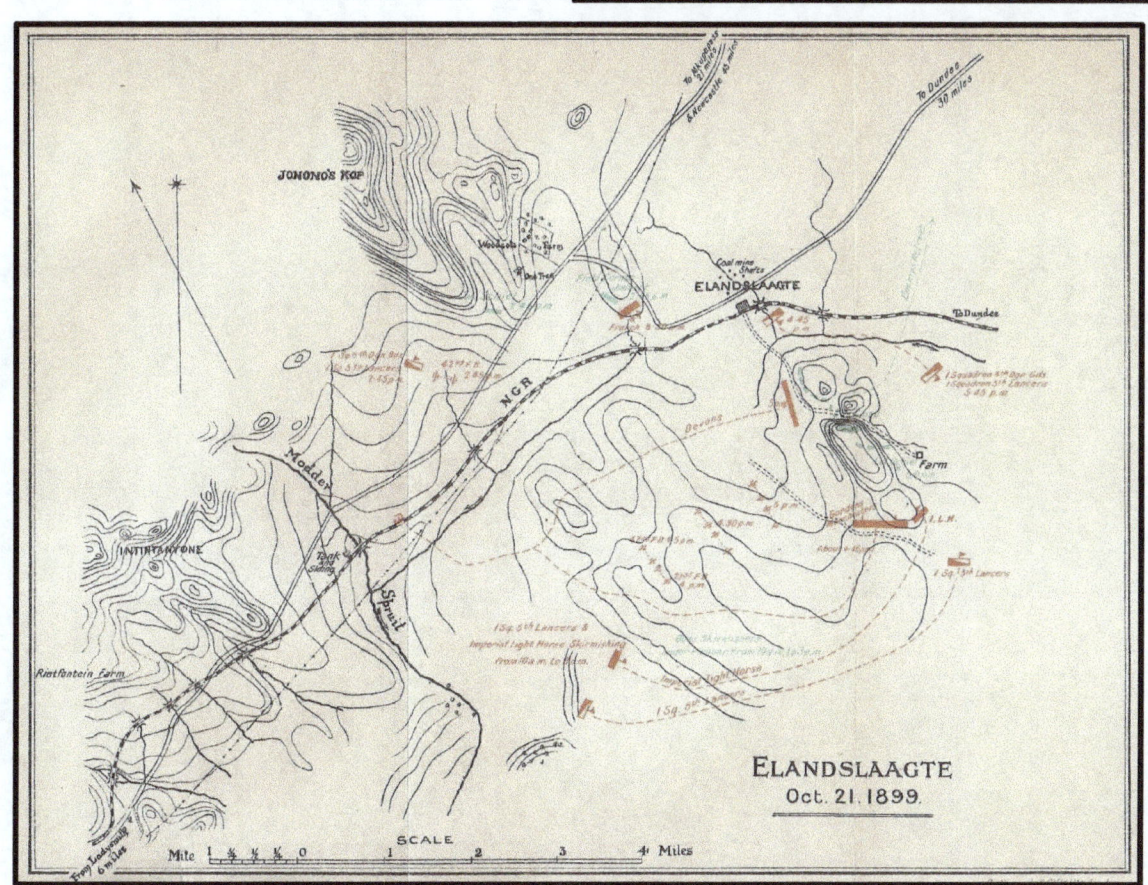

Accounts of the battle of Elandslaagte:

Chapter IV of George fleming Gibson in *The Story of the Imperial Light Horse in the South African War 1899-1902* has a detailed account which, naturally deals with the regiment's significant part in the action. There is also *The Times History of the War in South Africa* Volume II pp175-200. See also Chapter IX of Volume 1 of Major General Frederick Maurice's *History of the War in South Africa 1899-1902* (the Official History). A journalist's account is in H.W. Nevinson's *Ladysmith: The Diary of a Siege* Chapter IV. Douglas Haig, then Major and Major General John French's staff officer was present and made a detailed entry in his diary which may be found in Douglas Scott's *Douglas Haig: Diaries and Letters* pp124-131 which also covers Rietfontein. Here is a sketch he made.

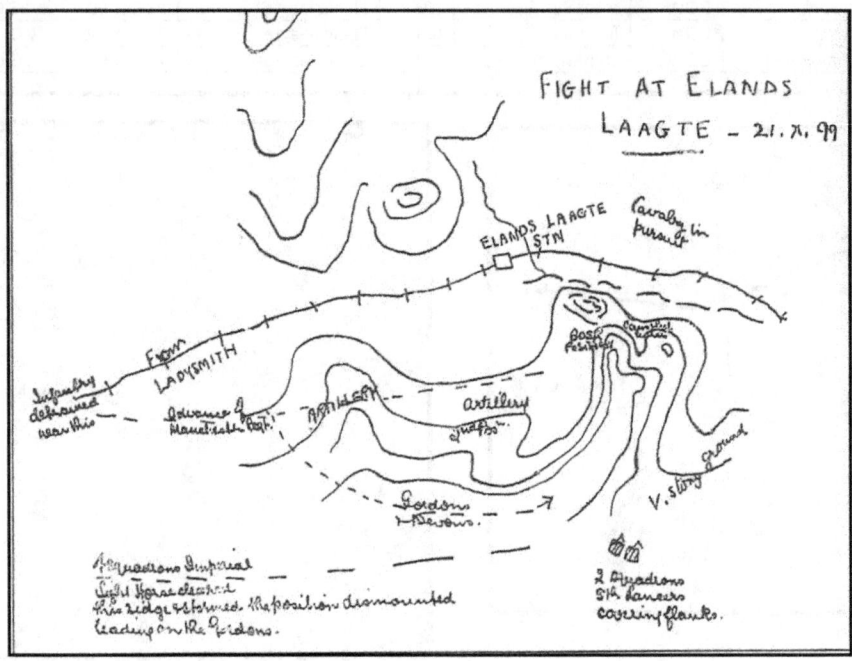

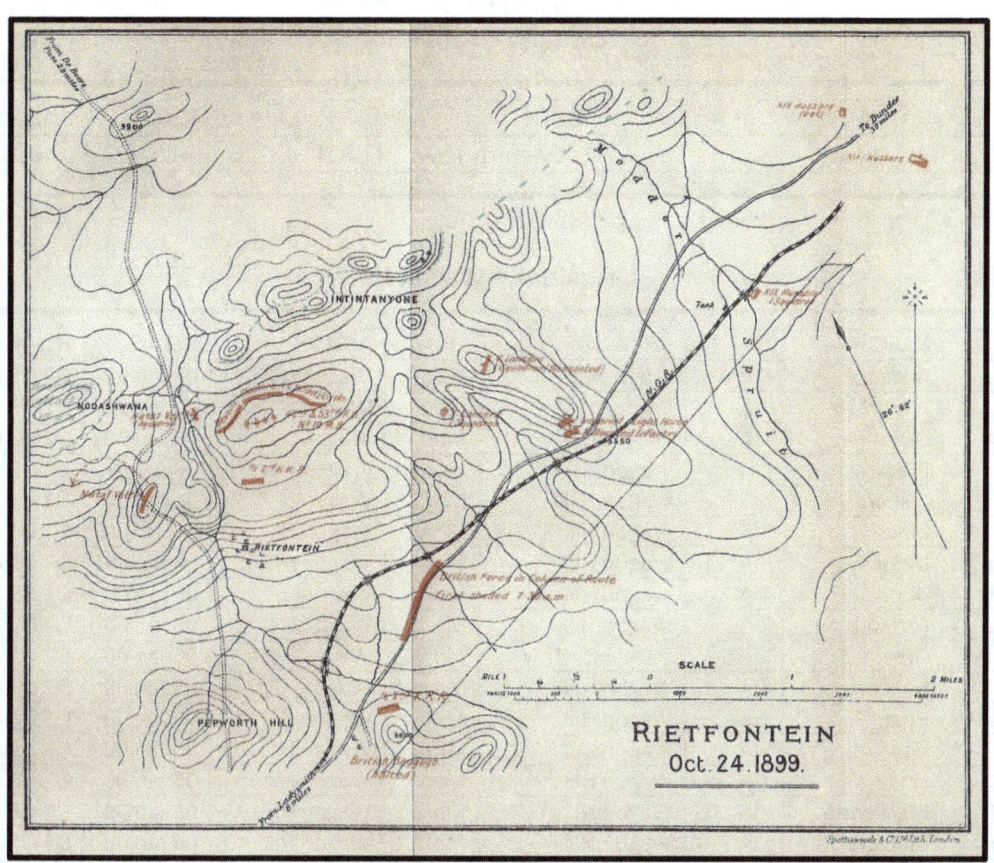

Accounts of the battle of Rietfontein:

Rietfontein has been largely ignored by historians but there is a detailed account in *A Little Bicker with the Boers* by R.W. Smith. See also *The Times History of the War in South Africa* Volume II pp203-7. H.W. Nevinson's *Ladysmith: The Diary of a Siege* Chapter V deals with Rietfontein which he calls Tinta Inyoni after the name of the mountain upon whose slopes the battle was fought.

We Rest Here Content

Ladysmith, the siege and the relief
Casualty – Gun Hill

RANK		NAME	BURIED		ACTION	Date	Hst/Mon
Tpr	R.G.H.	Nicol	DOW	Ladysmith Town	ILH	Gun Hill	08 Dec 99	G O5

Casualties – Wagon Hill

RANK		NAME		BURIED		ACTION	Date	Hst/Mon	Died
Lt	W.F.	Adams	KIA	Ladysmith Town	Mon *	Wagon Hill	06 Jan 00	O2 O5 A	06 Jan 00
Tpr	H.	Albrecht	KIA	Wagon Hill	Mon	Wagon Hill	06 Jan 00	O2 O3 A	06 Jan 00
Tpr	J.H.	Bewsher	KIA	Wagon Hill	Mon	Wagon Hill	06 Jan 00	O2 O3 A	06 Jan 00
Tpr	P.	Brady	KIA	Wagon Hill	Mon	Wagon Hill	06 Jan 00	O2 O3 A	06 Jan 00
L Cpl	G.G.	Cameron	KIA	Wagon Hill	Mon	Wagon Hill	06 Jan 00	O2 O3 A	06 Jan 00
Tpr	R.M.	Dawson	KIA	Wagon Hill	Mon	Wagon Hill	06 Jan 00	O2 O3 A	06 Jan 00
Cpl	E.deC.	Dickinson	KIA	Wagon Hill	Mon	Wagon Hill	06 Jan 00	O2 O3 A	06 Jan 00
Cpl	A.S.	Dunn	KIA	Wagon Hill	Mon	Wagon Hill	06 Jan 00	O2 O3 A	06 Jan 00
Cpl	G.A.	Ferrand	KIA	Wagon Hill	Mon	Wagon Hill	06 Jan 00	O2 O3 A	06 Jan 00
L Cpl	M.	Greathead	KIA	Ladysmith Town	Mon	Wagon Hill	06 Jan 00	O2 O5 A	06 Jan 00
Cpl	J.	Haddon	KIA	Wagon Hill	Mon	Wagon Hill	06 Jan 00	O2 O3 A	06 Jan 00
Tpr	W.S.	Hogg	KIA	Wagon Hill	Mon	Wagon Hill	06 Jan 00	O2 O3 A	06 Jan 00
Sgt	G.	Howard	KIA	Wagon Hill	Mon	Wagon Hill	06 Jan 00	O2 O3 A	06 Jan 00
Tpr	G.	Lind	KIA	Wagon Hill	Mon	Wagon Hill	06 Jan 00	O2 O3 A	06 Jan 00
Tpr	R.M.	MacKenzie	KIA	Wagon Hill	Mon	Wagon Hill	06 Jan 00	O2 O3 A	06 Jan 00
Tpr	E.W.	Mocatta	KIA	Wagon Hill	Mon	Wagon Hill	06 Jan 00	O2 O5 A	06 Jan 00
Cpl	G.H.	Moore	KIA	Wagon Hill	Mon	Wagon Hill	06 Jan 00	O2 O3 A	06 Jan 00
L Cpl	C.W.R.	Nettleship	KIA	Wagon Hill	Mon	Wagon Hill	06 Jan 00	O2 O3 A	06 Jan 00
Lt	J.E.	Pakeman	KIA	Ladysmith Town	Mon	Wagon Hill	06 Jan 00	O2 O5 O7 A	06 Jan 00
Tpr	T.T.	Preston	KIA	Wagon Hill	Mon	Wagon Hill	06 Jan 00	O2 O3 A	06 Jan 00
Cpl	A.M.	Robbins	KIA	Wagon Hill	Mon	Wagon Hill	06 Jan 00	O2 O3 A	06 Jan 00

Tpr	P.Y.	Tucker	KIA	Wagon Hill	Mon	Wagon Hill	06 Jan 00	O2 O3 A	06 Jan 00
Tpr	E.W.	Mocatta	KIA	Wagon Hill	Mon	Wagon Hill	06 Jan 00	O2 O5 A	06 Jan 00
Tpr	F.C	Rogers	KIA	Wagon Hill	Mon	Wagon Hill	06 Jan 00	O2 O5 A	06 Jan 00
Tpr	P.Y.	Tucker	KIA	Wagon Hill	Mon	Wagon Hill	06 Jan 00	O2 O3 A	06 Jan 00
Tpr	C.C	Atlay	DOW	Wagon Hill	Cross	Wagon Hill	06 Jan 00	G O2 A	28 Mar 00
Tpr	J.C.E.	Carter	DOW	Intombi	ILH	Wagon Hill	06 Jan 00	G O2 O4 A	22 Jan 00
Maj	D.E.	Doveton	DOW	Ladysmith Town	Mon	Wagon Hill	06 Jan 00	O2 O5 A	14 Feb 00
Tpr	F.H.C.	Gorton	DOW	Intombi	Mon	Wagon Hill	06 Jan 00	O2 O4 A	11 Jan 00
Tpr	W.G.B.	Saunders	DOW	Intombi	ILH	Wagon Hill	06 Jan 00	G O2 O4 A	08 Jan 00
Tpr	A.C.	Shortt	DOW	Intombi	Mon	Wagon Hill	06 Jan 00	O4 A	22 Jan 00
Tpr	T.C.	Chadwick	DOW	Ladysmith Town	ILH	Wagon Hill	06 Jan 00	G O2 O5 A	10 Jan 00
Tpr	J.F.	Wingate	DOW	Ladysmith Town	ILH	Wagon Hill	06 Jan 00	G O2 O5	08 Jan 00

- Lt W.F. Adams has an individual monument in the Ladysmith Town Cemetery.

Casualties – Long Valley

RANK		NAME		BURIED		ACTION	Date	Hst/Mon	Died
Tpr	F.	Dearlove	KIA	Ladysmith Town	ILH	Mtd Inf Hill	03 Nov 99	G O5	03 Nov 99
Capt	J.C.	Knapp	KIA	Ladysmith	Mon	Mtd Inf Hill	03 Nov 99	O5 A	03 Nov 99
Lt	A.E.	Brabant	DOW	Ladysmith Town	Mon	Mtd Inf Hill	03 Nov 99	O5 O6 A	05 Nov 99

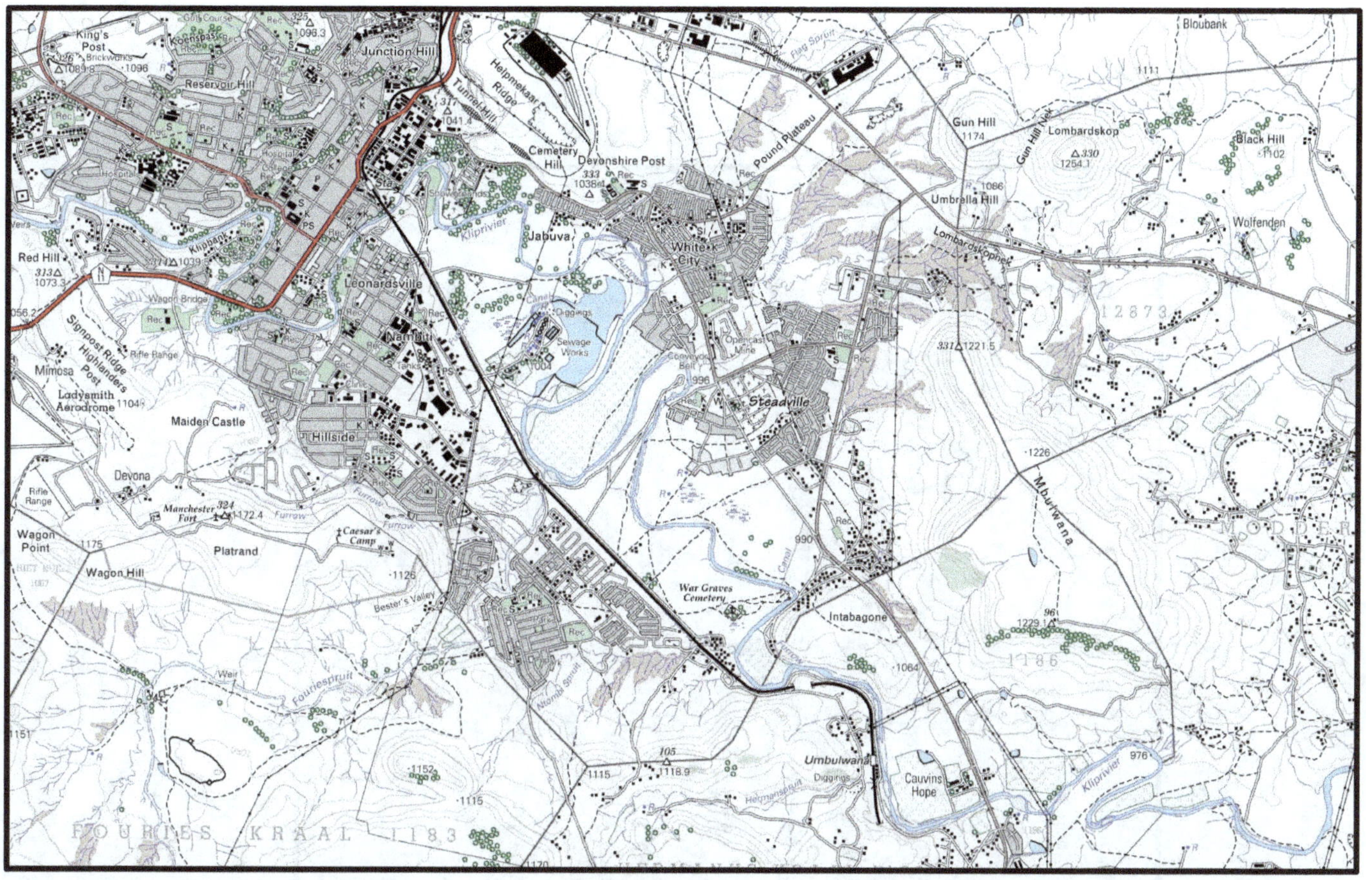

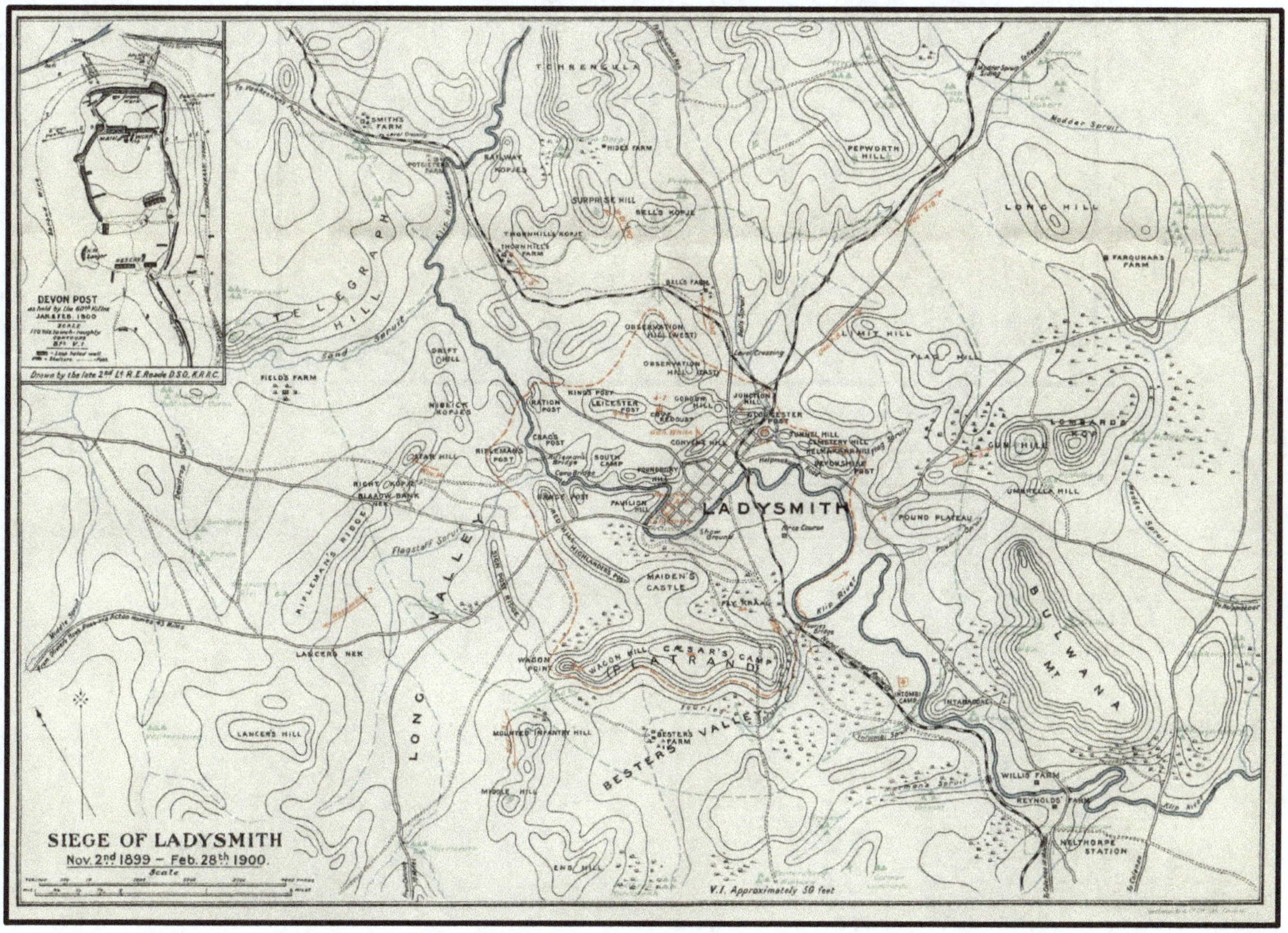

SIEGE OF LADYSMITH
Nov. 2nd 1899 – Feb. 28th 1900.

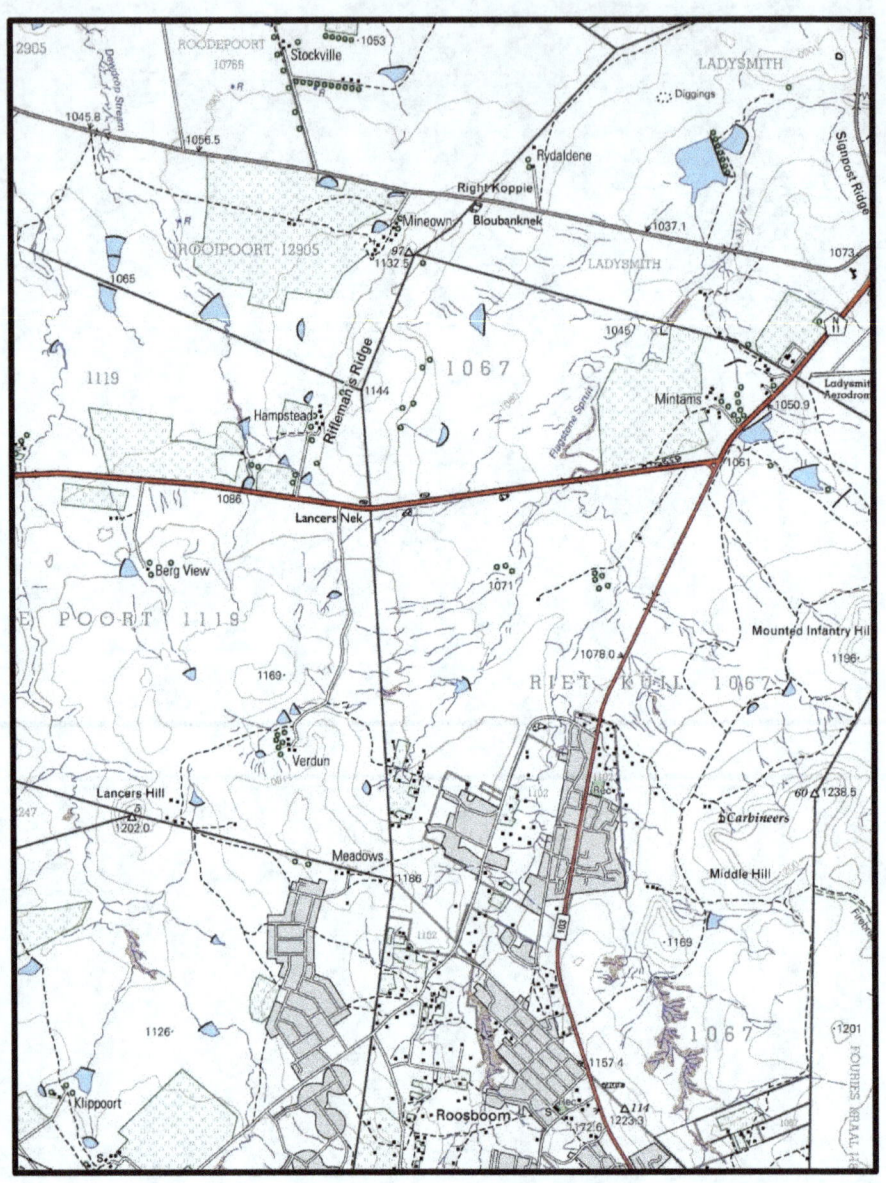

Ladysmith: Long Valley (to the south of the town).

Accounts of the actions around Ladysmith during the siege:

Gibson in *The Story of the Imperial Light Horse in the South African War 1899-1902* devotes many pages to the siege of Ladysmith. The I.L.H. was involved with other Colonial regiments in the attack on Gun Hill on the night of 7th/8th December 1899 when a number of Boer guns were put out of action. The breech block of a 12cm Creusot "Long Tom" was carried back in triumph to the camp and the regiment was complimented personally by Lieutenant General Sir George White. The regiment played a key role in the defence of Wagon Hill during the Boer attack on 6th January 1900.

Besides the *Times History* and Maurice's Official History there are accounts in numerous books in English and Afrikaans. Some of these include Denys Reitz *Commando,* G.W. Steevens *From Cape Town to Ladysmith,* H.W. Nevinson *Ladysmith: The Diary of a Siege,* J.F. Naudé *Veg en Vlug van Beyers en Kemp* and H.H.S. Pearse *Four Months Besieged* all by authors who were present in Ladysmith during the siege.

Ladysmith: The breechblock, a rammer and a projectile of the 12cm Creusot gun put out of action in the raid on Gun Hill displayed in front of the I.L.H. C.O.'s tent. The breechblock is now on display in the Ladysmith Siege Museum.

'A' Squadron with the Composite Cavalry Brigade
Casualty – Willow Grange

RANK		NAME		BURIED		ACTION	Date	Hst/Mon	Died
Tpr	G.	Fitzpatrick	KIA	Estcourt	Mon	Willow Grange	23 Nov 99		23 Nov 99

At Willow Grange, between Estcourt and Mooi River, the raid on southern Natal led by the Commandant General Piet Joubert and General Louis Botha was attacked by a British force from Estcourt commanded by Major General J.H. Hildyard. Only 'A' Squadron of the I.L.H. was present and Trooper George Fitzpatrick, younger brother of Sir Percy Fitzpatrick, was the only fatality. A few days previously the squadron had been involved in the celebrated incident with an armoured train where Winston Churchill was captured. Duncan McKenzie's *Delayed Action* tells of this. Willow Grange has, like Rietfontein, been somewhat neglected by historians and there is no one complete account of what happened in what was an indecisive action. Gibson *The Story of the Imperial Light Horse* gives some detail, as does the two major histories, and J.B. Atkins *The Relief of Ladysmith* devotes a chapter to the subject.

Willow Grange: Access to the battlefield is signposted off the R103 road. The action took place along a dry stone wall that stretches for a considerable distance and over Brynbella hill, the Boer position.

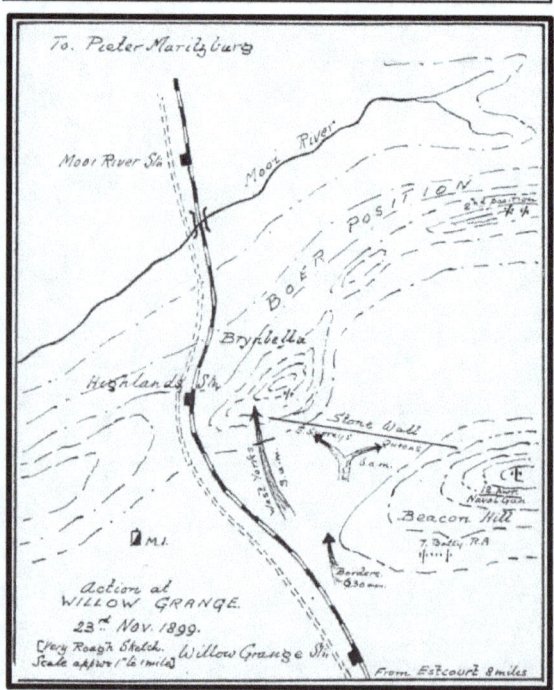

Willow Grange: The dry stone wall, a feature of the battlefield and the headstone of George Fitzpatrick now on the spot where he lost his life.

Imperial Light Horse Regiment – Anglo Boer war – 1899-1902

On 18th January, on the advance across the Tugela River on the left flank of General Redvers Buller's army, Lord Dundonald engaged a Boer commando near Acton Homes. Dundonald's *My Army Life* has a description of this action but without mentioning 'A' Squadron. The controversy surrounding Dundonald's foray is covered in R.L. Wallace *Imperial Light Horse (unpublished)*.

In the advance to relieve Ladysmith, 'A' Squadron, together with a squadron of Natal Carbineers, were the first of Buller's relieving force into Ladysmith. Once again, R.L. Wallace *Imperial Light Horse (unpublished)* covers this episode.

We Rest Here Content

The Relief of Mafeking
Casualties – Mafikeng and Maritzani

RANK		NAME		BURIED		ACTION	Date	Hst/Mon	Died
Tpr	T.S.	Cashman	DOD	Mafeking	ILH			G	02 Jun 00
Tpr	G.	Bonsey	KIA	Mafeking	Metal	Neverset	13 May 00	O10	13 May 00
Tpr	H.S.	Boome	KIA	Mafeking	Metal	Neverset	13 May 00	O10	13 May 00
Tpr	C.	Davis	KIA	Mafeking	Metal	Neverset	13 May 00	O10	13 May 00
Cpl	W.	Francis	KIA	Mafeking	Metal	Neverset	13 May 00	O10	13 May 00
Tpr	C.T.	Gardner	KIA	Mafeking	Mon	Neverset	13 May 00	O10	13 May 00
Tpr	H.E.	Taylor	KIA	Mafeking	Metal	Neverset	13 May 00	O10	13 May 00
Sgt	A.J.	Haynes	DOW	Mafeking	Metal	Neverset	15 May 00		16 May 00
Tpr		Gardner	D	Mafeking	Metal	Mafeking			15 Feb 01
Capt	C.H.	Mullins	DOW	Grahamstown	Cross	Maritsane	13 May 00		24 May 16

The Imperial Light Horse Regiment was shipped from Durban to Cape Town and thence to Kimberley by train. They joined the relief column of Colonel Brian Mahon at Barkly West. The column consisted of 900 mounted men, I.L.H. and the Kimberley Mounted Corps, and four troops of infantry from the Major General Barton's Fusilier Brigade, one each Royal Fusiliers, Royal Irish, Royal Scots and Royal Welsh. They passed through Taungs and Vryburg and were engaged by the Boer commando of Commandant Piet Liebenberg at Neverset farm. Mafeking was relieved on 17th May, 1900 after Mahon met up with the force of Colonel Herbert Plumer from Rhodesia. Both Gibson *The Story of the Imperial Light Horse* and the Imperial Light Horse by R.L. Wallace have detailed accounts but filson Young in *The Relief of Mafeking* tells the story of one who was in the relief column.

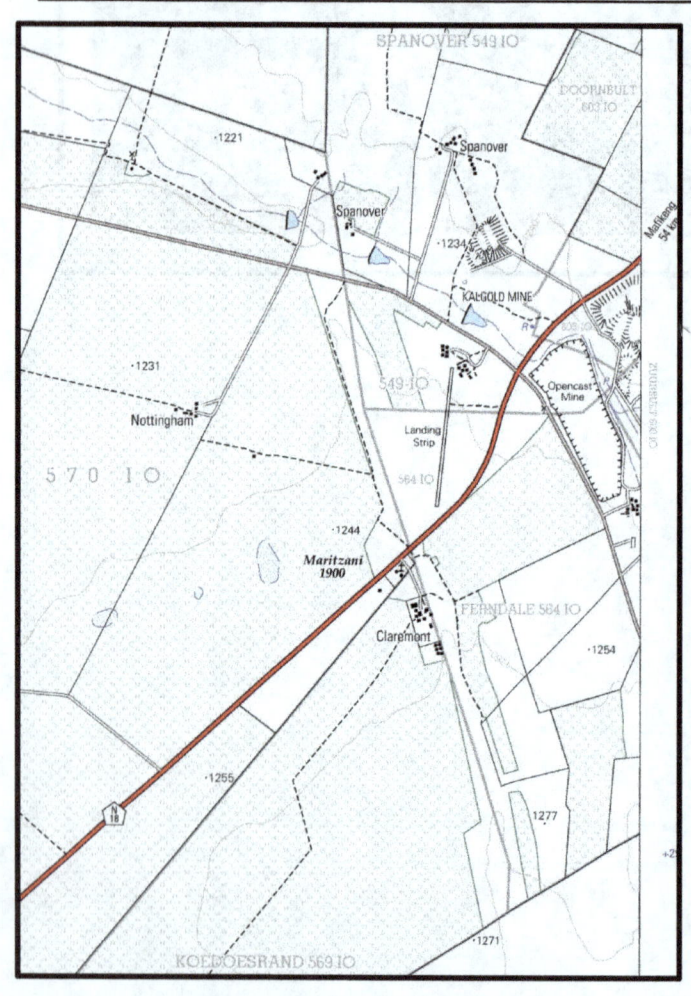

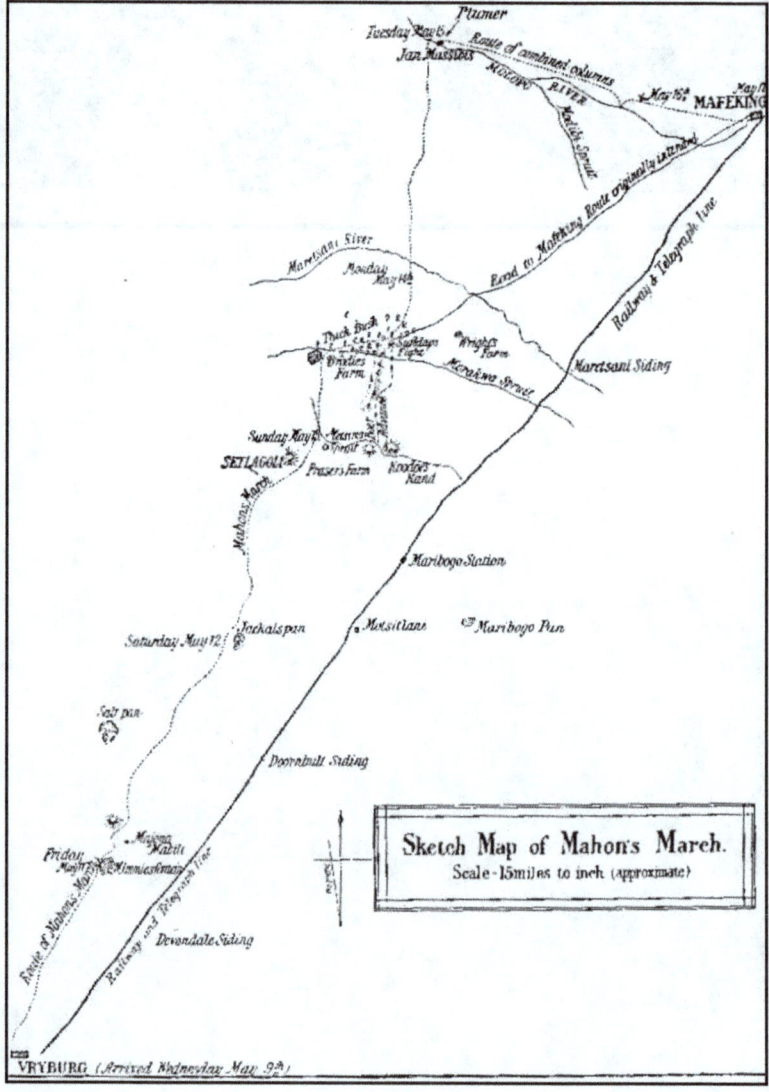

Maritzani – site of marble obelisk and filson Young's map of the relief march..

We Rest Here Content

Witklip – near Delmas

RANK		NAME		BURIED		ACTION	Date of action	Headstone / Monument	Yes	Other data	Died
Tpr	J.	McIniry	D	Braamfontein	Mon					CMR	
Cpl	E.O.	Atherstone	KIA	Braamfontein	Mon	Witklip	07 Jul 00	O8			07 Jul 00
Capt	W.M.	Currie	KIA	Braamfontein	Mon	Witklip	07 Jul 00	O8			07 Jul 00
Tpr	G.W.	Drennan	KIA	Braamfontein	Mon	Witklip	07 Jul 00	O8			07 Jul 00
Tpr	G.M.	King	KIA	Braamfontein	Mon	Witklip	07 Jul 00	G O8			07 Jul 00
Lt	E.E.	Kirk	KIA	Braamfontein	Mon	Witklip	07 Jul 00	O8		CMR	07 Jul 00
Sgt	J.	Marshall	KIA	Braamfontein	Mon	Witklip	07 Jul 00	O8			07 Jul 00
Farr Sgt	C.S.	Wooley	KIA	Braamfontein	Mon	Witklip	07 Jul 00	O8			07 Jul 00
Tpr	H.	Lane	DOW	Braamfontein	Mon	Witklip	07 Jul 00	O8			10 Jul 00
Tpr	A.P.D.	Moodie	DOW	Braamfontein	Mon	Witklip	07 Jul 00	G O8			10 Jul 00
Tpr	A.	Bouchier	DOW	Braamfontein	Mon	Witklip	07 Jul 00	G			14 July 00
Tpr	W.A.	Murray	DOW	Diamond Hill		Witklip	18 Jul 00			Hilton College	19 Jul 00

G = ILH headstone erected according to ILH Memorial Committee report (Appendix I in Gibson "The Story of the Imperial Light Horse".)
O8 = name inscribed on obelisk at Witklip moved to Braamfontein.

Major General E.T.H. Hutton's short campaign to clear Tiger Poort.
Wallace's untitled manuscript has an account of this engagement as does Gibson The Story of the Imperial Light Horse. It occurred when Lord Roberts had accumulated men and supplies and was ready to advance eastwards to Middelburg and beyond after the battle of Diamond Hill on 11th and 12th June 1900. Two officers and nine troopers were killed. Both General Louis Botha and Jan Smuts were present on the battlefield when the dead were buried the following day. The wounded were taken to hospital in Johannesburg. Arthur Bouchier dying after the amputation of an arm.

Braamfontein cemetery

We Rest Here Content

Casualties – Frederikstad

RANK		NAME		BURIED		ACTION	Date	Hst/Mon	Died
Tpr	H.L.	Aschmann	KIA	Potchefstroom	Mon	Frederikstad	16 Oct 00	G	16 Oct 00
Tpr	I.D.J.	Simpson	KIA	Potchefstroom	Mon	Frederikstad	20 Oct 00	G	20 Oct 00
Sgt	H.E.	Wellstead	DOW	Braamfontein	Mon	Frederikstad	25 Oct 00	G	24 Nov 00
Sgt	G.	Wileman	DOW	Braamfontein	Mon	Frederikstad	25 Oct 00	G	09 Nov 00

The battle to protect the railway line at Frederikstad, 17-22 October 1900.
Major-General Geoffrey Barton was ordered to head off General Christiaan de Wet who had crossed the Vaal River at Schoeman's Drift. De Wet's attack on the railway line at Frederikstad, north of Potchefstroom, was countered by Barton whose mounted men consisted of the I.L.H. and some Yeomanry. As usual, the Official History and the Times History give some detail but there are more detailed accounts in Gibson The Story of the Imperial Light Horse and Wallace's untitled manuscript/

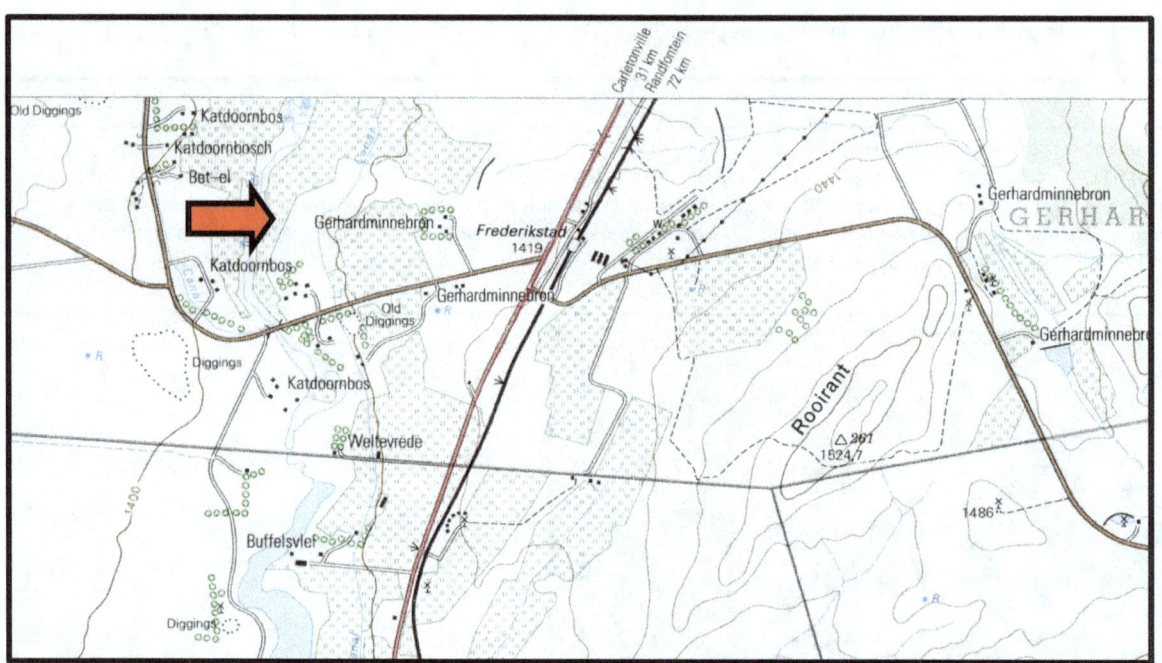

Frederikstad: Royal Welsh Fusiliers and I.L.H. fight side-by-side

We Rest Here Content

The rearguard action from Geduld Farm to Hartebeestfontein

Casualties – Hartebeestfontein

RANK		NAME		BURIED		ACTION	Date	Hst/Mon	Died
Lt	A.R.	Halling	DOW	Hartebeestfontein	Mon	Hartebeestfontein	18 Mar 02	011	23 Mar 02
Lt	J.	Ralston	KIA	Hartebeestfontein	Mon	Hartebeestfontein	22 Mar 01	011	22 Mar 01
Rgt Sgt Maj	A.E.	Hurst	KIA	Hartebeestfontein	Mon	Hartebeestfontein	22 Mar 01	011	22 Mar 01
Tpr	P.	Jones	KIA	Hartebeestfontein	Mon	Hartebeestfontein	22 Mar 01	011	22 Mar 01
Tpr	P.	Kennedy	KIA	Hartebeestfontein	Mon	Hartebeestfontein	22 Mar 01	011	22 Mar 01
Tpr	D.	Patterson	KIA	Hartebeestfontein	Mon	Hartebeestfontein	22 Mar 01	011	22 Mar 01

The six casualties around the hamlet of Hartebeestfontein are commemorated on one of the I.L.H.'s white marble obelisks.

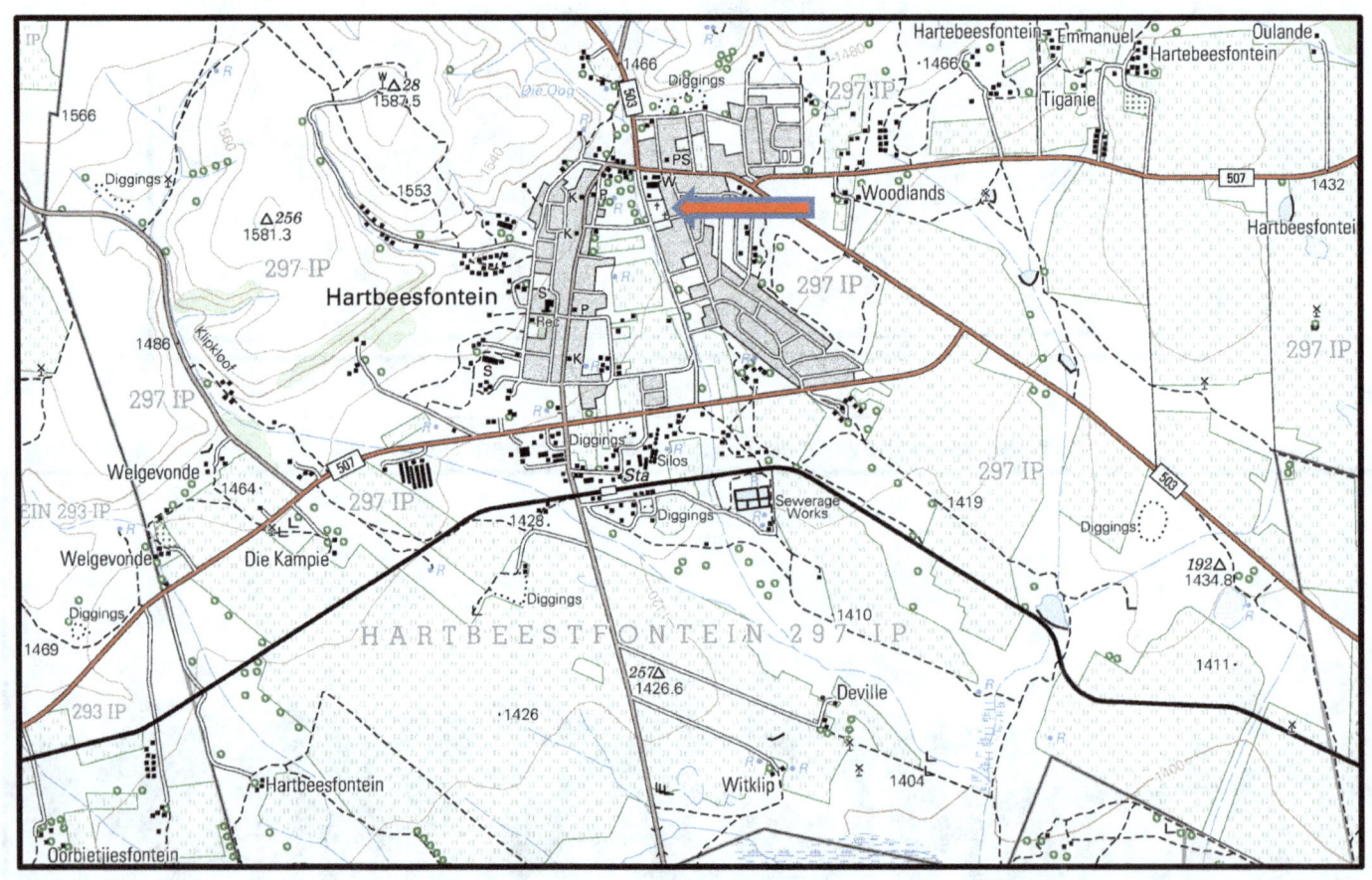

We Rest Here Content

The battle at Naauwpoort Nek on 5th January 1901

Casualties – Cyferfontein

RANK		NAME		BURIED		ACTION	Date	Hst/Mon	Died
Tpr	P.	Anderson	KIA	Krugersdorp	Mon	Cyferfontein	05 Jan 01	O9	05 Jan 01
Tpr	J.H.	Bentley	DOW	Krugersdorp	Mon	Cyferfontein	05 Jan 01	O9	06 Jan 01
Tpr	L.	Bromham	DOW	Braamfontein	Mon	Cyferfontein	05 Jan 01	G O9	16 Jan 01
Tpr	A.C.	Brown	DOW	Braamfontein	Mon	Cyferfontein	05 Jan 01	G O9	09 Jan 01
Tpr	R.O.	Butler	KIA	Krugersdorp	Mon	Cyferfontein	05 Jan 01	O9	05 Jan 01
Tpr	C.J.	Harding	KIA	Krugersdorp	Mon	Cyferfontein	05 Jan 01	O9	05 Jan 01
Tpr	M.A.	Langley	KIA	Krugersdorp	Mon	Cyferfontein	05 Jan 01	O9	05 Jan 01
Tpr	R.	Leak	DOW	Krugersdorp	Mon	Cyferfontein	05 Jan 00	O9	06 Jan 00
Tpr	J.W.	Maxwell	KIA	Krugersdorp	Mon	Cyferfontein	05 Jan 00	O9	05 Jan 01
Tpr	W.	Melville	KIA	Krugersdorp	Mon	Cyferfontein	05 Jan 00	O9	05 Jan 01
Cpl	H.	Nash	KIA	Krugersdorp	Mon	Cyferfontein	05 Jan 00	O9	05 Jan 01
Tpr	H.	O'Hagan	D			Cyferfontein	05 Jan 00		
Lt	A.	Ormond	KIA	Krugersdorp	Mon	Cyferfontein	05 Jan 00	O9	05 Jan 01
Tpr	W.	Pierce	KIA	Krugersdorp	Mon	Cyferfontein	05 Jan 01		05 Jan 00
Capt	T.	Yockney	KIA	Krugersdorp	Mon	Cyferfontein	05 Jan 00	O9	05 Jan 01

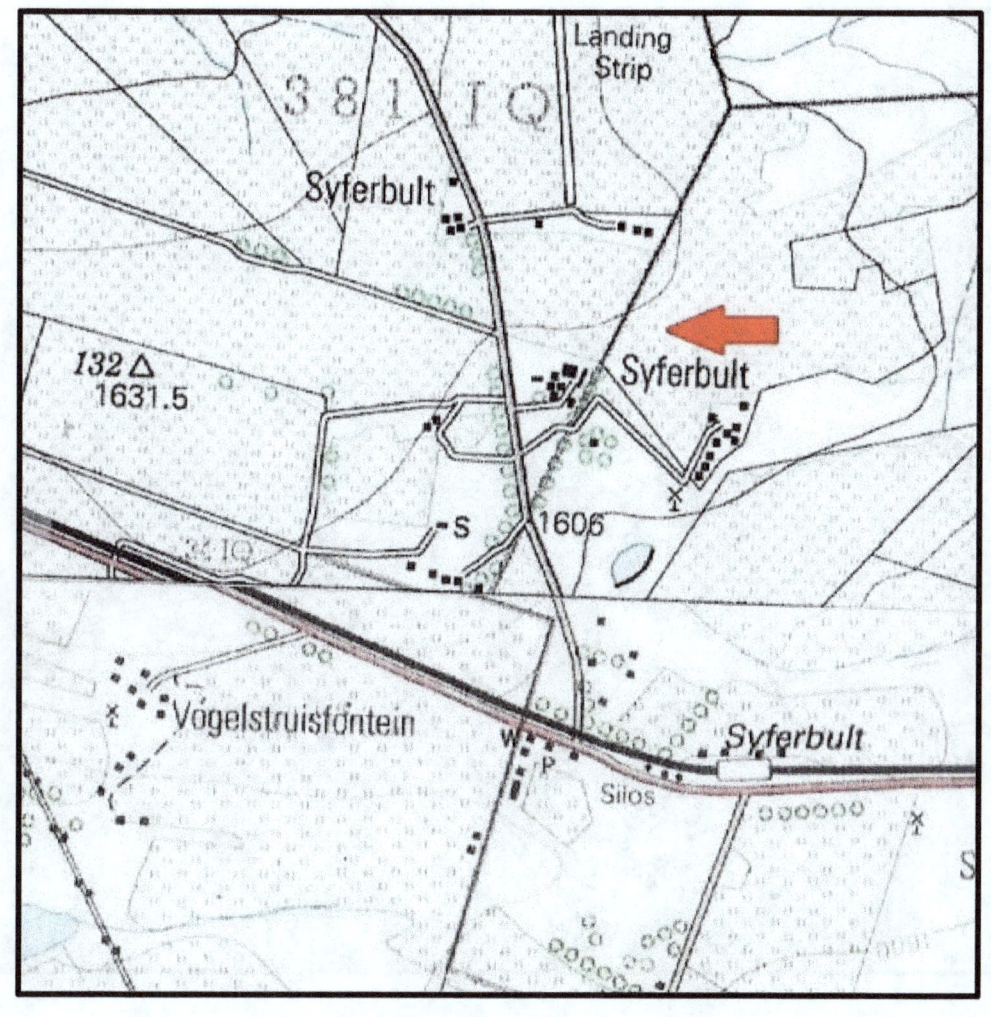

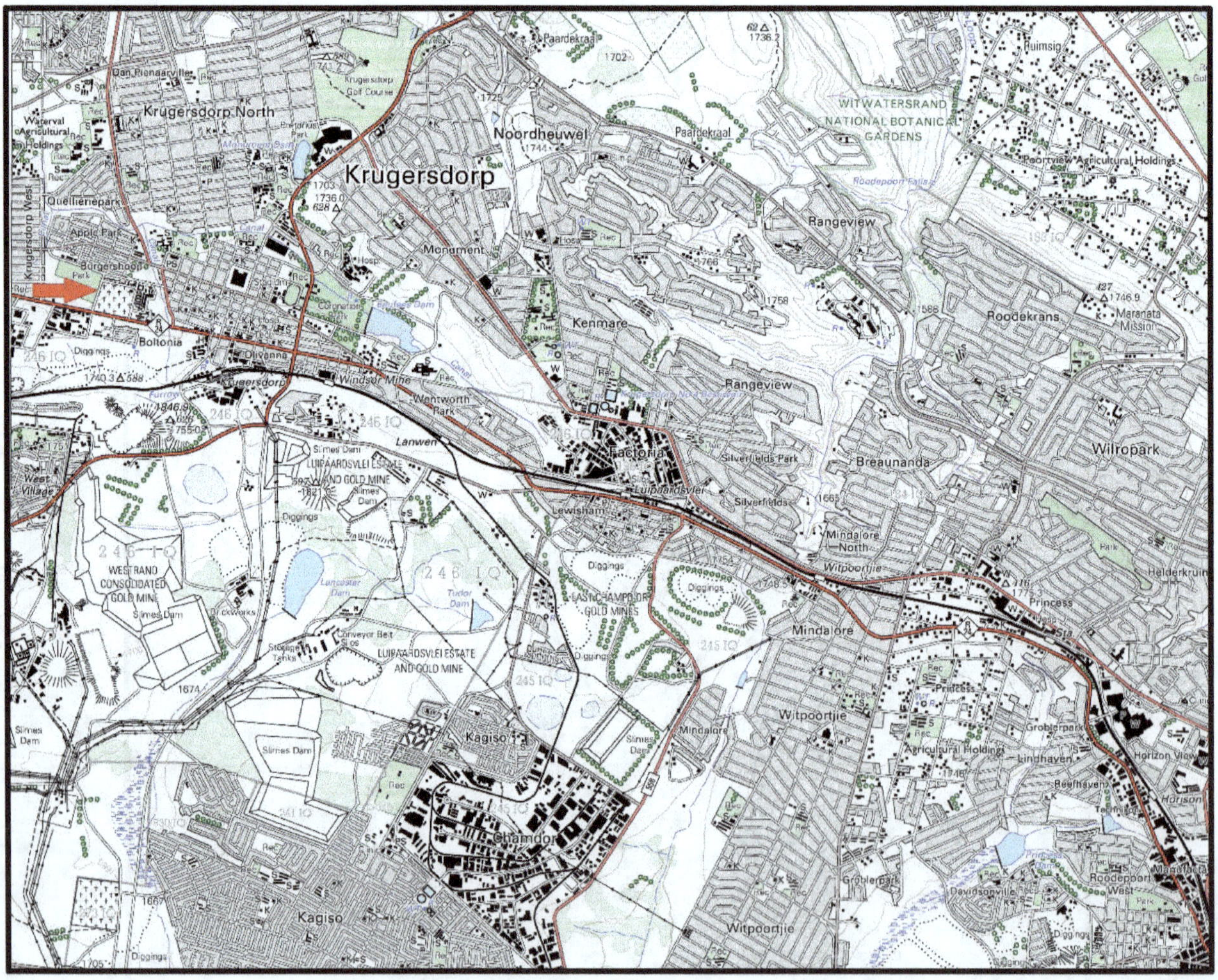

We Rest Here Content

Krugersdorp Garden of Remembrance

We Rest Here Content

General Louis Botha's attack on Major-General Horace Smith Dorrien's column at Bothwell.

Casualties – Lake Chrissie

RANK		NAME		BURIED		ACTION	Date	Died
Tpr	H.	Edmondson	DOW	Standerton	Mon	Lake Chrissie	06 Feb 00	25 Feb 00
Tpr	J.	Erasmus	DOW	Lake Chrissie	ILH	Lake Chrissie	06 Feb 00	06 Feb 01
Tpr	C.	Marsden	KIA	Lake Chrissie	ILH	Lake Chrissie	06 Feb 00	06 Feb 01
L Cpl	D.W.N.	Ritchie	KIA	Lake Chrissie	ILH	Lake Chrissie	06 Feb 00	06 Feb 01
Tpr	F.H.	Smallwood	KBL	Ermelo	Mon	Twyfelaar		25 Jan 01

Other fatalities

RANK		NAME		BURIED		ACTION	Date	Died
Tpr	J.W.	Lee	DOAB	Wakkerstroom	ILH	Piet Retief		15 Mar 01
Tpr	J.	Willcocks	DODE	Wakkerstroom	Mon			31 Mar 01
Tpr	C.	Harding	DODE	Wakkerstroom	ILH	Piet Retief		06 Apr 01
Tpr	F.H.	Hanks	DRO	Wakkerstroom	ILH	Amsterdam		22 Feb 01

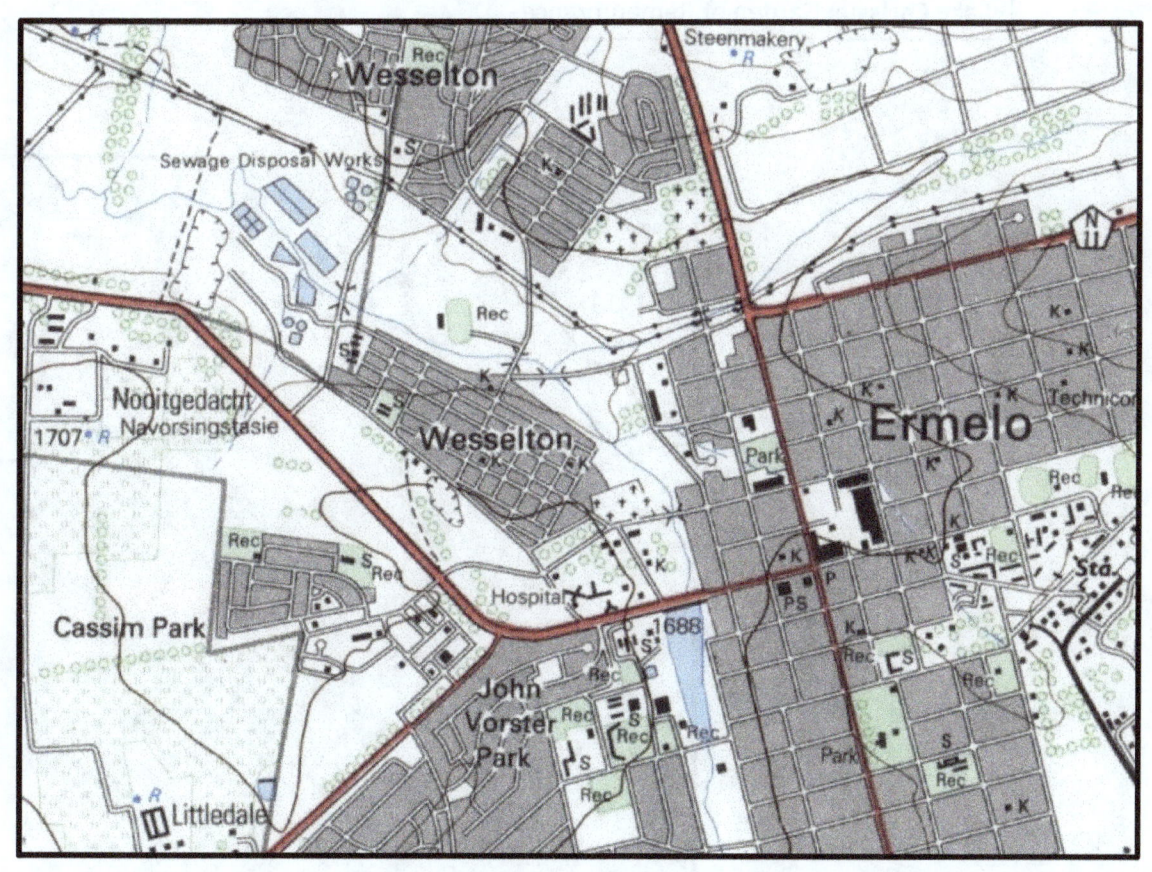

We Rest Here Content

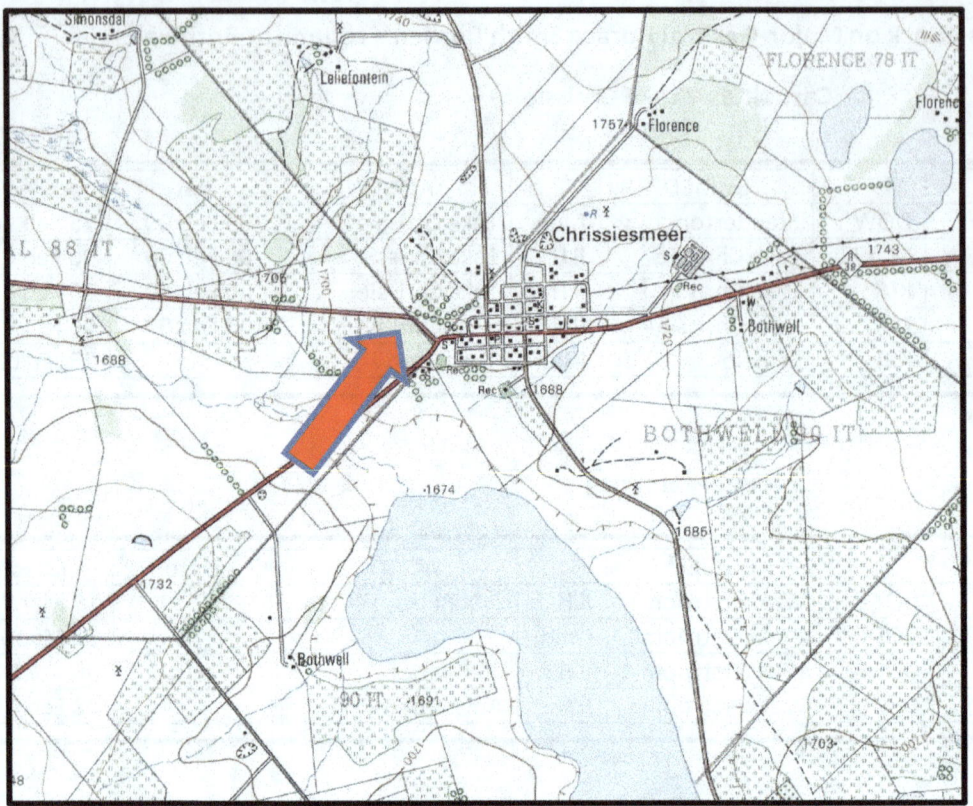

Lake Chrissie: Garden of Remembrance

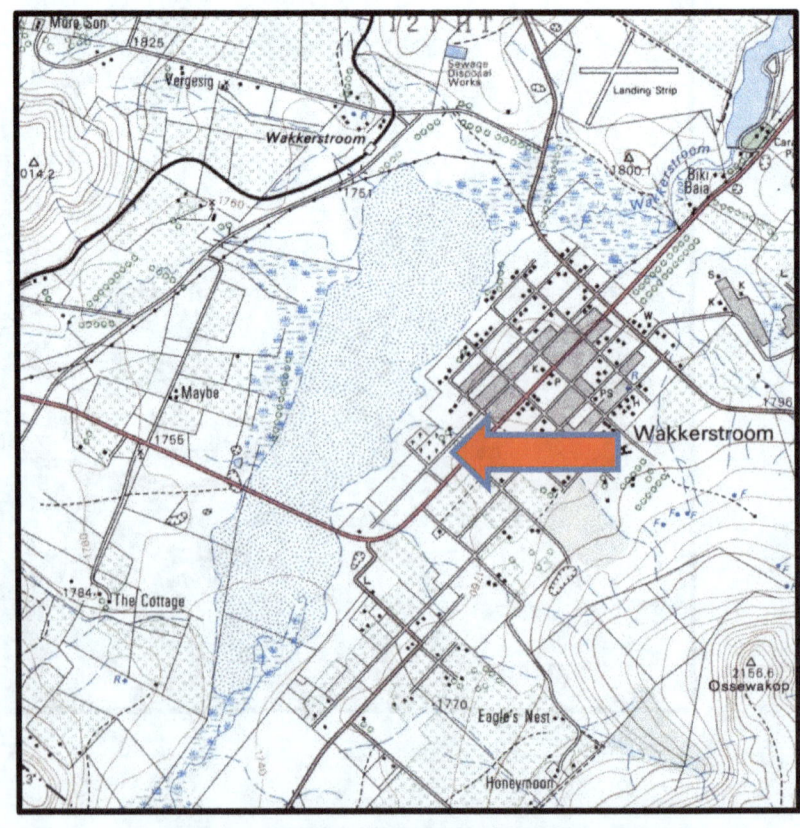

Wakkerstroom: Garden of Remembrance

We Rest Here Content

Casualties – Western Transvaal

RANK	NAME		BURIED		ACTION	Date	Hst/Mon	Died
Tpr	J.J.	Bailey	KIA	Ventersdorp	ILH	Elandsfontein	15 Feb 01	G	15 Feb 01
Tpr	D.S.	Burgess	KIA	Ventersdorp	ILH	Doornpan	01 Jan 01	G	01 Jan 01
Tpr	B.L.	Bristol	KIA	Ottosdal	Mon	Rietvlei	31 Jul 01	G	31 Jul 01
Lt	L.S.	Sanders	KIA	Ottosdal	Mon	Korannafontein	31 Jul 01	G	31 Jul 01
Tpr	A.	Cairns	KIA			Rietvlei	02 Mar 01		02 Mar 01
Tpr	F.H.	Ogston	KIA	Klerksdorp	ILH	Rietkuil	17 Apr 01	G	17 Apr 01
Sgt	H.	Parkin	DODP	Klerksdorp	ILH	Matjespruit		G	22 Aug 01
Lt	B.C.	Noel	DOW	Zeerust	Cross	Oog van Marico	06 Jul 01	G12	10 Jul 01
Tpr	E.	Clark	KIA	Treurfontein	ILH	Palmietfontein	09 May 01	G	19 May 01

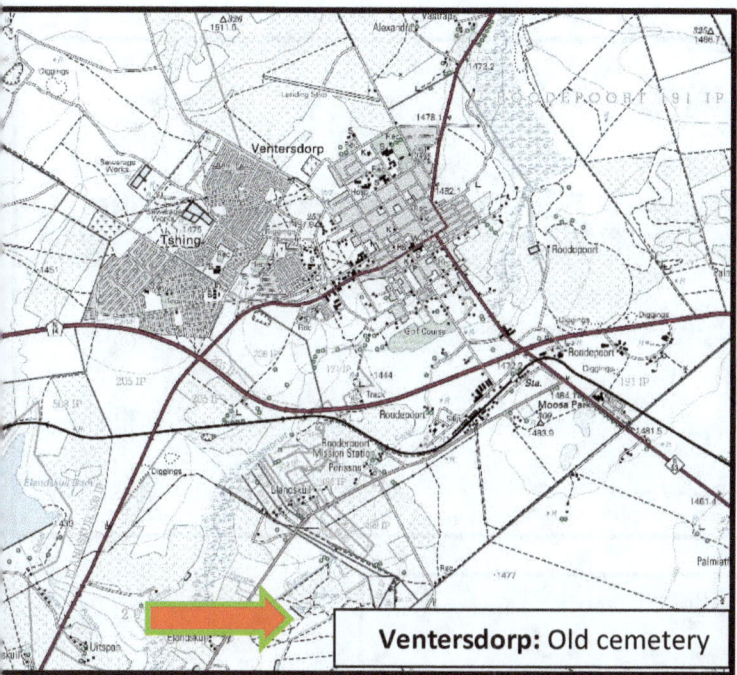
Ventersdorp: Old cemetery

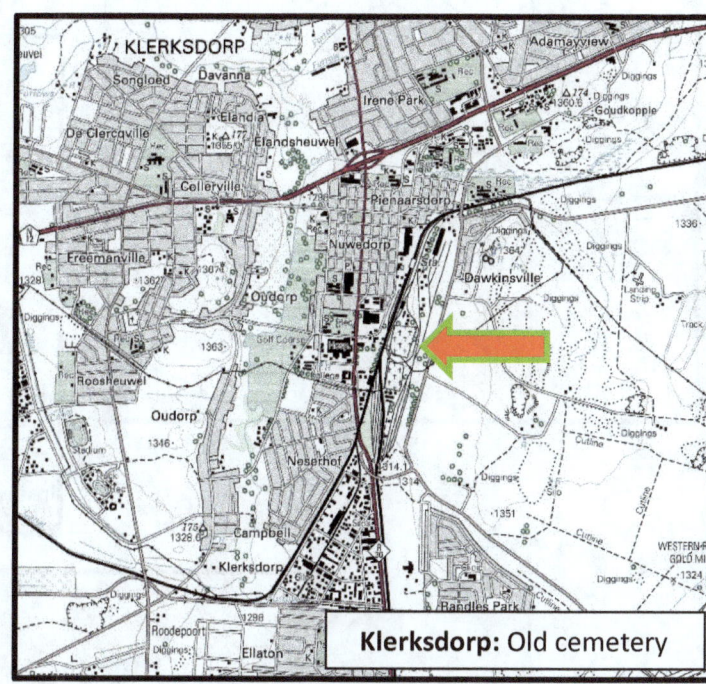
Klerksdorp: Old cemetery

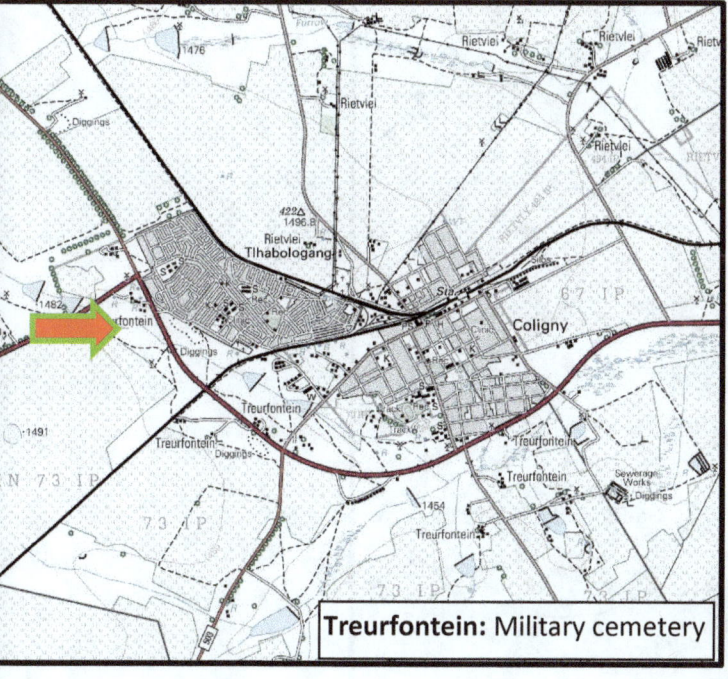
Treurfontein: Military cemetery

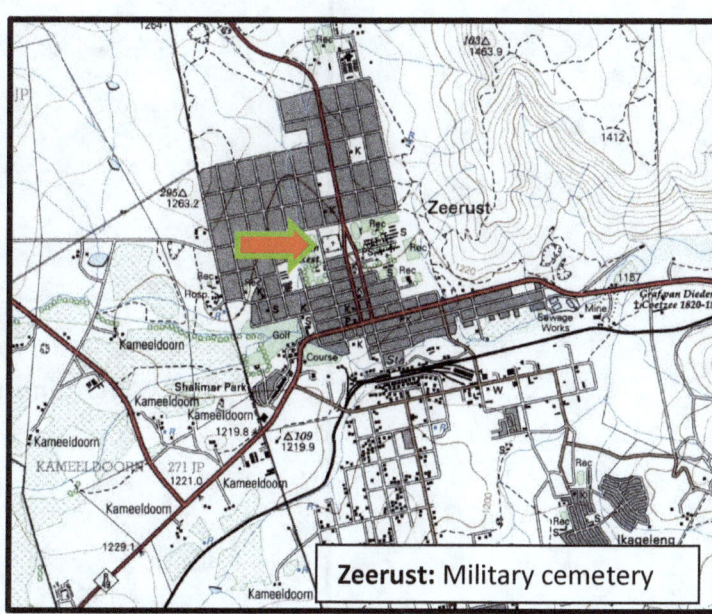
Zeerust: Military cemetery

We Rest Here Content

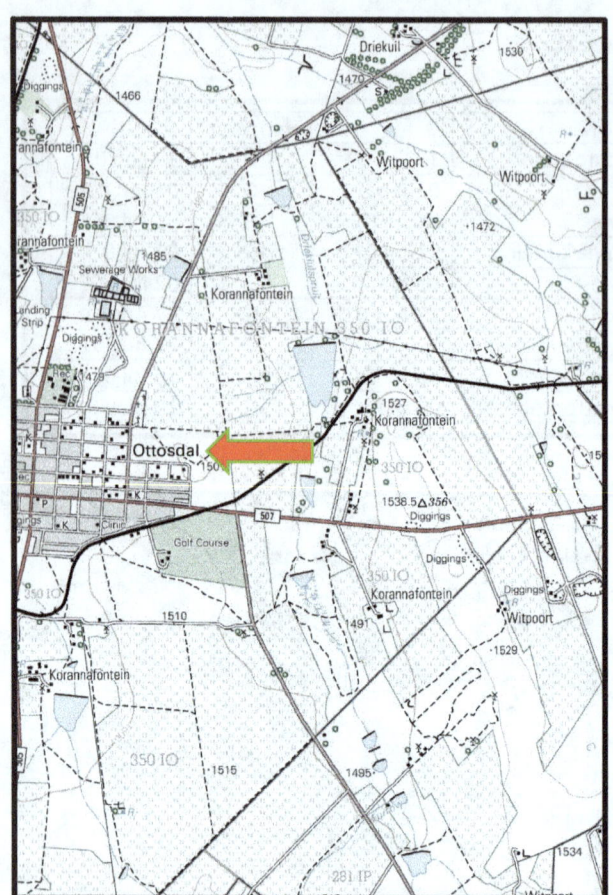

Ottosdal: Garden of Remembrance

We Rest Here Content

Casualties – Bethlehem Military Cemetery

RANK		NAME		BURIED		ACTION	Date	Hst/Mon	Died
Tpr	H.	Abercrombie	DOW	Bethlehem	ILH	Paardeplaatz	21Oct 01	G	25 Oct 01
Tpr	W.	Agar	DOD	Bethlehem	ILH	Bethlehem		G	30 Sep 01
Tpr	G.	Bremer	KIA	Bethlehem	ILH	Concordia	07 Sep 01	G	07 Sep 01
Cpl	F.	Connell	KIA	Bethlehem	ILH	Roodepoort	24 Sep 01	G	24 Sep 01
L Cpl	J.G.	Dixon	DOD	Bethlehem	Metal	Bethlehem			03 Nov 01
Tpr	V.G.	Hooper	KIA	Bethlehem	ILH	Vischgat	11 Nov 01	G	11 Nov 01
Tpr	E.H.	McChesney	KBL	Bethlehem	ILH	Vischgat		G	09 Nov 01
Tpr	V.	Miller	DOD	Bethlehem	Metal	Bethlehem			26 Dec 01
Tpr	M.	O'Shea	KIA	Bethlehem	ILH	Tygerkloof	28 Sep 01	G	28 Sep 01
Tpr	J.W.	Townsend	KIA	Bethlehem	ILH	Naauwpoort Nek	07 Oct 01	G	Accidentally

Casualties – Harrismith Military Cemetery

RANK		NAME		BURIED		ACTION	Date	Hst/Mon	Died
Tpr Guide	A.L.	Fraser	DOW	Harrismith	ILH	Tygerskloof	15 Jan 02	G	16 Jan 02
Cpl	W.	Gabriel	DOW	Harrismith	ILH	Newmarket Farm	29 Jan 02	G	05 Feb 02
Tpr	F.	Hutchinson	DOD	Harrismith	Head	Harrismith			13 Apr 02
Cpl	F.	James	DOD	Harrismith	ILH	Harrismith		G	07 Feb 02
Tpr	B.F.	Murray	DOD	Harrismith	ILH	Harrismith		G	17 Feb 02
Tpr	S.	Tennant	KIA	Harrismith	ILH	Klipkraal		G	25Jan 02
Tpr	F.	Wheeler	DOW	Harrismith	ILH	Ladysmith	04 Nov 99	G	01 Jan 1900

RANK		NAME		BURIED		ACTION	Date	Hst/Mon	Died
Cpl	J.H.	Renouf	KIA	Lindley	Mon	Craven's Rust		G	09 Mar02
Tpr	E.	Wiid	DOW	Fauresmith	Metal	Fauresmith	04 Mar01		08 Mar 01

RANK		NAME		BURIED		ACTION	Date	Hst/Mon	Died
Tpr	J.H.	Barry	KIA	Heilbron		Katkop	07 Feb 02	G	07 Feb 02
Tpr	W.	Evans	KIA	Heilbron	Mon	Katkop	07 Feb 02	G	07 Feb 02
Tpr	T.	Johnson	KIA	Heilbron	Mon	Katkop	07 Feb 02	G	07 Feb 02
Tpr	H.C.	Thirlwall	KIA	Heilbron	Mon	Katkop	07 Feb 02	G	07 Feb 02
Tpr	C.	KIA	KIA	Heilbron	Mon	Katkop	07 Feb 02	G	07 Feb 02
Tpr	J.	flanegan	DOW	Colesburg	ILH	Botha's Drift	23 Feb 01	G	08 Apr 01
Sgt	P.	Cawood	KIA	Vrede	Mon	Pramkop	27 Jan 02	G	27 Jan 02
Cpl	J.E.G.	Davies	KIA	Vrede	Mon	Pramkop	27 Jan 02	G	27 Jan 02

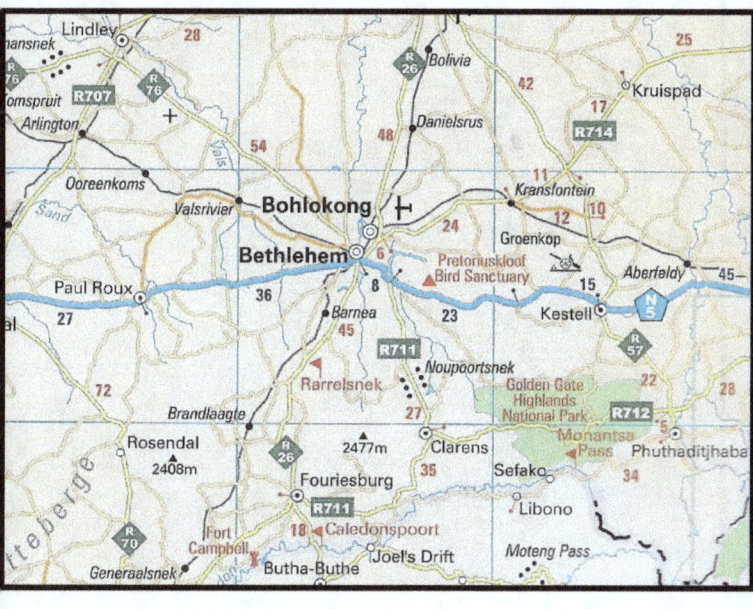
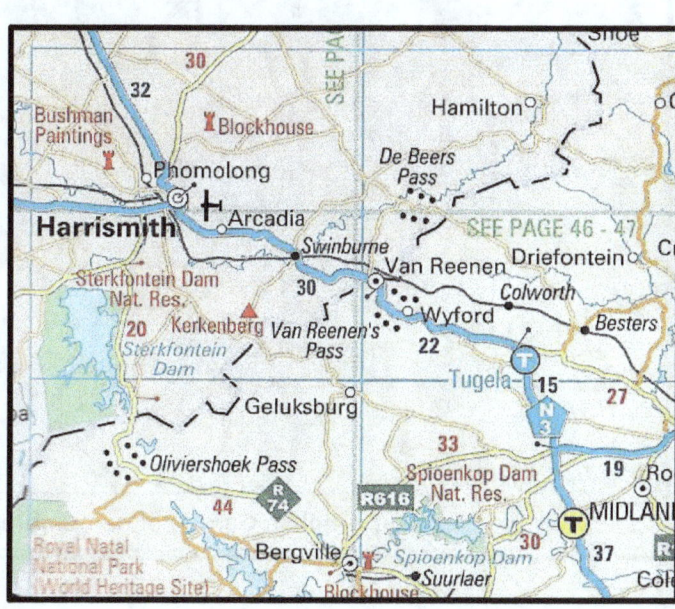

We Rest Here Content

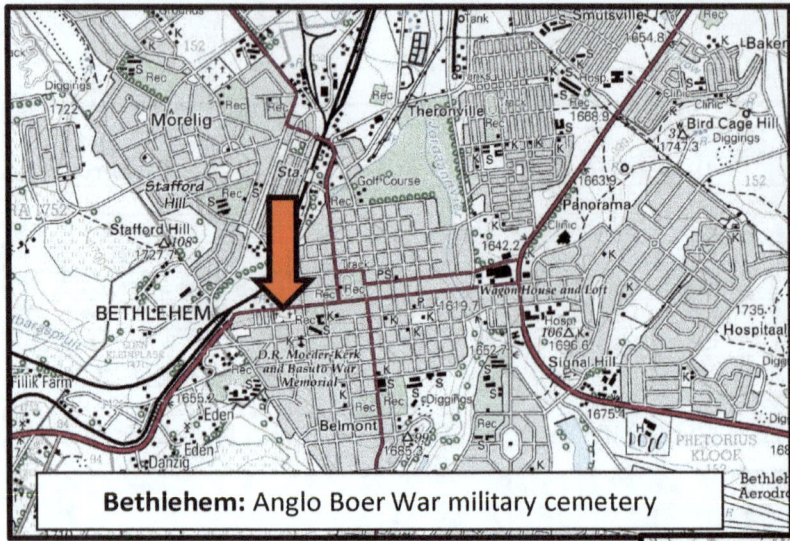

Bethlehem: Anglo Boer War military cemetery

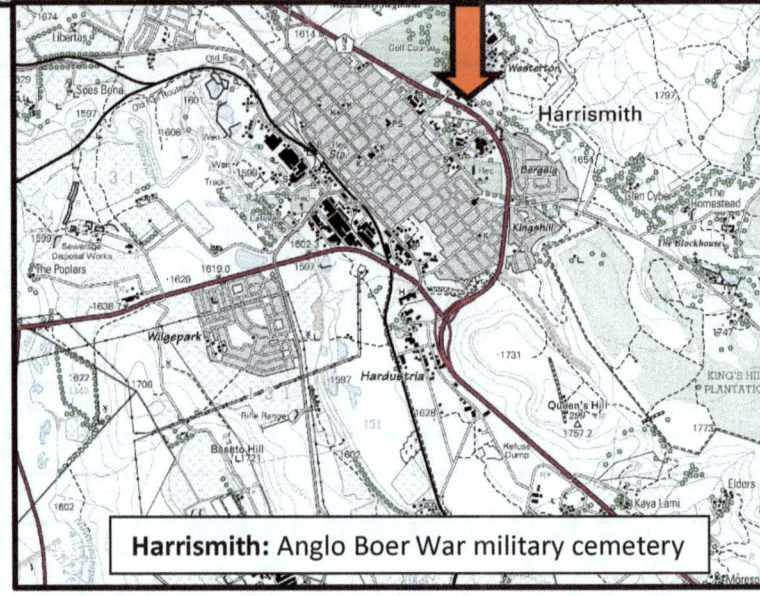

Harrismith: Anglo Boer War military cemetery

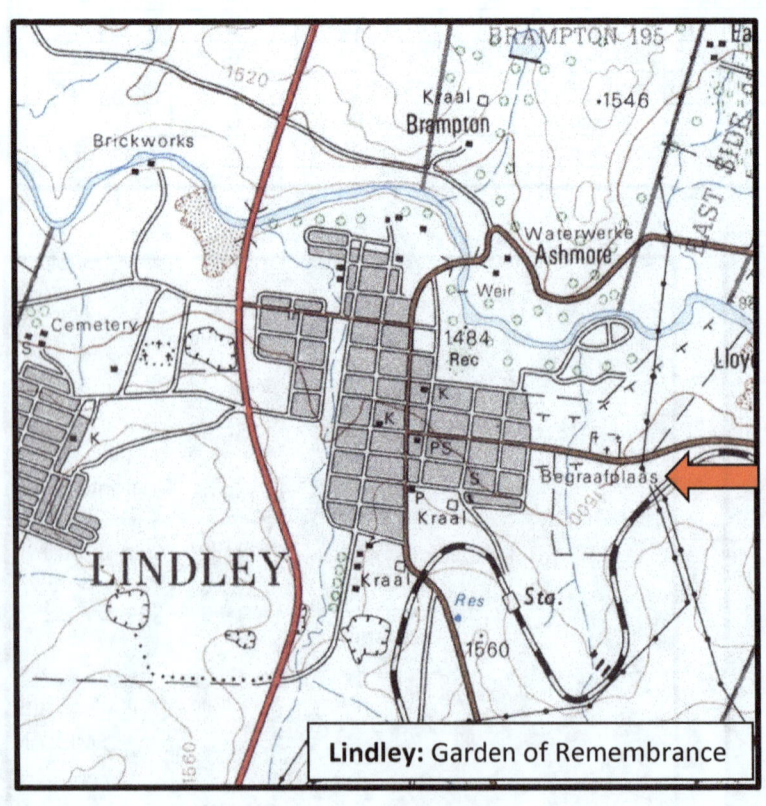

Lindley: Garden of Remembrance

We Rest Here Content

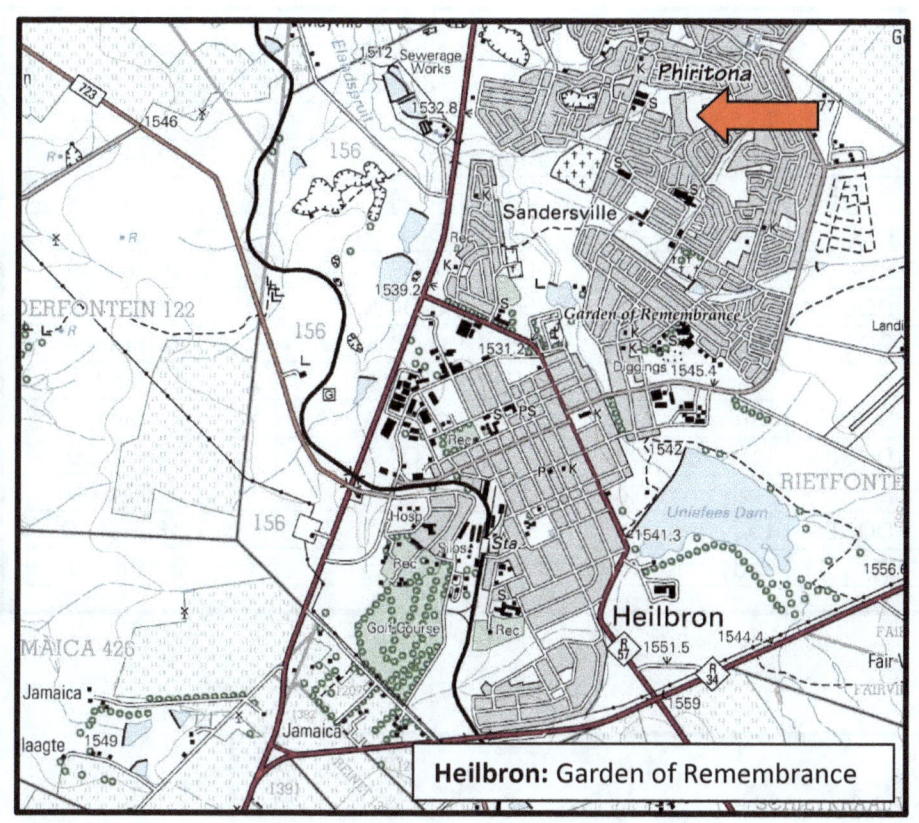

Heilbron: Garden of Remembrance

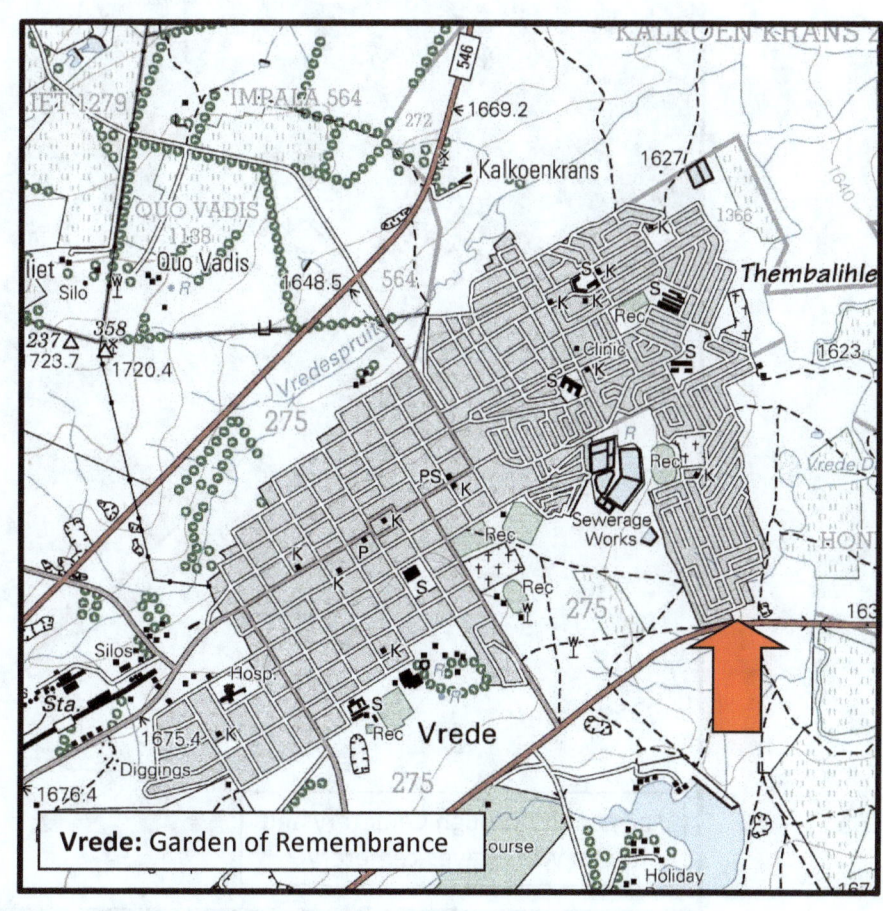

Vrede: Garden of Remembrance

RANK		NAME		BURIED		Headstone/ Monument	Yes	Died
Tpr	J.P.	Powers	D	Ladysmith Town	Mon	O5 A		31 Oct 99
Tpr	D.	Guthrie-Smith	DOW	Intombi	Mon	O4 A		12 Nov 99
Tpr	W.T.P.	Lawrence	DODE	Intombi	ILH	G O4 A	X	04 Dec 99
Tpr	B.	Stewart	DODE	Intombi	Mon	O4 A		11 Dec 99
Tpr	J.E.	Downing	DOD	Ladysmith Town	ILH	G O5 A	X	19 Dec 99
Tpr	J.G.	Taylor	DODE	Intombi	ILH	G O4 A	X	20 Dec 99
Tpr	R.A.	Foley	DODE	Intombi	ILH	G O4 A	X	18 Jan 00
Tpr	J.	Campbell	DODD	Intombi	ILH	G O4 A	X	23 Jan 00
Farr Sgt	W.	Burrows	DODE	Intombi	ILH	G O4 A	X	30 Jan 00
Tpr	F.W.	Pearce	DODc	Intombi	ILH	G O4 A	X	01 Feb 00
Tpr	J.	Ledingham	K	Ladysmith Town	Mon	A		21 Feb 00
Tpr	R.S.	Tute	DODE	Ladysmith		A		18 Mar 00
Tpr	J.	Pearson	D	Ladysmith Town	Mon			30 Jun 00

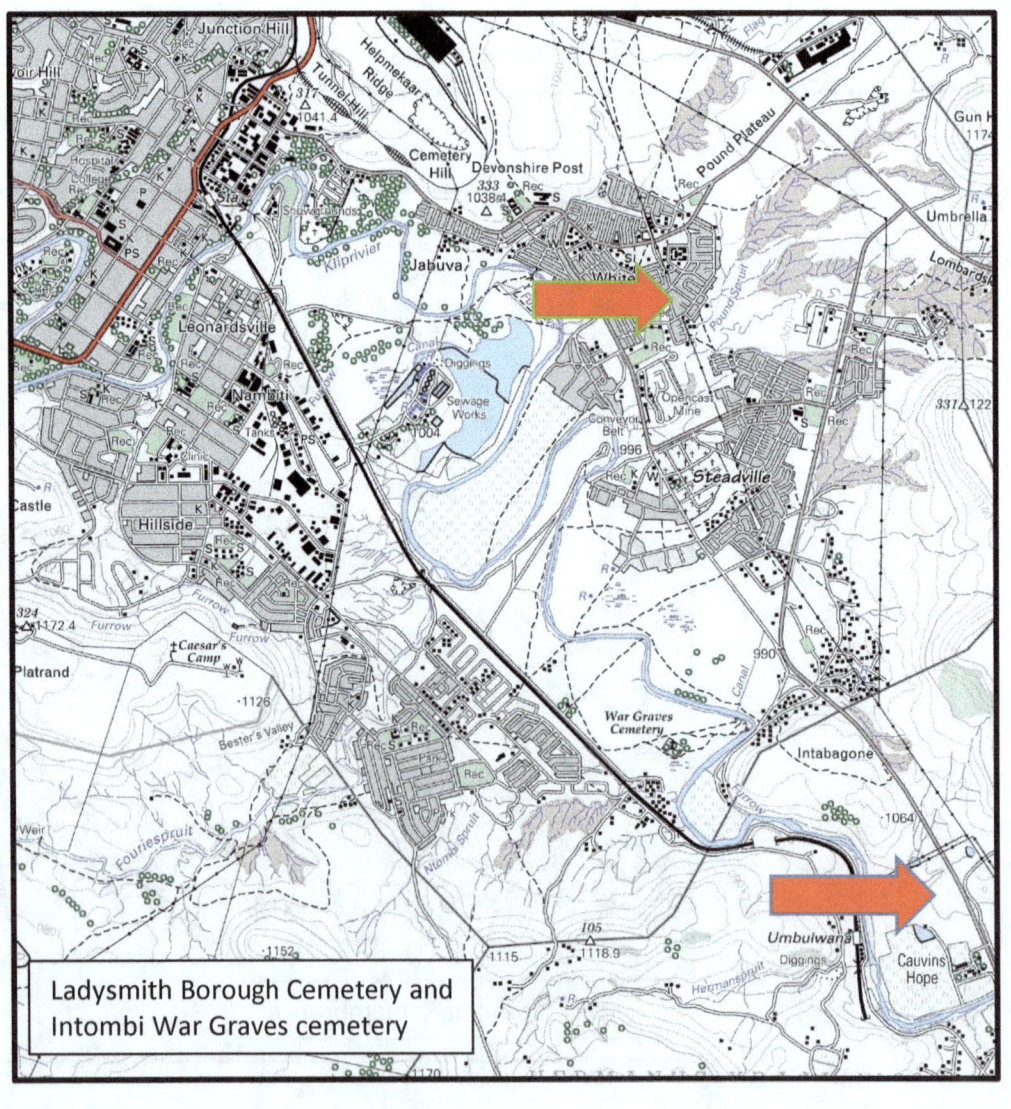

Ladysmith Borough Cemetery and Intombi War Graves cemetery

RANK		NAME		BURIED		ACTION	Headstone/ Monument	Died
Tpr	J.	McIniry	D	Braamfontein	Mon			
Tpr	E.H.	Wallace	D					
Tpr	J.P.	Powers	D	Ladysmith Town	Mon		O5	31 Oct 99
Tpr	D.	Guthrie-Smith	DOW	Intombi	Mon		O4	12 Nov 99
Tpr	W.T.P.	Lawrence	DODE	Intombi	ILH		G O4	04 Dec 99
Tpr	B.	Stewart	DODE	Intombi	Mon		O4	11 Dec 99
Tpr	J.E.	Downing	DOD	Ladysmith Town	ILH		G O5	19 Dec 99
Tpr	J.G.	Taylor	DODE	Intombi	ILH		G O4	20 Dec 99
Tpr	R.A.	Foley	DODE	Intombi	ILH		G O4	18 Jan 00
Tpr	J.	Campbell	DODD	Intombi	ILH		G O4	23 Jan 00
Farr Sgt	W.	Burrows	DODE	Intombi	ILH		G O4	30 Jan 00
Tpr	F.W.	Pearce	DODc	Intombi	ILH		G O4	01 Feb 00
Tpr	J.	Ledingham	K	Ladysmith Town	Mon			21 Feb 00
Tpr	R.S.	Tute	DODE	Ladysmith				18 Mar 00
Tpr	R.J.	Whittle	DODE	Wyatt Road	ILH		G	10 Apr 00
Cpl	W.G.	Downer	DODE	Fort Napier	ILH		G	12 Apr 00
Tpr	H.S.	Mapleston	DODE	Chieveley	ILH		G	16 Apr 00
Tpr	D.	Falconer	DODE	Mooi River	ILH		G	07 May 00
Tpr	W.B.	Bain	DODD			Albert Docks		20 May 00
Tpr	T.S.	Cashman	DOD	Mafikeng	ILH		G	02 Jun 00
Tpr	J.	Pearson	D	Ladysmith Town	Mon			30 Jun 00
Tpr	A.H.	Johnson	KIA					01 Aug 00
Tpr	D.H.	Cribb	DOI	Bloemfontein	Mon	Brandkop		07 Nov 00
Cpl	W.	Mackenzie	D	Braamfontein	Mon		G	10 Dec 00
Tpr	C.S.	Manning	DOD	Braamfontein	Mon		G	12 Jan 01
Tpr	M.G.N.	Norwood	DOD	Braamfontein	Mon		G	25 Jan 01
Tpr	F.H.	Smallwood	KBL	Ermelo	Mon	Twyfelaar	G	25 Jan 01
Tpr	J.I.	Thomas	DODE	Newcastle	Mon	/Charlestown		25 Jan 01
Tpr	G.	Simpson	DOW			Hamelfontein		15 Feb 01

Tpr	A.H.F.	Pinnick	DOD	Pretoria	ILH		G	19 Feb 01
Tpr	G.	Hanks	DRO	Wakkerstroom	ILH	Amsterdam	G	22 Feb 01
Tpr	H.	Muson	DOW	Standerton				25 Feb 01
Tpr	C.W.	Winter	DRO	Compies River				25 Feb 01
Tpr	A.	Cairns	KIA			Rietvlei		02 Mar 01
Tpr	J.W.	Lee	DOAB	Wakkerstroom	ILH	Piet Retief	G	15 Mar 01
Tpr	J.W.	Wilkes	DOW	Pretoria	Mon			24 Mar 01
Tpr	C.	Whittaker	DOIA	Krugersdorp	ILH			25 Mar 01
Tpr	W.R.	Willcocks	DODE	Wakkerstroom	Mon			31 Mar 01
Tpr	H.J.	Harding	DODE	Wakkerstroom	ILH	Piet Retief	G	06 Apr 01
Tpr	E.H.	Walshlager	DODD	Newcastle	ILH	Charlestown	G	18 Apr 01
Tpr	T.	Smith	DOD	Pretoria	Mon			30 Apr 01
Sgt	A.S.	Melville	DODE	Pretoria	ILH		G	04 May 01
Tpr	H.J.	Cox	DOD	Braamfontein	Mon			02 Jun 01
Sgt Maj	A.J.C.	Lang	DOD	Fort Napier	ILH	Victoria Hotel, Pmb	G	03 Jun 01
Tpr	H.	Parmenter	DODE	Braamfontein	Mon			26 Jun 01
Tpr	B.E.	Whittaker	DOIR	Colesberg	Mon	Norval's Pont		14 Jul 01
Tpr	T.	Knowles	DODH	Standerton	Mon	Standerton	G	14 Aug 01
Sgt	H.	Parkin	DODP	Klerksdorp	ILH		G	22 Aug 01
Tpr	L.T.	Hervey	DODE	West End	Mon	Kimberley		26 Aug 01
Tpr	W.	Agar	DODE	Bethlehem	ILH		G	30 Sep 01
Cpl	G.	MacKenzie	DODT	Braamfontein	Mon		G	08 Oct 01
Tpr	C.	Howell	DRO	Tugela River				17 Oct 01
L Cpl	J.G.	Dixon	DOD	Bethlehem	Metal			03 Nov 01
Tpr	E.H.	McChesney	KBL	Bethlehem	ILH	Vischgat	G	09 Nov 01
Tpr	V.	Miller	DODE	Bethlehem	Metal			26 Dec 01
Tpr	C.H.	Robinson	DODD	Mooi River	ILH		G	19 Jan 02
Sgt	P.	Cawood	KIA	Vrede	Mon	Pramkop	G	27 Jan 02
Cpl	F.	James	DODE	Harrismith	ILH		G	07 Feb 02
Tpr	B.F.	Murray	DODE	Harrismith	ILH		G	17 Feb 02
Cpl	J.H.	Renouf	KA	Lindley	Mon	Craven's Rust	G	09 Mar 02

Tpr	A.E.	Swanson	DOPP	Fort Napier	ILH		G	09 Mar 02
Cpl	A.H.	Twange	DODE	Howick	Mon		G	19 Mar 02
Rgm Sgt	C.E.B.	Belcher	DODE	Braamfontein	Mon		G	29 Mar 02
Tpr	S.	Goddard	DODT	Howick	Mon	Howick		02 Apr 02
Tpr	N.	Williams	DOD	Braamfontein	Mon	Elandsfontein	G	08 Apr 02
Tpr	F.	Hutchinson	DODD	Harrismith	Head	Harrismith		13 Apr 02
Tpr	W.H.	Davies	DOD	Primrose	Mon	Elandsfontein	G	29 Apr 02
Tpr	A.B.	Taylor	D			Diamantuur		08 May 02
Tpr	R.J.	Davies	DODD	Braamfontein	Mon		G	06 Jun 02
Tpr	P.	McCabe	DOAL	Braamfontein	Mon		G	25 Jun 02
Tpr	J.R.	Barrett	DODE	Braamfontein	Mon		G	26 Jun 02
Tpr	C.	Coltart	D	Braamfontein	Mon		G	13 Jul 02
Sgt	J.B.	Orrett	D	Maitland	Mon			23 Sep 02
Tpr	W.	Wood	D	Pretoria	Metal	Pretoria		21 Dec 02

Elandslaagte

Killed in action and buried in Elandslaagte cemetery:

Sergeant-Major E.H. Cuthbert (273).
Sergeant C.H. Hendley (321)
Trooper R.S. Farren (373)
Trooper F.C fisher (260)
Trooper F.J.T. Hunt (54)
Trooper K.R.G McClintock (621)
Trooper A.C.W Sillery (227)
Trooper H.J. Wolseley (465)

Died of wounds:

Trooper C.D.B. White (25) – taken to hospital at Fort Napier where he died on 25th October 1899 and is buried.
Sergeant H.C. Benson (527) – taken to hospital in Ladysmith; died in Intombi hospital on 7th December 1899 where he is buried.
Trooper H.C. Ochse (395) – taken to hospital in Ladysmith; died in Intombi hospital on 2nd December where he is buried.
2nd December 1899 where he is buried.
Trooper J.P.F. Cunningham (349) – taken to hospital in Ladysmith where he died on 24th October 1899 and is buried in Ladysmith Borough cemetery.

Casualties of other regiments at Elandslaagte:

	Killed in action *	Wounded*	Died of wounds*
Gordons	21	79	1
Devons	0	29	0
Manchesters	1	14	1
5th Lancers	0	2	1
5th Dragoon Guards	0	0	0
21st Battery R.F.A.	0	3	0
42nd Battery R.F.A.	0	3	0
* The figures from the Natal field Force casualty list as summarized above do not agree with those given in the official history.			

Elandslaagte, 21st October 1899: Imperial Light Horse obelisks in white marble – at left in the graveyard on the site of the Boer laager, at right on the summit of Battle Ridge where Colonel John James Chisholme was fatally wounded.

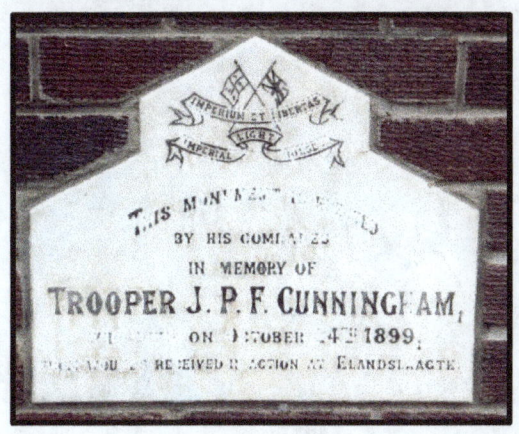

Elandslaagte casualties whose monuments are not on the field:
Top: The monument on the site of the Intombi hospital with the inscribed names of those members of the I.L.H. who are buried there. Trooper C.D.B. White's monument in the cemetery at Fort Napier, Pietermaritzburg.
Below: Sergeant H.C. Benson and Trooper H.C. Ochse in Intombi and Trooper J.P.F. Cunningham in Ladysmith Borough Cemetery.

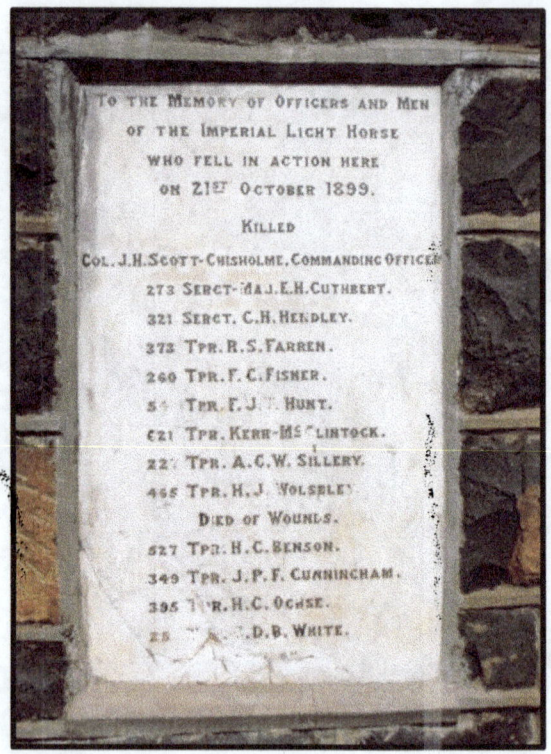

Elandslaagte 21st October 1899: The stone pyramid-obelisk on Battle Ridge erected in 1900 as memorial to the officers and men of the Imperial Light Horse who fell in action on that day. Below is W.B. Wollen's painting of the assault on the Boer position which hangs in the regiment's museum in Johannesburg.

The raid on Gun Hill

RANK		NAME		BURIED		ACTION	**	***
Tpr	R.G.	Nicol	DOW	Ladysmith	I.L.H.	Gun Hill	G O5	X

Above: Trooper R.G. Nicol's regimental headstone built into a wall at the Ladysmith Borough Cemetery.
Below: The Royal Engineers demolishing the 4.7in gun. Artist's licence shows what is evidently a Boer casualty in the foreground – there were no such casualties.

Ladysmith: (up to 3rd November 1899)

Killed in action: (buried in Ladysmith Borough Cemetery):

Captain J.C. Knapp – Mounted Infantry Hill on 3rd November 1899.
Trooper F. Dearlove – Mounted Infantry Hill on 3rd November 1899.

Died of wounds: (buried in Ladysmith Borough Cemetery):

Lieutenant A.E. Brabant – wounded at Mounted Infantry Hill on 3rd November 1899. Died in Ladysmith 11th May 1900.

Ladysmith Borough Cemetery

Top: I.L.H. monuments in Ladysmith Borough cemetery.
Left: Major David Doveton's headstone in Ladysmith – the metal cross is on the summit of Spion Kop. At one time a number of metal crosses were removed and repainted. Several of them were replaced in the wrong place – this is one of them.

Monuments to Lt A.E. Brabant and Capt J.C. Knapp, casualties of Maj Gen Brocklebank's reconnaissance in force outside Ladysmith on 3rd November 1899.

Ladysmith / Harrismith

Memorial in Ladysmith Borough cemetery to Lieutenant W.F. "Coffee: Adams who died on 7th January 1900 of wounds received in action at Wagon Hill on the previous day. The second picture is of the grave of Trooper F. Wheeler who was wounded and captured by the Boers in the acion at Long Valley on 3rd November 1899. Taken to Harrismith, he died there on 2nd January 1900

Wagon Hill

Casualties buried in Wagon Hill Cemetery

RANK		NAME		BURIED		ACTION	Hst/Mon	
Tpr	H.	Albrecht	KIA	Wagon Hill	Mon	Wagon Hill	O2 OC A	P
Tpr	J.H.	Bewsher	KIA	Wagon Hill	Mon	Wagon Hill	O2 OC A	P
Tpr	P.	Brady	KIA	Wagon Hill	Mon	Wagon Hill	O2 OC A	P
L Cpl	G.G.	Cameron	KIA	Wagon Hill	Mon	Wagon Hill	O2 OC A	P
Tpr	R.M.	Dawson	KIA	Wagon Hill	Mon	Wagon Hill	O2 OC A	P
Cpl	E. de C.	Dickinson	KIA	Wagon Hill	Mon	Wagon Hill	O2 OC A	P
Cpl	A.S.	Dunn	KIA	Wagon Hill	Mon	Wagon Hill	O2 OC A	P
Cpl	G.A.	Ferrand	KIA	Wagon Hill	Mon	Wagon Hill	O2 OC A	P
Cpl	J.	Haddon	KIA	Wagon Hill	Mon	Wagon Hill	O2 OC A	P
Tpr	W.S.	Hogg	KIA	Wagon Hill	Mon	Wagon Hill	O2 OC A	P
Sgt	G.	Howard	KIA	Wagon Hill	Mon	Wagon Hill	O2 OC A	P
Tpr	G.	Lind	KIA	Wagon Hill	Mon	Wagon Hill	O2 OC A	P
Tpr	R.M.	MacKenzie	KIA	Wagon Hill	Mon	Wagon Hill	O2 OC A	P
Cpl	G.H.	Moore	KIA	Wagon Hill	Mon	Wagon Hill	O2 OC A	P
L Cpl	C.W.R.	Nettleship	KIA	Wagon Hill	Mon	Wagon Hill	O2 OC A	P
Tpr	T.T.	Preston	KIA	Wagon Hill	Mon	Wagon Hill	O2 OC A	P
Cpl	A.M.	Robbins	KIA	Wagon Hill	Mon	Wagon Hill	O2 OC A	P
Tpr	P.Y.	Tucker	KIA	Wagon Hill	Mon	Wagon Hill	O2 OC A	P
Tpr	E.W.	Mocatta	KIA	Wagon Hill	Mon	Wagon Hill	O2 OC A	P
Tpr	F.C.	Rogers	KIA	Wagon Hill	Mon	Wagon Hill	O2 OC A	P

Casualties – Buried elsewhere

Tprl	G.G.	Cameron	KIA	Wagon Hill	Mon	Wagon Hill	O2 OC A	X
Tpr	R.M.	Dawson	KIA	Wagon Hill	Mon	Wagon Hill	O2 OC A	X
Tpr	E. de C.	Dickinson	KIA	Wagon Hill	Mon	Wagon Hill	O2 OC A	P
Tpr	A.S.	Dunn	KIA	Wagon Hill	Mon	Wagon Hill	O2 OC A	X
Tpr	G.A.	Ferrand	KIA	Wagon Hill	Mon	Wagon Hill	O2 OC A	P
Tpr	J.	Haddon	KIA	Wagon Hill	Mon	Wagon Hill	O2 OC A	X
Tpr	W.S.	Hogg	KIA	Wagon Hill	Mon	Wagon Hill	O2 OC A	X
L Cpl	G.	Howard	KIA	Wagon Hill	Mon	Wagon Hill	O2 OC A	P
Lt	G.	Lind	KIA	Wagon Hill	Mon	Wagon Hill	O2 OC A	P
Lt	R.M.	MacKenzie	KIA	Wagon Hill	Mon	Wagon Hill	O2 OC A	P

G = ILH headstone erected according to ILH Memorial Committee report (Appendix I in Gibson "The Story of the Imperial Light Horse")
O2 = Name inscribed on Obelisk on Wagon Hill
O3 = Name inscribed on Obelisk in Wagon Hill cemetery
O4 = Name inscribed on Obelisk at Intombi
O5 = Name inscribed on Obelisk in Ladysmith Borough cemetery
O7 = Name inscribed on Obelisk in Ladysmith Borough cemetery for Lt J E Pakeman
A = Name inscribed on plaque in All Saints' Church, Ladysmith
X = Headstone intact and photographed
P = Photograph of name on monument or obelisk

Imperial Light Horse obelisks on Wagon Hill:
Left: On the site of the redoubt that was defended throughout the day on 6th January 1900 with inscription above.
Right: The cemetery monument with inscription above

We Rest Here Content

The Imperial Light Horse obelisks in Ladysmith Borough cemetery which has the names of the regiment's casualties in the defence of Ladysmith, including the Long Valley, Gun Hill and Wagon Hill.

Intombi Cemetery: The I.L.H. obelisk has the names of those members of the regiment who are buried here – from Wagon Hill as well as a number who died of disease.

Durban: The West Street cemetery grave and monument to Trooper C.C. Atlay who died in hospital in Durban after being wounded at Wagon Hill. He was evacuated from Ladysmith after the relief.

Wagon Hill: Wagon Hill casualties' monuments in Ladysmith Borough cemetery.

Casualties – Fort Napier Hospital Cemetery, Pietermaritzburg

RANK		NAME		BURIED		PLACE	DATE	Hst/Mon	
Cpl	W.G.	Downer	DOD	Fort Napier	ILH	Fort Napier	12 Apr 00	G A	X
Sgt Maj	A.J.C.	Lang	DOD	Fort Napier	ILH	Victoria Hotel, Pmb	03 Jun 00	G	X
Tpr	A.E.	Swanson	DOP	Fort Napier	ILH	Fort Napier	09 Mar 00	G A	X

RANK		NAME		BURIED		ACTION		Hst/Mon	
Tpr	C.D.B.	White	DOW	Fort Napier	ILH	Elandslaagte	25 Oct 99	G MBR A	X

DOD = died of disease
DOP = died of pneumonia
DOW = died of wounds
G = ILH headstone erected according to ILH Memorial Committee report (Appendix I in Gibson "The Story of the Imperial Light Horse")
A = Name inscribed on plaque in All Saints' Church, Ladysmith
X = Headstone intact and photographed
MBR = Named on regimental monument on Battle Ridge, Elandslaagte

Fort Napier, Pietermaritzburg: At first an army base, later a hospital. Regimental headstones are still intact for Cpl. Downer, Sgt. Lang and Tpr. Swanson.
Trooper White has a similar headstone as well as a memorial erected by his family in the Easter Cape Colony. See Elandslaagte casualties for a picture.

We Rest Here Content

Memorial to Trooper Frederick Allen Freshney, Saltfleet, Lincolnshire

ST PETER'S, SOUTH SOMERCOTES, LINCOLNSHIRE (see photograph)
[now a redundant and deconsecrated church]

Decoration: Vine leaves and grape border and two standards with the inscriptions "Imperitum Libertas" and "Imperial Light Horse".

To the Glory of God and In Loving Memory of
FREDERICK ALLEN FRESHNEY
Trooper Imperial Light Horse
who was severely wounded at the Battle of Colenso,
December 15th 1899, and died at Salfleet. May 20th 1906.
This pulpit was erected by numerous friends as a tribute to
the fine character and self-denying patriotism of a Christian soldier.
And to his patience, fortitude, and cheerfulness
under sore and prolonged suffering.

Pro Patria
In
Memory of
FREDERICK ALLEN
FRESHNEY,
Trooper, Imperial Light Horse,
who was severely wounded
at the Battle of
Colenso, South Africa.
Decr 15th 1899
and in consequence thereof
died at Saltfleet,
May 20th 1906
aged 32 years.
Brave in action
Patient in suffering.
Erected by his many friends.

The Relief of Mafeking – the action at Neverset Farm, Maritzani

RANK		NAME		BURIED		ACTION	Date	Hst/Mon
Tpr	T.S.	Cashman	DOD	Mafikeng	ILH			G
Sgt	A.J.	Haynes	DOW	Mafikeng	Metal	Neverset	15 May 00	
Tpr	G.	Bonsey	KIA	Mafikeng	Metal	Neverset	13 May 00	O10
Tpr	H.S.	Boome	KIA	Mafikeng	Metal	Neverset	13 May 00	O10
Tpr	C.	Davis	KIA	Mafikeng	Metal	Neverset	13 May 00	O10
Cpl	W.	Francis	KIA	Mafikeng	Metal	Neverset	13 May 00	O10
Tpr	C.T.	Gardner	KIA	Mafikeng	Mon	Neverset	13 May 00	O10
Tpr	H.E.	Taylor	KIA	Mafikeng	Metal	Neverset	13 May 00	O10

G = ILH headstone erected according to ILH Memorial Committee report (Appendix I in Gibson "The Story of the Imperial Light Horse")
O10 = Name inscribed on obelisk at Maritzani

Maritzani: The marble obelisk apparently on the site where Corporal Hi;; found the body of Trooper C.T. Gardner and his horse "Billy". On the next page is the inscription on this monument.
Mafikeng: On the following pages are pictures of the metal crosses of the I.L.H. casualties who lie buried in Mafikeng as well as the Siege Monument in the Town Square, Mafikeng.

We Rest Here Content

Witklip (near Delmas)

RANK		NAME	BURIED		ACTION	Date	Hst/Mon
Cpl	E.O.	Atherstone	KIA	Braamfontein	Mon	Witklip	07 Jul 00	O8
Capt	W.M.	Currie	KIA	Braamfontein	Mon	Witklip	07 Jul 00	O8
Tpr	G.W.	Drennan	KIA	Braamfontein	Mon	Witklip	07 Jul 00	O8
Tpr	G.M.	King	KIA	Braamfontein	Mon	Witklip	07 Jul 00	G O8
Lt	E.E.	Kirk	KIA	Braamfontein	Mon	Witklip	07 Jul 00	O8
Sgt	J.	Marshall	KIA	Braamfontein	Mon	Witklip	07 Jul 00	O8
Farr Sgt	C.S.	Wooley	KIA	Braamfontein	Mon	Witklip	07 Jul 00	O8

RANK		NAME	BURIED		ACTION	Date	Hst/Mon
Tpr	A.	Bouchier	DOW	Braamfontein	Mon	Witklip	07 Jul 00	G
Tpr	H.	Lane	DOW	Braamfontein	Mon	Witklip	07 Jul 00	O8
Tpr	J.	McIntry	D	Braamfontein	Mon			
Tpr	A.P.D.	Moodie	DOW	Braamfontein	Mon	Witklip	07 Jul 00	G O8
Tpr	W.A.	Murray	DOW	Braamfontein			17 Jul 00	

G = ILH headstone erected according to ILH Memorial Committee report (Appendix I in Gibson "The Story of the Imperial Light Horse"
O8 = Name inscribed on obelisk at Witklip moved to Braamfontein

Witklip: This engagement was an extension of the bigger affair at Diamond Hill and was part of the pursuit as the Boers retreated eastwards. Trooper W.A. Murray was a casualty of an action on 16 July with Boer scouts north of Pretoria, His name therefore appears on the the monument at Donkerpoort, Pretoria on part of the field of the battle of Diamond Hill. He was an old boy of Hilton College and his name appears on a plaque in their Memorial Hall.

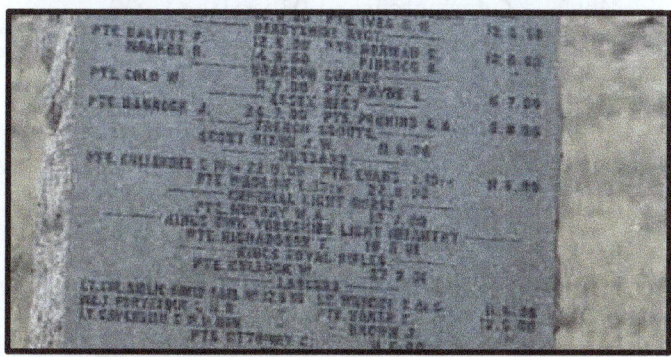

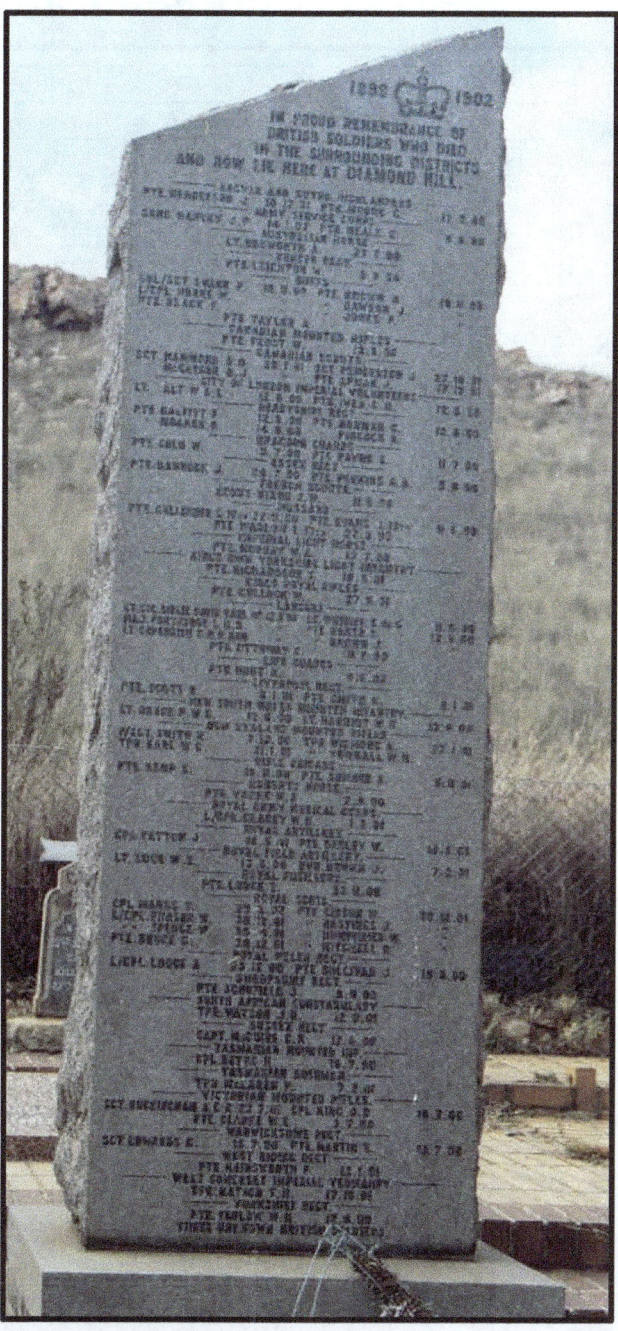

Top: Witklip casualties inscribed on the plaque in Braamfontein cemetery, Johannesburg
Below: The monument at Donkerhoek, Diamond Hill, Pretoria with Trooper W.A. Murray's name and the plaque in the Hilton College Memorial Hall.

Cyferfontein – the battle site, Krugersdorp and Braamfontein cemeteries

RANK		NAME		BURIED		ACTION	Date	Hst/Mon
Tpr	P.	Anderson	KIA	Krugersdorp	Mon	Cyferfontein	05 Jan 01	O9
Tpr	R.O.	Butler	KIA	Krugersdorp	Mon	Cyferfontein	05 Jan 01	O9
Tpr	C.J.	Harding	KIA	Krugersdorp	Mon	Cyferfontein	05 Jan 01	O9
Tpr	M.A.	Langley	KIA	Krugersdorp	Mon	Cyferfontein	05 Jan 01	O9
Tpr	J.W.	Maxwell	KIA	Krugersdorp	Mon	Cyferfontein	05 Jan 00	O9
Tpr	W.	Melville	KIA	Krugersdorp	Mon	Cyferfontein	05 Jan 00	O9
Cpl	H.	Nash	KIA	Krugersdorp	Mon	Cyferfontein	05 Jan 00	O9
Lt	A.	Ormond	KIA	Krugersdorp	Mon	Cyferfontein	05 Jan 00	O9
Tpr	W.	Pierce	KIA	Krugersdorp	Mon	Cyferfontein	05 Jan 01	
Capt	T.	Yockney	KIA	Krugersdorp	Mon	Cyferfontein	05 Jan 00	O9
Tpr	J.H.	Bentley	DOW	Krugersdorp	Mon	Cyferfontein	05 Jan 01	O9
Tpr	L.	Bromham	DOW	Braamfontein	Mon	Cyferfontein	05 Jan 01	G O9
Tpr	A.C.	Brown	DOW	Braamfontein	Mon	Cyferfontein	05 Jan 01	G O9
Tpr	R.	Leak	DOW	Krugersdorp	Mon	Cyferfontein	05 Jan 00	O9
Tpr	H.	O'Hagan	D			Cyferfontein	05 Jan 00	

G = ILH headstone erected according to ILH Memorial Committee report (Appendix I in Gibson "The Story of the Imperial Light Horse"
O8 = Name inscribed in Krugersdorp cemetery.

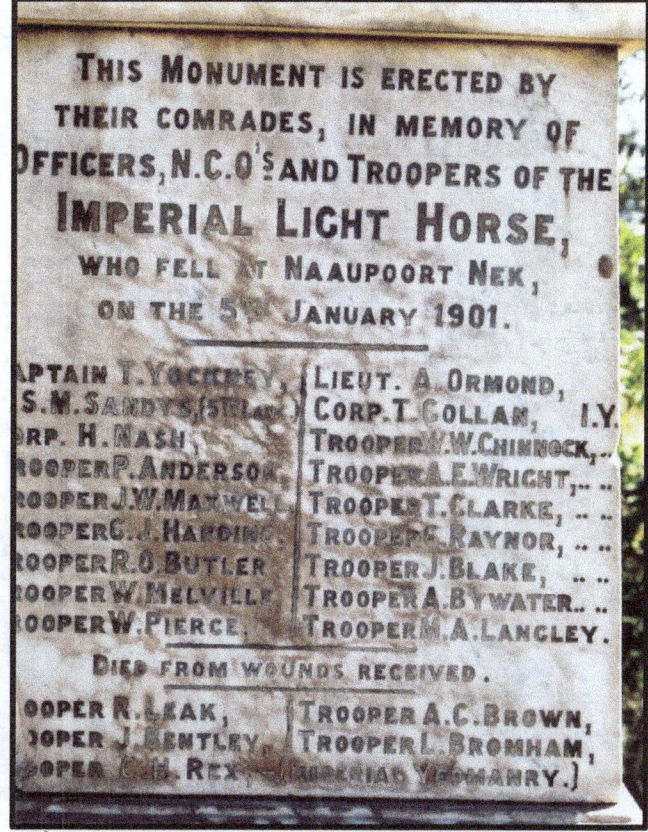

THIS MONUMENT IS ERECTED BY THEIR COMRADES, IN MEMORY OF OFFICERS, N.C.O'S AND TROOPERS OF THE IMPERIAL LIGHT HORSE, WHO FELL AT NAAUPOORT NEK, ON THE 5TH JANUARY 1901.

Captain T. Yockney	Lieut. A. Ormond
S.M. Sandys (Staff)	Corp. T. Gollan, I.Y.
Corp. H. Nash	Trooper W.W. Chinnock
Trooper P. Anderson	Trooper A.E. Wright
Trooper J.W. Maxwell	Trooper T. Clarke
Trooper G.J. Harding	Trooper G. Raynor
Trooper R.O. Butler	Trooper J. Blake
Trooper W. Melville	Trooper A. Bywater
Trooper W. Pierce	Trooper M.A. Langley

DIED FROM WOUNDS RECEIVED.

Trooper R. Leak	Trooper A.C. Brown
Trooper J. Bentley	Trooper L. Bromham
Trooper G.H. Rex	(Imperial Yeomanry.)

	GIBBARD W.	15. 5.01
	POWELL F.	5. 2.01
	PRIOR G.	17.10.01
IMPERIAL LIGHT HORSE		
SGT.	WELLSTEAD H.E.	24.11.00
	WILEMAN G.	9.11.00
TPR.	BOURCHIER A.	14. 7.00
	BROMHAM L.	17. 1.01
	BROWN A.C.	10. 1.01
	COX H.J.	2. 6.01
	LANE H.	11. 7.00
	MANNING C.S.	12. 1.01
	MOODIE A.P.O.	11. 7.00
	NORWOOD N.G.	25. 1.01
	PARMITER H.	27. 6.01
IMPERIAL LIGHT INFANTRY		
CPL.	McKENZIE W.	10.12.00

Top: The I.L.H. obelisk in Krugersdorp cemetery, very badly eroded, probably from the corrosive industrial atmosphere in the area, and the inscription.
Below right: The marble plaque which now lies in Braamfontein cemetery with the names of the two casualties of Cyferfontein who died in hospital in Johannesburg.

Lake Chrissie

RANK		NAME		BURIED		ACTION	Date		
Tpr	H.	Edmondson	DOW	Standerton	Mon	Lake Chrissie	06 Feb 00	G	
Tpr	J.	Erasmus	DOW	Lake Chrissie	ILH	Lake Chrissie	06 Feb 00	G	X
Tpr	C.	Marsden	KIA	Lake Chrissie	ILH	Lake Chrissie	06 Feb 00	G	X
L Cpl	D.W.N.	Ritchie	KIA	Lake Chrissie	ILH	Lake Chrissie	06 Feb 00	G	X
Tpr	F.H.	Smallwood	KBL	Ermelo	Mon	Twyfelaar		G	
Tpr	J.W.	Lee	DOAB	Wakkerstroom	ILH	Piet Retief			
Tpr	J.	Willcocks	DODE	Wakkerstroom	Mon				
Tpr	C.	Harding	DODE	Wakkerstroom	ILH	Piet Retief			
Tpr	F.H.	Hanks	DRO	Wakkerstroom	ILH	Amsterdam			

G = ILH headstone erected according to ILH Memorial Committee report (Appendix I in Gibson "The Story of the Imperial Light Horse")
X = headstone intact and photographed

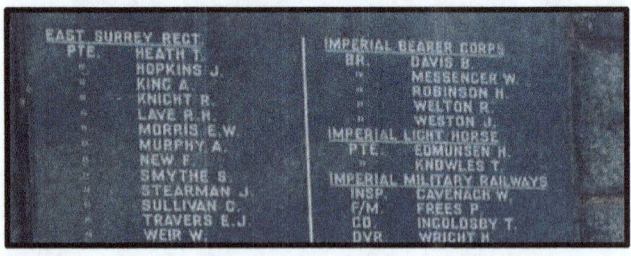

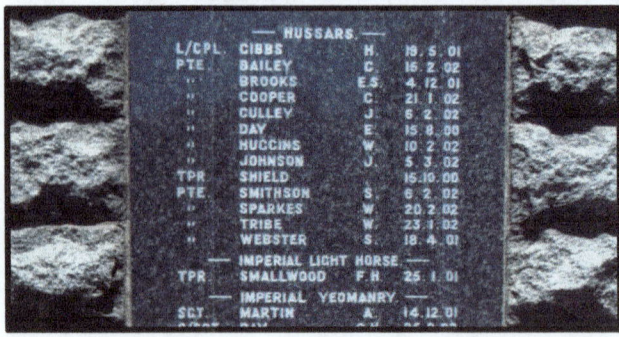

Hartebeestfontein – the rearguard action from Geduld farm

		NAME		BURIED		ACTION	
Lt	A.R.	Halling	DOW	Hartebeestfontein	Mon	Hartebeestfontein	O11
Lt	J.	Ralston	KIA	Hartebeestfontein	Mon	Hartebeestfontein	O11
RSM	A.E.	Hurst	KIA	Hartebeestfontein	Mon	Hartebeestfontein	O11
Tpr	P.	Jones	KIA	Hartebeestfontein	Mon	Hartebeestfontein	O11
Tpr	P.	Kennedy	KIA	Hartebeestfontein	Mon	Hartebeestfontein	O11
Tpr	D.	Paterson	KIA	Hartebeestfontein	Mon	Hartebeestfontein	O11

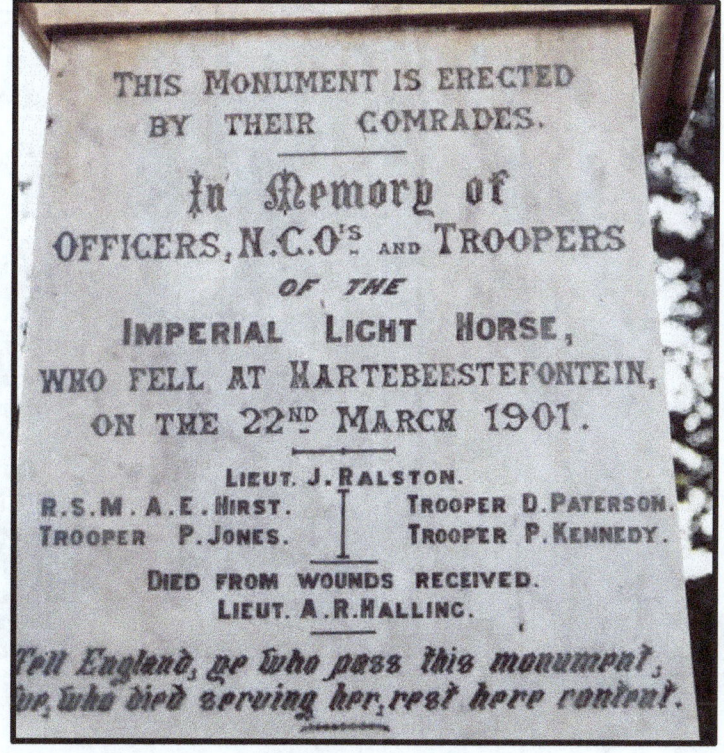

Heilbron – the action at Katkop

RANK		NAME		BURIED		ACTION	Date	Hst/Mon
Tpr	J.H.	Barry	KIA	Heilbron		Katkop	07 Feb 02	
Tpr	W.	Evans	KIA	Heilbron	Mon	Katkop	07 Feb 02	G
Tpr	T.	Johnson	KIA	Heilbron	Mon	Katkop	07 Feb 02	G
Tpr	H.C.	Thirlwall	KIA	Heilbron	Mon	Katkop	07 Feb 02	G
Tpr	C.	Upton	KIA	Heilbron	Mon	Katkop	07 Feb 02	G
Tpr	J.	flanegan	DOW	Colesberg	ILH	Katkop	07 Feb 02	G

G = ILH headstone erected according to ILH Memorial Committee report (Appendix I in Gibson "The Story of the Imperial Light Horse")

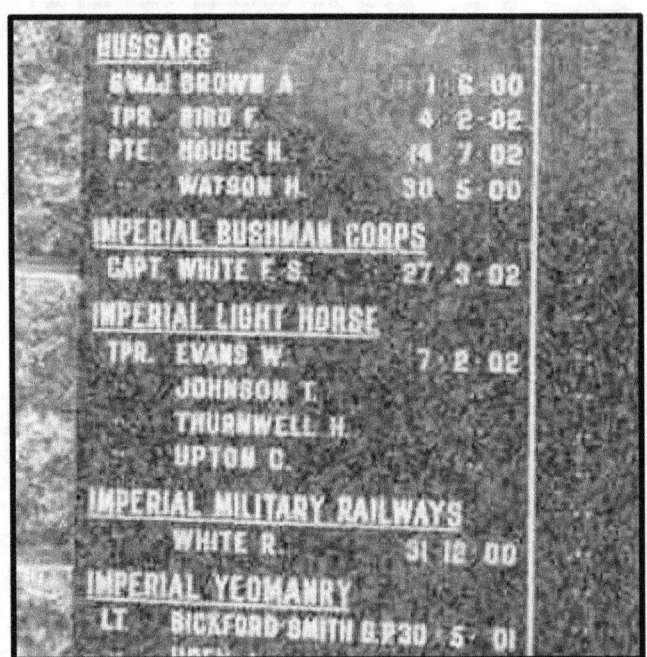

Heilbron: Only four names appear on the Wargraves Commission monument in Heilbron military cemetery. The I.L.H. headstones are nowhere to be found.

Bethlehem – Harrismith

Casualties – Bethlehem Military Cemetery

RANK		NAME		BURIED		ACTION	Date	Hst/Mon
Tpr	H.	Abercrombie	DOW	Bethlehem	ILH	Paardeplaatz	21 Oct 01	G
Tpr	W.	Agar	DOD	Bethlehem	ILH	Bethlehem		G
Tpr	G.	Bremer	KIA	Bethlehem	ILH	Concordia	07 Sep 01	G
Cpl	F.	Connell	KIA	Bethlehem	ILH	Roodepoort	24 Sep 01	G
L Cpl	J.G.	Dixon	DOD	Bethlehem	Metal	Bethlehem		
Tpr	V.G.	Hooper	KIA	Bethlehem	ILH	Vischgat	11 Nov 01	G
Tpr	E.H.	McChesney	KBL	Bethlehem	ILH	Vischgat		G
Tpr	V.	Miller	DOD	Bethlehem	Metal	Bethlehem		
Tpr	M.	O'Shea	KIA	Bethlehem	ILH	Tygerkloof	28 Sep 01	G
Tpr	J.W.	Townsend	KIA	Bethlehem	ILH	Naauwpoort Nek	07 Oct 01	G

Casualties – Harrismith Military Cemetery

RANK		NAME		BURIED		ACTION	Date	Hst/Mon
Tpr Guide	A.L.	Fraser	DOW	Harrismith	ILH	Tygerskloof	15 Jan 02	G
Cpl	W.	Gabriel	DOW	Harrismith	ILH	Newmarket Farm	29 Jan 02	G
Tpr	F.	Hutchinson	DOD	Harrismith	Head	Harrismith		
Cpl	F.	James	DOD	Harrismith	ILH	Harrismith		G
Tpr	B.F.	Murray	DOD	Harrismith	ILH	Harrismith		G
Tpr	S.	Tennant	KIA	Harrismith	ILH	Klipkraal		G
Tpr	F.	Wheeler	DOW	Harrismith	ILH	Ladysmith	04 Nov 99	G

Harrismith: Trooper F. Wheeler in the civilian precinct.

Frederikstad

RANK		NAME	BURIED		ACTION		Date	Hst/Mon
Tpr	H.L.	Aschmann	KIA	Potchefstroom	Mon	Frederickstad	16 Oct 00	G
Tpr	I.D.J.	Simpson	KIA	Potchefstroom	Mon	Frederickstad	20 Oct 00	G
Sgt	H.E.	Wellstead	DOW	Braamfontein	Mon	Frederickstad	25 Oct 00	G
Sgt	G.	Wileman	DOW	Braamfontein	Mon	Frederickstad	25 Oct 00	G

Frederikstad: I.L.H. headstones were erected over the graves of Troopers H.L. Aschmann ans J.D. Simpson in a graveyard in the yard of Frederikstad station. On reinterment to Olin Park in Potchefstroom in 1962 the headstones were lost.

Trooper J.J. Bailey (wrongly spelt "Baillee" on this plaque) has a regimental headstone in the Ventersdorp cemetery and is presumably buried there.

The inscriptions for Sergeants H.E. Wellstead and G. Wilemn are on the plaque in Braamfontein – see the Cyferfontein casualty pictures.

Bloemfontein

President Street cemetery: Names on the granite column.

Braamfontein

Braamfontein: Various marble name plaques.

Clouston, Chieveley – Colenso

Pretoria – Church Street

Ottosdal

Lindley, Vrede, Fauresmith

RANK		NAME		BURIED		ACTION	Date	Hst/Mon
Cpl	J.H.	Renouf	KIA	Lindley	Mon	Craven's Rust		G
Tpr	E.	Wiid	DOW	Fauresmith	Metal	Fauresmith	04 Mar01	
Cpl	J.E.G.	Davies	KIA	Vrede	Mon	Kalkfontein		G
Sgt	P.	Cawood	KIA	Vrede	Mon	Kalkfontein		G

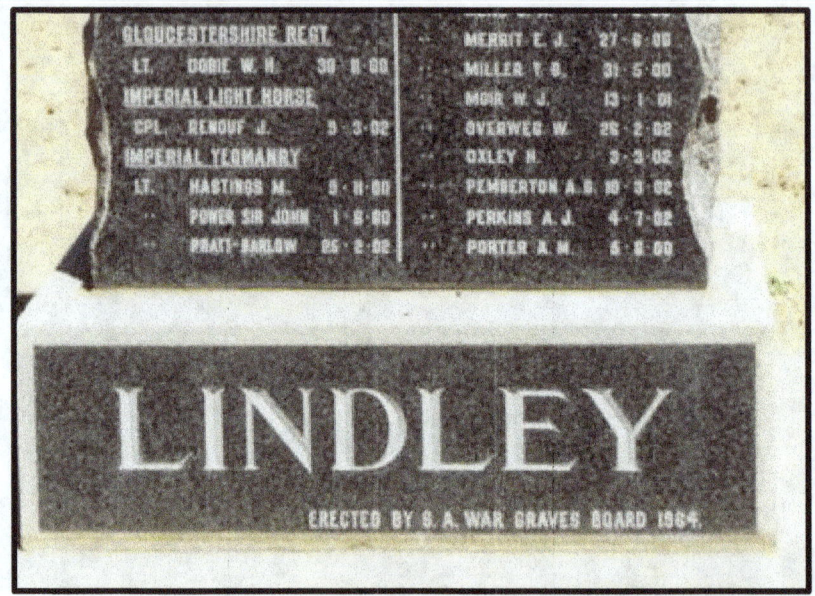

Fauresmith: There is no monument or I.L.H. headstone at Fauresmith.

Newcastle

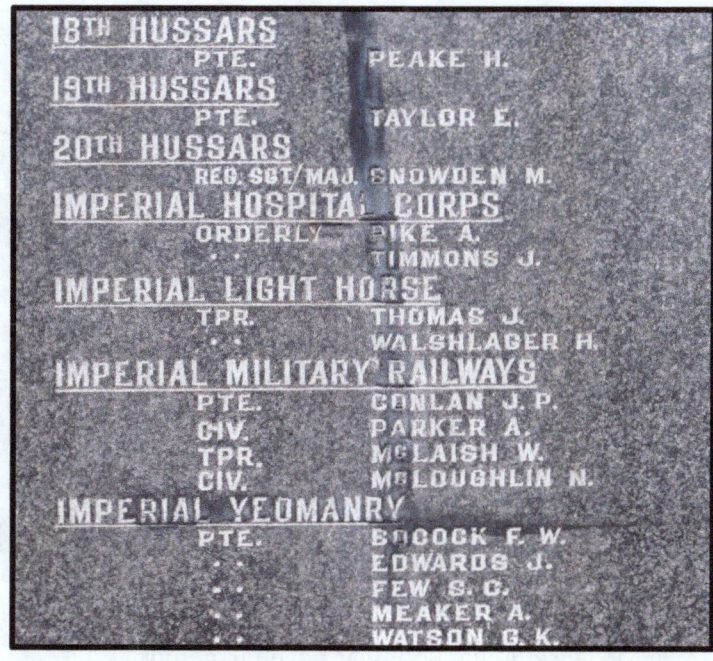

Howick and Mooi River

Mooi River: I.L.H. headstones

Howick: Anglo Boer war hospital memorial.

Ventersdorp and Treurfontein

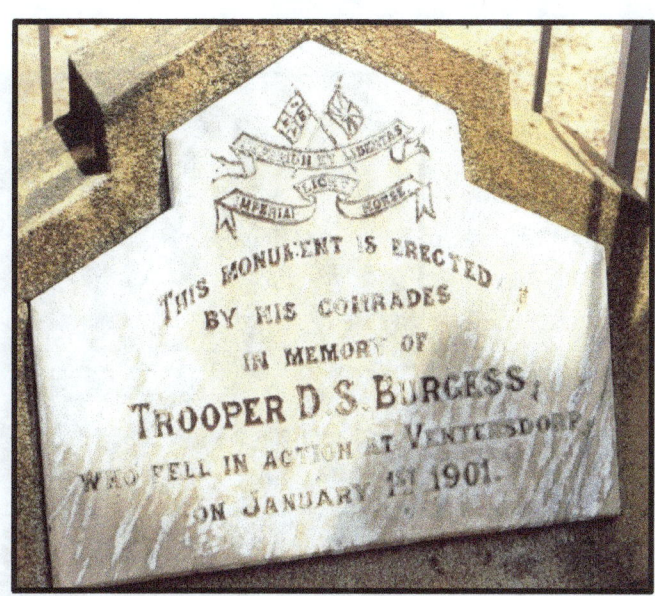

Ventersdorp: I.L.H. headstones

Treurfontein: I.L.H. headstones.

Colesberg and Cape Town

Above: Colesberg
Below: Maitland, Cape Town

Klerksdorp

Grahamstown

Grahamstown cemetery:
The grave of Captain Charles H. Mullins VC.

Wakkerstroom

Zeerust

Ladysmith

All Saints' Anglican Church, Ladysmith: All those who gave their lives during the Siege of Ladysmith have their names engraved on marble panels inside the church. Trooper Herman Albrecht's name had not included the VC. This was recently corrected.

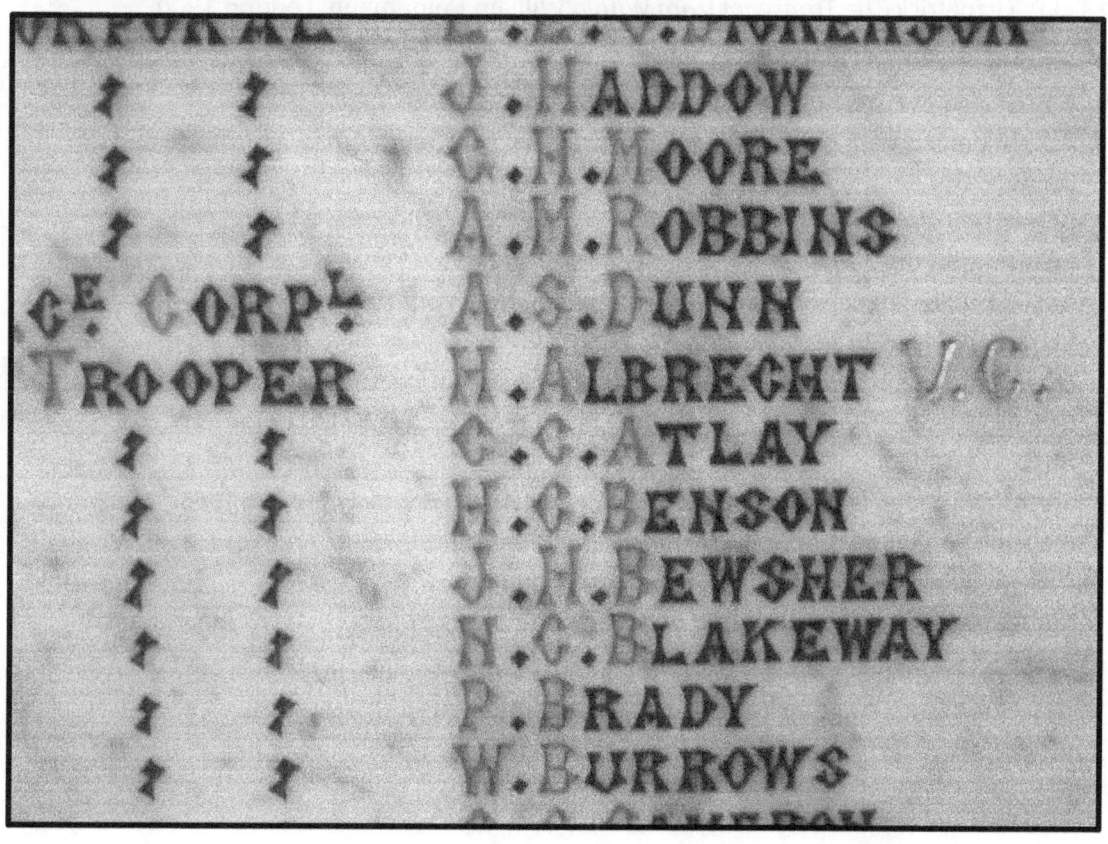

Bibliography

<u>Published books.</u>

1. L.S. Amery *The Times History of the War in South Africa* volumes II, III, IV and V. Sampson Low, Marston and Company, Ltd, London 1902 to 1907.
2. J.B. Atkins *The Relief of Ladysmith* Methuen & Co, London 1900.
3. The Marquess of Anglesey *A History of the British Cavalry Volume 4: 1899–1913* Leo Cooper, London 1986.
4. Ron Bester and Associates *Small Arms of the Anglo-Boer War 1899–1902*, Kraal Publishers, Brandfort 2003.
5. J.H. Breytenbach *Die Geskiedenis van die Tweede Vryheidsoorlog in Suid Afrika*, 1899-1902 Government Printer, Pretoria 1969.
6. Bennett Burleigh *The Natal Campaign* George Bell & Sons, London 1900.
7. Major Charles Burnett *The 18th Hussars in South Africa* Warren & Son, Winchester 1905.
8. Diana Cammack *The Rand at War 1899–1902* University of Natal Press, Pietermartizburg 2000.
9. Ruari Chisholm *Ladysmith* Jonathon Ball Publishers, Johannesburg 1979.
10. Arthur Conan Doyle *The Great Boer War* Smith, Elder & Co., London, October 1900.
11. Lionel Crook *Artillery of the Anglo-Boer War 1899–1902*, Kraal Publishers, Brandfort 2003.
12. Lieutenant General the Earl of Dundonald *My Army Life* Edward Arnold & Co, London 1926.
13. J.P. Fitzpatrick *The Transvaal from Within* William Heinemann, London 1900.
14. G.F. Gibson *The Story of the Imperial Light Horse* G.D. & Co 1937.
15. C.S. Goldmann *With General French and the Cavalry in South Africa*. Macmillan and Co. London 1902.
16. Darrell Hall *The Darrell Hall Handbook of the Boer War* University of Natal Press, Pietermaritzburg 1999.
17. Archie Hunter *Kitchener's Sword Arm* Sarpedon, New York 1996.
18. J.H. Kestell *Through Shot and flame*
19. Elizabeth Longford *Jameson's Raid* Weidenfeld & Nicholson 1982.
20. Donald Macdonald *How we kept the flag flying* Ward Lock & Co Ltd., New York and Melbourne 1900.
21. Brigadier General Sir Duncan McKenzie *Delayed Action* Privately printed 1965.
22. Maj-Gen Sir Frederick Maurice *History of the War in South Africa* volumes I, II, III, IV. Complied by direction of His Majesty's government.
23. Martin Meredith *Diamonds, Gold and War – The Making of South Africa* Jonathon Ball Publishers, Johannesburg 2007.
24. J.F. Naudé *Veg en Vlug van Beyers en Kemp* (translation in Afrikaans from "Vechten en Vluchten van Beyers en Kemp" Nijgk & van Ditmar, Rotterdam, 1903.)
25. H.W. Nevinson *Ladysmith: The Diary of a Siege* Methuen & Co, London 1900.

26. Thomas Pakenham *The Boer War* Weidenfeld and Nicholson Limited, London 1979.
27. H.H.S. Pearse *Four Months Besieged* Macmillan and Co, London 1900.
28. Denys Reitz *Commando* Faber & Faber, London 1929.
29. Victor Sampson and Ian Hamilton *Anti-Commando* Faber & Faber Limites, London 1931.
30. Douglas Scott *The Preparatory Prologue – Douglas Haig, Diaries and Letters 1861-1914* Pen & Sword Military, Barnsley 2006.
31. General Sir Horace Smith Dorrien *Memories of Forty-Eight Year' Service* E.P. Dutton and Company, New York 1925.
32. G.W. Steevens *From Cape Town to Ladysmith* The Copp Clark Co., Limited, Toronto 1900.
33. John Stirling *The Colonials in South Africa 1899–1902* William Blackwood and Sons, Edinburgh & London, 1907.
34. Ian Uys *Heidelbergers of the Boer War* Ian Uys 1981.
35. Dietlof van Warmelo *On Commando* A.D. Donker/Publisher, Johannesburg 1977.
36. R.L. Wallace *The Australians at the Boer War* The Australian War Memorial, Canberra 1976.
37. S.A. Watt *In Memoriam – Roll of Honour Imperial Forces* University of Natal Press, Pietermaritzburg 2000.
38. E.J. Weeber *Op die Natalse Front* Nasionale Pers, Beperk Cape Town, Bloemfontein and Port Elizabeth 1940.
39. Walter Temple Willcox *The fifth (Royal Irish) Lancers in South Africa 1899–1902* Boer War Books, York 1981.
40. Filson Young *The Relief of Mafeking* Methuen & Co., London 1900.

Unpublished manuscripts, articles and diaries.
1. Untitled manuscript with detailed history if the Imperial Light Horse believed to be an original manuscript, possibly written in the 1920s by R.L. Wallace. There is a copy in the Ladysmith Siege Museum.
2. *Diary of Lieutenant E.I.D. Gordon*, 2nd Battalion, The Royal Scots Fusiliers. Unpublished annotated diary in the possession of his son, Major Antony Gordon.
3. *Diary of Captain P.H. Normand, D.S.O.* The original is on display in the museum of the Light Horse Regiment in Johannesburg.

Official documents:
1. The South African War Casualty Roll: *The "Natal field Force" 20th Oct. 1899 – 26th Oct. 1900.* J.B. Hayward & Son, Polstead, Suffolk 1980.
2. The South African War Casualty Roll: *The "South African field Force" 11th October 1899 – June 1902.* J.B. Hayward & Son, Polstead, Suffolk 1982.

www.ingramcontent.com/pod-product-compliance
Lightning Source LLC
Chambersburg PA
CBHW081435300426
44108CB00016BA/2375